PRAISE FOR
THE POLITICS OF TRAUMA

"Somatics is a freedom-inducing framework. The central idea is that the natural living body—with its sensations, memories and emotions, triggers and pleasures—is a complex system that carries our whole lives, including trauma and healing, boundaries and risks, patterns and transformation. Staci Haines is one of our central teachers weaving the Somatics lineage with social justice and being in the body in community, increasing the possibility that we can be in collective bodies of justice. This book maps the cycles of healing that shift us from being victims of systemic injustice to being shapers of constant change and liberatory systems."

—ADRIENNE MAREE BROWN, author of *Emergent Strategy* and *Pleasure Activism*

"If I've discovered anything in several decades of social justice work, it's that the body never lies. If we can embrace her, change can happen. Grounding in my body, not just in my words, has turned out to be a critical source of humility and courage, preconditions for any significant change. The ideas and tools in *Politics of Trauma* allow us to listen to our bodies, and then make choices about what we do rather than constantly reacting to what we think are external pressures. A must read for anyone trying to lead anything."

—RINKU SEN, activist and author of *Stir It Up: Lessons in Community Organizing and Advocacy*

"*The Politics of Trauma* is an essential read for every social movement leader, healer, therapist, and newly 'woke' person responding to this moment in history's calling. Movement leaders know firsthand the level of trauma we have experienced in our personal lives, our families, communities, and across generations; and we often carry out our work at great personal expense. Haines brings a political clarity desperately needed and reminds us that we must courageously embark on our own healing journey, grounded in racial, economic, and gender justice. Then and only then will we be able to live whole, vibrant, resilient lives and bring about the transformation we seek in society."

—MARIELENA HINCAPIÉ, executive director of the
National Immigration Law Center

"*The Politics of Trauma* is a bold and important response to a long-existing split between those who work on individual change and those working to change the institutions of society. The profound gift of Staci's book is that rather than diagnosing what doesn't work, it offers us a remedy: Somatics—a body-centered approach to transformation that fully integrates the healing of individuals with the creating of a more just and equitable society."

—ROBERT GASS, EdD, co-founder of the Rockwood Leadership Institute and the Social Transformation Project

THE
POLITICS
OF
TRAUMA

Somatics, Healing, and Social Justice

Staci K. Haines

North Atlantic Books
Berkeley, California

Published by
North Atlantic Books
Huichin, unceded Ohlone land
aka Berkeley, California

Cover design by Rob Johnson
Book design by Happenstance Type-O-Rama
Printed in the United States of America

The Politics of Trauma: Somatics, Healing, and Social Justice is sponsored and published by North Atlantic Books, an educational nonprofit based in the unceded Ohlone land Huichin (*aka* Berkeley, CA) that collaborates with partners to develop cross-cultural perspectives; nurture holistic views of art, science, the humanities, and healing; and seed personal and global transformation by publishing work on the relationship of body, spirit, and nature.

North Atlantic Books's publications are distributed to the US trade and internationally by Penguin Random House Publisher Services. For further information, visit our website at www.northatlanticbooks.com.

Library of Congress Cataloging-in-Publication Data
Names: Haines, Staci K., author.
Title: The politics of trauma : somatics, healing, and social justice /
      Staci K. Haines.
Description: Berkeley, California : North Atlantic Books, [2019] | Includes
      index.
Identifiers: LCCN 2019019241 (print) | LCCN 2019022272 (ebook) | ISBN
      9781623173876 (pbk.)
Subjects: LCSH: Psychic trauma—Social aspects. | Mind and body. | Healing.
      | Social conflict. | Social justice.
Classification: LCC BF175.5.P75 H35 2019 (print) | LCC BF175.5.P75
      (ebook) | DDC 155.9/3—dc23
LC record available at https://lccn.loc.gov/2019019241
LC ebook record available at https://lccn.loc.gov/2019022272

4 5 6 7 8 9 KPC 26 25 24 23

North Atlantic Books is committed to the protection of our environment. We print on recycled paper whenever possible and partner with printers who strive to use environmentally responsible practices.

For Jamie, Sam, and Torie,
thank you for being amazing humans
and all you bring to my life.

For my Mom, Mary Kay Haines,
for staying in the healing and complexity
all these years, and for your love of justice.

CONTENTS

Part 4: Healing and Social Change: We Are in It Together

Critical Context

FOREWORD

The work of #metoo is about healing. It's about healing as individuals and healing as communities.
—TARANA BURKE

Beware that, when fighting monsters, you yourself do not become a monster ... for when you gaze long into the abyss, the abyss also gazes into you.
—FRIEDRICH W. NIETZSCHE

There are things we have control of in life and things we don't. But a mentor of mine used to say we always have choices. We cannot control the actions or behavior of others—but we do have agency over how we respond to those actions. We cannot control what systems or culture we are born into, but we *can* control how we engage with or attempt to change those systems.

The organization I lead, the National Domestic Workers Alliance, serves the more than two million women—mostly women of color—who work in our homes as nannies, cleaners, and home care workers. This is the workforce we count on to care for our loved ones and whom we entrust with many of the most precious parts of our lives. And despite their importance to millions of families, they are among the most undervalued workers in our economy today. Excluded from basic labor protections and working under extreme isolation, this workforce is vulnerable to a range of abuses from the everyday violence of poverty to the more extreme—including human trafficking and sexual violence. Many of the women who do this work are survivors in every sense of the word—literally carrying the suffering and the dreams of their families across borders and on their shoulders.

Most of us experience some form of trauma in the course of our lives. It shapes us in conscious and unconscious ways. For many of us—the events that cause trauma are deeply rooted in our culture and society, reinforced by a set of beliefs, norms, and policies that are structural and hierarchical in nature. While we experience them as individuals, they are not caused by individual choices or failure.

We have many tools to heal from trauma as individuals. And we also have some tools to change policy, systems, and culture. But rarely do the two meet; somehow the minute we are talking about violence and trauma at a systemic level, the human element gets lost. And when we're trying to heal as individuals we often attempt to do so in a vacuum, as if the therapist's office or the meditation cushion were islands in a sea devoid of systems of power and privilege.

For those of us working toward social change and justice, it sometimes occurs to us that we may be missing something. When you realize that meeting you attended about inclusion feels exclusive. Or the rally for justice features speakers who dehumanize one group to humanize another. The truth is that we are all, as human beings, a work in progress. We are shaped by trauma, deeply and profoundly flawed and imperfect. We've internalized our trauma and adapted in healthy and unhealthy ways including judgments against ourselves and others. But if you claim to seek progress and social change, you will be held to a higher standard of intentionality about how you manage that imperfection and proactively seek to develop, evolve, and heal.

At the National Domestic Workers Alliance, we knew that if we wanted the people with the most at stake leading the way in transforming domestic work, we would need to address trauma head-on and create a movement that would not only *not* re-traumatize us, but help us heal. Not only win policy change to heal social injustice, but support individual change and resilience. We believed it would be impossible to achieve one without the other. With the help of the author of this book, we created leadership programs that promote healing from trauma. We created a culture that includes practices to help us stay centered and connected—to one another and to our shared purpose; practices that support our individual well-being and our ability to truly be powerful collectively. And it's made all the difference in our ability to be powerful together.

We live in a time of profound change in every aspect of our culture, economy, and politics. Deep divisions are being sown by people in the highest levels of elected office. Violence and trauma show up everywhere—and it's nearly impossible not to internalize it. The #MeToo movement has shown us the potential to wrench change out of trauma in positive ways—opening an unprecedented cultural conversation and truth-telling about the reality of sexual violence, and moving us toward healing and long-overdue solutions. The activism of women is powering a new movement to protect and expand our democracy. Much of the work of this time is to ensure that in the midst of so much change and volatility, we begin to set new patterns, new relationships, and a new culture that allows us to heal through all the change.

Unfortunately, harm is part of the human experience. Healing, in our systems and in ourselves, is core to realizing the human promise. It's not easy. In fact, it may be some of the hardest work we have to do.

That is why we need this book—full of insight and ideas at the intersection of personal transformation and social change. As you seek to make change in this rapidly changing world, take it with you and keep it close.

—AI-JEN POO, Director of the National Domestic
Workers Alliance

GRATITUDE

Thank you to the many, many people who have partnered with me in this depthful and wacky path of somatics. Particularly, thank you for your partnership in interfacing somatics and social and environmental justice movements—Spenta Kandawalla, Raquel Laviña, Chris Lymbertos, Nathan Shara, Alta Starr, Denise Perry, Xochitl Bervera, Sumitra Rajkumar, RJ Maccani, and Morgan Bassichis. Thank you to the "originals" Vassi Kapila, Elizabeth Ross, Lisa Thomas-Adeyemo, Liu Hoi Man, and Jennifer Ianniello ... it only happened once! Thank you all for being creative, bold, and willing to take risks that don't make sense at first glance. A special gratitude to Spenta Kandawalla for co-creating the Somatics and Social Justice Collaborative and gs! I'll be forever grateful, and we have things to laugh about for the rest of our days.

Thank you to Richard Strozzi-Heckler for your decades of committed practice, and the generosity with which you share your arts. I am impressed by how you hold the depth and mastery of the work in a highly commoditized world, and pass it beyond your known worlds. Thank you for being a lifelong learner and creative force.

Thank you to those of you who read this along the way, and supported this being done amidst so much else. Lisbeth White, you were a steady invitation for chapter after chapter. Thanks to Shayna, Tim, and the folks at North Atlantic Books for being supportive, enthusiastic, and holding down all you do as a small press.

Lastly, thank you to my sister, Wendy, for all the conversations, week after week, year after year. I am grateful for you.

INTRODUCTION

Two questions have been with me most of my life: How do people change? How do social systems change?

It took me time to craft these questions. When I was young, I just hated things being unfair. When there was another way that seemed available and sometimes so obvious, why didn't we make it fair? Why were people so mean to each other? Perhaps some would have called me sensitive. Maybe I was. I just felt things, and people, and nature.

I grew up in a small mountain town in the Rockies. Nature and wildness were larger than humans. I think this often saved my heart and my lucidity. Beauty was all around me, and I noticed it. I listened to the creeks and smelled the sweet grasses and spruce. I spoke to the mountains and sky and they communed back. I loved the snow. I loved the billions of stars in the night skies.

At home I watched my parents fight. Sometimes over things that seemed inane to me as a child. They seemed so solvable, if they would talk or listen. I understand much more about what shaped them now ... about trauma and triggering. About sexism and the ongoing pressures of money and debt and working hard. About being pregnant at nineteen with no means for an abortion, and having three children by their mid-twenties. My family swerved in and out of the working and middle class, and ended with a house lost to the bank and my mother living below the poverty line after the divorce.

As I followed these feelings, which would eventually become crafted questions, they became the guide for much of my exploration these last thirty years.

Healing and Activism

In my experience, healing and activism went together. I won a scholarship for "future leaders" and spent my last year of high school in Hamburg, West Germany, before reunification. I applied for that scholarship not because I even knew where West Germany was, but because it would get me out of my house for a year. I was politicized being outside of the United States, and saw a global economic and cultural view for the first time. I also started thawing from the violence in my family. That thawing came in the form of depression and wondering what was wrong with me.

In 1985 I went to college, and in 1986 I dropped out to walk with the Great Peace March for Global Nuclear Disarmament, across the United States. I learned about the wide diversity of communities in the country, the utter beauty of the land, and about what it would mean to build a peace-based economy, rather than one fueled by war and defense/offense. It struck me that the poorer communities were the most generous and welcoming, while the wealthier neighborhoods we walked through often pulled their curtains closed as we passed. In retrospect, walking ten to fifteen miles per day, and being a part of a purpose so much greater than myself, somatically opened my system to the healing that was to come.

Back at college I got into activism and had the honor of learning third-wave feminism, getting to meet and study with some of its influential teachers: Audre Lorde, Chandra Mohanty, bell hooks, Mary Beth Krouse, and others. I was also fortunate to have teachers who began to unpack class for me, and ones who validated the importance of relationship to land, indigenous rights, and intuition as another way of knowing. I am grateful. So much of my political understanding of the

2

world and perception of oppression, privilege, and power-over systems were grounded here. My life experiences began to have names and context greater than me, my family, and my town. I began to unpack my own shaping from patriarchy, white supremacy, class, and heterosexism. I also started having my first flashbacks of child sexual abuse by my father and some of his friends. Not fun.

In this context I tried to get help. Having never been exposed to therapy or personal development, I didn't really know what to do. I tried the college's psych services and was told that child sexual abuse is very rare, and if I wanted support, I would need to find other survivors on campus—then they'd run a group for us. I was putting myself through college, had no other insurance, and worked washing dishes on campus. So ... in what was the "emergency stage" of healing, I outed myself on campus, put up flyers with my phone number, and did outreach to find other survivors of child sexual abuse who might want to heal. In two weeks there were eight of us who wanted a group. I went back to psych services ... they were surprised. And, a therapist ran a group for us. In retrospect, I am grateful for my drive and perseverance, and pissed at the lack of consciousness and care. My self-reliance wedged itself in a level deeper. That group became a lifeline. Much of my healing happened in groups from there on out, and eventually I found somatics.

In those days of studying, working, being an activist, and trying to survive through all the pain and loss, healing and social change wove themselves together more deeply inside of me. When I could not heal for myself, I could for others. Through my learning I could see that others had worked for change, for freedom, before me—that I was a link in a very long chain—and I could do my part for the future. I saw that I was freer than my mother because of how others had organized for change, and that could be true for the generations after me. I could do my part. This gave me courage.

Many, many experiences unfolded from there. I studied Neuro-Linguistic Programming (NLP), was invited to ceremonies, and stayed close to land and beauty when I could. I waitressed, worked banquets, and eventually landed myself in San Francisco with $300, two friends, and then a job at Good Vibrations—at the time a woman-owned and -run, sex-positive, sex store. I have learned so much since then.

Healing

As I found my way in the Bay Area, I connected with a somatic practitioner who revolutionized my understanding of healing and what was possible. Through somatics practices and bodywork—the same processes I would later study—experiences of abuse, violation, grief, and fear fell off and out of me. I faced a level of loss, shame, rage, and the isolation that comes with things you have to keep secret—that I didn't think I'd survive facing. The deep self-reliance I had developed was sometimes at odds with the sheer vulnerability that emerged through this healing work. Yet, I was amazed at what my body had held for me, and when given the chance and the somatic support, my body/mind/emotions/being knew how to heal. Anyone who knows the healing process from violence and trauma, knows there are so many other things you'd rather be doing and feeling. It is hard and painful work. It is also freeing work.

I didn't spend my twenties partying. I spent my twenties healing, finding broader purpose and community, and working hard.

In 1997 I formally began to study somatics, first through the Lomi School with Robert Hall and Richard Strozzi-Heckler, and then through the Strozzi Institute. Again, it was amazing for me to see how the body and self are interdependent, and how we can deeply change as the survival patterns and adaptations in the body and tissues are transformed. I saw people change there that I never would have expected to transform … namely older, privileged white men who seemed unfeeling. I saw in a profound way that everyone has a story, is shaped by their context, has survival strategies, and that all of this is embodied. Our adaptive and inherited embodiment can radically change when these strategies are somatically addressed and people's authentic longings are accessed. I often see people now as an embodiment of their history and experiences, with a long trail of stories and adaptations behind them, and some longing drawing them forward. Lots more on this in the book.

It was a complex space, as well, in that there was not a social analysis integrated into the work or the training rooms. The broader conversations of how we are shaped by social conditions, about oppression and privilege, about our individual and collective survival strategies that come from these conditions, were missing. While people were empowered in their empathy, longings, and to take bold new actions, the conversation of collective accountability and collective action was not there. Individual change was the ground, and even as people felt desire to make a difference for others, even support social change, the analysis of broader systems was absent and the support defaulted to individualism and unreflected-upon privilege.

I would often choose what to say and what not to, taking many conversations home to my more political community. The space was primarily white, middle to upper middle class, and heterosexual. Usually I was the youngest in the room, one of the few queer people, and I was on a work exchange/scholarship, meaning I was again doing dishes and cleaning up after folks. I did attempt to have these conversations at the time. They did not go well. I chose to learn and gain all I could through somatics, and then find other ways to integrate somatics with a social analysis, and serve people committed to equity, social justice, and a radically different relationship to the earth.

I became a somatic practitioner within this lineage and methodology, I ran somatic healing groups for survivors of violence, I have now worked with thousands of people, and I became a teacher in the work. Eventually, in connection with what you'll read below, I developed the somatics and trauma work you'll see here. I ran the first Somatics and Trauma course in 2000, and continued developing the work from there. This was both an innovation on and extension of the work that Richard Strozzi-Heckler had continued to develop. We were in conversation through these years, and he was continuously supportive of me taking the work into places he didn't or couldn't—both the healing from trauma and oppression, and politicizing the work. I appreciate him very much for that.

Activism

I did not grow up in a family that was socially active, or that had a social analysis. I have often thought that my mother would have thrived if she had been exposed to a feminist and social analysis earlier. My guess is she would have become an organizer if she knew what that was. I have also reflected that my father would have been more empowered, and likely less violent, if he had known about labor unions and been a part of one. He strove for the "American Dream," and what he thought that would give him; while the skills, education, finances, and network he would need to do that were not available to him. But, one doesn't know that, and all the loss and failure become so personal. I think he too would have thrived working for something bigger than himself. Born-again Christianity found him instead, although that's mellowed with age.

After activism in college, I looked for a number of places to get active in social change. I started with San Francisco Women Against Rape (SFWAR) and trained as a volunteer. This turned out to be too raw for me, given the stage of healing I was at myself. I went to many actions and meetings, from queer to feminist, from antiwar to environmentalist. I tried to bring my politics to where I worked. I never quite found my political home in that era. I often wished I would have trained as an organizer in this phase of my life. It would have given me a lot more ground for my work going forward.

By the mid-1990s I wanted a place to address child sexual abuse (CSA) as a social and political issue, not just as a therapeutic one. While so many of the activists and organizers I knew were survivors of child sexual abuse, it was not integrated into their social movement work. It lived in conversations we'd have on the side, as I became more and more public as a survivor. I spent a lot of time trying to find good healing resources for these folks. I could not find a group or organization that was taking on CSA from this political bent, so talked a close friend of mine into starting an activist group with an intersectional analysis, called RunRiot! Survivors Activist Coalition. Because this was the era of the "false memory" backlash (more in the book on this too), we held actions at book readings of false memory authors (life before podcasts), talked to healing groups about activism and the connection to healing, tried to influence the emerging sex offender registry, and joined marches as a public group. I know it might seem strange, but it was during the 1996 San Francisco LGBT Pride Parade when the sheer numbers of people sexually abused as children really hit me.

We decided to join the parade as a contingent for a number of reasons … to be public about such a silenced and hidden issue, to repoliticize it, to counter the homophobic reaction that "you must be queer because you were sexually abused," and to be sex positive. Whew. We had stickers, placards, a banner, you get the idea. Most of us were also freaked out because the stretch from being a secret, hidden, unacknowledged issue to a parade with 450,000 spectators, was a lot. As we walked down Market Street toward the Embarcadero cheering and yelling, a consistent reaction happened block after block. You could see people reading our signs and banners, looking over our diverse crew (gender and race), and taking a moment to process. Then people would start waving, yelling, "Me too! Me too!" or break down crying, or touch their partner or friend's shoulder, pointing to us … and eventually that person would wave, yell, or cry. It was amazing, and it was utterly emotionally overwhelming. To move away from numbers like one in three girls and one in six boys (with no statistics for trans folks), to faces and people and partners, waving, was deeply impactful. We wanted to mobilize them, to have a strategy where we could impact root causes of CSA, and to have this be a healing experience. I did not know then that this would mean a lifetime of work.

We founded generationFIVE in 2000 after eighteen months of hosting community groups about how we might end child sexual abuse.

These groups were with targeted communities, Asian Pacific Islander, LatinX and Black, mixed raced providers, adult survivors of CSA, activists, folks who worked with CSA offenders, and more. We sat with over three hundred people and cold-called twice as many to invite them. generationFIVE grew into a leadership and capacity-building organization, developing a transformative justice (TJ) approach toward ending the sexual abuse of children. It was the survivor's groups that let me know we were ready for and committed to a radically different approach, outside of the state incarceration systems. All of the survivors did NOT want incarceration for the people who had violated and abused them. They also did NOT want to go through the criminal/legal system themselves, given how they'd be treated, and what evidentiary laws require. It is a setup; the evidentiary laws are contrary to the lived dynamics of CSA. They wanted healing, accountability, and social change so that we can end the abuse of children, and so that they could heal.

Child sexual abuse is deeply traumatizing. It is also very early training in power-over, in victim and offender, in coercion, in silencing, and in adapting to violence and domination. This is training related to all systems of oppression and power-over social conditions.

generationFIVE and our CSA and TJ work were the first places we began to integrate somatics in theory and practice. We used it as staff, we understood the trauma and shaping from CSA through a politicized somatics lens, we integrated healing and the TJ approach, and we did somatic practices in all of our trainings. We saw we needed all of it to address child sexual abuse. As we were more and more out as leaders around CSA, many, many people told us their stories of abuse. People wanted to take action, and as they did they got triggered and needed healing, then that healing would serve their leadership and action, and back again to healing. Even non survivors that got involved in the work needed personal and emotional development, because of the intensity of the work and the stories. It was clear that to address CSA as a social issue, we had to integrate personal and systemic transformation.

In 2007–2008 I shifted from being all in with generationFIVE, to looking at somatics as having a wider contribution for social justice movements. I had been running the Somatics and Trauma course for seven years and, as more and more social movement folks studied it, they were encouraging wider application and access within social and environmental justice spaces. In 2008, we gathered community again, organizers and healers who worked in various social justice organizations, and explored where to bring somatics and who and what to serve through this.

In 2009–2010 we ran a sixteen-day (four, four-day sessions) somatics program for movement leaders from across the United States. We wanted to test a wider application and get folks' feedback. Is this relevant beyond generationFIVE? That year, and over the few years of expanding programs and partnerships, we got a resounding "Yes." This was the first project Spenta Kandawalla and I worked on together, which grew into us co-founding and launching generative somatics (gs). This is the organization that now houses and continues to develop a politicized somatics supporting social and environmental justice organizers, leaders, organizations, and alliances in the United States. We continue to run the Somatics and Trauma programs through gs. Many of the folks who participated in the 2009–2010 program have continued within the work and practice and are now somatic movement leaders doing transformative organizing, and lead teachers for generative somatics. To find out more about our work at gs, go to www.generativesomatics.org.

In the early days of exploring the wider application of somatics within social movement spaces, we also got to partner closely with some key leaders and organizations. The rub between personal and systemic transformation became a dynamic tension. We learned from and deepened the work through this tension. I want to acknowledge Social Justice Leadership (SJL), Black Organizing for Leadership and Dignity (BOLD), the National Domestic Workers Alliance (NDWA), and the Racial Justice Action Center (RJAC) for our partnership and joint exploration in these early years. I also want to appreciate Spenta Kandawalla, Raquel Laviña, Sumitra Rajkumar, Xochitl Bervera, Chris Lymbertos, Denise Perry, and Ai-jen Poo for looking for what can truly meet and serve the needs of member leaders, organizers, and systemic change today. I deeply appreciate all of the risks each of you have taken, and the co-creating we do together!

The depth of the somatics and trauma (S&T) work initially was not always welcomed in social justice spaces. Tapping into trauma and embodied healing, when so many of the conditions people were living in were precarious, needed to be done well and respectfully. The relevance needed to be shown and proven in spaces that were working class and majority people of color, across languages, and with people who had had very little access to healing. S&T trained teachers and practitioners needed to understand and blend with the context of organizers, activists, and movement builders. On the other hand, the relevance of emotional depth and competency and healing to social change had been thrown out of many organizing models over the last decades. This created an attitude toward healing and personal development as "soft skills." I heard more than one organizer talk about emotions and trauma not being well held, or not being "allowed" in their organizations.

NDWA really took the first big leap with us, bringing key aspects of the somatics and trauma methodology and practice, including somatic bodywork, to nannies, housekeepers, and home health care workers. Please see Raquel's story about NDWA in the final chapter of the book. I'll always be grateful for NDWA's seeing and pragmatic commitment to meeting members' needs and building collective power.

This Book Is for You

This book really has two imagined audiences. One is healers, therapists, and somatic practitioners and the other is people committing their time and lives to social and environmental justice—members, leaders, organizers, staff, campaigners, visionaries. Some of you are in both of these groups.

In this book are the theory and process of somatic transformation and healing, after the impacts of trauma and oppression. Here you will learn about how essential the soma is to transforming trauma, cultivating resilience, and embodying new practices, actions, and ways of being. Embodied healing means we can make choices based on what we care about, rather than react from survival strategies, even under the pressures of living, loving, and social justice work. Somatics allows us to heal, find wholeness, and be on a purposeful path of transformation. It does much more than help us understand what happened to us and why we are as we are. It lets us live, choose, be, and act differently. It lets us get better at loving and being loved, at generating safety, and at taking bold purposeful action. It pragmatically and authentically helps us know how to build more trust together, and work with conflict in a way that's generative. It helps us to heal shame and internalized oppression.

This book also asks the question of what causes trauma. What experiences, family and community dynamics, and social and economic conditions cause most traumas? It looks to social justice as the *primary prevention* of trauma, while also acknowledging how essential healing from trauma and oppression is to that goal, to decreasing suffering and to increasing safety, belonging, and dignity. If we do not understand and integrate the shaping power of institutions, social norms, economic systems, oppression, and privilege alongside the profound influences of family and community, we will not fully understand trauma or how to heal from it. We will not understand how to prevent it.

This book unpacks why healing, and a politicized, grounded methodology for healing and transformation, are a supportive part of creating social and environmental justice. Organizing to transform social and economic conditions and healing are very different processes, and take very different skills and strategies. Yet, they are related. While personal and systemic transformation require unique methods of change, they are deeply co-serving. I believe they need each other to be successful.

Oppressive social and economic conditions cause traumas that need healing. Social change requires masses of people building together toward collective safety, belonging, and dignity, and systems that support this. Healing can serve that goal. Systemic transformation can serve healing.

The Stories, and More

Most chapters end with a story. These are written by people who have trained and practiced deeply in this work. Many of them have ten or more years of time in and practice together. Most of the authors are senior somatic teachers or practitioners now, serving social and environmental justice leaders and organizations. Most are long-term social change organizers or healers. They speak to the work of somatic healing, collective healing, and the relevance of personal and systemic transformation. Given their influence on and practice of the work, it felt very important to have their voices, experiences, and wisdom here.

To support you in reading this book there is a glossary in the back that includes both healing and somatics terms as well as social justice terms. And, for those of you who do not spend the majority of your time in social and environmental justice movements, I suggest reading Critical Context, following the final chapter of the book. This can help to give more grounding in understanding the "rules" of our broader social and economic systems. This is good to read after chapter 2. I hope both of these are helpful in reading this book.

Good News

I am glad you have this book in your hands. The integration of personal and systemic transformation, and what a politicized somatics has to offer—healing from trauma and oppression—are ahead. And, I want to offer a perspective on learning this work. If you are moved by the content and theory presented here, there is a path. I call it a path because it can become lifelong development and engagement. This, to me, is the good news. If you are so called, this path includes training with competent and embodied teachers, daily somatic practices, doing and deepening your own transformational work, practice clients, feedback and assessments, and more practice. It also includes beginning, or continuing, to be involved in systemic change, with a community of practice and action, a social justice organization. Reading this book alone, or mental understanding alone, will not make you competent in somatics and trauma, or a politicized somatics. It's like anything embodied—riding a bike, or becoming a surgeon, an organizer for social equity, or a healer—it takes vision, embodied practice, teachers and guides, and feedback to become good, really good, at such important work.

I hope you enjoy and are engaged by what's here.

Part 1

Somatics and Social Conditions

1

Somatics—
A Radically Different
View of Who We Are

The Church says: The body is a sin.
Science says: The body is a machine.
Advertising says: The body is a business.
The body says: I am a fiesta.

—EDUARDO GALEANO, from
"Window on the Body"

Somatics is a holistic way to transform. It engages our thinking, feeling, sensing, and actions. Transformation, from a somatic view, means that the way we are, relate, and act become aligned with our visions and values—even under pressure. More than understanding and insight, it supports us in embodying new ways of being, aligned with a broader vision. Somatics is very effective in both healing trauma and embodying new skills for leadership, organization building, and social change.

A young Vietnamese immigrant woman I met recently at a somatic training said, *"This is so exciting. I intend to be someone, to make a difference, and I don't know how to. This teaches me how to be able to do the things I want to, to be myself."*

Somatics introduces us to an embodied life. It reminds us that we are organic and changing people. There are vast amounts of information within our bodies and sensations. When we learn to listen to the language of sensation, to live inside of our skins, a whole new world opens. What is most important to us, what we long for, is found and felt through our sensations, impulses, and an embodied knowing. Through the body, we can access ourselves, develop self-knowledge, and change.

The habits and survival strategies we develop through life are also bodily phenomena. One of the most effective ways to interrupt reactions, and instead respond based on what we care about, is through the felt senses. This is where we can learn about and retrain our nervous systems, and develop ourselves.

Lastly, somatics can remind us that we are human, connected to a much wider fabric of life. Objectification of others and disconnection from the land and our living environments require us to numb, separate, and dissociate. Sadly, we as a species are fairly good at this. Not feeling ourselves allows us to not feel others. Opening to our own senses, perceiving, and aliveness allows us to develop and remember our empathy and interdependence.

Let's dive in.

What Is Somatics?

Somatics is a holistic methodology and theory of change that understand both personal and collective transformation through a radically different paradigm.

It differs from approaches to change that might say a change in your thinking will change your life, or a change in your framing and language is all you need, or even adding a mindfulness practice alone will transform you.

Somatics understands both the individual and collective as a combination of biological, evolutionary, emotional, and psychological aspects, shaped by social and historical norms, and adaptive to a wide array of both resilient and oppressive forces.

Somatics is an intentional change process by which we can embody transformation, individually and collectively. Embodied transformation is foundational change that shows in our actions, ways of being, relating, and perceiving. It is transformation that sustains over time.

Any transformation happens within a social context. We are shaped by and embody the social conditions we live in. This is so, whether we believe in these conditions or not. The social conditions include the political, economic, and historical systems, as well as the cultural norms, beliefs, and practices by which we are surrounded. The impact of the shaping from these broader forces is often what we are looking to heal from and transform, individually and collectively.

Most psychological and somatic approaches focus on individual healing and do not integrate a social analysis into their understanding of how we are shaped and what needs changing. This is a limitation that, I propose, perpetuates the oppression and trauma that we are trying to heal.

First let's clear up a common misunderstanding. Somatics is *not* adding a "body-based" exercise to psychotherapy or leadership development. It is not a workout class, or even a yoga class. It is not solely bringing your attention to your bodily sensations and following these—although this can be a powerful part of somatics. In Western(ized) cultural and economic systems, we fundamentally live within a disembodied set of social beliefs and practices. This means we have learned to hold the body as an object separate from the self, rather than a living organic process inseparable from the self. Thus, the distinctions around body-based work can get unclear and sloppy. Anything that has to do with the body can be called "somatics." I'd like to get more nuanced to make this grounded and useful.

The word *somatics* comes from the Greek root *soma*, which means "the living organism in its wholeness." Although it can be cumbersome, it is the best word we have in English to understand human beings as integrated mind, body, spirit, and social, relational beings. In somatic speak, we call this embodiment "shape." One's shape is one's current embodiment of beliefs, resilience and survival strategies, habits, and actions. We can somatically perceive an individual's shape, or the collective shape of a group. In a group this is the embodied and practiced culture, norms, and dynamics, especially those that you see when the group is under pressure.

Somatics essentially sees the self as indistinguishable from the body. The body is an essential place of change, learning, and transformation. You can think of it as muscles having memory and tissues having intelligence. We often can forget that the brain is an organ within our bodies. It is not a hard drive with software. We don't work like that.

Our embodiment, our shape, is developed in interaction with our experiences and environments. Our adaptations to these experiences and environments—both resilience and survival strategies as well as social and cultural practices—become embodied and then automatic. We think and act, relate and imagine from a certain embodiment. This opens some choices and reduces others. Once something is embodied, it is familiar and feels "normal." It can also seem permanent or "just the way we are." What we embody deeply connects to our identity and how we see ourselves.

Lastly, somatics understands people as a compilation of practices. Embodied practices are mostly unconscious to us—we have been doing them so long that we no longer have to think about them. Most of our practices are inherited through our families, communities, and social systems. Some practices we learned purposefully, like riding a bike or how to greet a new person, and others were driven out of survival and safety. They are then trained into our psychobiology over time. They become habits or skills—some useful and others not. Embodied practices are both individual and collective.

Because of how we are built, we *can't not* practice something, be it the pattern of our breathing or our response to a new love. Somatics asks, "What are you practicing? And, is what you are practicing aligned with what you most care about?"

The good news is that we have an incredible capacity for change. As the neuroscientist might say, we have an "incredible neuroplasticity." As the meditation or aikido teacher might say, "Through embodied practice, we can deeply cultivate ourselves."

Somatics pragmatically supports our values and actions becoming aligned. Somatics works through the body, engaging us in our thinking, emotions, commitments, vision, and action.

Somatic Transformation

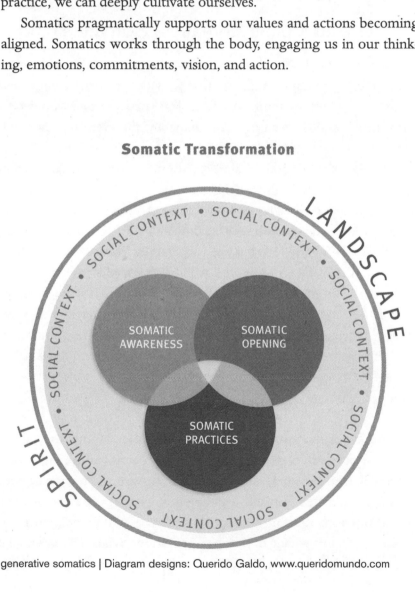

generative somatics | Diagram designs: Querido Galdo, www.queridomundo.com

21

It helps us to develop depth and the capacity to feel ourselves, each other, and the life around us. It builds in us the ability to act from strategy and empathy. It teaches us to be able to assess conditions and "what is" clearly. Somatics is a practicable theory of change that can move us toward individual, community, and collective liberation.

What Makes Somatics, Somatics?

The key aspects of somatic methodology include: somatic awareness, somatic opening, and somatic practices, within a social context and connected to land and spirit. For spirit, please use whatever word works for you. By spirit I mean the vast unknown, the ever-expanding universe, the energies, beyond human, that we are living within.

These aspects of somatics are used interdependently to create a shift in embodiment. In somatic speak, this is a shift from your *current shape* to a *new shape*. The ground for the change is your vision and longings. What do you want? What do you want to become skilled in, or cultivate in yourself? What needs healing or change? We ask these same questions of a group as well, whether it is a collective, an organization, or a community. What do we want? What creates more justice, connection, and freedom? What allows us to have the impact we want to have? The body learns on "Yes." This is the guide for transformation.

Here's more about each aspect of the somatic methodology.

Somatic Awareness

Somatic awareness involves learning to both pay attention to, and live inside of, our sensations and aliveness. This means connecting to sensations like temperature, movement, and pressure, in an ongoing way. Through increased somatic awareness, sensations become sources of information. You can think of sensations as the foundational language of life. Overriding or numbing sensations, while a good survival strategy, leaves us disconnected from a key source of information and satisfaction. Feeling our organic aliveness lets us connect with ourselves; feel what we care about and long for; build empathy and connection with others; and feel what needs to be attended to, acted upon, or healed.

There are levels to how we experience and interpret life. Sensations are the building blocks of our experiences—meaning, at the base of every internal experience is sensation. Understanding sensations as a foundational language, we can then feel emotions. For example, I may feel sad, and I can feel the sensations of pressure in my chest, warmth in my throat, and wetness in my eyes. I then experience all this as sadness. Emotions are deeply meaningful to us and can also act as guides to our commitments, connections, healing, and growth.

Since many of us have needed to turn away from our sensations because of trauma and oppression, or have been trained out of paying attention to them, here are some things you can pay attention to, to feel more of them: temperatures—more warm or more cool; movement—pulsing (heart, pulses), breath (in and out), tingling, streaming, twitching; and pressure—places you feel more contracted and places you feel more relaxed. When you notice your sensations try and be inside of them, rather than being an outside observer.

We also have internal narratives—or stories and interpretations of the world that run through us. Some are inherited; others habitual; others have wisdom and information for us to better understand, create, and navigate by. Language is a very powerful aspect of being human. Research of children born deaf shows that when we are not exposed to language early on, certain aspects of our brain do not develop (Sacks 1989). This is one reason it is important to assess deafness early, and expose deaf and hard of hearing children to sign language. Thinking and language are also bodily phenomena, although we can often remove ourselves from our sensations through language. What I mean here is that we can separate ourselves from sensations and bodily experiences by talking ourselves out of them, thus denying other information.

Lastly, we also perceive others and things that are happening around us. This happens through various senses from visual and auditory to kinesthetic and sensing. When we feel our sensations and emotions, we can also perceive the aliveness in others, or a situation. Many of us can relate to feeling tension in a room, or between people, even when everything "looks fine." We can also feel the effect of peacefulness or ease in a person, space, or in nature.

Somatic awareness invites us to attend to all of these sources of information—sensation, emotion, thinking, and external perception. It asks us to learn to feel ourselves, others, and the environment, at the same time. We can develop our skill to feel deeply, and assess what is needed internally and externally. We can then have conversations and take actions that serve what is needed based on what we, and others, care about.

Dissociation, minimization, and numbing are normal responses to trauma, oppression, and difficult life experiences. These are all ways to remove ourselves, or aspects of ourselves, from feeling. In turn, being connected to sensation helps to bring us back into contact with ourselves. It also brings us back to what we have been avoiding or protecting ourselves from. This can mean feeling physical and emotional pain that made us want to leave or numb in the first place. Thus, returning to sensing and feeling can also require support, training, and/or purposeful healing.

I know this may sound strange, but so often what we are reacting to is not being able to tolerate what is happening in our own sensations, emotions, and experience. We react to get rid of the feeling, to push away the sensations, because they are associated with something intolerable, painful, and uneasy. Increasing our ability to "allow for" sensations and emotions gives us more choice and decreases our reactivity.

Somatic awareness and ongoing *embodiment*—living inside our own body and aliveness—give us more choice. They grow our ability to be present in more and more situations. They help us act connected to what matters to us rather than react to get away from something.

Somatic awareness often reintroduces us to what we most care about … what's in our hearts or our gut feelings.

A group can practice this as well, together attending to the sensations in the body and the information it brings, in our conversations, coordination, and collective action.

Somatic Opening

Somatic opening is another core aspect of somatic transformation. In many ways, somatic transformation is not possible without somatic opening. We can increase our somatic awareness and take on new somatic practices, yet if we do not open and process the contractions that have held a certain embodiment in place, transformation does not happen. This is true for individuals and groups. A level of disorganization happens in moving from one shape to another, one embodiment to another.

Somatic opening helps to deconstruct embodied shapes and habits that no longer serve us. This means disorganizing habitual ideas and beliefs, emotional patterns or avoidance, and reactive ways of being. While this all sounds good, somatic opening can be … well, disorganizing of what's familiar. Even when what is familiar isn't working, it's still familiar. We tend to gravitate toward homeostasis. Somatic opening places us in unbounded terrain, where we can find ourselves between known self-concepts. Between known ways of being. Between known ways of interacting or coordinating.

We need a strong purpose and vision for change during somatic opening. In this disorganized place, we—as people or as groups—can feel unmoored. People can often grab onto the familiar, the habitual, and revert to what no longer works.

Our deep patterns, survival strategies, beliefs, and reactions live in our somatic structures. By this I mean, live in our tissues, muscles, and organs in patterning that includes, but is not limited to, our well-traveled neuronal pathways. These embodied patterns are supported by our habitual practices and are often reinforced by the structures and systems in which we operate; organizations as well as the broader social structures. The embodied or survival-based habits cannot be changed through conversation or thought alone. The language centers in the brain have very little influence over the survival centers in the nervous system and brain. At the same time, language and thought are important. In the big picture we want to align the head, heart, gut, and actions.

Somatic opening works through the body to access and transform survival reactions, experiences that have shaped us, and emotions or numbing that has become automatic. Our bodies tell stories. Our muscles hold memories. Somatic opening allows us to listen to, somatically process, and transform these stories. Somatic opening allows more aliveness, purpose, love, and power.

A very cool sign of somatic transformation is when you find yourself responding to something in a way that's not at all like "you." Or you find yourself taking actions and making moves you were not able to before. One of my favorites is when I find myself having new thoughts and interpretations that I did not intend or learn.

Groups that are focused on transforming also go through somatic opening. This too is a disorganization of the group's norm and embodied patterns. This deconstruction is guided by the group's commitment to something more transformative and effective or toward more choices.

Let me offer an example:

A progressive social change organization recently confronted a very difficult situation of sexual harassment amidst its leaders. The cis-male leader fired the cis-female coworker when she confronted him about his behaviors. Within the organization, all agreed ideologically on an intersectional analysis of structural power—meaning they shared values about equity and an analysis about how different forms of oppression can be challenged and changed. Like many organizations, they did not have the collective embodied skills to deal with the situation in a way that was aligned with their vision, analysis, and values. The processes, the collective practices, the conversations were not in place to find a way through that took care of the organization and the leaders within it.

Overall, this situation required the organization to reorganize its ways—meaning they had to engage in a deep level of collective change. They had to confront the fact that they did not have the collective know-how to respond, they did not have the processes in place, to handle this situation. It asked them as an organization to change, deal with their reactions, and restructure to be aligned with their values, vision, and analysis.

There are many somatic processes that support somatic opening. The processes are based on the "rules of the soma," or how embodiment works, not how we think it should. The shaping in the soma has its own deep intelligence. As we understand these adaptations and shaping on their own terms, there are many ways to work toward change. Three key principles in somatic opening are: supporting the contraction, or blending; connecting more resilient places in the soma with more stressed or numb places; and allowing more aliveness to move through the soma connected to purpose, which includes opening the tissues to allow for this aliveness and sensation to flow.

Let's unpack these principles.

Blending is the principle of joining with. This is joining with a contraction or habituated shaping in the soma, rather than trying to break it up or unlock it. The assumption behind this blending is that there is intelligence in the protective patterning. We want to be curious in our conversations and touch. What has this somatic contraction been taking care of? What has it served? When did it get established, or how long has it been around? How does it work? In supporting the contraction, slackness, or numbness—physically and verbally—the soma will begin to tell its story. We can discover how the somatic pattern works and what its key purpose has been.

The second principle is connecting more resilient places or states in the soma with those more numbed or contracted. The resilient places and states are usually more relaxed, allow for more aliveness to be felt and moved, and tend to have more flexibility and possibility. Connecting these places in the soma with places that are more numb, terrified, contracted, etc. allows an introduction to other possibilities at the feeling level—like the unconscious mind getting to talk to itself.

The last principle of somatic opening is about reminding the tissues how to allow for more aliveness and sensation to flow. This can happen through practices, using various breath patterns combined with particular somatic bodywork points. More detail on each of these is in chapter 10, the chapter on Somatic Opening.

Somatic bodywork is a powerful process for somatic opening. In this approach to somatic bodywork, we include conversation, touch, breathing patterns, gesture, and emotional processing. The bodywork is on a mat or massage table and fully clothed. Somatic bodywork allows us to work directly with the places in the soma that have held traumatic experiences or patterns for safety or are hypervigilant or numb.

Practically, this means processing the experiences stored in the soma *through* the emotions and body. Massage can temporarily relax a muscle or contraction, but the "shaping" or "armoring" in a body will not shift unless the concern that contraction is taking care of (safety, love, protection, shame, terror) is worked through. From a neuroscience perspective, the body is the easiest doorway into working with those reactions, emotions, and memories that are primarily run by the reptilian brain, and the limbic and stress centers in the brain. This is an integral part of the somatic transformation process.

Through somatic opening, change is revealed from the body up, not from thinking down. New thinking appears from changes within embodied patterns. Trying to use new thinking alone to change embodied patterns tends to be unsuccessful and unsustainable.

Somatic Practices

Somatic practices help to build new skills and competencies that are relevant to what we care about. Somatic practices allow these new skills to become embodied, so that we can count on them, even under pressure. We can ask ourselves what skills and options do we, or the groups we are a part of, need to embody to align with our callings, our vision and values? To make the impact and difference we want? The answers to these questions show us the purposeful practices we need to do.

Both individuals and groups already have default embodied practices. These may or may not be aligned with the purpose of the group. A group can also shift into purposeful collective practices that serve their joint aims.

At generative somatics, we worked with a social justice organization whose overall commitment was to be bold in their work. Being bolder would allow them to take bigger risks, attempt different strategies, and organize larger numbers of people. Being bold is a great idea, and HOW do we do that? Part of the embodied collective shape at this organization was to hold back, take care, perform well, not be messy, etc. Much of this was shaped through internalized oppression and culture. So, just saying "we are going to be bold," while important, did not shift into new actions and ways of being. New individual and collective practices were needed. These practices were both exciting and uncomfortable, given that they invited folks out of their comfort zone. As we took on these practices, other things needed to be faced as well—certain strategies of appeasing and agreeing that historically had taken care of safety, belonging, and dignity; and protecting oneself and community from targeting. These were now getting in the way of being bold, and required change.

Embodied practices are mostly unconscious to us—we have been doing them for so long that we no longer have to think about them. Some practices we learned purposefully and others we modeled from our environment (family, culture, and society). Still others were driven out of survival and safety. Many embodied practices or automatic reactions are derived from stress responses to loss, hurt, trauma, and the need for safety. These experiences can range from very personal experiences to the impact of our social, economic, and environmental conditions.

New practices tend to invite somatic opening. As we develop new skills, often previous embodied strategies may need to be shifted. What we do know is that adding new practices on top of an older embodied strategy won't work. Given enough pressure, the older embodied habit will emerge, unless it has been resolved or processed through somatic opening.

Given our community and family experiences, and because of oppressive social conditions, there are fundamental skills that many of us don't learn to embody, such as: having boundaries that take care of yourself and others, mutual contact and intimacy, moving toward what is important to you, or building trust amidst conflict. Other survival skills become embodied, including: hypervigilance and distrust, appeasing, and aggression. Trauma and oppression can leave people with a deep sense of powerlessness, isolation, and shame that you can't "talk" someone out of.

New skills are developed somatically so that they become more than good ideas—they become natural actions and habits. We want to not only know about boundaries, but be able to take the action of having boundaries in the course of our days, relationships, and work. We don't want to leave centered accountability as a good theory, but rather embody it and be able to act from this place under pressure. Somatic practices allow us to begin to build a "new shape" aligned with our values and purpose.

There are many embodied practices that are useful to a person, community, or organization. To develop a new embodied practice it takes:

- Meaningful narrative or purpose—what are you looking to embody and why?

- The practice needs to be based in the soma, or holistically engage the sensations, tissues, muscles, organs, emotions, and thinking.

- Somatic opening so that the new practice can root.

- Repetition of the new somatic practices—three hundred times creates muscle memory and three thousand times creates embodiment.

- The practice shows up as change in your actions and life, and others notice.

Again, not every physical practice is a somatic practice. In fact, some physical practices can be training us to dissociate rather than develop a new embodied skill. All of the screens and places to go virtually that have been added to gyms are an example of these invitations to a practice of dissociation rather than embodiment.

Some of the foundational embodied practices that we have found vital to healing from trauma and oppression, and to building powerful organizations for justice are:

- **Presence and Embodiment:** being able to feel and engage with a wide range of sensations and emotions

- **Generativity:** creativity, vision, possibility, chosen values, extending trust, holding complexity, and purposeful action

- **Setting Limits:** embodied boundaries with others and self, including saying "no," insistence, and discipline

- **Mutual Connection:** presence with self and other simultaneously, felt sense of belonging, intimacy, and community

- **Impacting and Leading:** influencing, choosing, intending, and taking action based on chosen values

- **Centered Surrender:** trust of self, other, and Spirit; being influenced from center

- **Compassion and Love:** giving and receiving, permeability, and appreciation with self, others, and the world

- **Unknown and Contradiction:** being with death, change, contradictions, and unanswered questions

- **Centered Accountability:** being responsive to self, others, and wider community; able to differentiate intention from impact; apologize, repair, and forgive

We will dive into these more in chapter 12, on Embodying Change. Somatic practices, combined with somatic awareness and somatic opening, let us engage a holistic, sustainable transformation.

Social Context

Any transformation is happening within a social context or social conditions. We are shaped by and embody the social conditions in which we live. These conditions include the political, economic, and social systems as well as the cultural beliefs and practices we inherit, live, and function within daily. The institutions and social norms we are surrounded by are currently shaping and have historically shaped us. We embody these just as we are shaped by and embody our family practices and culture, those of our communities, and the land and environment. We are in both a current social and political moment, and strongly shaped by the flow of history before us.

When we are looking at transformation, social context is one of the most influential shaping forces, whether we are focused on personal, community, or systemic change. The impact of the shaping from these broader forces is often what we are looking to heal from and transform, individually and collectively.

Spirit and Landscape

Spirit and landscape are forces that are beyond humans, and shape us deeply, as well. These forces are more lasting than what humans can do or create. The earth was formed 4.5 billion years ago, the Milky Way galaxy 11–13 billion years ago. Six hundred million years ago the ozone layer formed. During the Cambrian explosion, 580–550 million years ago, the most modern phyla of animals began to appear in the fossil record. A hundred million years ago the earliest bees appeared, 80 million years ago came the ants, and 50 million years ago the first deer. *Homo sapiens* appeared in Africa 250,000 years ago. Around 50,000–100,000 years ago, they began moving to other continents, replacing the Neanderthals in Europe and other hominins in Asia. Time is vast compared to a human lifetime.

We can forget this in our modern and technological world, yet we are still shaped by these broader forces. Even as we are degrading essential parts of our natural environment and collectively becoming less connected to sources of our food, water, and energy, we are completely dependent on the earth for our existence. Land, the atmosphere, the global weather systems, the water cycle—these allow us life. It is only very recent in human evolution that many of us are not centrally connected to land and landscape. Throughout most of human history, our deep relatedness to the earth and stars was reflected in our cosmologies and social and religious practices. No matter what, however, whether we are in a wilderness, rural area, or cityscape, landscape shapes us.

Nature and land are repeatedly shown to be a central resilience factor for humans, as is our connection to something more vast, felt yet unknown, which here I am calling Spirit.

By Spirit, I mean the larger forces of energy, the vastness of the cosmos and unknown, and the harmonizing forces of nature. One of the 2011 winners of the Nobel Prize in astrophysics, Saul Perlmutter, reports that what we can see in the universe (stars, planets, nebulae, etc.) is under 5% of what is out there. Roughly 68% of the universe is made up of antigravity dark energy, with dark matter making up the remaining 27%. Scientists know how much dark energy there is because of how it affects the universe's expansion. Other than that, it is a complete mystery.

People across cultures report direct experiences of this vastness as profound and meaningful. Across cultures and time, it is named in different ways and a variety of practices have been cultivated in connection with it. Religions have attached ideology to this sense of the unknown.

So, as we consider what shapes us, what we are made of, what resilience we can cultivate individually and collectively, it is vital to include land and spirit.

Embodied Transformation

This model—somatic awareness, somatic opening, somatic practices, within social context and landscape and spirit—helps us to see the methodology of somatics as a whole. Any one of these components alone or separated from the others does not allow for embodied transformation. When integrated, these components support deep and actionable change that lasts.

To transform, to create sustainable change, we need to perceive and come to know our individual and collective "shapes." We need to increase our awareness of the automatic reactions and ways of being we have embodied. Then, we get to open or deconstruct these, often healing and developing a much more substantial capacity through the opening. This somatic opening allows for new ways of acting, feeling, relating, and knowing. It is the pragmatic process of deep transformation, of shedding in order to change.

Somatics then moves us toward embodying new ways of being and action that align our values, longings, and actions. Often our social conditions and our family and community experiences do not teach us the embodied skills we need. This focus on developing embodied skills—whether it's centered accountability and liberatory use of power, building deeper trust through conflict, or the capacity to be with the unknown or love more deeply—is essential to sustainable change.

The bad news, from a social justice perspective, is that we inadvertently embody societal norms we don't believe in, and often don't embody the values we do believe in. From a somatic vantage point, this is completely understandable and there is a lot we can do about it.

When we look at transformation from an embodied approach, we say: A person has transformed when their ways of being, acting, and relating are aligned with what they most care about—even under the same old pressures. This is also true for a group, collective, or organization. Embodied transformation is foundational change that shows in our actions and ways of being, relating, and perceiving. It is transformation that sustains over time.

Social transformation is a more complex beast. Social transformation requires many things—base building and organizing, leadership development, empowered democratic engagement, policy change and implementation, and much more. It requires a radical transformation of our economic system. We could say society, or the political economy, has transformed when the economic, social, and political systems (institutions, practices, and norms) are designed for equity for all people and sustainability with the planet. These are radically different economic, social, and political structures than what we currently have.

Since we are so deeply shaped by and embody the social and economic conditions in which we live, somatics would ask this question about social change: *What economic and political structures do we need to have masses of people embody cooperation, interdependence, and equity? This translates into systems that hold your well-being as mine, just as your demise is mine, and the well-being of the earth's living systems the same destiny as our own.*

Soma

Throughout the book I will be using the word *soma*. I know it is a little weird, and I am trying to distinguish something more than our default associations with the word *body*.

When I say "soma," here is what I mean: the soma is the interconnected thinking, emotions, actions, relating, and worldview, embodied. All of this lives in, through, and with the body. I tend to use the word *soma* instead of *body*, because body is generally defined in an objectified and utilitarian way. Body is mostly seen as a physicality and parts, separate from the self. It is seen as something to manage, steward, control, keep healthy, or feel ashamed about.

Somatics, instead, holds the body as inseparable from the Self and how we live, act, and relate.

Somatics is fascinated with embodiment—what is embodied, and is that working? Do we have the embodied options we want for love, boundaries, dealing with conflict in a life-affirming way, equity, and more? Somatics looks for aliveness—what allows for more life, more connection, more wisdom, more effective action, and relations? Somatics looks to increase choices—based in agency and empowerment—to becoming more individually and collectively whole and skilled at living.

There are rules of the soma. The soma will not let go of an embodied pattern that has been protecting safety, belonging, or dignity, if a better embodied option is not available. From the soma's point of view, that would be abandoning survival. Bad move! The soma will release and process protective embodied patterns if healing is accessible, or if new embodied choices and moves become available that better take care of the original need. The soma responds to resilience, to an organic pace, rather than a sudden insight or breakthrough experience, and to practice with meaning and community. The soma responds to practice connected to purpose. The soma responds to support and core needs being met by opening, changing, and awakening. We get to learn from and follow the way the soma works.

I also use *soma* to distinguish from the culturally defined "model" or normative "body." This is the culturally defined idea of how a body should look, function, appear, and work. While every culture has a "normative body," these norms vary greatly. Some cultures have lots of room for human variation, and others very little. The current Westernized and capitalized normative body, the "right" body, is white(r), European in build, cis-male, heterosexual, sporty, able-bodied, "attractive," and wealthy. Or cis-female, thin, large-breasted, etc.

Somatics, with a social analysis, challenges this norm. It holds that all bodies, all people, have aliveness, form, a shape, the impulses to live, connect, and make meaning. That all bodies, all people, have adaptations to their experiences that leave them with more and less choice. The socially constructed objectified and narrowed idea of body leaves us with less aliveness and an attempt to adapt to a norm that is not possible for most people. This also leaves us with less of a sense—and for many, actual lived experience—of safety, belonging, and dignity.

Somatics works through the body, and has been influenced by ableist social conditions. Disability justice is a framework and set of principles, created by queer, disabled people of color, that challenge these notions and offer a vision for what else is possible. I am a student and learner here. The integration of these principles is vital for a politicized somatics.

Following are the 10 Principles of Disability Justice as written by Sins Invalid.

INTERSECTIONALITY "We do not live single issue lives." —Audre Lorde. Ableism, coupled with white supremacy, supported by capitalism, underscored by heteropatriarchy, has rendered the vast majority of the world "invalid."

LEADERSHIP OF THOSE MOST IMPACTED "We are led by those who most know these systems." —Aurora Levins Morales

ANTI-CAPITALIST POLITIC In an economy that sees land and humans as components of profit, we are anti-capitalist by the nature of having nonconforming body/minds.

COMMITMENT TO CROSS-MOVEMENT ORGANIZING Shifting how social justice movements understand disability and contextualize ableism, disability justice lends itself to politics of alliance.

RECOGNIZING WHOLENESS People have inherent worth outside of commodity relations and capitalist notions of productivity. Each person is full of history and life experience.

SUSTAINABILITY We pace ourselves, individually and collectively, to be sustained long term. Our embodied experiences guide us toward ongoing justice and liberation.

COMMITMENT TO CROSS-DISABILITY SOLIDARITY We honor the insights and participation of all of our community members, knowing that isolation undermines collective liberation.

INTERDEPENDENCE We meet each other's needs as we build toward liberation, knowing that state solutions inevitably extend into further control over lives.

COLLECTIVE ACCESS As brown, black and queer-bodied disabled people we bring flexibility and creative nuance that go beyond able-bodied/-minded normativity, to be in community with each other.

COLLECTIVE LIBERATION No body or mind can be left behind—only mobbing together can we accomplish the revolution we require.

The Objectified Body

Where did the idea of Body as Object come from? We, in the West, have inherited a deeply rationalistic and objectifying view of the body, and therefore of ourselves and each other. It is an interpretation of the body as separate from the (more important) thinking mind. The body is seen as muscles, sinews, bones, and a series of functions that move the mind or the "Self" around. We are quick to objectify, productize, devalue, and try to manage the body as a "thing," an "it." Many of us have also inherited, whether Christian or not, a deep orientation toward the body as sinful, or as base and shameful. This sets us into a very complex and confusing relationship with the most intimate aspects of life, and the organism we and other humans actually *are*.

We are taught to distance from sensations and the body, rather than living inside them. This distancing from lived experience, from feeling aliveness, also prepares us to be quick to objectify others and other types of life (soil, air, trees, animals). The dismissal or degradation of sensing and feeling atrophies our empathy. Sensing comes with lots of information including impulses and needs, habits, current time experiences, historical patterns, deep cares, and wisdom. The disregard of sensing dismisses a realm of information that holds both evolutionary wisdom and interdependence.

There is a history within Western philosophical tradition that led us here, and a whole series of power-over/oppressive social conditions that this history serves.

The contemporary interpretation of the body that has led us to the marginalization of feeling has its roots in the work of the French philosopher René Descartes. Descartes was convinced that it was possible to alleviate (social and religious) chaos by providing certainty through rational means.... The Scientific Revolution—the essential distinction in the rationalistic tradition is the division of the universe between matter, which is governed entirely by mechanical laws, and the mind, whose lofty territory comprised thinking, ideas, and will. In an intellectual turf war whose reverberations we're still riding, Descartes and his colleagues staked out mind, matter, and science, which included the body; and the Church claimed spirit and religion.

In this interpretation mind and body, spirit and matter, are two separate worlds that are vaguely and mysteriously linked. This was the beginning of the Western model of mind, body, and spirit existing in separate compartments.

Once the notion of an inner animating principle was dismissed, a vigorous, reductionist quantification of the material world began. The operating metaphor is that the material world, which includes the body and nature, is machine-like, similar to a huge clock, and by understanding its mechanisms we can dominate it, oppress it, and control it to our advantage.

(RICHARD STROZZI-HECKLER, PhD, *The Art of Somatic Coaching*)

The Cartesian worldview and a rationalistic tradition are defining forces in our understanding of the self, others, the body, the earth, and even knowledge and *how* we know.

I took a college philosophy class called Subjectivity and Reality. The name of the class compelled and fascinated me. We proceeded to read Kant, Nietzsche, Descartes, and other white European and American male philosophers. In a discussion on how it is we experience knowing, I shared that knowing for me often came through images and sensing. An understanding would appear through feeling first. The professor proceeded to lecture me publicly on the impossibility of that. Thinking ONLY happens mentally and in words, was his stance. I did try again to explain my experiences of knowledge and thinking through other means. I was dismissed. I don't think I spoke up again that semester. I knew my experiences were real. I just had no idea how to validate my reality or explain it to unsympathetic ears.

Rationalism separates the self from the body, and the thinking or rational mind from the aliveness and experiences of the emotional and physical self. This philosophy moves us toward an objectifying view of the body and the physical world as parts, devoid of or separate from a person's holistic and lived experience. This objectification, and mind-body split, have far-reaching consequences.

The rationalistic separation puts us at deep odds with ourselves. As we learn to dismiss our lived experience, to be rational instead of "too emotional," we necessarily learn to numb, to dissociate, and to override the feelings of ourselves and others. This distancing truncates our ability to know what we deeply care about, how to relate within complexity, and how to feel and validate experiences—whether our own or those of another. Rationalism as a primary way of being tends to side with control when it comes to working skillfully with our biological/spiritual/social/psychological selves.

The mind-body split reifies a particular power-over system as well. We can consider who and what is associated with being rational—science, maleness, whiteness, education, and wealth—the "right people" to decide, advance, and rule. Consider also who and what is associated with body and feeling—sin, irrationality, emotions, "hysteria," women, transgender, people of color, the exotic (read racist), indigenous, earth, desire—the "wrong" people to decide and lead. You can hear the multiple forms of oppression informing these and, in turn, how they are supported by rationalism.

This is not a vote dismissing rational thinking altogether or to rid us of science and scientific inquiry. Rather, it is to awaken to what is shaping us. What have been the costs of rationalism and who has repeatedly been thrown under the bus by its precepts? What of this do we want to question and change? What of rationalism as a cultural norm is deadening, disconnecting, or harmful?

The power-over economy will have us be consumers before people. Most anything we can think of to edit and manage the body is being sold to us—from a multibillion-dollar diet industry to chemicals to cover any smell. The traditional Church presents the body and human desires and sexuality as a sin. It is easier to control a person if you have made their inherent impulses toward life and contact shameful or punishable.

> All over the place, from the popular culture to the propaganda system, there is constant pressure to make people feel that they are helpless, that the only role they can have is to ratify decisions and to consume.
>
> (NOAM CHOMSKY, *Manufacturing Consent*)

Lastly, a note about neuroscience and rationalism. There have been thousands of amazing findings within neuroscience over the last twenty years. In its current popularity, many people assume that because we can explain what happens in the brain, we understand behavior or how to change behavior. Many also interpret the brain as the most important organ—if we understand the brain, we understand humans. There are many organs without which we cannot live, like the heart, the lungs, and the large intestines. Interpretations of modern neuroscience can get caught in the same rationalistic tradition of objectifying the body as now merely carrying around the more important brain. It can also promote the idea that mental understanding alone lets us know how to change.

> We like to think of the brain as this incredible computing device, that's designed for creativity and actualizing our purpose. The brain's primary function is to keep you breathing, keep you alive, and keep you safe. It evolved in order to predict danger, to predict threat.... We need to hijack that machinery, and apply it in a deliberate and specific way. The good news is that your brain is a highly plastic device.... We have planning and imagination. Practices to engage the neuroplasticity will truly rewire your brain and its ability to function, so that you are set in alignment with purpose.
>
> (ANDREW HUBERMAN, neuroscientist and tenured professor in the Department of Neurobiology at the Stanford University School of Medicine, "Presence: Living and Working on Purpose")

A somatic understanding of the body/self is radically different. It holds the body, self, thinking, emotions, action, and relating as an interconnected whole. We, this human organism, have evolved for over three billion years. That's a long, long time, from a human point of view. We have many capacities that we inherit through this evolutionary history, through having a human body, and many we can learn and cultivate. Listed below is an amazing range of our human capacities. Asking us to deny or compartmentalize aspects of being full humans can leave us longing for our humanity.

The human organism, body / self has:

- Emotions: Inherent and foundational experiences that hold deep meaning for us. We can develop our emotional skills over a lifetime.

- Sensing and interpreting: We do this through our sense organs and through feeling. We sense ourselves, others, our environments, and the mystery (Spirit).

- Thinking, analysis, and the cultivation of critical thinking through learning and study.

- Touch and capacity to develop skilled touch: Touch is an inherent aspect of healing and bonding.

- Relating: We are social animals. We can develop our skills of relating over a lifetime. Much of how we relate is based on our own experiences of safety, belonging, and dignity—both personal and social—and the social, economic, and cultural systems we live within.

- Resilience: We have inherent resilience, and we can cultivate it.

- Presence: We have inherent presence, and we can cultivate it.

- Action: We can take action in many ways—from having conversations, to coordinating with others, to physical actions.

- Communication and language: Being exposed to and learning language is essential to our brain development. We can learn new languages throughout our lifetimes.

- Spirit: We can see this as consciousness or an animating force. This is interpreted in many ways across culture and time.

Somatics is not just an effective and potent set of tools by which to heal and transform deeply. It is also an invitation to mend a profound personal and social mind-body split, which has consequences that are more harmful than life affirming. I posit that returning or reintegrating into the life of our bodies allows us to return to a greater connection with each other, life, and land. It is a practice to help us deobjectify life. It lets us sense and feel life more readily.

Somatics: The Field

We are in an institutionalizing phase in the field of somatics. Within the last fifteen years, numerous universities have begun to offer graduate degrees in somatic psychology. However, the majority of the foundational development of somatics and somatic training institutes are still independent of the university setting. There are a variety of quality somatic approaches.

As many of these somatic approaches are being integrated into the discipline of Psychology, an *attention-based* somatics is being prioritized. This is a somatic approach that attends to the sensations in the body, through conversation, imaging, and cognition. Through tracking sensations, it uses the body as a base of knowledge and change. Because of the historical bias in the institution of psychology *away from the body and touch,* essential aspects of a holistic somatic approach—including somatic practices and somatic bodywork—are being deprioritized. In this, the full potency of somatics is being missed. There is a debate within somatic psychology circles about the ethics of *not* using touch when it is such a powerful tool for healing and transformation.

The mainstreaming of somatics is, for the most part, without a social analysis and does not acknowledge the deep shaping caused by social conditions. Somatics is primarily being understood and promoted inside of an individualized healing framework. Much of the current research is focused around the use of somatics in healing trauma, at which it is very effective. But the question of why there is so much trauma and oppression to heal, and what somatics can do about it, is often left unasked. While somatics has much to offer in healing, a somatic approach without an analysis of social and economic institutions, unequal distribution of power, and use of violence and coercion, excludes some of the largest forces that shape us. Without a social analysis much of the trauma that people withstand is either left unnamed—racism, gender oppression, homophobia, class oppression—or only partially addressed.

Even when somaticists and somatic therapists are well meaning, without this analysis, we often do not explore how we too embody oppressive and individualistic ways of being, and can perpetuate this through the work.

A somatics with a social analysis can see the multiple experiences and systems that shape us, both individually and collectively. It is therefore more effective at supporting healing and change. A somatic trauma analysis can be applied to both personal and systemic violence, and give us a much deeper understanding of the violence as well as how we can effectively address it. A somatics with a social analysis can be used to build vision, strategy, and practices that serve systemic transformation, toward equity and sustainability. This is the somatics I would like to see institutionalized—somatics with its full contribution.

Somatics with a social analysis has powerful and relevant uses at a larger scale—in community, for leadership development, alliance-building, and more. Somatics can support collective practices of building power, deepening presence and capacity, increasing our emotional skills and range, and developing the embodied skills we need to generate large-scale change. Without a political analysis, this collective practice doesn't get leveraged.

The somatic methodology I am discussing here takes into account these social conditions, and also holds as its aim personal and collective equity and liberation, in interdependence with the earth and its living systems.

I began training in somatics in 1997 with Richard Strozzi-Heckler and Robert Hall, in what was then the Lomi School. I continued studying and then began teaching at the Strozzi Institute with Richard. The focus on trauma healing and the integration of a social analysis into the work began in 2000 through generationFIVE. There, we integrated somatic principles and practices into transformative justice work, addressing child sexual abuse. Beginning in the same year, I developed and ran independent Somatics and Trauma programs. This politicized somatic methodology has continued to be experimented with, tested, and practiced within generative somatics since 2009.

A politicized somatic theory addresses the need for deep personal transformation, aligned with liberatory community and collective practices, connected to transformative systemic change. One is inseparable from the next, and each should serve the other. We need all three to generate strong and grounded strategy, to build compelling alternatives, and to mend the deep wounds of oppression and violence. We need all three to build collective power that has wisdom, and to act and organize in accordance with liberatory values. My hope is that the use of a politicized somatics by social and environmental justice movements and healing practitioners will help to advance large-scale systemic change.

2

Sites of Shaping, Sites of Change

As we start to orient to somatics and trauma healing, I want to introduce a model to help us understand how we are shaped by many layers of our experience from the genetic and uniquely personal to social norms that shape millions of people, including you and me. Social norms are communicated, taught to us, and practiced at each Site.

This model helps us ask questions and understand how we are shaped at each Site. It reveals how these Sites inform and interact with each other. We can explore how each Site either shapes us into, or in contradiction to, the social norms and historical forces we live within.

This Sites of Shaping, Sites of Change model is based on a public health framework, and was developed by Alan Greig and generationFIVE to help understand the multiple layers of child sexual abuse—its causes, its impacts, and how to end it. generationFIVE's mission is to end the sexual abuse of children within five generations. One of the powerful phrases they use is, "offenders (people who sexually abuse children) aren't born, they are built. How are our social conditions building them?" You can learn more about the transformative justice approach to ending child sexual abuse at www.generationFIVE.org.

Any large society will have all of these Sites. The ways in which they are organized can look very different, however. Family can be constructed in a wide variety of ways, as can the ways broader democracy or decision making is practiced. These Sites do NOT have to be organized for power-over or exploitation. Each Site can be organized to build and train cooperation, interdependence, and deep regard for the earth. The PURPOSE the Sites are organized toward can be equity and sustainability; this means the practices, ideas, institutions, and economic exchange would be in support of "power-with," instead of power-over. This type of organization would result in less individual and collective trauma too. In this chapter we will focus on how we are shaped by each of these Sites, and in turn have embodied that shaping. Later in the book we'll explore how we create change at each Site. Through a better understanding of how we are affected and shaped by multiple Sites, we can also better understand trauma, healing, and embodied transformation.

Sites of Shaping
Sites of Change

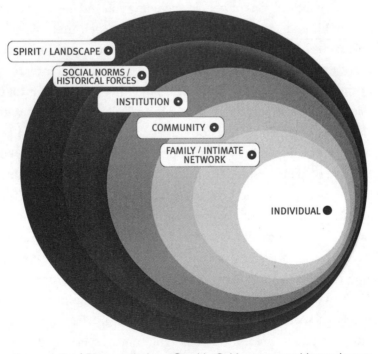

generative somatics | Diagram designs: Querido Galdo, www.queridomundo.com

Let's break this down.

Individual: We can think of this as the constitution or nature with which we are born. As we can see, different children have different ways of being and different constitutions from the beginning of life. Different cultures and people interpret this differently—some say it is genetics or the mother's diet and exercise. Others say it depends more on the safety of the mother and infant. Still others say it is the influence of previous lifetimes and reincarnation. I don't think we can definitively answer *why*.

Questions: What do you feel your constitution is? What did you "come in with"? What about your family or friends—how would they answer this question for themselves?

Families and Intimate Networks: These are people close to us with whom we form bonds, or attempt to, both in our youth and our adult lives. These are the people we are a part of or "belong to" through biology, circumstance, or choice. This is the Site that many forms of therapeutic work focus within.

Questions: How have your experiences of family shaped you? In your younger development? Now? What did you learn about safety, belonging, and dignity? About resources? About equity? How were the larger social norms taught to you through your family and intimate networks?

Community: This can be many things, such as the region or place in which you grew up or live (i.e., the South, West, Southwest, New York, rural, or urban areas). Community can also be a racial or cultural identity (Black, LatinX, Arab, Jewish) as well as a community organized around gender or sexual orientation (queer, trans, LGBT). It can be connected to a practice (martial arts, sports, meditation, etc.). Community often has institutions and regional or cultural norms connected to it.

Most of us have a number of communities by which we have been shaped and may identify with. For me, I identify with the rural mountain community in which I was raised. The community identity included being hearty and sturdy, and had the attitude that "nature bats last." The mountains, rivers, pine trees, and night sky there live deep inside of me. I also identify with the queer community, particularly the progressive/left parts of that community as well as more radical left communities who are feminist, anti-racist, and actively engaged in social change. I am white, my ancestors are primarily from Scandinavia and Ireland, and I have been shaped by white supremacy and that privilege. I was raised working class, and am now middle class and one of the more resourced people in my family—some who live at poverty-level income for the United States. My class experience shaped a "share what you have" and "work very hard" orientation in me, and was very coupled with male supremacy and violence.

Questions: Who are your communities? How have they shaped you? How have others you know been shaped by those same communities? How does your community position itself toward communities that are different than yours culturally, racially, or economically?

Institutions: Institutions are larger systems that affect many people and communities. This includes: private and public education, banks and other financial institutions, health care, military and paramilitary, religious institutions, media, corporations, agriculture and agribusiness, criminal/legal and prisons, communications, technology, energy and transportation, government, and social services—from local to national and international.

Our institutions and systems are currently based within a power-over paradigm. Global capitalism promotes massive national and international institutions and social narratives that concentrate wealth with the few, and use the labor of the many to do so, exploiting them and the earth.

Questions: Consider two institutions that have shaped you and others you care about. How have these shaped your ideas, actions, and relationships?

What have you gained through this institution? How has this institution harmed you, those you care about, and others? Which of these institutions can cause trauma and to whom? Which of these perpetuate oppression? How do these institutions orient to the natural environment and sustainability?

Social Norms and Historical Forces: Social norms are the "rules of engagement" and the definitions of "reality" that we are swimming in. Who and what is considered the norm or normal or valid? What are the collective stories we live in that are presupposed? How are these stories weighted to give some more deservedness and others less? Social norms and institutions are mutually reinforcing.

Historical forces are the large trends of history that are shaping us still, even though they seem to be in the past. Examples of this are chattel slavery and Jim Crow, *Roe v. Wade*, the reservation system for indigenous peoples in the United States, the 1980s and 2008 billion-dollar bailouts of financial institutions, World War II, and Japanese internment camps.

Questions: What did you learn was normal and not normal? What's the grounding for that? Who did you learn "naturally" deserves more safety, belonging, dignity, and resources? Who has more inherent worth? Who is more disposable? Who are you or any "group" assumed to be? What relationship to the earth and nature did you learn? To money and the economy?

Spirit and Landscape: The largest circle and final Site is landscape and spirit. These are forces beyond human. We just explored this in chapter 1.

Humans can affect landscape and spirit; we can mine the earth, warm the oceans, and put satellites into space. And yet, landscape and the expanding universe are beyond our full understanding and control, while shaping us deeply. Landscape and spirit will outlast us, if 4.5 billion years of history have anything to tell us.

The landscapes (wilderness and cityscape) we are raised and live within get into our sinews. Often this sense can span intergenerationally as well, such as finding a deep sense of reso-nance in a land one's peoples migrated from. It shapes our thinking and our boundaries, whether we look nearby (forests and cities), far away (plains), or up (mountains). Wilderness, even city parks, and a relationship with a greater mystery rate as two of the main resilience factors for humans. As resilience factors, they tend to bring us a sense of coherence, more calm, hope, and connection. Research shows other key resilience factors to be positive connec-tion to another person or people, art and creativity, and being able to make a difference for others.

Questions: How has landscape shaped you? How does it live in you? How has it shaped your communities? How has a connection to the vastness or unknown shaped you? What are your experiences with this mystery that are not interpreted through social norms? Do you find resilience in land-scape or spirit? Does your community?

We tend to experience all of these Sites acting within our lives at once. The larger the circle (social norms and historical forces), the more difficult it can be to perceive and understand its complexities, without training. Perhaps this is true for every Site.

The larger the circle on this model, the more people it impacts. The larger the circle, the more people it also takes to change the sys-tems and norms of that Site. Each Site necessitates a different method of change. For example, we might engage family systems therapy or ceremony to change the Site of family and intimate networks. This would involve five to twenty-five people depending on the size of the family or intimate network, and one to five skilled guides. Used effectively over time, this can have a huge impact on a family system, culture, and practices. To change something like the economy, or the massive use of fossil fuels, or to end incarceration ... this takes social movements, new policies, changed financial and corporate institutions, radical changes in the dominant social narrative, and hundreds of thousands of people in various roles. It takes organizing, campaigns, building scalable alternatives, and movement-building to create mass systems change. We'll explore more of this in chapter 13, the final chapter.

I have heard healers and therapists say that the world would be different if people would do their deep healing work so as to not pass on their wounding to their kids and coworkers. I have heard meditation practitioners say that if we all meditated, we could bring about peace. I have also heard social change leaders say that if we change the economic conditions, the rest will take care of itself. To me, each of these holds a partial truth, yet is incomplete on its own.

While engaging in healing and personal transformation is vital for our lives, actions, and relations to become more loving, purposeful, and skillful, it does not create social justice. In fact, I see many wealthy and privileged people engage in personal or leadership transformation, and *NOT* engage in changing institutions and social norms that cause harm to others and the planet. Even though this is allegedly aligned with their values. I rarely see teachers or leaders of transformation, meditation, therapy, or neuroscience call their organizations and students to engage in social justice movements, or integrate a social analysis. Rather, the social norms and systems of individualism, capitalism, white supremacy, and others confine and coopt the transformation. These same norms and institutions continue the concentration of wealth and consumerism, and allow practices like mindfulness and yoga to emerge as products of capitalism stripped of their history and original intent.

Engaging in social change asks us to do deep internal work, uprooting and recognizing how social conditions have shaped us through privilege and oppression. Most people do not intend to be racist or sexist or transphobic, yet are anyway. Most of us have a wide variety of experiences (from resilient to traumatic) and occupy varied social locations—some with more privilege and some with less. This does not equalize our various social locations. We need to recognize our complex participation in social systems, rather than flattening everyone's experiences by saying we have all experienced hardship.

The way we decide to use transformative work, and toward what end, is also shaped by the social context and economy. We need to ask ourselves, what do I want to serve through forwarding transformative processes and practices? Whom do I want to serve through healing?

I worked for over a decade with generationFIVE, and with many survivors of child sexual abuse from a broad range of communities and class backgrounds. Child sexual abuse is a highly traumatizing experience, and is both a psychological and social issue. Many of the white, cisgendered women survivors really struggled with seeing white supremacy or their white privilege as something they had to contend with. Mostly because they had been so victimized, it was hard to see the structural power they had through being white. To do so, they needed both the education and conversations. They needed a level of healing that would allow them to hold this complexity emotionally, then act on it. Without this, an individual may experience deep healing personally, while continuing to perpetuate oppressive behavior and uphold harmful systems at the expense of others. That's not healing.

Changing policy, winning campaigns, and organizing goes a long way in helping folks change their material conditions and have more safety, resources, and choice. At the same time, it does not mend the impact of trauma and oppression, or necessarily change interpersonal dynamics that can be harmful in our groups and communities. Because we are all shaped by power-over conditions, I have seen interpersonal harms within progressive organizations either go hidden and unaddressed, or blow up and polarize groups, because the healing and facilitation skills needed weren't present or acknowledged as necessary.

These Sites work interdependently—we need to use change methods that can also work interdependently.

Again, the Sites that we just unpacked don't inherently need to be based on a power-over system or domination and exploitation. They can be based on social norms, economic systems, and practices of cooperation and social equity. At some level, the ways in which we operate, whether power-over or power-with, separation and domination or interdependence, will be our collective choice over time. Humans have shown both capacities across cultures and societies. And, Nature will bat last.

Power-Over: Systems That Harm

As we see, we are shaped by power-over conditions and we come to embody them, both unconsciously (mostly) and consciously (some). Power-over economic, political, and social systems concentrate safety, belonging, dignity, decision making, and resources within a few elite, and particular nation-states. This is done by taking from and exploiting others and the natural world. Those who are harmed and made poor are blamed in broader social narratives. We can see how power-over systems do harm and cause trauma.

Power-over systems dictate that some peoples, nations, ethnicities, genders, and lives are more worthy of safety, belonging, dignity, and resources than others. Power-over declares that it is okay to leave many in poverty, hurt and exploited, while we concentrate money, energy, power, and decision making over others and the commons to a very few. The social and economic distribution of dignity, safety, and belonging is how we construct who is seen as worthy of existing and who is considered expendable.

Power-over depends upon violence, threats of violence, coercion, and a steady stream of misinformation to work. People(s) don't inherently want to give up their dignity, self-determination, or safety, or to be without resources. This must be taken through many forms of denigration and violence. Power-over is supported by vast cultural narratives, including media, religious beliefs, and government propaganda (e.g., the Patriot Act) that validates and uplifts inequity, war, nationalism, patriotism, and the worthiness of these few, while suppressing and minimizing information that shows us otherwise.

Power-over also encompasses a worldview about the earth, our planet, and its billions of life forms. It creates a worldview in which the plants, animals, water, air, seeds, microbes, etc. that are here are primarily for the use of humans. It suggests that humans are inherently more worthy than all other life. It is assumed that natural ecosystems can be manipulated, devastated, or recreated to serve the ever-expanding human population. Aspects of the earth's ecosystem are "owned" and profited from, while the remaining devastation is most often left to the earth alone to recover from, for poor communities and countries to face and contend with the wreckage upon their lives, and for wealthy individuals and families to benefit from the resources.

This is the situation we have arrived in and it is ours to contend with. To live skillfully, to heal, to act in accordance with our values, we have to be awake to our conditions. To decrease suffering and prevent trauma, we need to organize or join organizing efforts that are working to transform social and economic systems.

While all human societies have social norms and systems, not all societies have been based on power-over structures. There are many examples, in the history and the geological record, of societies constructed on power-with dynamics. These social structures have small wealth gaps, gender equality and role flexibility, few war-related weapons, relatedness to nature as if humans are an interdependent part.

Power-Over and Trauma Healing

For the master's tools will never dismantle the master's house. They may allow us to temporarily beat him at his own game, but they will never enable us to bring about genuine change.

(AUDRE LORDE, "The Master's Tools Will Never Dismantle the Master's House")

What we tend to think of as individual traumas, such as intimate part-ner violence, child abuse, harmful drug and alcohol use, and more, are not so individual when we look at the numbers and the social condi-tions in which they are happening. Intergenerational traumas can be best understood within this broader view as well.

Let me pose these questions:

- How can a woman heal from child sexual abuse without address-ing sexism and gendered targeting, sexualization, and violence toward girls, women, and transgender people?

- How can a young Black man organize for social justice for his peoples without also addressing the intergenerational trauma of US slavery and racism? Where is his space to heal?

- How can people engage in spiritual awakening practices, yoga, mindfulness, or meditation practices and not become agents for social justice, actively organizing for the dignity and well-being of all life? How is it that the cultural appropriation, white supremacy, and classism in many of these practices is mostly left unaddressed?

- How can an immigrant domestic worker organize for equal pay without having an accessible and relevant place to heal from the pain of leaving her family in order to provide for them?

When we look at healing something as intimate as family violence or child sexual abuse, very quickly we find ourselves in the midst of social conditions and norms. Here are some things to consider:

What creates offenders, or people who sexually abuse children? Yes, we can give them a diagnosis, find them deplorable, or react through vigilantism or denial. If people are not born sexual abusers, what makes them that? Why are 96% of them men? This requires a complex answer. The statistics will tell us that a majority of people who sexually abuse children were neglected or physically abused as children. Those in treatment consistently report having felt helpless as adults, yet able to easily assert control over children. Typically, it takes a year of treatment for people who have sexually abused children to begin to thaw out enough to empathize with those they hurt. If we look to male gender socialization, we find lots of training in power-over beliefs and behaviors with little permission to feel afraid or vulnerable, to not know, to not be in control, to have needs for connection. There is encouragement to control, win, fight, and know more, to earn one's worth and identity. Even the benevolent patriarch forms of these messages are power-over: protect, save, know, assure. There is deep social training in sex as power, sex as violence, and very little training in the social conditions of sexual empathy and mutual consent.

Why do so many people surrounding child sexual abuse not notice, deny it, or do nothing? Again, a complex answer. We have automatic survival responses to horrors and trauma. Denial and numbing are some of these. Running and hiding are others. The vast majority of child sexual abuse happens to children by their families and other people they know. There is a strong social stigma against intervening in the family. We are not supposed to comment on others' child-rearing. We have all kinds of shared social denial—they (children) don't remember anyway, kids are resilient, I would have known if it was happening, or I know him (offender) and he could have never done that, and more.

The social consequences are very high for discussing with a family or community member your concern about child sexual abuse in their family. Most of us can't even imagine the conversation. The social and criminal consequences are high for outing child sexual abuse, especially if you are poor or working class, from a community of color, or are undocumented. The more class status you have, the easier it is to buy your way out of child protective services by promising to do private therapy. Most people do not want to engage the criminal legal system in their families. The criminal legal processes are not designed for healing, accountability, and mending relationships. The evidentiary laws (proof) of the criminal legal system have very little to do with the facts and dynamics of child sexual abuse (i.e., physical evidence, a witness, child development, social denial, traumatic amnesia). And there are almost no treatment services within the US prison system for sexual offenders. Whew.

By looking at this situation holistically, we can see why child sexual abuse continues. How do we then heal this violation and the ensuing trauma? How do we prevent it from happening again? We can see that personal, family, and community healing are needed in consort with broader organizing efforts for social and environmental justice. In the case of child sexual abuse, organizing for transformative justice responses is central.

Because most of the root causes of trauma stem from power-over social conditions, we need to both heal and organize for social justice. We need to mend from deep hurts and violations *and* we need to change social and economic conditions that are causing the next generations of trauma.

After twenty-five years in both social justice and somatic work, I believe that we cannot heal, or help others heal deeply, unless we integrate into this work an analysis of social conditions and how they are shaping us. Theories and practices of trauma healing cannot end at the impacts of family or community, or integrate only war or natural disasters. Healers and therapists need a strong social and economic analysis to understand and successfully address healing, and help to prevent further trauma.

I also believe that our work to create widespread social and economic change can be served by addressing trauma and healing. Those we are organizing with, as well as ourselves, have been shaped and often traumatized by social conditions that require healing and transformation. What we believe and how we relate to each other can be at odds—and we need to continue to close the gap. An understanding of the impacts of trauma from both intimate experiences and social conditions, and the processes of healing and building resilience, have a place in our social change strategies and tactics.

Deepening Understanding

There are many ways to learn more about Sites and the PURPOSES they are organized around. Here are some questions we can ask to help us perceive the power-over social and economic conditions we are collectively shaped by:

- Who is (systemically) offered safety, belonging, dignity, and resources? Whom is it taken from, to do this?

- Who is (systemically) denied safety, belonging, dignity, and resources? And then, blamed for it?

- Who benefits from this system/policy/norm/war? Which people, communities, and nations benefit?

- Who suffers from this system? Who pays—with their health, labor, and lives?

- Who decides? Who defines reality, the dominant narrative, history, possibility?

- Which peoples and what natural resources are exploited to concentrate wealth, power, and decision making in the few?

- Who is poor and who is wealthy? Which people, which countries? How is this perpetuated? Whom does this serve?

- How are the poor, the exploited, and the victimized described by or blamed in the dominant narrative?

For those of us working in trauma healing or social change, I invite us to also ask:

- What does it take to transform how power-over social conditions have been embodied in us, even when they are not what we believe in?

- Even when our thinking might have shifted, have our actions changed? Has how we spend our lives, time, and resources changed to align with these values?

- What does it take for us to work collectively, when there has been so much wounding between us and our peoples? When these power differences still operate? If, when under pressure, we tend to polarize and make each other wrong?

- If you are a healer, therapist, or practitioner, have you joined organizations and organizing for social justice? If not, why not?

- If you work in social movements, have you integrated an understanding of trauma and healing into your strategy and work? Have you accessed healing and transformation for yourself and your organization?

After the final chapter, I have included an introduction to power and systems—Power-Over: An Intersectional Analysis. There are definitions, stats, quotes, and some stories to begin to grapple with how broader systems work, and work together, to perpetuate oppression and harm. If this type of work is newer for you, please go check it out.

Other ways to deepen our understanding and integration of a systemic analysis are through study—reading, discussing, watching movies; through formal political education through organizations like Catalyst, The Center for Political Education, The School of Unity and Liberation, and more; and through joining social justice organizations and becoming active members. There are many organizations and resources listed on this book's website (www.thepoliticsoftrauma.com).

To be a part of change, whether personal healing or widespread social change, we need to be awake to how we embody and participate in social conditions that harm, consciously and unconsciously. We have been and are shaped by power-over social and economic conditions, rather than ones based on *power-with,* or the interdependence of life. To move toward more healing, systemic equity, and sustainability on the planet, we need to transform these conditions into ones that are life-affirming, just, and sustainable.

We need to change ourselves to change society, and we need to change the structures of society to change ourselves, at scale.

SUMITRA RAJKUMAR, longtime political educator and movement builder, somatic practitioner, teacher for generative somatics, and writer.

When asked to consider the impact of social conditions on my psyche, my body, my development of selfhood, I immediately recall the deep disorientation I felt in the city where I grew up. Often, stories of migration are stories of separation, lack of access, loss, exclusion, outsider syndrome, exile, or disorientation to one extent or another contingent on race, gender, and class advantages or limits. After a second migration to the United States later on, I became doubly troubled. But, I believe my upbringing in Dubai in the United Arab Emirates was its own particular, surreal case and I want to focus on that. I want to talk about the broader social dynamics more than intimate ones, partly to protect my family's privacy, and also because I think in our world of healing trauma, we tend to focus on intimate violence often without the impact of broader geopolitical forces and structures, which can shape our bodies intimately too.

The city of Dubai rose out of the sand around me at a soaring pace that the world had never really seen. My parents, brother, and I moved there in 1979. My dad had studied to be a chartered accountant and believed this was the place where the family could find their fortune. This was a middle class aspiration, to be clear, not one made out of desperation for survival. Dubai was the promised land: no taxes, free trade, and just a stone's throw from family in India, since we would be well off enough to travel back now and then. Businesses were about to flourish there and he wanted a piece of that. That was his story, he stuck to it, and we lived by it. He was relentless about wanting the best of the world for us. It gave him his sense of purpose.

Dubai was a grand experiment in wealth creation by warring Bedouin tribal leaders turned neocolonial elites. They were ready for the stability and the caprices of modern capital and so created it hand in hand with the British. The British in turn were ready to make new deals with Third World leaders to retain some hold on money and power in a changing world. Everyone was willing to share some pie, or *lahmbajin,* if you will. The city became a blueprint for a cosmopolis drafted out of the twinkles in these men's eyes and in perfect sync with the excesses of late capitalism. We all exist amidst the contradictions of our societies, but what made Dubai so damn special was the acceleration of its growth at a time when that kind of capitalist momentum was still new for the world. As a tourist economy to boot, with its glorious beaches and powdery sands, Dubai became a "liberal" jewel in the crown, suffused with money from rich tourists and businessmen who drank their cocktails and slapped each other's backs in the many watering holes freely allowed in the hotels. Meanwhile, Dubai was built completely on migrant labor of all classes, but especially from South Asia. There weren't enough locals to build it, especially since the elites did not want to work. In fact, we South Asians outnumbered all the local Emiratis as well as the Arabs and Iranians from neighboring countries. We were migrants, but denied any stable migrant status or security, in a blueprint of a city that was just being pieced together. I think it's important for me to communicate how "special" the politics of this city was. My own hypervigilance and paranoia to be understood as well as my growing penchant and skill for understanding the complex and contradictory shapes of other people were born from this difficult to translate "specialness."

Dubai was and is a highly stratified, unequal society and I strongly felt the impact of all these unequal relationships, coming from India as well, which was also very class- and caste-striated and feudal. I remember being deeply sensitive in relationships with people higher in social status and in those below us and I did not know what to do with my sensitivity. We had upper middle class family on my mother's side back in India, and always had that security, but my father did not have much of an inheritance, according to family lore, and as can often happen with migration, we were demoted in class and social status when we got to new shores. Meanwhile, the city ran on an underbelly of exploited labor in order to reproduce itself—construction workers and domestic workers whose passports were hijacked, who were exploited, abused, their pay withheld—many of whom may have perished in the building of Dubai's many lofty skyscrapers. To add terrorizing insult to injury, men who built this city with their hands were hidden in camps deep in the desert rather than have them blemish the tourist scene that was important for Dubai's status in the global economy as the liberal bastion of the Middle East.

From the beginning, I had an unsettled feeling of not belonging, uncertain about where I did belong. I was constantly reminded that this was not my country and my parents constantly reminded us, in the manner of immigrants who cautiously play by the book, that we should be grateful for being allowed to be here to make our money. We started out in an old working class Indian enclave, Karama. My father began a series of jobs, in the slow climb of upward mobility, eighties-Dubai style. We were in a different apartment almost every year, each in a slightly different neighborhood, as the neighborhoods themselves became neighborhoods. Some streets had names; some did not. My father worked incredibly hard for long hours and to put it obliquely out of respect for my father's efforts to care for his family in this place, the household surely felt the intense emotional impact of his stress and any indignities he suffered. This was hardly the only way in which patriarchy impacted my sense of self as a young woman in a violent city, with rigid gender binaries, run by rich men.

I remember how rich Emirati men careened around the streets in expensive sports cars all the time, the sound of a Lamborghini or

Porsche screeching, taunting women in the street. Everyone was terrified to be in an accident with these cars especially if they were connected to the royal family, which most of them were. It would always be your fault. I was barely allowed out alone for fear of rich men and what they could do. Cars would slow and roll down their windows and men would taunt me, invite me to get in. Going to the supermarket was an ordeal. I was always drawing surreal images of women in chains and covered in thorns as a child, with faceless men. Grounded or ungrounded as that fear may have been, it was pervasive, widely shared, and it shaped my psyche.

To me, Dubai society seemed baroque and almost cartoonish in its contradictions and power dynamics. Dubai was an authoritarian theocratic society run by monarchs but it was also a liberal tourist economy and tax-free business hub run by free trade cosmopolitan capitalists. I went to a madrassa and then a Catholic school. My parents were Hindu, nonreligious, and we always had a mixed group of friends from different religions but our community was South Asian, mostly North Indian—although we were from the South so I spoke more Hindi and Urdu than I did my own language, Tamil. The British, Europeans, and elite Arabs rarely mixed with South Asians in those days, whatever class background they were. As a schoolteacher, my mother was paid half as much as her white colleagues while she was still on my father's visa—she had no civic identity of her own beyond "wife." I remember being in the midst of fights when my friends and I were denied entry into "members only" spaces that were obviously set up on the basis of race. Those nineties Benetton ads had not made it to Dubai yet to instill a shallow "anti-racism," inviting diversity for profit. I was dark-skinned and had a strong feeling that I was looked down upon by whites and Emiratis but also by light-skinned South Asians and Arabs. But it seemed like no one else had the paranoia I did or they did not admit to it. I was always told I was too angry or that I was exaggerating and perhaps it was best that I go to the United States where apparently, I could express my ideas more freely. I remember this as painful and I became loud and shy in erratic turns. I felt that everyone was always shushing me out of fear and telling me to be grateful for the sheikh's generosity. My rage grew even as my family became more comfortable. There seemed to be a Faustian trap in all this.

There were people a lot more objectively impacted by social conditions. My family was relatively privileged in many ways. I was fascinated and tormented by class hierarchies and confused about my family's changing role within them, along with the violence we had experienced or witnessed. Class differences felt stark, arbitrary, and wrong and I felt helpless, like I did not have any say in how fairness could be structured into society. It was true: I did not, since we lived in an authoritarian society that imprisoned people who spoke against the state. My righteous outrage was large and live within me. At the same time, my resilience built up from a warm family that loved to laugh, tease, be bawdy, and eat well together; and in my own secretly nursed love of art, literature, and music that would only grow over the course of my life.

When I came to the States as a student it did not take long for me to get involved in social justice work, to be particularly interested in anarchist and communist anti-colonial traditions, to engage in solidarity struggles around police brutality and racial injustice, to build with queer and feminist artists and youth media workers. But, as the US nonprofit-based left grew in the nineties, they had their own contradictions. I always had a big mouth and wanted to use it but I was young, new to political work and its turfs, and clumsy. What I needed was kind guidance but was about to encounter the authenticity policing that accompanied the American social movement left in the 1990s. Most people seemed to posture their way through it, playing up wherever they had felt victimized as a way to ensure their belonging. I did not hide my hedonism (my love for literature, art, food, bawdy humor) or my class privilege in being able to come to this country even though I was ashamed of it at times, and defensive, knowing people were suspicious of me. All it took was a woman in leadership whom I deeply admired publicly accusing me, my accent fresh from British medium schooling, of being an outsider and an interloper. It plummeted me into a sudden panic. All my outspokenness vanished.

As I grew to facilitate popular and political education work in large groups with more serious and judgmental organizers who thought more categorically, and frankly less imaginatively but with a ton of provincial American authority about how people's identities were shaped, the fear of being in front of a room consumed me. It kept me from my purpose. I was convinced my voice had no right to be heard. I could not brush it off. It settled into my body, my bones. I stayed doing the work because I regarded it as my duty and purpose. My entire focus was in my attempt to continue to understand the structures of the world but keep all my ugly un-belonging behind the scenes. To make matters worse, every time I returned to visit family, I recognized where I grew up less and less. After I watched the towers fall in September 2001, someone almost immediately told me to get out, to go back home. Where would I go? In my memory was a pastiche of mismatched corridors and streets with no names. Global development causes many cities to gentrify for the rich but Dubai had transformed in the blink of an eye to a disorienting sci-fi landscape. I couldn't recognize it. I couldn't even recognize my family and what it had made of them. I was unmoored. I became more belligerent when I returned home; I lost childhood friends. We mutually judged one another's life choices.

The erasure was so thorough that I felt completely lost and took complete refuge in my intellectual and political pursuits. I stayed up in my head then panicked when I felt emotion in my body like it was wrong or shameful to feel it, sometimes erupting in a fit of hard disconnecting anger that left me lonely. I liked people and made friends easily wherever I went, always had a good intuition and empathy for a range of people's experiences, and was never surprised by any stories, only curious. This would eventually help me be a good practitioner. But I was also hypervigilant, feeling all the time but refusing to admit it, policing myself, criticizing myself viciously, mistrustful and paranoid, convinced that my alleged friends secretly thought I was a sham and did not understand or trust me. This made me lonely and sometimes misanthropic, always halfway out the door of all relationships, of all places. When under pressure to speak, my mouth would dry and I would assume that people were coming for me. I could be intellectually battle-ready but I longed to speak from more than that, from my heart, my guts. I knew I had something to say and yet that I was not special. Like everyone else, I wanted to be known for everything good and bad about me, loved for my contradictions and efforts, and to be free enough to love back.

Once I found somatics, I realized my work was in the body. It was literal. I had to tolerate the blankness in my brain and the sensations in my insides and look people in the face without being scared of them until my breath and thoughts came back. I had to allow that trusting people was not necessarily dangerous. I had to face the terror and the longing to be seen all at once—to reveal myself, to be more vulnerable. I opened my ribs up, sat in my seat more, eased up on my hypervigilant eyes and throat. I had to talk about and face all the fear and shame of growing up in Dubai, the disorientation and inability to connect the dots of my own life and realize that I, like everyone else, had a story. In the midst of this, I opened up my original love for literature and my passion to write but I was terrified of the irrelevance of my voice: again, the blank, dry loss of words. I had to ease my armored system to be more porous, allow for relationships with trust in lovers, friends, family, readers. I had to get over myself. I had more choice once I did this. I could choose to be less lonely, to not press the eject button, to stop collecting the evidence of loss and hurt to build the case against relationship, as though loss only happened to me, to dare to stay and build love and community and even share my own voice. Even now, I'm scared to write this but writing feels so much more alive than staying silent. That awareness deepens my embodiment of courage to help build our collective radical will to change our individual lives and the world itself.

Part 2

Trauma and Oppression

3

Individual and Systemic Trauma: A Somatic Understanding

*History, despite its wrenching pain, cannot be
unlived, but if faced with courage, need not be
lived again.*

—MAYA ANGELOU, "On the Pulse of Morning"

Let's delve into understanding just what individual and systemic trauma are.

There are many experiences that can cause traumatic impact in people. Since trauma has become a widely used word, I want to dig in and make some distinctions.

In daily speech, I often hear people say things like, "I was traumatized by that," or "That's traumatizing," often meaning that it was an unexpected or intense experience. Or that they feel uncomfortable and are unsure how to process feelings of sadness, fear, anger, or even uncertainty. Having feelings (emotions and sensations) in life and about our world is normal. Developing our ability to be emotionally present and skillful is also a good thing.

Feeling, in and of itself, is not "traumatizing"—even when those emotions or sensations are intense. Often, intense emotions and sensations are actually part of healing, and a realistic, humane response to our world. In the big picture, I think becoming more and more skillful, able to feel and make choices that take care of ourselves and others with the aliveness of sensation and emotion, is both part of healing and part of being responsible people and leaders.

So what is trauma, what are traumatic experiences? Why are they so impactful? I want to invite you to look at trauma from a holistic perspective with an understanding that our emotions, thinking, physiology, actions, and relations are integral or inseparable. Thus, when the soma is impacted, all aspects of the self and relationship are impacted.

Here is a somatic definition of *trauma*:

Trauma is an experience, series of experiences, and/or impacts from social conditions, that break or betray our inherent need for safety, belonging, and dignity. They are experiences that result in us having to vie between these inherent needs, often setting one against the other. For example, it might leave us with the impact of "I can be safe but not connected (isolated)," or "I have to give up my dignity to be safe or connected." This is untenable, because all of these needs are constitutive or inherent in us.

We have built-in psychobiological (mind/body/evolutionary) ways to protect ourselves when our safety, belonging, and/or dignity are threatened. These are mobilized automatically; we don't have to think about it. You have likely heard about the instinctive responses of fight, flight, freeze, appease, and dissociate. We'll dig into these deeply in the next chapter.

At a profound level, two things are happening with trauma. First: We have an inherent instinct to mobilize to protect ourselves and often others. This is holistic and somatic; it engages all of us. We are either only partly successful at the protection/escape, or not successful. This mobilization and the harm of the violation are then left incomplete in our somas. They don't go away, though—they are stored there and shape our experience, interpreting the world for us.

The second is this: Once threatening and harmful experiences have happened, we have mobilized to protect and this is left incomplete— the sensations of the trauma and mobilization can be overwhelming, and we shut them down. What the soma needs is to complete the excitation, and process and mend the break and betrayal. What we do instead is over-contain it, or move away from the pain and fear. In some very foundational way, we cannot tolerate the sensations and emotions that are evoked and shut them down instead. This becomes further shaping, contraction, and numbing on top of the wound and survival reactions.

One aspect of healing is widening the range of sensations and emotions we can feel, be present with, and allow to move in us. Primarily our reactions are to help us not feel the things we cannot tolerate. We'll explore this more in the following chapters.

> I became what I am today at the age of twelve, on a frigid overcast day in the winter of 1975. I remember the precise moment, crouching behind a crumbling mud wall, peeking into the alley near the frozen creek. That was a long time ago, but it's wrong what they say about the past, I've learned, about how you can bury it. Because the past claws its way out. Looking back now, I realize I have been peeking into that deserted alley for the last twenty-six years.
>
> (KHALED HOSSEINI, *The Kite Runner*)

Thus, traumatic experiences cause a somatic contraction and "shaping" that becomes unresponsive to current time experience. This means that when our natural survival reactions cannot be processed through to their completion at the time of the event(s), these reactions, and resulting shaping of the self, become generalized. The soma organizes itself around the experiences and the caught survival reactions—"If it happened once, it can happen again!" The intention is self-protection or prevention of further harm. Yet, the result is the overgeneralization of survival strategies.

Most importantly, this survival shaping does not take in new or current time information. Rather, the psychology, physiology, and relationality all remain organized around protecting from the same or a similar harm, without taking in new information. We become organized for danger, abandonment, and humiliation—without a way to regain safety, belonging, and dignity holistically.

This "survival shaping" impacts identity, interaction, relationship, physiology, emotions, behavior, and thinking or interpretation. The shaping remains, even when it is no longer useful or relevant to the current context. It is preparation for the worst, rather than being able to assess for danger, safety, connection, and dignity; and the nuances of each.

What are some examples?

- A successful Black woman in the United States who is a leader, published author, and looked up to as a mentor by others. She has been dealing with the impact and misrepresentations of racism and sexism for her entire life. She has a deep sense that she is not worthy, or must prove herself. A sense of never fully belonging, that something is wrong with her—that she has to "earn" her place.

- A male survivor of child sexual abuse, now an adult, in a vibrant, choiceful, and communicative partnership, has a deep sense of readying himself for betrayal and abandonment.

- A gender-queer person, who is also a survivor of rape, is left with a deep sense of shame. A sense that something is wrong with them. The shame of rape, and the shame of authentically expressing their gender in a world that doesn't dignify them, are interwoven. Something as harmful and degrading as sexual assault is intertwined with something as life-affirming and full of agency as self-discovery and -definition.

Survival shaping can become so familiar that we can think it is "just the way we are." We end up acting and reacting from our survival shaping, even when it does not take care of what matters to us. These survival strategies live deep in our nervous systems and psychologies. We embody them. By embodying them I mean that they have become habits, not only in our neuronal pathways, but also in our muscles and tissues. We can't *not* be them (until we heal and transform them).

Some ways that survival shaping may look in the physiology are:

- Someone who consistently hangs their head or casts their eyes down, not taking up space. It may seem that they apologize with their bodies. This can be a survival shaping of appeasing, or one shaped by a deep sense of shame.

- Someone whose eyes are more fixed or held wide, like they are shocked or scared. Someone who knows where the exits are, and may be "on the move" a lot. This can be survival shaping of unprocessed shock, or one who is looking to escape, to run.

- Someone who gets angry, defensive, or controlling quickly. They may seem sharp or cold in their eyes, or jaws. The chest and jaw may protrude. This can be a survival shaping of "fight" or defense, when defense is not needed in the current situation.

- Someone who has a hard time staying "here" or present. It may seem like they are not paying attention, or that they don't care, or that they are "checked out" a lot. This can show up in the eyes, in not "hearing" or tracking what's going on. The person may somatically appear more airy or floating. This can be a survival shaping of dissociation, of staying away from feeling or experiencing life.

You may ask any of the above people about this shaping, and most would say they don't know what you are talking about. Once a survival strategy is embodied, it becomes less and less conscious to us, and more "just how things are." At this point, the soma has few other options than this shape.

Evolutionarily, this all makes sense. Humans are very adaptive. Our somas (mind, brain, body, emotions, and the ways we relate) are organized through these devastating experiences. We are adapting to survive, to connect, to be dignified, and to matter, through traumatizing situations and/or conditions. Whichever survival strategies worked best in the traumatizing context, our soma will generalize and continue to use. This is naturally not a fully conscious process—we are mostly not choosing our survival strategies. Rather, the deeper and unconscious parts of the brain and nervous system, the muscular system, endocrine system, our being (sense of self, soul, and resilience), and the context we are in, all become a part of the "decision." In fact, our conscious minds may get frustrated with the consequences of these survival reactions, and not be able to stop them.

Survival strategies are taking care of something very deep in us: our need for safety, for belonging, for dignity, and significance. These are vital. Often, these same survival strategies also cause struggles, breakdowns, and limitations in our lives.

Trauma can be caused by many experiences, including experiencing or witnessing violence.

- Examples of intimate violence include: child abuse (physical, sexual, emotional, and neglect), intimate partner violence, having a caregiver with severe mental health issues, sudden loss or abandonment, severe or ongoing harm from siblings or extended family, etc.

- Examples of community violence include: bullying, physical, sexual, or emotional violence, financial abuse, and many aspects of state or institutional violence that are enacted at the community level.

- Examples of state or institutional violence include: poverty, racism, sexism, heterosexism, transphobia, ableism, war, political torture, imprisonment, police violence, surveillance, unnecessary medical procedures, forced migration (economic violence or political repression), xenophobia, etc.

- We can also be traumatized by accidents and natural disasters, and necessary medical procedures, among other experiences.

Most traumatic experiences are caused by humans and/or by human-designed cultural and institutional systems. Because we are social animals and need one another, this is even more deeply impactful.

Lastly, trauma is an individual and social experience. This is vital to the clear understanding of trauma, as well as how we heal and transform its effect. We'll explore more of this below.

I know this is a lot of bad news. Hang in there. We must know the problem well, in order to know the solutions well.

Systemic Trauma

Just as it is vital to get a holistic understanding of trauma, we also need to look at the larger context of systemic trauma. I am calling it *systemic* because many aspects of society interact to perpetuate this broader trauma. They include: our economic system, and the assumption that unending growth and concentration of wealth are its highest purpose; our institutions that focus the resources and decision-making power with the wealthy (corporations, owners of corporations, financial institutions, and politicians), and blame and institutionalize the poor; and social norms that teach us collectively that some human beings have more worth and dignity, are more deserving of safety, and have the inherent right to belong (e.g., men, whites, heterosexuals, the wealthy). The rest are left to prove their worth, their dignity, their belonging, and try to find safety amidst these inequitable social norms and conditions.

We delve into these power-over social and economic conditions more deeply in Critical Context at the end of the book

What is systemic trauma?

Systemic trauma is the repeated, ongoing violation, exploitation, dismissal of, and/or deprivation of groups of people. State institutions, economic systems, and social norms that systematically deny people access to safety, mobility, resources, food, education, dignity, positive reflections of themselves, and belonging have a traumatic impact on individuals and groups.

The ongoing violence of colonization, slavery, imperialism, human trafficking, war, and genocide and the resulting dynamics of forced migration, criminalization, and displacement are all examples of systemic trauma. Other types of systemic trauma include the ongoing negative portrayal in the media of Blacks, Muslims, Arabs, LatinX, and indigenous peoples, of women, transgendered people, and poor white people that is backed by government and economic policies. For instance, women's airbrushed bodies are being used to sell us everything from shampoo to cars, from weapons to war, while women's actual bodies are scrutinized, criticized, legislated, and violated. Another example is the demonization of queer people by most major world religions. This lack of safety, belonging, and dignity traumatically impacts individuals and whole groups of people.

Climate change–induced disasters and environmental destruction are also a part of systemic trauma. Because of rising sea levels and the ensuing contamination of freshwater, many island communities may be forced to migrate by 2030. The Republic of Kiribati, Tuvalu, Tokelau, the Maldives, and the Marshall Islands are all at risk. *Anote's Ark*, an Official Selection at Sundance 2018, tells the story of the Republic of Kiribati. Land and place are central to the culture and identity of many of these communities. The collective impact of displacement is traumatizing.

Like individual trauma, systemic trauma overwhelms and breaks down safety, connection, and dignity in the minds, bodies, and spirits of individuals and communities. Collective survival strategies can "shape" whole communities across generations. Certain survival strategies can become embodied in cultural practices; some cultural practices may develop out of trauma rather than resilience.

When we live inside of economies and social norms based on a model of power-over (domination), rather than power-with (interdependence and cooperation), many peoples and communities are traumatically impacted.

Here are further examples.

Slavery and Anti-Black Racism

As a result of twelve years of quantitative and qualitative research, Dr. Joy DeGruy has developed her theory of Post Traumatic Slave Syndrome, and published her findings in *Post Traumatic Slave Syndrome: America's Legacy of Enduring Injury and Healing*. The book addresses the residual impacts of generations of slavery and opens up the discussion of how the Black community can use the strengths gained in the past to heal in the present.

This is a theory that explains the etiology of many of the adaptive survival behaviors in African-American communities throughout the United States and the Diaspora. It is a condition that exists as a consequence of multigenerational oppression of Africans and their descendants resulting from centuries of chattel slavery. This is a form of slavery that was predicated on the belief that African-Americans were inherently / genetically inferior to whites. This was then followed by institutionalized racism, which continues to perpetuate injury. This results in what Dr. DeGruy has articulated as M.A.P.: **M:** Multigenerational trauma together with continued oppression; **A:** Absence of opportunity to heal or access the benefits available in the society; leads to **P:** Post Traumatic Slave Syndrome. (From Dr. DeGruy's website at www.joydegruy.com.)

The Multigenerational Impact of Colonization

Dr. Eduardo Duran, a noted Native American psychologist, has done groundbreaking work in the area of postcolonial healing.

81

Hozhonahaslíí: Stories of Healing the Soul Wound is part of a healing process occurring in the Navajo Nation, and in many other parts of the world, in regard to historical trauma. He has created a series of videos in which personal testimonies, memories, and reflections of the Diné (the Navajo) from a community in Northern Arizona are interwoven with his own commentaries. While it focuses on the Diné, the story is true for many Native peoples who have been colonized. This collective healing process focuses on healing from what Duran calls the "colonization of the native life world."

> Most of the time people say that alcohol is the problem, marijuana is the problem, suicide is the problem, and these old people say, no that's not the problem ... it's the soul wound.
>
> ... When somebody gets injured in the heart, in their spirit, and they get real sad, if they do not get a chance to take care of that through some kind of a treatment, some kind of therapy, that this is passed on to the children, the grandchildren, the great grandchildren.... A lot of the problems that we face now are a direct result of the soul wounding that happened.... Almost every time I have told people about this, they feel a great relief, because they start realizing that they are not a defective Indian, they are not a defective person.... Colonization ... when you are colonized that means your identity is taken away from you.
>
> (DR. EDUARDO DURAN)

Targeting Muslims and Arabs as "Terrorists"

There are long-standing stereotypes in the United States targeting Arabs and Muslim peoples as terrorists. These have been fueled by political agendas intending to build a viable "enemy" for war and the securing of resources (oil) and US positioning toward the Middle East. Most recently we have seen aggressive immigration policies targeting Muslims. Executive Order 13769, titled "Protecting the Nation from Foreign Terrorist Entry into the United States," often referred to as the Muslim ban or the travel ban, was an executive order by President

Trump in January of 2017. The executive order banned foreign nationals from seven predominantly Muslim countries from visiting the country for ninety days, suspended entry to the country of all Syrian refugees indefinitely, and prohibited any other refugees from coming into the country for 120 days.

> A new analysis from the Cato Institute—based on data from the State Department—makes the facts clear. On refugee policy—the area where the president has the most discretion to enact his vision—his administration has almost completely shut out Muslims. From 2016 to 2018, the government cut admissions for Muslim refugees—which Trump has called a "Trojan horse" designed to bring down America— by 91 percent. In 2016, the government accepted nearly 40,000 Muslim refugees around the world, compared with just 3,000 in 2018. And while refugee admissions overall have plummeted, the Muslim share dropped from 45 percent to 15 percent, meaning it's fallen at an even faster rate.
>
> (DAVID BIER, immigration policy analyst at the Cato Institute, "Trump Might Not Have Gotten His 'Muslim Ban,' But He Sure Got His 'Extreme Vetting'")

Systemic Denial and Reparations

These examples reflect current and historical social and economic violations. Mainstream US society continues to be designed to deny and minimize this history, and to continue to degrade and to exploit Black, indigenous, Arab, Muslim, and other people of color. There has been no collective apology and amends. No radical restructuring of society to assure safety, belonging, and dignity for these peoples. Just as in intimate violence or sexual abuse, the denial and dismissal of the violation, the retaining of the power-over by the person doing harm, the lack of accountability, authentic apology, and restitutions, does not allow for a transformation of the relationship, or the harmful power dynamics.

Those harmed need healing, agency, and structural power. And those who enact harm need transformation so as to shift from domination to equity, to take ongoing actions to rebuild trust, to demonstrate trustworthiness. At the level of systemic trauma, with which most personal traumas are interconnected, this requires both individual and collective healing, as well as structural change, both social and economic. These become inseparable for truly transforming trauma, and minimizing further trauma.

> Won't reparations divide us? Not any more than we are already divided. The wealth gap merely puts a number on something we feel but cannot say—that American prosperity was ill-gotten and selective in its distribution. What is needed is an airing of family secrets, a settling with old ghosts. What is needed is a healing of the American psyche and the banishment of white guilt.
>
> (TA-NEHISI COATES, "The Case for Reparations")

Connecting Individual Trauma with Systemic Trauma

While we may have traumatic experiences that are very personal, and may live alone with them for years, traumas such as child sexual abuse, intimate partner violence, harassment, and police violence reveal themselves to be systemic due to their sheer numbers and spread across regions. Violations that occur frequently, and across many communities, show us that there is something happening in the social and economic fabric that actually supports, or allows for, their occurrence.

Thus we need to see the trauma in a more complex way. The immediate violation has impact, the relationship to the offender(s) has impact, the social denial or blaming of the victim has impact, and the overall lack of effective collective response has impact. The broader social norms that feed this narrative of who's to blame and who can remain unaccountable have impact. These are all connected.

Here are two situations to unpack using this lens of the interdependence of individual and systemic trauma.

Let's look at the sexual abuse of children. One in four girls and one in six boys will be sexually abused before their eighteenth birthdays, and 34% of people who sexually abuse a child are family members (National Sexual Violence Resource Center 2015). That's a big and painful set of numbers. As we know, around each child who has been sexually abused, there is the person who violated them, the other adults who may or may not be intervening, and then other children, teachers, and people in their lives. Child abuse, both sexual and physical, and neglect stun me because it is so prevalent, yet there is so much silence. It's so hidden. How do we do that? What social norms and practices allow for both the abuse and the silencing of it? Given the statistics of child sexual abuse, and that the vast majority of people who abuse are known to the child, most of us know someone who has sexually abused a child.

> In order to escape accountability for his crimes, the perpetrator does everything in his power to promote forgetting. If secrecy fails, the perpetrator attacks the credibility of his victim. If he cannot silence her absolutely, he tries to make sure no one listens.
>
> (JUDITH LEWIS HERMAN, *Trauma and Recovery: The Aftermath of Violence—From Domestic Abuse to Political Terror*)

Over the last years, we have been witness to repeated police violence against Black communities in the United States. While this is sadly nothing new to Black communities, more has been caught on video and phones—and made public. This has helped to source a new wave of resistance movements, like Black Lives Matter. This intimate and systemic violence can be traced back to slavery, to community policing of enslaved people, and those trying to get free. Black families and communities need healing from loved ones being killed, all while there is little opportunity to gain accountability or apology for the death. How do we deal with these contradictions? How do families and communities heal?

> We see *healing justice* as necessary in a society that criminalizes Blackness, and structurally ensures trauma for *Black people*.
>
> (BLACK LIVES MATTER [www.blacklivesmatter.com])

For those of us for whom the above scenarios are not part of our communities, let's imagine and bring on our ability to empathize. Imagine it is our family, our extended family, our community who were not assessed as important enough, by a system so much larger than us, to have access to clean water (as in Flint, Michigan). To have thousands of treaties broken by the government that calls itself the freest in the world (First Nations peoples). To have the majority of our community killed or our peoples enslaved for profit (genocide and slavery). Imagine that our peoples are deemed terrorists, and those judging have few to no distinctions between Sikhs, Muslims, Arabs, Pakistanis, and others—that this narrative is used to drive wars that profit the wealthy and forward imperialism—but it is you that is blamed. What does trauma healing look like in these contexts?

Power-over social conditions shape and impact all of us, but not in the same ways. People and communities in positions of systemic privilege are also shaped by systemic trauma. The impact here is often to stay separated, disconnected, and "better than," which results in breaking safety and connection. They often seek real and emotional power, or perceived safety through retaining their privilege. Fear, other experiences of trauma, and blame can be misplaced based on the negative stereotypes and structures of oppression. Safety can be sought through domination and degrading others—while this may protect one's access to resources, which is a type of safety, and one's perceived identity, this is not sustaining safety. It limits choices and limits connection and belonging, rather than increasing these.

The following is an excerpt from *The Physiology of Sexist and Racist Oppression* (2015), by Shannon Sullivan. In a course she was teaching on introductory feminist philosophy, she was discussing racism. A young white woman replied, "But I am afraid of black men! ... I can't help it: I tense up and get knots in my stomach." While this is her experience, and feels deeply authentic to her, it has been shaped by oppressive social conditions, not the truth. This speaks clearly and painfully to the embodiment of social conditions and the shaping of privilege.

Most of us live in multiple social locations when it comes to oppression and privilege. We may be transgender, working class, and white, or Black and upper middle class, or a documented immigrant, etc. While we have all inherited the social conditions in which we were born, while we have embodied them, and been shaped by them, we have many choices—and accountability—about what we do with them once we have more choice and agency as adults.

As we can see by the examples throughout this section, trauma is an individual and social experience. Healing requires an individual and social response. Engaging this interdependence is vital to the clear understanding of trauma, as well as how we heal and transform its impacts.

Relevance for Social and Environmental Movements

Understanding this somatic definition of trauma, as well as how to generate healing, is vital to the success of social and environmental justice movements. As activists, organizers, and politicized healers, we are impacted by individual and systemic trauma and are often reacting out of our survival strategies. The same is true for the communities, members, and the organizations we work with.

These reactions shape the culture, strategies, and visions of our movements. Our experiences of trauma can be a source of compassion and wisdom, and also can have us bring increased suspicion, reactivity, and distrust to our work. Doing our own deep healing can dramatically strengthen our leadership and effectiveness. It can dramatically improve our relationships. It can help us align our actions and skills with our visions. Being able to integrate an understanding of trauma and a way of working with it into our movements can increase the well-being of our constituencies, our ability to effectively coordinate and connect with one another, and the relevance of our strategies for change.

As movements, we are committed to transforming oppressive conditions that damage our communities and planet, toward a more equitable, life-affirming future. Working with trauma somatically allows us to better understand *how* to generate change, *how* to build more agency and collective action, and *how* to sustain it over time. The somatic impact of trauma is predictable, as are the things that encourage transformation. We can incorporate these insights, principles, and practices into our work.

Relevance for Therapists, Clinicians, and Healers

Understanding trauma through somatics, and acknowledging the social conditions we live in, can be a lot of bad news at once. And, for therapists and clinicians, it is essential to our success. When we can join our clients in their individual experiences as well as the social conditions that have shaped and are still shaping them, we can better serve their healing, witness their experiences, and choose effective approaches that meet them and serve their transformation.

Most healers and therapists are primarily trained in a Western and individualistic view of trauma, and/or family systems. This is vital, and it is also limited. Practitioners are often not trained in perceiving the social conditions, either historical or ongoing, that are a part of the trauma, or even the cause. These broader circles are both the container in which life, healing, and harm are happening, and those that the client is and will be navigating as they transform. Community, social institutions, and social norms have great influence in trauma, resilience, and healing, and in a client's navigation of life.

To Close

The somatic definition of trauma, set within our social conditions, can be a big chew. But, it is what *is*. We are physiologically, psychologically, and relationally affected by traumatic experiences and social conditions. We are all shaped by our experiences and the social conditions in which we live. I hold that a deeper understanding and an ongoing curiosity as to what actually works for transformation let us all live better and do the real work of healing and social change more effectively.

ELIZABETH ROSS, artist, somatic practitioner, longtime harm reduction organizer, and teacher for generative somatics.

I grew up in the 1950s during the McCarthy era, when J. Edgar Hoover, director of the FBI, was determined to eradicate the voices of union organizers and progressives. My parents were targeted because of their membership in the United States Communist Party, and my father was an organizer with the International Typographical Union. Under the Smith Act of 1940, advocacy for Marxism was equated with advocating for the overthrow of the US government. Activists—and those swept up in the climate of suspicion—were summoned before HCUA (House Committee on Un-American Activities). In 1953, the year after I was born, the Rosenbergs were executed. The McCarran Act (Subversive Activities Control Act of 1950) made it possible for suspected immigrants to lose their citizenship and be deported. In the wave of fear, my cousins went underground. This was the environment of my early years. My experience of safety was limited: life inside the family was safe; life outside was unsafe. The world was riddled with danger, and an irreconcilable fact that my community and specifically my loving, marvelous parents—who had committed themselves to creating a world of peace and equity—were considered a threat.

For the first eight years of my life, as the multiple charges brought against my father progressed through the legal system, my family was deeply isolated. The persecution was multilayered: from individuals threatening my father at work ("two red hot Rosenbergs on the grill, one more to go"), to systemic public attacks through newspaper articles. Activists were frightened to associate with us as suspicion and isolation were an important tactic of the government. My sister and I were ostracized at school. Even though I was extremely young, I had few childhood friends. I remember my father meeting with other parents as lines of association were, sadly, drawn.

Safety was entwined with silence to protect people. Because of this, I developed a rigid sense of self-reliance at a young age. I grew up having very little experience with asking for help or depending on others outside of my parents, which continued well beyond their deaths. My childhood view of protection was limited: I felt safe with my parents, I trusted them, and I also had a duty to protect them and others. My parents hid people who were underground. The FBI regularly came to our home; our address was printed in the media. The dominant quality in the household was fear of what might happen. The unknown became a frightening prospect, at odds with my parents' positive ideology regarding change. While in actuality the result of a conviction would have been deportation, the acceleration of hate in the country made it clear that the unthinkable was possible. I was increasingly alert to this ubiquitous danger, in body and psyche.

Throughout their childhoods and youth, my Jewish and Quebecoise parents persevered through poverty, starvation, discrimination, and genocide. These were the social conditions of their families and communities. Violence was part of my parents' lives, confirming the belief that discrimination was an integral component of structural domination. Growing up working class, alongside the difficult story of my parents' immigration and political life, led me to accept and believe that trauma was part of the terrain: to be fought against but persistent and inevitable. I experienced trauma as simply part of what happens to us. The normalization of violence became both a very important and very difficult survival strategy.

The decade of the McCarthy era left my family asunder; the conspiracy charges were dropped but my father lost his job as the first Jewish typesetter at the *Long Island Star Journal*. My mother's fragile health was compromised. All organizing ceased; relationships with other organizers were destroyed.

Well into my youth I was told I was "intense" and "serious." I did not feel ashamed of these attributes; I felt I was different, separated from my peers. The magnitude of trauma, fear of losing my parents, my community, and all I knew, alongside the perception of my parents as enemies of the State, resulted in my developing a buoyant, strong, creative inner life. I constructed an alternate world: a refuge of art and nature, a forecast of my becoming a printmaker, painter, and denizen in a rural area. My parents deeply loved and wanted me, which has to this day been an unparalleled resource in surviving trauma. But it would be many years before I would tackle emotional intimacy with another person outside of my family. The idea of voluntarily depending on a person, telling my story, was years away.

After the 1950s and relocation to California, family life was full of rigorous political study and love of the arts. This flourishing was an altogether new experience, as robust joy had been submerged in the shadows of the McCarthy era and the devastation of the political community. I attended college and widened my circle of friends, yet it became clear I had no healthy sense of dependency or boundaries, only a continued sense of protecting my loved ones. But protectiveness did not create an awareness of my body, and my emotional state was remote—an enigma to me—while I longed to connect. I was adept at conflict with adversaries but a novice at productive conflict with intimates. I replicated the stern demeanor of my father, with the nonjudgmental and sensitive aspects of my mother reserved for those I knew. I was unable to tolerate even minor discord within the family, as well as with my close friends. In my teenage years I had been told not to upset my mother due to her increasingly fragile emotional state, underscoring the taboo of any problems at home. I knew how to fight with the outside world; I had honed skills as an activist but was immobilized in my intimate life. I tried to manage difficult emotions by managing others. My familiarity with danger was a poor guide in choosing intimate partners.

I rarely felt an emotion without taking action. A significant part of my life was located in problem-solving. At work, my chin jutted forward and I worked on the edge of my chair, ready to spring into action. I worked in the dire early years of the AIDS epidemic and harm reduction; fighting and advocating were familiar modus operandi. I had a high threshold of tolerance for catastrophe. I was good at it. This came to the foreground in 1986 when my mother was raped and brutally murdered by a man in the neighborhood in which she lived.

The young man who raped and murdered my mother pled guilty in a plea bargain to murder in the second degree, with no rape charge. This bargain was without my consent due to a mishandling on the part of the investigating officers. There was never any accountability for this profound error. I was unrelenting in the early years at parole hearings as I possessed keen insight into the nature of sexual violence and murder. Throughout the years I felt alone, despite the support of friends, with the criminal justice system adding to the harsh experience. I knew that the system would never be part of my healing or learning to live with the tangle of violence and grief, but I was unprepared for the chronic harm I encountered at each parole hearing; engaging with the criminal justice system was an additional trauma I had to navigate. Every three to five years I armored myself as the parole date approached, barely able to contain the agony during the hours of testimony. It took another year, sometimes two, to gain back the lost ground after each hearing. The emotional cost of attending hearings was significant: I often dreamt I was killed, I struggled mightily with loss, I fought off bitterness in the face of a rigid, inhumane criminal justice system.

I grew up with the conviction that you protect the ones you love. I was both unable to protect my mother, which threw me into turmoil, and I had yet to include myself as someone who needed protection even though I was sustaining a high level of secondary harm. I started to consider—at what point do I need to preserve my own well-being? In the first twenty-five years after my mother was killed, I had not considered not fighting or if there was a different method of fighting, much less who I would be without fighting. The years of victimization and overnormalization from trauma had taken a toll. My life in the arts and on a rural farm kept me buoyant, but it was not until I began to delve into the impact of trauma that I turned toward my own history and development.

Not surprisingly, it was through the needs of others that I encountered somatics. I distinctly recall a workshop in which trauma and somatics were presented in harm reduction context. I was aware that clients needed this healing awareness available to them, as well as staff. At long last, I put myself in the picture—setting a new stage of exploration and hope in my life.

I have been a politicized Somatic Practitioner for fifteen years now. Training and working in this area deepened my knowledge of trauma, and widened the aperture onto my courageous political family history, allowed me to reestablish my artistic life, and instilled in me a renewed aliveness in my body. The hidden corners of my life were brought to daylight. There is calmness and confidence while moving from my internal life to the outside world. It is no small achievement that through somatics I gained the ability to deeply connect with others, reveal myself, and discern when and how to fight, and to relish the wonder of life.

4

The Impact of Trauma and Oppression

It is easier to build strong children than to repair broken men.

—FREDERICK DOUGLASS

Traumatic experiences and oppressive social conditions cause us to move into a series of automatic, holistic, and incredibly creative means of first surviving then adapting to the harm, ruptured connection with ourselves and others, and betrayal. We are built for safety, belonging, and dignity. We are built to be connected to and make a difference for others, to have meaningful lives. When any of these core needs are disrupted through trauma, we automatically attempt to protect ourselves. We instinctively adapt. To the superficial gaze, it may not look like adaptation, but with a deeper view it becomes understandable and obvious. Individual and social experiences of trauma are discussed as separate experiences, but they are not, in essence, separate. Traumatic experiences are always happening within a social context and shaped by social conditions. They are nearly always perpetuating the "rules of engagement" of our social conditions.

The Wisdom of Protection: Automatic and Adaptive Responses to Trauma

Inherent in our physiologies and in ourselves are automatic, protective, and adaptive responses to traumatic experiences and social conditions. We did not have to learn these. They are in us and function in wise and adaptive ways. These protective responses are well beyond our conscious capacity to control them. We have inherited them through both evolution and the particular biology of who made and birthed us. In turn, they work with the interpersonal, cultural, and social context in which we live. People often develop prominent strategies for survival, for safety, belonging, and dignity. While these reactions are automatic and stored deep in the body, they are also adaptive to the environment and thus shaped by culture, gender, class, etc. Fundamentally, we hold these survival reactions and adaptations as wise, intelligent, and essential.

Fight, flight, freeze, appease, and dissociate are protective and adaptive responses that come with the package of being human. These protective responses aren't perfect. Usually once we have been hurt or endangered, our automatic defenses generalize and assume the harm will come again. When this happens, we can't "put down the defense" to see trustworthy, good people and situations. It feels more like we are waiting for the next bad thing to happen. When these defenses "generalize," they become a foundational embodiment from which we are functioning. These survival reactions can then create suffering and breakdowns, mistrust and disconnection. We can mis-assess safety, love, dignity, and others' actions.

If we look at the purpose of automatic protective responses being generalized, this makes sense. Being prepared for your environment and its stresses means you are better able to survive. This is adaptive. And it has its costs—generalized survival reactions are hard on our bodies as stress increases; hard on our relationships as suspicion and mistrust can occur; hard on our families and communities when there is a lack of empathy, boundaries, and accountability; and lastly, hard on our organizations and social movements when feeling helpless, critiquing to a destructive degree, and when lack of trust and a generalized distrust of power arise. You get the point.

Matt Ridley, the author of *Genome: The Autobiography of a Species in 23 Chapters,* writes dynamically about stress, which has many implications about trauma, healing, and our shaping from it.

> On chromosome 10, there's a gene which makes an enzyme which creates cortisol from cholesterol. Cortisol is the body's stress hormone. When you feel very stressed, it's caused by having cortisol in your blood system. Cortisol goes around switching on and off genes and that changes your behavior and your sensations. This means that external events in your life, which change the stress you're under, can actually change your genes. It can switch on some genes and switch off others. So our genes are at the mercy of our behavior, as well as our behavior being at the mercy of our genes.
>
> (MATT RIDLEY, from an interview online)

In his chapter on stress, he discusses that when this stress gene is "turned on" in the pregnant mother, the infant will be born with it turned on as well. That blew my mind, thinking about intergenerational trauma. The good news is that our behavior, healing, and practice can also switch the stress gene "off."

Our aim in understanding and honoring these automatic protective responses is to get to know them on their terms, honor how they have protected us, and through somatic processes, free up the contractions and withheld energy so that these survival responses are not "over-applied." They do not become who we are; rather, they are there in times of danger, and can relax and let go again once the acute danger has passed.

We want to be able to make choices, based on current time and situation, accounting for our current skills, power, and competencies today. To take actions and build relationships centered in our values and what is important to us instead of reactions based in trauma calling the shots.

This allows us to become life-affirming agents in our own lives and the world. This is a key aim of healing and embodied transformation.

Many people and communities are living in social and economic conditions that are not full of safety, belonging, dignity, and resources. Can we build more resilience, heal, and uplift more choice and agency, even in these environments? Yes.

Let's more deeply explore each of the built-in survival responses. Which do you recognize in yourself or those you care for?

Fight, Flight, Freeze, Appease, and Dissociate

FLIGHT

I am starting with *flight,* even though it doesn't match our rhyming order, because it can be more easily described. Human fight response is complicated, because we use fight for many reasons, both protective and offensive. So, to start, *flight.*

"To flee: to escape by running away, especially because of danger or fear." (*Cambridge Learner's Dictionary*)

Flight, fleeing or running away, is the impulse and action of getting out of or away from a threatening person, experience, or situation. This is a holistic impulse that engages our musculature, chemistry, brain, emotional state, relational state, and energy. This can happen at a subtle level (increased attention and a slight turning away), or at a gross level (literally running away, moving away, leaving someone or some situation).

Sometimes it's easier to look to the animal world for clear examples of the flight response. What animals run away as a main protective response? The cool thing is that *all* of them do. From insects to spiders, fish to amphibians, and four-leggeds to us humans. It's a good move.

The mammals that are built to run as their major defense strategy usually have hooves and don't have claws and fangs. We can look to deer, cows, horses, antelope, and others. While these animals also know how to fight (hooves kicking, horns charging), the hooved animals are more equipped to run as a primary defense strategy. Let's imagine a deer. If something gets its attention, first it assesses (ears up, head turned, still and listening), then if it assesses danger, off it leaps and runs. It goes as far as it assesses is necessary for safety. This is all an integrated deer process—not a cognitive assessment process—which is how we might think of it.

Even the clawed animals tend to flee before they fight. You can think of a domesticated cat. It does the same thing—a moment of assessing, then off. Mice, rabbits, flocks of birds also do the same. There is a disturbance, it is checked out, and then they go, running, flying, swimming. This can happen individually or collectively, flocks of birds, schools of fish, herds of horses, and us.

We are the same as the deer. As people, we also take flight, or internally mobilize to do so. If the circumstances allow for it, fleeing is a core protective response. We run. We leave. We go.

Flight: In seventh grade, I and the girl who was sleeping over were allowed to walk at night to the 7-Eleven, on our own. It took some convincing of my mother, but we did, and were excited. I lived in a rural mountain town and we walked down a dirt road, to the main street. The town didn't have street lights; rather car headlights and the brightness from stores offered the only light. It was maybe a ten-minute walk. We went to 7-Eleven and, I am sure, got Tootsie Rolls and Red Vines.

On our way home, a car honked, then circled round again, as if it was following us. We needed to turn off into a more sparse area to get home. When we did, the car again turned around to enter the neighborhood. We saw this and then started to run. We ran as fast as we could. We ran into the woods to get off the dirt road, where the car could not see us or follow us. The car circled a bit, then left.

We stood hidden in the woods, breathing hard, and laughed with excitement, relief, and energy. And safety. We were okay. We walked home still paying close attention and also a little giddy. It was the adventure of our night. Of course, I did not tell my mother because I wanted her to let us walk to 7-Eleven again by ourselves, sometime before I turned eighteen. The protective flight response took over, ran through us, was used to a successful end, and while we recounted the story to each other, it wasn't traumatizing for us.

As an adult I look back at that situation, and terrible things run through my mind about the vulnerability of young girls. (And, sadly both of us were already living in homes with intimate violence.) That evening, the car following us could have been high school students who knew our older siblings, and were just trying to scare us. But I'll never know.

The flight response can also be held at a sustained level over time. Or perhaps it was mobilized repeatedly in your soma and did not get to be expressed or completed. You may then embody a flight response that shapes your soma. It can show up in your soma and life like this:

- Leaning away from contact or engagement in your somatic shape. A backing up, or angling away from, that feels "normal" to you.

- Leaving, ending a conversation, relationship, not hanging in—is a relief. May feel "safer" even though it does not take care of your life and your commitments.

- A repeated internal dialogue that is about leaving, escaping, planning for how to and when to leave uncomfortable, but not threatening, situations.

- An identity built around the above. "I am just not a person who hangs on," "I don't like staying around for the end," "I am better alone," etc.

When a protective strategy becomes a generalized embodied tendency, it can seem like fleeing or leaving becomes the solution over and over again. Your range of choices may be more limited, with leaving apparently the most obvious choice, again and again.

There are other situations when those protective impulses of flight go off in us, and our circumstances do not allow it. A child dependent on their parents, a partner financially dependent on the other perhaps with children, a person in prison, a situation of violence in which you cannot get away, and more. Even though you were not able to flee, the chemicals, physiological impulses, and mobilization were still there. These get caught or unexpressed in the mind-body and "stored" there, still needing to be processed. These survival impulses get trapped, unexpressed, and stored in the tissues and somatic shape.

The flight response can get engaged even in situations that don't necessarily call for it. This response can "take over" under pressure, even though we may have more choices or power now. The response then shows up in our automatic and unconscious actions, nonactions, our beliefs, our ways of being, and ways of relating. Again, this is not a conscious choice; rather it is automatic and well-practiced in the nervous system.

Social and cultural conditions tend to accept and encourage particular survival response in certain peoples, genders, and groups, and not in others. Flight may be affirmed in some and discouraged in others. Think of gender training in a US context: "Men fight, not run." "Man up." Or men are called names if they do flee (e.g., "pussy," "fag"). This social shaping gets integrated into our biological impulses, encouraging some and suppressing others.

Our biologies and psychologies are always interacting with our relations, and our broader cultural and social conditions. We are reading for safety, belonging, and dignity, and making complex and unconscious assessments as to what may help us toward those outcomes. These decisions are not uninformed; rather they are complexly informed by our senses, impressions, reading of others and the environments, and more. If flight does not work, or is discouraged, we may shift to freeze or fight. There are multiple biological, social, cultural, and psychological pressures intermixing to shape us and our survival strategies.

Dr. Andrew Huberman, a neuroscientist at Stanford, states that our abilities to perceive, and make adjustments and adaptations, are a stunningly refined set of skills. In it we use our entire nervous system and brain, our organs (skin being the largest organ), our muscular system, and our abilities to perceive and read our environments. He adds that exporting our perception to handheld devices abdicates these profound skills to objects much less adept at perceiving.

FREEZE

"To freeze: To become fixed or motionless; *especially:* to become incapable of acting or speaking." (*Merriam-Webster Dictionary*)

Freezing is the protective mobilization to be deeply still, not move, and wait until it is over. This too is a holistic impulse that engages our musculature, chemistry, brain, emotional state, relational state, and energy. This can happen at a subtle level (slight holding of the breath, and stillness) and at a gross level (literally being unable to speak or act, and often dissociating within the freeze response).

Let's look to the animal world. Which animals use a freeze response as a key protective mechanism? My very favorite is the opossum. We talk about opossums "playing dead," almost like they're pretending, "I'm dead, I'm dead, I'm dead, don't eat me!" That isn't exactly what's happening in them, however. When threatened, opossums go into a state called *thanatosis,* or tonic immobility. They appear limp, they drool, and are temporarily paralyzed and unresponsive to external stimuli. You can think of it as if they are in a temporary coma. This can last from forty minutes to four hours. And opossums take it a step further. They also excrete a stench that makes them smell as if they are dead or rotting. Thus, a predator sees a limp, unresponsive, and stinky opossum, and goes to find its lunch elsewhere. Eating a dead or rotting carcass will make most other animals sick. Freezing is a brilliant protective strategy.

We too experience tonic immobility. We freeze under threat.

In humans, when we look at the freeze response, I often think of those bad "B" horror movies. Usually a woman is standing in a corner, shrinking and still, while the attacker is coming. I remember as a kid

I'd yell at the TV, "Run, run, run!" That was a great model of a freeze response.

Many people, especially children, tend to employ a freeze response. They are often not big enough to fight back, or there's no place to run. Especially if there is violence in their homes or violence with someone that they know—where is there to run to? The freeze response is often reported in sexual assault and rape. It is also often socially misunderstood (even promoted through sexism) as passive consent. Freezing is not passive consent. It is a sign of intense threat and danger.

Often people will be frustrated with themselves, wondering, "Why didn't I scream, why didn't I fight back, why didn't I run?" Even supportive friends or healers may ask those questions. These are not the right questions, though. It is so important to know that, during a freeze response, you can't do any of those things. You are temporarily immobilized—cannot speak or move, so as to survive. Our deep evolutionary survival assessment "chooses" the protective response—it assesses what will most serve our safety, belonging, and dignity, our survival, even though you feel like another option may have worked better.

Freeze is unique. Fight and flight are mobilizing us into action. Freeze is mobilizing us into *non*action.

The freeze response can also be engaged over time, or repeatedly mobilized in your body. You may then see that the freeze response shapes your soma. Like other survival responses, a freeze response can be learned young, then can be generalized, and will show up in adulthood too. Freeze as an ongoing shaping in the soma can look like:

- A general numbness, not feeling, or a stillness in your body and emotions. Sensation or emotions may feel overwhelming, and numbing may feel "normal" to you.

- Conversations that have conflict, too many choices, or even pleasure may have you go "blank," when you can't think of what to say or do.

- Being away from stimulation, even positive situations, may feel "safer," even though it does not take care of your life and your commitments.

- An internal dialogue that is about numbing, not feeling, or shame of inaction.

- An identity built around thinking, "I am self-contained," "I don't have many needs," "I am detached," or "I can't act."

- Allowing for little stimulation or aliveness somatically (including pleasure), even when it does not take care of you or your life. This can be read as a lack of authenticity because you cannot come out to allow for contact and connection.

There are other situations when the protective impulses of freeze go off in us and do not serve our circumstances. Sometimes people who have been harmed as children through intimate, community, or state-based violence have a deeply practiced freeze response. This response can "take over" under threat, even though people now may have more choices or power. The response then shows up in our automatic and unconscious actions, nonactions, our beliefs, our ways of being, and ways of relating. Again, this is not a conscious choice; rather it is automatic and well practiced in the nervous system.

Social and cultural conditions tend to accept and encourage certain survival responses in certain peoples, genders, and groups, and not in others. Freeze may be affirmed in some and discouraged in others. If we think of cultural training that encourages being quiet or proper, not speaking up, being seen and not heard, these can show up in both gender and cultural norms.

Freeze: About a decade ago, I was working in Ramallah, Palestine, at the Palestinian Counseling Center. We were on a monthlong journey, learning of the systematic colonization of Palestine by the Israeli State—with vast financial and policy support from the United States and Britain. Overall, the trip was devastating and grounding as to what is actually happening, rather than what we hear on the news in the United States. We were bringing this somatic approach to working with trauma and learning much from the therapists and psychologists there. The work was simultaneously interpreted into Arabic and many of the clinicians also spoke English.

These therapists are operating in a very intense and complex set of circumstances. Often they were seeing clients or families in which there was domestic violence or child abuse, the family had been forcibly displaced from their town or community, many of their extended family had been killed by the Israeli military, and their town was under curfew. How do we resource and support healing in these conditions?

Just before we arrived, Ramallah had been under curfew. This meant that there were only two to four hours per day when people were allowed to leave their homes for supplies and water or to see one another. Children were not in school; shops and livelihoods were closed. A military enforced curfew means that if you're caught out during undesignated hours, live bullets are used. Just trying to live within this context is traumatizing.

We were talking about the fight, flight, freeze, appease, and dissociate responses as automatic, protective responses, and how they show up psychologically, physiologically, and socially. One of the young male therapists got very animated as we talked about the freeze response. He said, "Oh, wow, this is amazing, because me and my friends ..." and continued with this story. When he was nineteen years old (he was in his thirties when we met), Ramallah was also under curfew, and he and two friends were caught out after the designated hour for curfew. They had been delivering water and had not made it back home in time. As they were making their way home, they spotted the Israeli military and hid. They waited for them to pass and made a plan. They would run together from one hiding place to the next until they got home, and in this way, avoid being shot. First, they ran over to a ditch and burrowed down into it. The soldiers made another pass. The next spot was behind a building. When they thought the coast was clear, they counted to three and ran. Except this time, one of the young men did not run. He still lay in the ditch and didn't move. The therapist described how upset they were: "Oh, no, why didn't he come with us?

What's he doing?" Again, watching for patrols, they went back to get him and took him to the next hiding place.

That young man was experiencing a freeze response; he literally couldn't run. It was not that he did not mean to stay with his friends, or did not want to run—it is that survival reaction took over and the physiology, the self, was unable to move.

The therapist was thrilled because he knew exactly what a freeze response was firsthand, and better knew how to understand what happened to his friend. He then shared, "My friend felt so ashamed because, as a man, he froze and we had to come help him."

Here is where our evolutionary wisdom, our physiological capacity for survival, and social belief systems collide. We are taught through the social norm within a patriarchal system that "men are supposed to act," "men are not supposed to be afraid," or "men don't need help." So this young man had an intelligent response to his life being threatened, responded accordingly, and then felt ashamed for his actions. Not only was he struggling with a traumatic experience, but also thinking he did it wrong and was embarrassed in front of his friends. This is where PTSD begins to set in and we begin to develop a self-identity out of trauma.

The telling of the story also shook me. The therapist was so animated and excited about understanding the freeze response. He had had to live amidst the curfews, live bullets, and military occupation. He had developed survival strategies to deal with these conditions—I, on the other hand, had not. I felt devastated about the insanity of colonization, what adults and children are required to live in and how the State can validate violence by making others less than human, en masse. This is true for any imperialist nation, including the United States.

Some communities within the United States are sadly more used to police violence and a "police state." I am white and was raised in a rural mountain town. While there was plenty of intimate and community violence, we were not under occupation and the police were not shooting the young men in my community. In many Black, poor, indigenous, and migrant communities in the United States, this experience is more familiar.

APPEASE

"To appease: to pacify or placate (someone) by acceding to their demands" (*Oxford Dictionary of English*); "to make concessions to (someone, such as an aggressor or a critic) often at the sacrifice of principles." (*Merriam-Webster Dictionary*)

Appeasing is the protective mobilization to pacify, placate, become smaller than and less threatening, so as to ward off threat or dissipate it. This is a holistic impulse that engages the whole of us, body, identity, relationship, and thinking. This can happen at a subtle level (making oneself smaller, nodding in agreement, smiling), or at a gross level (taking actions to assuage aggression or danger that do not take care of you or others, or are not aligned with your ethics).

Let's again look to the animal world. Let's think about dogs. What do they do when they are appeasing? They get lower (smaller), roll onto their backs and show their bellies and throats, and avert their gaze. The basic communication is, "I won't hurt you, don't hurt me." That's the basic communication of appeasing—"I'm not threatening, don't hurt me." When dogs turn their bellies up, they are exposing their vital organs. This is a very vulnerable position. A bite to the belly or neck could be fatal. In the dog world, this communication is usually met with an establishment of dominance and then they're off and running and sniffing.

We too appease. It is very similar to the dog's moves. Humans appease by making ourselves smaller in shrinking our height and width, by getting lower, by averting our gaze, by smiling, being agreeable, shrugging our shoulders, apologizing often, and more. Just as dogs show their bellies, one way we appease is by tilting the head to one side. This shows our jugular vein. This is also a vulnerable exposure. These are human ways of saying, "I'm not threatening. I won't hurt you, please don't hurt me." Or saying, "Keep me as part of the herd/pack/family/community."

We don't have to learn this. It comes with our evolutionary history. Appeasing is a brilliant protective strategy.

When appeasing is generalized as a consistent strategy, it can both be useful and have a high cost. It can help us stay safe, decrease violence, and keep us more connected. But, it can also have us not stand up for ourselves and others, not have boundaries, and not give others feedback as to their actions and behaviors. We can also be hurt.

People can get frustrated with themselves when appeasing is automatic. "Why did I agree, when I don't really agree?" "Why didn't I stand up for myself? For them?" "I am not telling the truth." Others may say, "Why do you let that person do that to you?" "Why don't you say something?" There are lots of answers to those questions. One is that you may be seeing an embodied appease response that was originally used as a way to survive. Once these responses have been generalized, it is hard to recognize that other moves are available.

You may then see that the appease response shapes your soma. Like other survival responses, an appease response can be learned young, then generalized, and can show up throughout one's life. Appeasing as an ongoing shaping in the soma can look like:

- A shape of apology—a more collapsed chest, automatically nodding in agreement and conceding space to others. Apologizing often.

- Making oneself small, not taking up space physically, relationally, with one's voice or presence. This may feel "normal" to you.

- Not having direct boundaries based on your own needs and concerns. Shaping your self to fit others' needs and desires, while often abandoning your own.

- A lack of feeling or access to your self and body. Or, a pressure and collapse in the chest, stomach, and tissues feel "normal" to you.

- Avoiding conversations and situations that have conflict, difficult decisions with others, finding yourself trying to "keep the peace."

- Appeasing, apologizing, letting others have their way may feel "safer" even though it does not take care of your life and your desires.

There are situations when the protective impulses of appeasing are evoked, but they do not serve our circumstances. This response can "take over" under threat, even though people may now have more choices or power. Again, this is not a conscious choice; rather it is automatic and well practiced in your psychobiology. It is embodied. Through healing we can shift this automatic reaction, and embody other responses.

Again, social and cultural conditions affect which survival reactions get more practiced and embodied. Appeasing may be more affirmed in some and discouraged in others.

Appease: generative somatics has worked for many years with the National Domestic Workers Alliance (NDWA). This amazing and innovative organization, as mentioned in the Foreword, works for labor rights for domestic workers such as nannies, housekeepers, and home health care workers, and a care-based economy (www.domesticworkers.org). We partnered with NDWA to create an embodied leadership development program called SOL—Strategy, Organizing and Leadership. The program includes political education, somatic trauma healing, embodied leadership, and some organizing training.

As we worked with domestic worker leaders over time, we saw something that was totally understandable and contradictory. Many of the leaders, under pressure, appeased while they were simultaneously organizing state by state for labor rights like a minimum wage, paid vacation, sick leave, and dignity and safety in their work. Because this also required pressuring policy makers, dealing with elected state officials, and, many times, direct actions, appeasement was not exactly what they currently needed for their well-being and rights.

The appease response was highly effective and earned/learned through other social and life experiences. This group is nearly all women. Many immigrated for lack of opportunity in their home countries, many survived poverty, many have not seen their own children for years—even as they take care of others' children. The shape of appeasement, because of the lack of social power, tends to serve and is particularly expected from domestic workers. The history of domestic work in the United States goes back to slavery and indentured servitude, and carries that deep cultural expectation. Human trafficking is today's indentured servitude, and domestic workers are vulnerable. Lastly, many of the leaders we worked with have experienced domestic violence and/or sexual assault in their homes, communities, or by employers.

And these women are very powerful. The appease response was useful for survival and navigating oppression, but it got in the way of their agency and power when it was automatic. We worked together to shift this and open more options.

So, sexism, anti-immigrant sentiment, racism, intimate and state-based violence all conspire to support an appease response. Mostly, I am so impressed with the sheer commitment, resilience, and power of these leaders. We can see why appeasing is not just a good survival strategy within their individual somas, but also required by the social conditions. As women, as immigrants, and Black, Latina, Filipina women, as poor people—what would a strong, dignified, or defiant stance have produced? Likely, more violence. Appeasement becomes required by the social conditions.

Lucky for all of us, through organizing, political education, and somatic transformation—dignity, healing, collective action, empowerment, and more can be restored, learned, and acted upon. These are some of the fiercest and most loving women I know. I am proud to be able to work with them.

FIGHT

"To fight: Verb: Struggle to overcome, eliminate, or prevent. Noun: A violent confrontation or struggle" (*Oxford Dictionary of English*); "Verb:

To contend in battle or physical combat; to strive to overcome a person by blows or weapons. Noun: A struggle for a goal or an objective (i.e., a fight for justice)" (*Merriam-Webster Dictionary*); "The ancient root of fight comes from the Proto-Indo-European prefix *pek,* meaning 'to pluck out'" (Vocabulary.com). Picture a hair-pulling fight, and this makes complete sense.

Flight, freeze, appease. Now, let's dig into the fight response. What is interesting about fight is that very few other animals besides humans use fight proactively. Animals will hunt for food, will fight for and defend territory, and sometimes will fight to compete for mates or establish dominance. Yet, most of these are using fight defensively or for short-term gains.

Wild and even domesticated animals know it is a risk to fight, even if they win. Animals can get punctured and harmed and not recover, even if they won the fight. When you think about the intelligence of survival, the evolutionary, biological intelligence of survival, fighting is not that strategic.

Humans, on the other hand, will proactively fight and kill, torture and maim. What is this? Sometimes it's for the same reasons as other mammals: establishing dominance, trying to establish safety, or access to a resource or a person. Much of this, however, is not for survival. Instead, this is cultivated and trained by social, economic, political, and cultural systems that are based on power-over and exploitation of people, land, and other natural resources. This organized fight serves to concentrate wealth and decision making in the hands of a few. It is about hoarding of power and resources. To do this, violence and manipulation must be engaged. People do not want to be exploited, demeaned, and degraded. People do not want to be hungry or to have their children be hungry. This violence, this systemic trauma, is strategically employed and trained into masses of people by use of violence such as war, prisons, policing, rape, intimate partner violence, torture, and exploitation. This often leaves natural allies harming one another and the elite protected. Trauma comes to both the victims and the perpetrators of violence, yet in very distinct ways.

That said, fight as a survival response is this: the best defense is a good offense. If I threaten, perhaps you will not harm me. Or, because you are harming me, I will fight you off.

Fighting, in this way, is the protective mobilization to threaten, get bigger than, position and defend, and intimidate to ward off or dissipate threat. Again, this is a holistic impulse that engages our musculature, nervous system, chemistry, brain, emotional state, relational state, and energy. This can happen at a subtle level (puffing up one's chest, setting the jaw, making oneself bigger), or at a gross level (taking aggressive and threatening actions, doing violence or harm either in self-defense or proactively, in ways that do not take care of you or others, or are not aligned with your ethics).

Let's again look to the animal world. Let's look at grizzly bears. What do they do when threatened and moving to fight? If you have not seen *National Geographic* specials on grizzlies, they are definitely worth watching. The bears get bigger, their fur stands out, they often stand up on their two back legs (making them up to eight feet tall). They extend their claws, bare their teeth, growl … you get the point. I am already afraid and ready to run.

We do similar things when we fight. The human fight reaction includes making ourselves bigger by getting taller, puffing up, by "staring someone down," jutting the jaw, setting the teeth, making threatening sounds, and more. Just like grizzlies, these are human ways of saying, "I am threatening. I will hurt you, don't mess with me. Stay away."

Again, we don't have to learn this. It comes with our evolutionary history. Fight (and defend) is a brilliant protective strategy.

When fight is generalized as a consistent strategy, it can be both useful and costly to our lives. It can help us stay safer, decrease violence by dissuading violence through threat, and help us keep control of and defend what is important to us when triggered. A generalized fight response can also cost us connection, decrease others' trust in us, have us harm people we do not mean to harm, and even engage more violence.

People can get frustrated with themselves when a fight response becomes the default. "Why did I pick a fight again?" "Why did I hurt someone I love?" "Why can't I stop defending, and be more flexible?" Others may say, "They are hard to be with. I don't really like working with them." "They always seem defensive/aggressive. They need to be right all the time."

One way to understand this as an embodied fight response is that it was originally used as a way to survive. Once these responses have been generalized and embodied, it is hard to recognize that there are other choices.

You may see that the fight response shapes your soma. Like other survival responses, a fight response can be learned young, then generalized, and show up throughout one's life. Fight as an ongoing shaping in the soma can look like:

- A defensive or positioned, immovable shape—jaw and/or chest stuck out slightly, making yourself bigger, clenching your fists.

- A hardening or thickening of the body—organizing to be impermeable.

- Making yourself bigger and louder. Taking up space physically, relationally, with your voice or presence. This may feel "normal" to you.

- An automatic "no." Having automatic avoidance and boundaries that don't take care of you or those you care about.

- A lack of feeling or access to your self and body. Or, a tension, pressure, and pushing outward, feeling "normal" to you. A pressure internally to act externally.

- Engaging or creating conversation and situations that have conflict, or are difficult. These may feel like "safer" ways to relate, even when they do not take care of your life and commitments.

- Distrusting people "getting along" or agreeing. Only trusting people who can fight with you.

- Separating, critiquing, hardening as an automatic way of being. The critiquing or separating feeling "safer" than connecting or softening.

There are situations when the protective impulses of fight are evoked, and it does not serve our circumstances. The fight response can "take over," even though you may now have more choices or power. An example is the person who, nine times out of ten, brings discord, distrust, or challenge to a conversation and either leaves it in distrust, or is calmed only by the conflict being engaged. This can have a high cost on a relationship and a group. When we are deeply shaped by a generalized fight response it affects how we see and interpret people and situations, our mood and emotions, and our overall physical state.

There are also situations where the fight response was evoked but the person wasn't able to act. This often happens when a child or adult is physically overpowered. Even though you were not physically able to fight, the chemicals, impulses, and mobilization were still there. These survival impulses get trapped, unexpressed, and stored in the tissues and somatic shape. They are there, still needing to be processed. It is like the soma "holding a punch" or wanting to kick someone off of you, and not being able to.

Lastly, social and cultural conditions tend to encourage certain survival responses in some peoples, genders, and groups, but not in others. Fight may be affirmed in some and discouraged in others. These are often tied to racist and gendered social norms that are targeting and harming these same peoples.

Fight: I had the opportunity to work with a Black man from a poor community in the United States, in which nearly all of the young men had been harassed by the police and most had spent time in prison. He was put in at seventeen years old and spent twelve years imprisoned. This is not because most of the young men in this community are "criminals"; rather it is because the social

*conditions targeting their community channeled the young men toward prison
and poverty.*

> *Decades of data show that the journey to racial disparity begins when
> black men are boys. Black boys are policed like no other demographic.
> They are policed on the street, in the mall, in school, in their homes,
> and on social media. Police stop black boys on the vaguest of descrip-
> tions—"black boys running," "two black males in jeans, one in a gray
> hoodie," "black male in athletic gear." Young black males are treated as
> if they are "out of place" not only when they are in white, middle-class
> neighborhoods, but also when they are hanging out in public spaces or
> sitting on their own front porches.*
>
> (ANGELA DAVIS AND KRISTIN HENNING, "How Policing
> Black Boys Leads to the Conditioning of Black Men")

*To survive, both in his community and in prison, it was important that he
harden, learn to fight, and show no vulnerability. This showed up in him
somatically as hardening his chest and back, stilling his face and showing little
through his facial expressions or eyes. He said it was hard to feel himself, even
though he knew the people in his life were very important to him. This shaping
was now getting in the way of the connection he wanted. Softening his chest
and back, however, felt counterintuitive to staying safe and alive.*

DISSOCIATE

"To dissociate: The action of disconnecting or separating or the state of
being disconnected." (*Oxford Dictionary of English*)

Dissociation is the protective mobilization to get away without
physically leaving, to numb awareness and feeling, to check out so as
not to be there for whatever is happening. Dissociation engages all of
us, our thinking, self-identity, body, and how we relate and act.

Dissociation can happen at a subtle level like leaving your eyes,
spacing out briefly, shrinking inside of yourself, thinking of someplace

else while someone is talking to you, or just not quite remembering the interaction. Or, it can happen at a gross level, such as leaving your body or present time to "come back" later, numbing yourself to an experience by removing some vital part of your awareness, disappearing outside or inside yourself where no one can get you. It can often be combined with feeling foggy, and not clearheaded, by not remembering short or long periods of time.

Sometimes, we quit feeling so much that we deny feelings exist, or deny and minimize feelings in others. Sometimes we can feel others' emotions deeply, but not feel ourselves. In healing, many of us have to learn again to feel and sense, both physically and emotionally. We need this to connect to ourselves and to others. We need it to connect to life.

Dissociation is literal, not metaphoric. It is amazing to me that most survivors of abuse and violation, when asked, can tell you how they leave their bodies (or present time), and where they go. It is a very somatic experience. Many will say they move up and out of their bodies, behind their left shoulder, and go away. Some will leave their bodies and watch the incident from above, as if floating, while others will "go" someplace else, away from the violation. Some people report dissociating by going into their heads, disconnecting from the rest of the body. Yet others will talk about tucking themselves deep within themselves (guts, intestines) where no one can reach them, hiding in the caverns and dark folds. Amazing, really. And so pragmatic. Dissociation is a way of fleeing without leaving the room.

Somatics will ask you *how* you dissociate, not necessarily why. Trauma and threat are why. The *how one leaves* also reveals *how one can return.*

We don't have to learn this. Like the other survival strategies, dissociation comes with our evolutionary history. Dissociation is a brilliant protective strategy. It often goes along with other survival reactions. We may fight and dissociate. Flee and check out. Freeze and numb out. You get the idea.

When dissociation is generalized as an automatic strategy, it can both be useful and have a high cost. It can help us feel safe, go away, stay checked out, or go to an alternative world that feels more safe, soothing, or controllable to us. On the downside, it can leave us compartmentalized and disconnected. We can be out of touch with what is happening with our own experience, as well as others. We can misassess people and situations, because we are not very present to pay attention. This can cost us, and others, safety and connection, intimacy and trust.

Dissociation, as a strategy used over time, shapes your soma. Like other survival responses, a dissociation response can be learned young, then generalized, and show up throughout one's life. Dissociation as an ongoing shaping in the soma can look like:

- A shape that is more floaty, otherworldly, not quite there. A dispersed energy up (toward the head) and out.

- Not very present in the eyes, or to the touch. Pulled out of the eyes and away from the surface of the skin.

- Very sensitive to others' moods, emotions, and shifts in energy and movements, but not present to your own, or not feeling yourself or others deeply.

- Physically, emotionally, and/or relationally checked out or numb feeling more "normal."

- A somatic organization of being tucked deep inside the guts and body—where no one can reach or find you.

- Avoiding or at times not remembering conversations and situations that have emotional intensity—from conflict, to difficult decisions with others, to love.

There are situations when the protective impulses of dissociation are evoked, and it does not serve our circumstances. This response can "take over" under threat, even though we may now have more choices or power. We may be checked out when we really want to be present, and not be able to control this. What does it cost us to split ourselves like that over time? What does it give us to bring ourselves whole again?

Again, social and cultural conditions tend to accept and encourage certain survival responses in some peoples, genders, and groups, but not in others. Often children and adults who "can't pay attention" are tracked or punished. There are many different reasons for not being able to attend consistently, dissociation being one.

Lastly, dissociation asks us to consider Who is leaving, and who is left behind when we dissociate? People have different answers to this, and it often depends on the circumstances in which the dissociation was needed. People often talk about an aspect of themselves, their spirit or core, leaving the violence in order to remain intact or not shattered. There can be a spiritual sense in the leaving—like going someplace wiser and kinder. Or, there may be a sense of just dissipating or evaporating.

Dissociation separates ourselves from ourselves. Who remains? The other aspects of the self, including: the body, nervous system, tissues—our corporeality. These aspects of ourselves are registering the experiences. They are surviving the experiences—adapting, adjusting, and surviving. When the part of us that left returns, we also return to the experiences.

Dissociate: Another client I had the chance to work with over time is queer and Latina. Dissociation was a primary safety shaping for her. She, like all of us, came by it honestly, through experiences of rape, racism, and sexism. She had a strong spiritual life and practice, and this was a very big resource for her. One of the complexities of her style of dissociation was that it would get collapsed with her spiritual life. Pressure, conflict, and even closeness could send her into a more dissociated state, which then would often pivot to a spiritual interpretation, overriding the more difficult emotions or situation. She described her dissociation as first a kind of shrinking and backing up and then leaving her body, then dissipating. This let her get away from what was intolerable. This dissipating would often connect her to a calmer, more spiritual space.

The resource and perspective of a spiritual space can deeply build resilience. Dissociation connected to this is tricky. In her healing process she had to build more tolerance to stay present in herself and feeling during times of pressure, closeness and intimacy, and conflict. Her automatic impulse to leave was strong, and learning to hang with a wider range of sensations and emotions was key. She also needed to build different skills in recognizing her emotions like fear, guilt, and anger, and how to work with them, with others. As in all healing, she also had to touch and deal with the core wounds that made her learn to dissociate so well. The impulse to leave through dissociating is wise, and it is caused by experiencing harm. Those experiences needed to be touched, felt, and deeply attended to.

Traumatic Amnesia

Traumatic amnesia can be understood as a deep type of dissociation, or a shutting down of what is intolerable. Again, its adaptive intent is saving us from what we cannot live through. Traumatic amnesia is when we do not remember what happened until a time in the future, in which it is safe enough to do so. The remembering often comes through visual or physical flashbacks. These often do not make any sense to the person because they have built a self-identity that does not include these experiences. The thawing and remembering process from traumatic amnesia can be very jarring to the self-image and one's constructed sense of invulnerability. Traumatic amnesia tells us that something so traumatic happened that one's self and survival were deeply threatened.

What neuroscience is telling us thus far about traumatic amnesia is this: we do not yet understand a lot about memory and how it works. We do, however, understand that memory and emotions are linked. We tend to remember, long-term, emotionally meaningful experiences more than non-emotional ones. Whom have you loved? Whom have you learned from? What life-giving, challenging experiences made you who you are? We tend to remember those meaningful experiences.

Unless those experiences are so overwhelming, threatening, or debilitating that our systems move into a kind of survival override. Sometimes we will just not remember the feelings of the experience: "I was raped, it wasn't a big deal. I'm over it." Or, we don't register the experience as we would a regular memory. Then, we do not remember the experience(s) mentally, or in our self-concept. We do, however, remember them in our tissues, emotions, and survival reactions. Often people with traumatic amnesia are perplexed by their own reactions to threat or fear. They may over- or under-react to a challenging situation and their own behavior makes no sense to them. They may have an overwhelming sense of shame when showing fear, sadness, or anger that conflicts with their current self-concept. Often this points to traumatic experiences that are compartmentalized, literally put away, in the soma.

Often through somatic opening work, these experiences will show themselves to resolve and heal. We'll explore this more in chapter 10.

TRAUMATIC AMNESIA AND SOCIAL CONTEXT

In the 1990s, child sexual abuse (CSA) was being acknowledged at its epidemic scale. *The Courage to Heal* was a best seller, and more and more stories about child sexual abuse were being publicly acknowledged. A former Miss America, Marilyn Vanderbilt, came forward with her experiences of child sexual abuse within her elite, white Denver family. It was a modern-day breakthrough of the cultural silence. This was not the first, and given the current #MeToo movement, it will not be the last.

During the nineties, many groups organized to create social change regarding CSA. Some focused on changing laws to acknowledge child sexual abuse and rape, and the real dynamics of traumatic amnesia.

They are called delayed discovery laws. This means that the statute of limitations was suspended, allowing survivors to seek legal and criminal retribution, once the violation was known to the person. That means survivors of sexual violence who had traumatic amnesia and began to remember, to feel, to heal, had some options. This was a big cultural and legal acknowledgment of the real impacts of trauma, dissociation, and the processes of healing.

In response to the public opinion and power shifts toward survivors, there was a backlash led by an organization called the False Memory Syndrome (FMS) Foundation (FMSF). The premise of the FMS was that therapists were "planting" false memories in the minds of vulnerable, primarily female, clients and, in turn, ruining families. While there is no proof of this phenomenon, it took off like wildfire. The idea of false memories allowed the cultural denial to reengage. We collectively did not have to confront child sexual abuse and the millions of children who were and are experiencing it. We did not have to collectively grapple with what to do and how we might need to change to prevent this. FMS took hold, got media coverage, and started reversing delayed discovery laws, again silencing the wave of collective awareness.

For some background: the founders of the False Memory Syndrome Foundation are parents whose daughter privately confronted them about her father's sexual abuse of her. The father, Peter Freyd, denies the allegations, while others in Jennifer Freyd's extended family support her, and are confident the abuse happened. One of the members of the foundation's scientific advisory board resigned after it was discovered that he had an article in *Paidika: The Journal of Paedophilia*. The article contained statements that were interpreted as supportive of pedophilia. And yet, to this day the concept of false memories— particularly questioning child sexual abuse—stuck. The FMSF, while supporting lawsuits and training for therapists, and pushing legislation, worked to maintain a nonpolitical scientific image.

It is interesting to me that the parents' response was not to try to help their daughter in any way they could. It is also telling that the social response was to question, deny, and blame, but not to believe and help survivors.

> Whether child sexual abuse occurs, and how often, has been debated for centuries. Public concern and intervention have peaked and declined multiple times, sometimes springing from feminist activism and sometimes growing from other medical or political frameworks. The most sizable of the previous efforts, the child protective movement of the 1880s, was populated by feminists.... Nevertheless these previous efforts had slipped out of view by the time feminists took up the issue again nearly 100 years later.
>
> (NANCY WHITTIER, *The Politics of Child Sexual Abuse: Emotion, Social Movements, and the State*)

Combining Survival Strategies

Each of us is born with the innate capacity to fight, flight, freeze, appease, and dissociate as protective responses to threat and violence. We are deeply adaptive and creative in how these are applied and used. Most of us are using a combination of these as our key survival strategies. The primary survival strategy may be different, based on the context. You may defend with fight and then flee in more intimate situations, and appease in more public dynamics. Most importantly at this phase is to get to know how these work in you, how you have been shaped by and embody each.

Some ways you can explore these protective responses are:

- Consider each one: fight, flight, freeze, appease, and dissociate. What do you relate to with each one? Which are familiar? Which are unfamiliar? If you become reactive in a more public or group setting, what happens? How about in a more intimate setting? What would your friends say about what you do or how you are?

Just as a reminder, see if you can bring a little compassion to yourself and your strategies. We have taken on these embodied habits both for survival and in trying to adapt for safety, belonging, and dignity.

- *HOW* do these operate in you—not only conceptually, but how you hold your breath, what contracts in you, what moves away, etc.? If you are organized to appease, how do you do that somatically? Where do you feel the impulse to defend or fight?

- Begin to recognize and know these in others. How are they organizing themselves to survive and adapt? Beginning to see this shaping in each other gives a different ground for compassion and accountability with each other. We can understand these reactions, and also ask each other to transform so that they are not running the show.

- As we get to perceive and know these shapings more clearly, we can let that inform our work. Whether you are a healing practitioner or a leader doing social movement work, seeing the patterns of impact from trauma and oppression is key. What embodied survival strategies do you see in your clients, given their traumas; or in the communities or sector you are organizing, given their traumas and locations of oppression and/or privilege? We can use this wisdom to inform more effective approaches, actions, and interventions.

Learning to feel and perceive safety shaping lets us more clearly see what we are working with. Given the embodiment of the shaping, we can know that trying to "fix" it, talk someone out of it, or override it will not work. Something deeper and more transformative is called for.

A note on the neurobiology of survival. I will not dive into the current writing and research regarding trauma and neuroscience here. There are many people doing it, and doing it well. If you would like to read more about the brain and organ functions during and after trauma, please check out Bessel van der Kolk, *The Body Keeps the Score: Brain, Mind, and Body in the Healing of Trauma;* Pat Ogden, *Trauma and the Body: A Sensorimotor Approach to Psychotherapy;* and Dan Siegel and his many books. FYI—none of these researchers/practitioners deeply integrate a social analysis, or consider the impact of trauma on or the resilience building of social movements.

What Happens When Our Survival Reactions Get to Do Their Job?

Something kind of amazing happens when our survival reactions get to enact and express successfully. Imagine this: There is a potential threat. We assess the threat and confirm it. The impulse is to flee. Our environment allows for fleeing. We flee and get away successfully. We flee to an environment with safety, belonging, and dignity, and are welcomed there. All of the mobilization to flee is spent (muscles, breath, adrenaline, brain chemistry, etc.). The breath and body relax and we are alive and connected.

We don't have symptoms of PTSD, ongoing contraction, and trapped energy from the escape.

In the embodied healing process, accessing these stored survival reactions and making somatic space for them to process and complete are core aspects of transformation. Putting new interpretations, or even new practices, on top of these generalized survival reactions alone does not work. Under the pressures of love, conflict, success, or failure, the history will press forward and again drive our reactions, rather than us getting to choose what form we care about, and our values.

The Force of Harmony and Healing

What is amazing to me in all of this is that most of us still have a deep yearning to heal, to be more whole, to be more alive. And we also want that for others. Some of that comes from wanting the pain and suffering to decrease or end. Most of it, I think, is something else. What is it that draws us toward healing, even when we know the road will be difficult? What has us want love and justice for ourselves and others, when ignoring this seems to be the easier path? I think it is a positive and life-affirming force that draws us. I experience it like something inside of me and outside of me is pressing and inviting toward more harmony, more interconnection, more love, and capacity to love. By this, I mean love in action. It seems that Life wants to keep Living.

These twenty-five years into somatics, trauma healing, and social justice work, I have seen over and over again that there is a draw and pull toward life deep within our somas. As we un-numb, allow more aliveness, relearn to feel ourselves and others, this draw increases. By becoming more embodied, we are invited toward more life, even when the road to healing and getting there may be difficult and take courage.

I see so often a deep and powerful move toward transformation and harmony within us. We can purposefully heed it, and use our courage to follow it. We can nourish it through our attention (individually and collectively), our practices, and our gratitude.

> Not everything that is faced can be changed, but nothing can be changed until it is faced.
>
> Love takes off masks that we fear we cannot live without and know we cannot live within.
>
> People are trapped in history and history is trapped in them.
>
> (JAMES BALDWIN, in conversation with Nikki Giovanni)

CHRIS LYMBERTOS, organizer with the Arab Resource and Organizing Center, lead teacher for generative somatics (gs), and gs program director.

Is it possible that trauma lives so deep inside our bodies that it is integrated into our DNA? And what does that mean for what lives inside of me: the genocide of Armenians, the devastation and displacement of Aleppans, the exile of non-Muslim Iranians displaced after the 1979 revolution? What about slavery for Black people, the genocide and colonization of indigenous Americans, the active settler colonial project and the genocide of Palestinians, the current assault on migrants on US borders, the Holocaust of Jews?

Can we heal? What does that look like? And how does that happen when some of these traumas are ongoing? Examples include: anti-black racism, the invisibilization of Native Americans and the environmental racism that comes with oil pipelines and uranium discharges, making Palestinian freedom fights (i.e., free speech) illegal through "anti-terrorism" and anti-BDS laws.

I am not supposed to tell you what I'm about to. Growing up in a constantly displaced family meant you packed your life into suitcases small enough to travel with you, and you left the rest untouched. Life was safer that way. Keep yourself to yourself, and the family secrets even closer. We didn't discuss the obvious aberrations, let alone actual trauma.

When I look at old photographs of my parents, they look like they're having more fun than I ever had—connected, laughing, confident. But I know this was unsustainable. The aliveness they tried pulling toward in these photos couldn't keep up with the conditions they were living in (poverty, racism, war, etc.). The moment life got good, that was taken away, or they took themselves away before it could get taken. That was the inherent expectation—nothing this good can last for long.

My parents embodied the fracturing of their homelands, and with it their identities. They were both torn away from their homes violently, through racism and classism. My dad leaving Aleppo, Syria, and my Armenian mom leaving Baku, Azerbaijan. Both escaping unlivable economic and political conditions. Upon arriving in Iran as very young refugees, they settled into a new life in a new and unfamiliar land. They both embodied a deep resourcefulness in making a life from nothing; they knew how to build strong relationships with others who were struggling; they were adventurous and fearless. There was no challenge that couldn't be met. I got this from them.

They also embodied the deep split from their homeland, the violence of poverty, and an expectation that life at its core was about tearing and losing. By the time I was born, they had already experienced loss upon loss upon loss. Even though they wanted a better life for my sister and me, we were taught not to have grand expectations for life. Through their words, beliefs, and actions, they showed us that life was about violence, misery, and that we would not be valued because of who we were. It was the opposite of what they longed for, but they didn't know any other way to be.

My mom's insistence that we not talk about our lives wasn't to punish us, or protect her. It was out of sheer survival and the desire to protect us. Safety isn't inherent to a queer Syrian-Armenian born and raised as a foreign national in Iran. It only got worse when I immigrated to the States just before the Iran hostage crisis. All of my mom's lessons had prepared me for this moment. Fit in, keep our secrets close to the chest, like Mom taught me.

So that's what I did. For a good fifty years I followed my parents' instruction and ignored pain. They told me not to give power to these emotions, keep moving on, and build a life as far away from these feelings as possible. There was no point to facing something that lives so deep inside. I think they honestly believed that was the salve for our wounds. Either way, I didn't even know that what I was experiencing was trauma. I had lived through everything from war to racism to sexual abuse; I even worked and organized in these fields, but I didn't identify as a trauma survivor. Even if I did, it wasn't something to talk about. It was something to work on ending, not feeling.

And then my life fell apart.

In that moment, shattered and alone, I had two options: keep spiraling downward, or figure out a way to heal. I chose the latter, by starting with a trip to Palestine. It was here, with children living as refugees in their own country, that I began to confront my own healing. The second thing I did was to start learning about trauma and its impact on us and how it can heal if we attend to it. Immediately I understood this healing wasn't just for me. Within hours of confronting my own healing, I made a commitment to learn this healing for my people, namely Arabs. A healing that can not only transform our lives, but change how we strategize, how we can be with each other in struggle, and how we win.

Once I opened the door to healing, I reconnected to all the ways our ancestors had healed. Earlier generations, our ancestors may not have had access to "healing," but they still knew how to be resilient and survive. I started to see how their and my protective mechanisms for survival were a true gift. An armor against what has come, and what will continue to come, from the traumatic impacts of oppression.

So then, why heal? Why pull off the bandage that acts as armor to see what's underneath?

Tucked inside of us are our connections to the things we care about the most. Political longings, connections to our legacies, our families, longings around relationship, or the kind of life we want to live. Trauma can take us so far away from all of that. Tucked inside of me were my worth and dignity. I had no access to it. I did everything I could to protect it without even knowing full well what I was defending. Somewhere inside of me, I didn't believe my life was worth living without suffering. I felt set up to live a life of misery, and that life was *only* about suffering. I had no idea life could be about happiness, connection, positive, long-lasting relationships that could include me and what I wanted. That was for other people.

Tucked inside of me were my words. Words to connect instead of fight. Words to stand up for myself. Words to express what I love and long for in this world. Words that include me in the whole, that have deep experiences and stories, that know history, that have sharp analysis, that love my people so deeply I would die for them. These words were swallowed up whole, so no one could get close to knowing what matters to me, who I am, or why I exist. It was safer that way. Lonely, but safe and reverent to my parents.

I also threw people away—people that made me feel bad about myself or challenged something in me that I didn't know how to face. I didn't want to feel that kind of pain, so I would remove myself from relationship and connection. I would leave jobs, unmoor; it felt safer than staying in. Being unmoored was no way to live, but it felt better than having to confront all the possible loss and betrayal of actually longing and losing it. Loss upon loss upon loss. My parents had known it so well. I was going to avoid that at all costs.

In all of the avoidance, what I actually lost was a sense of my own humanity. I could see for others what I wanted for them, but I couldn't access that for myself.

Once my life fell apart, it was a contradiction I couldn't sustain. I felt my purpose was to be in service of our collective freedom, but I wasn't included in that. I couldn't include myself because I didn't know what to include. I still didn't have access to my own longings. For those of us who are literally fighting for the freedom of our people, I think we're limited if we don't know what freedom feels like inside of ourselves. If we don't know how to access it on an individual level, in our families, in our communities, then how do we sustain the larger, harder, more emboldened fight for our people? I know what freedom feels like now. I have a sense of it, a taste of it. And I know my own embodiment of it is critical to how I fight for my people's freedom.

We see it in others too sometimes. Those struggles that embody some aspect of freedom, that give us a sense of hope toward the future. We are drawn to them. We want to learn from them. I think we need to create that space authentically in all our movements. Not as catch phrases, or momentary slogans; but an embodied sense of hope, resilience, connection, of possibility and freedom that is trust-worthy and compelling. Facing into pain, contending with our healing, takes courage, patience, and valuing of ourselves and each other that we all already long for. These are the movements we need. These are the movements I know are possible.

Through healing, I realized I have value. My humanity is inherently valuable. I have something genuine to offer, something to contribute. I learned that I'm lovable, and my love for others has meaning. That I'm dependable and can depend on others. That my worth isn't defined by being someone's workhorse, but that I have value because I exist. When things get hard, instead of throwing people away, I stay in. My sense of safety isn't challenged by conflict and struggle. I can feel in discord with someone and still sense my own worth and value, and theirs. I don't throw either of us away.

This is critical for us in our fights for freedom. The systems trying to take us down leverage these splits; they rely on weakening our bonds; stripping our humanity; playing us against each other. Why give them more power to do that than they already have? My healing is reclaim-ing our right to stay in relationship, even through struggle. Our biggest act of resistance is to fight for our humanity, to fight for our connection to what and who we care about. It may be all we have in this lifetime, but it's ours for the taking.

Even though healing is such hard work, I know now life was harder before. I am more at ease in myself, in my relationships, and in my life. Healing makes us feel pain, devastation, terror, loss, but the other side of it is a much easier life. I want that for everybody, especially the people I care about in my personal life and my political/movement life. I want it for everyone who is targeted, for everyone thrown away by capitalism and imperialism, for everyone who is deemed unworthy of being whole, so that we can create the systems that dignify us and our lives.

When we look collectively, we see that the impacts of trauma and oppression can leave whole communities with a limited capacity to respond effectively to violence and harm, both within the community and from outside the community. We see these limits as the direct results of systemic injustice and abusive power, as communities are repeatedly and calculatedly denied the very resources and supports they need most.

Our biggest act of resistance is to heal our traumas.

5

Safety, Belonging, and Dignity

The only dream worth having is to dream that you will live while you are alive, and die only when you are dead. To love, to be loved. To never forget your own insignificance. To never get used to the unspeakable violence and vulgar disparity of the life around you. To seek joy in the saddest places. To pursue beauty to its lair. To never simplify what is complicated or complicate what is simple. To respect strength, never power. Above all to watch. To try and understand. To never look away. And never, never to forget.

—ARUNDHATI ROY, *The Cost of Living*

Safety, belonging, and dignity. These are inherent needs in human beings. We are tracking for safety, adapting to belong, and organizing ourselves to find dignity. We are at our best when we have, and can offer, all three. We need to understand these more deeply to understand the impacts of trauma and oppressive social conditions, as well as how we heal and create equitable social change.

These needs come with the package of our complex physiologies and psychologies, and are deeply influenced by our social conditions. They aren't learned or negotiable; rather, our orientation toward safety, belonging, and dignity as needs is part of our biologies, our identities, our communities, and our lives.

Humans adapt in many ways to address these needs within their contexts, from family and community, to culture, landscape, and social conditions.

Trauma and oppression negatively impact all three of these needs. We may be physically or sexually harmed; targeted by racist or classist ideas, actions, and policies; told we are worthless and do not belong; and/or objectified through social norms or family practices. Our survival strategies to navigate these experiences may need to prioritize connection over ongoing safety, or dignity over connection. We are then trying to survive and navigate our experiences while internally set at odds with our own nonnegotiable needs. Traumatic symptoms set in: depression, anxiety, lack of self-trust, distrust of others, shame, numbing, and more.

Trauma and oppression leave safety, belonging, and dignity harmed or unmet. It splits safety, belonging, and dignity from each other, so that they are no longer co-supportive. We are then in an unwinnable internal struggle. We are fighting ourselves, because each of these needs are inherent. None can win out over the others.

In its simplest form, healing is the embodied ability to reconnect safety, belonging, and dignity and have them serve one another, rather than be at odds with one another. It is bringing our selves (body, actions, emotions, relations) into current time ... not as a concept, but as a felt reality. The survival strategies mobilized through trauma will hold on and recreate themselves, until the experiences of deep threat are processed and completed, and new updated skills are learned to replace those survival reactions.

What do we really mean by safety, belonging, and dignity, and why is it so essential to understand these when healing trauma? Why is it vital to perceive these core needs when working for social and environmental justice? Let's dig in to what we mean by safety, belonging, and dignity.

Safety

Let's begin with safety, because it is complex. How do we understand safety as material needs (housing, clean water, resources, education, etc.); a feeling, a triggered feeling; and a physical, emotional, relational, and spiritual need—all at the same time?

Safety, at its foundation, means physical and material safety. This is having nourishing food, shelter, health care, access to education and learning, clean water and air, and freedom from physical and sexual violence and neglect—not only to your own being, but to those around you.

Looking solely through this lens of material safety, we can already begin to see that we are in trouble, given the state of our world and the amount of violence many people are exposed to. The vast majority of the world's population experiences war, colonization, environmental destruction and toxins, and family and community violence. When looking at material safety we can also begin to see how traumatizing poverty can be.

Often, when people are harmed and traumatized, the standard for safety drops considerably. One might say they are "safe" because they are not being beaten today. Or that a sexual assault was "in the past, and doesn't affect me," even though the same person is struggling with shame, self-esteem, choosing partners that disrespect them, or other impacts of trauma. When we are looking at safety, we want to look over time—past, present, and into the future—to see what needs addressing to establish or reestablish safety.

By safety, we also mean emotional, spiritual, and relational safety. This means being in connection with people, environments, and your definition of God(s) that are fundamentally interested in your well-being and the well-being of life. Safety gets created when your agency, your interdependence, and your autonomy are affirmed. Emotional and relational safety is created when people acknowledge and support your emotional life, your empathy, and your capacity to act on your own behalf, as well as on behalf of others.

When I was a kid, we had cats, dogs, a stray raccoon, and other animals. Our animals lived primarily outside and came in to visit and sometimes for the night. Our cat, Tigger, had "an accident" in the house and my father angrily threw him out the back door and over the porch railing. I could feel the discord between them and the punishing nature of my father's actions. I began to cry, and wanted to find the cat. My father was upset by my upset and said something like, "They don't have feelings!" Well, I knew this was not true. I could feel the situation and all of what was in it. I also knew, however, to not speak back to my father. I said okay, waited for him to leave, and went to find and comfort Tigger.

While this was not a traumatizing experience for me, it stayed with me. It was a point where my sensitivity, my feeling another's feeling, was beginning to be dismissed and pruned out of me. My emotional and relational development was being pressed into a direction that was about decreasing my capacity to feel and empathize. We can and do empathize. We can and do feel ourselves and others, emotionally. The problems come in stopping ourselves from feeling and connecting emotionally to others.

Safety is also a feeling or state. One way to see it is as a state in which one is able to be both secure and vulnerable, authentic and without fear that this vulnerability will be used against them. Another way to understand safety is as the ability to assess one's environment, other people, and mutual concerns in a relaxed and open way. Once assessing this, safety also means we are able to take the relevant corresponding actions.

What is tricky about describing the "feeling of safety" is that, when one has experienced trauma and oppression, our "feeling state" of safety can get mixed up and cross-wired with traumatic states. For some who have experienced trauma, a feeling of safety cannot be accessed even when their environment and relations are safe.

We can be in a safe place, with a safe person, and *"feel unsafe,"* to the extent that we assess them, their actions, and intentions as harmful, when there is little or no grounding for this. Other times, we can be in an unsafe place or with a person who is harming us, and *"feel safe."* In other words our "feeling" of safety can be a mis-assessment based on the familiarity of harmful environments, and the effects of trauma and oppression on our somas. Tricky.

There is an impactful study of Vietnam veterans who were brought together and shown combat footage from this war. They were monitored through various means—measuring heart rate, temperature, breathing, blood pressure, and more. The scientists expected an increased stress response while viewing combat footage. What they saw instead was that the nervous systems of the vets calmed down, relaxed, and showed all the measurements of being "safer" in the face of combat footage. This is a complex result and one that reveals the adaptations to and impact of trauma.

Often, with great intent, in progressive political spaces or healing spaces, people attempt to create "Safe Space," or declare "This is a safe space," or "You are safe." I have never known what they mean by that, really. This is a nearly impossible claim, if what you mean is to have all participants "feel safe," or if you are declaring safety in community and social conditions that do not allow for material, physical, or relational safety for most people.

I remember a therapist saying to me in the early days of my healing from child sexual abuse and sexism, "You are safe now." I said in return, "That is not true. People are raped every day. You cannot tell me I am safe, now." I still agree with the statement. Luckily, she could roll with this, and deal with the reality of the social conditions, while also continuing to support my healing.

I fully support intentional spaces, and generative agreements within groups that are coming together for a purpose. To make these agreements real, we need to be in practices aligned with these agreements and with the purpose of the group. Most of us need to learn how to align our behavior and practices with these agreements. We come to spaces with a complexity of experiences. Purposeful agreements, collective practice, and engaging in our own reflection, transformation, and accountability can give us the ground for building safety that allows for the complexity of trauma and systemic oppression. It can give us the space in which to learn, heal from trauma, and navigate ongoing oppressive conditions toward more equity and liberation.

I encourage healers, activists, organizers, and therapists to be rigorous about what we mean by safety. I encourage us to expand our understanding beyond either just the material aspect of safety, or just the "feeling" of safety. A more expanded understanding of safety includes understanding the power of social and economic conditions. It integrates the view that safety includes the need to heal, to learn to regenerate safety, and to build the skills needed to create safety for ourselves and others. A broad understanding of safety naturally leads us to work to change social conditions so that all people are systemically granted safety.

Fundamentally, what I am saying is:

1. All people, as well as other beings, deserve safety—material, emotional, relational, social, and spiritual.

2. The vast majority of people, because of our social conditions and global economy, are not granted safety.

3. Because of the experiences of trauma, most people need to relearn and heal around safety. We need to learn to assess safety based in current time, generate safety from the inside out, and develop a wide range of skills to take care of our own and others' safety and well-being.

4. "Feeling safe" is complex. We need to be able to respectfully assess for ourselves and with each other whether the "feeling unsafe" or "feeling safe" is based on what is happening, or on wounds and hurts that are predisposing us to feel afraid or distrustful, and where we may have more choices, allies, and power than we recognize.

Lastly, our states and emotions are changeable and varied. We may be in a safe partnership (by all the above definitions) and be upset or triggered for some reason and feel unsafe. While, after a conversation or resolution, we feel safe in the same circumstances an hour later. We may be in a group, such as a healing group, organization, or social justice alliance that has dynamic disagreement. A group may engage in deep and meaningful questions that we may not have the answer to, and sometimes feel enlivened by this and sometimes feel unsettled and even unsafe.

Because of traumatic experiences and conditions, many of us need to relearn how to distinguish internal, relational, and external safety. We often need to relearn how to generate safety from the inside out, rather than waiting on others to be and do what we need to "feel safe." We often need to find more choices amidst dynamic and complex environments.

Somatics helps us to understand how and why this mix-up happens, and how to heal around this inherent need for safety. Through healing trauma we can generate safety and choices to act on our own and others' behalf ... even in social and economic conditions that are not supportive of our safety. We'll get to all of this in the regenerating safety and resilience chapters of the book.

Belonging

The moment we choose to love we begin to move against domination, against oppression. The moment we choose to love we begin to move towards freedom, to act in ways that liberate ourselves and others.

(bell hooks, *Outlaw Culture*)

Belonging. We are social animals. Being a part of the herd or pack is necessary for us. It is deep in our knowing, our desire, and in our biology. We also want and need an "I," an authentic experience of a self that is dignified, discovered over time, known by others, and belongs in the "we."

We gather in tribes, towns, and cities, and coordinate life together. There is lots of complexity in how well this goes, and many people are lonely and isolated, even amidst others. Yet, being near each other, being a part of the group, is inherent to our very beings. We thrive in supportive connection, in being a part of, in cooperation, and in giving and receiving love. We have a deep biological expectation to belong, and in this, an expectation to be protected by the group.

Even those people who have purposefully spent large swaths of time alone (months, years) often are in a spiritual practice that is about connecting to what is more vast—to God, Nature, Mystery. Across cultural and spiritual traditions, experiences of deep interdependence and oneness are reported as some of the most profound experiences of Truth.

Belonging reaches from the intimate to the social. It is vital with our intimates and family, and reaches more broadly to our communities, neighborhoods, schools, and workplaces. Our belonging also needs to be reflected as a welcomed and meaningful part of society. Belonging reaches to place, culture, and landscape. Where do we belong? Where do we yearn to belong? We need to be part of the pack. What happens to our sense of belonging when the pack hurts us? Or when one pack continually harms another?

Traumatic experiences and systemic oppression betray belonging. This means one's sense of connection, of interconnection, and of "mattering" is deeply affected. Trauma and acts of harm are most often at the hands of another human being such as a parent, family member, teacher, coach, religious leader, soldier, or policy maker. Trauma can also be caused by human designed and operated systems such as prisons, police, military, immigration policies and enforcement, corporations, financial institutions, media messages and images, and governments.

The impact of trauma and oppression on belonging is very hard for people. For some there is a profound sense of isolation, of not being understood or understandable. For others it is a sense of abandonment and being left alone, or not chosen. For others there is a sense of being cut out, not seen or acknowledged, or unloved or unlovable. Because belonging—being deserving of and able to give and receive love—is an inherent need, this causes many hardships for those navigating trauma and oppression.

To reflect on belonging, we can ask ourselves:

- Who in your immediate and extended family is held as belonging, meaningful, and loved? Who is not?

- Who is reflected in the media as belonging, meaningful, and loved? Who is left out?

- Have you seen or heard yourself, or people like you, reflected as belonging, meaningful, and loved in the mainstream media?

- Who is held by our broader social and economic systems as worth including, and who is seen as disposable, as not belonging?

When people or systems look to harm or control others, isolation is a key tactic. In other words, taking people out of belonging and contact. In prisons, war, and torture, the use of isolation and solitary confinement is standard practice. This is also typical in situations of intimate or domestic violence—isolating the person from their networks of support and family is used to break down, hurt, and control the person. It essentially sequesters them with the person harming them. Also, in human trafficking, whether it is for labor or sex, isolation and disconnection from others is a key form of control. Isolation is traumatizing.

I also want to talk about land and belonging. This does not mean owning land, or even living in a particular nation-state. Rather, this is a connection to place, to land, that forms an aspect of our identity, our community, our belonging. For most of human history we have been deeply connected to, and a part of, the land. I believe this lives deep in our cellular memory.

Even in post-industrial and high-tech societies, many speak of the yearning for place and connection to land, and knowing our part in it. Many will speak of the resonance and homecoming of wilderness, or returning to a deeply known place—even when that place is urban. In the research on resilience, connection to land and nature is shown again and again to be healing and restoring for us ... when that environment also feels safe and culturally relevant. Land and place may be the original and deepest belonging. Cultural practices, healing practices, language, and identity are often deeply connected to land.

Power-over social and economic conditions often use colonization, forced migration, and the destruction of a community's connection to land and place. The consequences of global capitalism are often economic migration from land that one has been connected to for generations. In this system land is now held as an own-able resource. Each of these systems separates our belonging to land.

Attachment Theory

Lastly, I want to include some thoughts on attachment theory. Secure attachment is an embodied sense of belonging and security, an ability to self-regulate, and the capacity to form intimate connections as well as have separation from those with whom we are intimate. Trauma negatively impacts or prevents secure attachment. One of the things I appreciate about this work is its acknowledgment of humans as inter-dependent and needing each other to thrive. Attachment theory under-scores that our bonds and connections with one another are central to our development through many stages of life. In most cases, when this bond is disrupted, there are healing approaches to help mend and reestablish positive or secure attachment.

I'd also like to challenge this work to look further—to the lack of dignified connection and belonging offered to many communities by the broader social norms. Attachment is not just to our primary care-givers or our family and children—while it is key there. We also need to belong within our communities. Our communities need to belong to the broader social fabric. There is a broader circle of belonging that also affects attachment, a sense of security, and real choices for connec-tion and interdependence.

Let's consider this:

What happens to people within a community who are regularly tar-geted by the police, where children have typically been detained by the age of eleven? What is happening to their attachments and belonging? This is regularly happening in poor Black and Brown communities in the United States. How does this environment allow for secure attach-ment, even if the child has it at home?

> It's from behind that gate that I watch the police roll up on my broth-ers and their friends, not one of whom is over the age of 14 and all of whom are doing absolutely nothing but talking. They throw them up on the wall. They make them pull their shirts up. They make them turn out their pockets. They roughly touch my brothers' bodies, even their privates, while from behind the gate I watch, frozen. I cannot cry or scream. I cannot breathe and I cannot hear anything. Not the sirens that would have been accompanying the swirl of red lights, not the screeching at the boys: Get on the fucking wall!
>
> (PATRISSE KAHN-CULLORS, *When They Call You a Terrorist: A Black Lives Matter Memoir*)

What happens to attachment and belonging when one in three women and one in six men experience some form of contact sexual violence in their lifetime (National Sexual Violence Resource Center 2015)? What happens when this is denied and dismissed by the president of the United States, Congress, and many political commentators, along with the newest justice confirmed to the Supreme Court? Belonging is deeply impacted when our lives and experiences are continually denied and made irrelevant by the broader governing powers.

What happens to secure attachment when your peoples are colonized and disappeared in the colonizer's telling of history? How can we understand and support trauma healing for indigenous peoples or Palestinian peoples without deeply integrating the broader social and political contexts? I'd say we can't.

For many people, the social norms and narratives do not include our communities in positive and whole ways ... or do not reflect our communities at all. Having our personhood and communities reflected positively, considered as belonging to the broader social fabric, is essential for belonging and interdependence. I say this too is essential for secure and positive attachment.

Dignity

Dignity is our inherent value and worth as human beings. Dignity is a sense of worthiness. We thrive when we are dignified, and when we know how to dignify others. Everyone is born with it. Everyone needs it.

We can think of respect, on the other hand, as earned through one's actions.

Some know their own dignity. Some know how to dignify others. Sadly, many of us don't have a deeply embodied experience of either our own or others' inherent dignity. Trauma and oppression profoundly affect a person's and community's sense of worth. I see often that the processes of leadership development in social justice organizations, building a social analysis and understanding history, are deeply mending for people's dignity. One begins to see behind the curtain of social and economic power-over systems and realize that so much is not personal. You and your community are not bad or wrong. In fact, you and your community are inherently worthy. We begin to see that a power-over system is designed to leave us feeling worthless rather than empowered and dignified.

Dignity and privilege or entitlement are very different.

We can think of privilege as something given by social and economic systems, that can leave people with more access and a deeper sense of worthiness. Their dignity has not been systematically targeted. But, I would not call this an embodied sense of dignity, because it's built on a false ground. Privilege depends on oppression and power-over. In that sense, the dignity it grants is always limited.

Entitlement is an attitude that assumes value and deservedness. While entitlement can drive many actions, policies, and even philanthropy, at its core it has little to do with dignity. It's an assumed sense of deservedness based on one's social location or privilege, and is often promoted by the social norms. Entitlement, fundamentally, is at the expense of others, and depends on not seeing the whole.

Like safety and belonging, our need to be dignified is part of our somatic and human inheritance. We want to be of value, to live as inherently worthy, to not question our right to exist. We want to have merit, to be known to have skills, presence, and worth that contribute to others.

We can see the traumatic impact of oppression on dignity. When society, through images, collective narratives, and institutions from schools to Immigration and Customs Enforcement (ICE), says you and your communities are worthless, don't matter, or are less than, it has a traumatic impact. Revoking or diminishing one's dignity is destructive. It's like stealing the right to exist, the right to be, the right to take up space. When people are invisibilized, degraded, and undignified, it impacts their choices and sets the stage for an uphill battle. This same battle does not have to be fought by those who are systematically granted dignity by society.

Peoples and governments most often go to war or colonize to gain resources, wealth, and the power to declare and decide reality. One of the strategies used to do this includes challenging or degrading a people's inherent dignity. They are perceived as less than, evil, or made into an enemy. The degradation is then used as validation to harm or kill, to steal land and resources, to appropriate and commodify culture, and take over the governing of those people and resources.

Not being dignified can leave us with a sense of shame, that something is inherently wrong with us, and that something is wrong with people like us. The odd thing about shame is that most often the person harmed is left with the sense of shame, rather than those harming.

Along with safety and belonging, healing also looks to restore dignity, a deep sense of worth, and the feeling that your existence matters. One of the most powerful healing declarations that I have heard over these years is from Lisa Thomas-Adeyemo, a somatic practitioner and teacher for both generative somatics and Black Organizing for Leadership and Dignity. Lisa is a queer Black woman. Her declaration is fundamentally about dignity: "I am a commitment to being in my skin without apology."

This declaration, this aim of healing, is to counter and mend from the traumatic impact of white supremacy. To restore an embodied dignity.

Reconnecting Safety, Belonging, and Dignity

We have all adapted to try to address safety, belonging, and dignity—from trying to meet them in relationships that cannot again and again, to numbing ourselves to our needs, and everything in between. It can be a relief to recognize that we all have an inherent need for safety, belonging, and dignity, and begin to explore our own adaptations. Recognizing our own survival strategies can, in and of itself, begin to open more choices. These behaviors may not be "who I am," but rather how I best adapted for safety, belonging, and dignity.

Mending safety, belonging, and dignity, somatically, and having them work in conjunction with each other, is the central purpose of healing. This shifts us from the more limited reactions stemming from survival strategies—to a more coherent and resourced embodiment. This leaves us with more choices, more aliveness, and being more able to take actions based on what we care about. This reconnection eases the unresolvable tension from these inherent needs being at odds with each other. Safety once again can support connection, connection can support dignity, and dignity can support belonging and safety.

SPENTA KANDAWALLA, acupuncturist, co-founder of generative somatics (GS), member leader of the Arab Resource and Organizing Center, and lead teacher for GS.

Assimilation may be defined as the cost of one's dignity for the sake of their safety and belonging. At least, this was true in my story.

I grew up in a suburb of Columbus, Ohio. It was very white, middle to upper class, and reflected the earnest but conservative sentiment of the rest of the state. My family stuck out like a sore thumb. Divorced when I was five, my mom worked one job and went to night school while raising me and my two brothers. We went from eating *dhansak* and rice to chicken nuggets overnight. We were Zoroastrians, an ancient Persian religion. My parents were born and raised in Pakistan, but that was only talked about in hushed tones around our house. Being Pakistani was dirty, scary, foreign. Being American became the goal. More explicitly, becoming white.

One of the first splits I can remember between my safety, belonging, and dignity happened when I was in first grade. My class was lined up at the door waiting to go outside for recess. I was good. Always good. For my teacher, for my mom, for my friends. By the time I was seven, I was already trained to not rock the boat, cause a disruption, or upset someone else's reality in any way. So when this boy started whispering slurs to me about my body hair, namely my mustache that was already burgeoning on my upper lip, I froze. I stilled.

My breath stopped, suspended in my sternum, my chest collapsed, curling my shoulders in around my heart, my ears scanned for who else may have heard him, and the rest of my self got sucked into my solar plexus (that place right below your rib cage where your diaphragm is) like a vortex into a black hole. In an instant my dignity became compromised. This concession would last for over twenty years.

But, I had done it. I had disappeared in plain sight. Over time I learned how to spot him from a distance, and invisibilize before these encounters would even begin. Pull yourself in, back, away. Scan for how many people are a part of this, and find an exit as fast as you can. Then wait and endure. It'll pass, and the goal is to have as few witnesses as possible. The fewer people involved, the less people realize you're not actually white. That way, I could still have friends, fit in, belong. Even though his violations lasted and escalated through high school and my tormentor enlisted others to join him, I still found an ample amount of belonging among many of my peers.

I was liked. At least, as a friend. He made sure I was too undesirable for more than that. But, I made it so I was liked as a friend, a confidant. I comported my body into a smaller version of itself. A deeply appeasing version of itself that knew how to laugh at the right times, sound like an Ohioan, and never talk about anything related to my brown skin and where it came from. I had real, depthful, and sincere friendships that had major limitations. My friends loved me, but they never defended or protected me from my bullies. They probably didn't even know a defense was needed. They knew a lot about me, and they knew nothing about me. I made sure of that. And the longer I played this role, the further I got from myself, from my people, from my lineage, from my inherent beauty and longing.

This story, of course, isn't unique to me. It's as old as empire. The stripping of one's dignity is a tool of colonization, of slavery, of occupation. We internalize and reproduce oppressive conditions through our behaviors and ways of being. The attempt to destroy a whole people's dignity while denying access to material needs (food, shelter, education, employment) is part of a calculated strategy to steal land, exploit labor, and desecrate culture and traditions. This is in my diasporic lineage as it is in the majority of people of color, including the peoples' land we currently occupy here in the Americas. Many of our peoples have been shaped by this move that demands our collusion, our capitulation, our integrity, in the face of our own survival.

But this is not just a story of how safety, belonging, and dignity get broken. It is also a story about healing. How weaving these three components back together is critical to finding ourselves again. At least, it was a key for me to re-find the self I stored way back in grade school.

The first place I started to find my dignity, even before somatics or personal healing work, was in organizing. It was working in a group of people who shared my desire for freedom; who helped me learn and hone how the State has constructed me and my life—both the unearned privileges it grants me because of class and education, and the oppression it requires me to face because of race and gender. It was here that I understood a much larger force had been chipping away at my dignity even before I was born. It was in these collective bodies that I learned to first resist the state-sanctioned diminishment of my and our worth. To me, dignity is interchangeable with our worth. What oppression is doing is trying to render us worthless. If we are worthless, you can just do whatever the hell you want to us. It was out on the streets organizing and in political work that I was able to tap into a feeling of "We're worth something. We're worth a lot."

Organizing is healing, and it was the first way I began to heal.

Suddenly, I could belong *and* be brown. It was revelatory and started awakening a life in me that had been dormant, stale, covered up, and piled on. This was the first time I started to uncover what I had so expertly hidden years earlier. In my organizing work today, I fight for the liberation of Palestine and the rest of the Arab world. I get to see and be a part of the resourcefulness of oppressed peoples and movements to create safety, to embody dignity, and to sustain connection in the midst of everything trying to shatter it. It is remarkable.

Then, there is healing. The work of transformation that is about unwinding and uprooting the old traumatic stories to make way for new realities that are more congruent and integrous with who we are and what we care about. Different stories create different splits in our safety, belonging, and dignity. When safety has been broken in ourselves, when our boundaries have been profoundly crossed or violated, as mine had, as yours have, I think there's a way that we don't even know how deeply we end up mistrusting ourselves. We start to believe we did something wrong because that boundary, that thing we were using to protect ourselves, got violated or crossed, and we didn't stop it. It doesn't matter that we couldn't stop it. We've betrayed ourselves, and start to think: "Well, I betrayed myself once. What's to say I'm ever really trustworthy?"

Many experiences, including violence and harm, helped shape my body into a "C." Curled in on myself, shrunken, eyes cast down, my real desires tucked deep away, and a constant and thorough questioning of myself and everything I did. That was the lasting shape of trauma and oppression. Through somatic work I have taken on commitments to get me reconnected with my longings, rebuild trust in myself, and become a powerful woman of color in my organizing and healing work. I have risked revealing more of myself with people I care about. I have learned to embody my dignity through the eyes of other women of color who either modeled theirs for me, or looked to me to show them a different way forward. We are such unspoken gifts to each other. We don't even know how we constantly lift each other up when we live from our freedom, aliveness, faith, and knowing. We're still here. That's a big deal. They don't want us to see that, but we're still here.

I have taken on daily practices. I have worked with shame, depression, and despair. I have let my body open to feelings I never wanted to feel, like terror, rage, and longing (that was the worst … until it wasn't). I talk about being a Zoroastrian now. I teach my niece about it. I let myself feel as big as my hero(ine), Freddie Mercury—as full of life, as authentic, as contradictory, as bold, as alive. I trust myself as an acupuncturist, as a comrade, and as an ally. I have let myself fall in love and stay in love. None of these things have been easy, but they have been worth it.

This intersection of healing and organizing has been, to me, the only way forward to mend these fissures between safety, belonging, and dignity, in ourselves as individuals and also collectively. Both individual and collective work are required. I don't think you can just do one and not the other. To get free, we have to understand more clearly in ourselves what that means. Simultaneously, it's not enough to just free ourselves, while so much is in peril. I think in some ways we are at the core always fighting for safety, belonging, and dignity, in our own lives and in our organizing work. A more healed sense of safety, belonging, and dignity is when we get to a place where we realize we can generate those things, not just be the effect of them.

I/we can generate my sense of safety, I/we can generate my sense of belonging, I/we can generate a sense of dignity. I don't sit in organizing meetings and wait for everyone else to say everything exactly right so that I feel safe enough to speak. I extend trust to the people I work with by offering my thoughts, and I deal with disagreement or conflict as it comes. I don't automatically shrink myself for the sake of connection or being liked. I sink into the bigger work we are all in together, and remind myself I am a part of these commitments.

At some point in my history, all three of these components were threatened in one way or another, and they still are today through oppression and political repression. But on the whole, I feel more whole. I have found ways to not sacrifice one for the sake of the others. I can be relatively safe and stay in my dignity while being connected. I feel happy often, with my people, loved, and on purpose. I continue to learn and grow, unfold and unfurl, but I can honestly say that I live a life I never thought would feel this good.

Part 3

Transforming:
I, You, and We

6

The Arc of Transformation— Overview

Part 3 is about the *how* of embodied transformation. This section will dive into the different aspects of the change model. As with any embodied competence—be it healing or organizing, leadership or facilitation, this change model is best learned through study and practice, and with training and mentorship from those embodied in the work.

This is a model that we have been using at generative somatics for many years. It evolved out of the somatics work of Richard Strozzi-Heckler along with the Somatics and Trauma programs that I launched in 2001. The model has been used for individual transformation and healing and within groups, organizations, and alliances through generative somatics since 2009.

The Somatic Arc of Transformation is a two-dimensional map that would be better shown as a moving hologram. It is dynamic and its components are interdependent. We'll explore it in a linear fashion here, though that does not mean it always works that way. All of the components are vital and we are organic. Our embodiment, protection strategies, resilience, and shaping are unique and dynamic, and don't fit easily into lines and frameworks.

Embodiment can and does transform, however. Many aspects of healing are both unique to the person or group, and predictable or able to plan for. The soma operates by its own rules. When we learn them, listen to them, and understand their processes, we can readily invite and support embodied healing and transformation.

The Arc of Transformation is always held inside of social conditions and systems, and acknowledges the variety of causes of trauma, from individual to systemic.

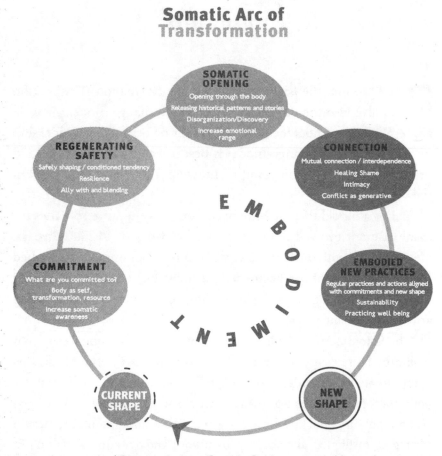

Somatic Arc of Transformation

SOMATIC OPENING
Opening through the body
Releasing historical patterns and stories
Disorganization/Discovery
Increase emotional range

REGENERATING SAFETY
Safely shaping / conditioned tendency
Resilience
Ally with and blending

CONNECTION
Mutual connection / interdependence
Healing Shame
Intimacy
Conflict as generative

COMMITMENT
What are you committed to?
Body as self, transformation, resource
Increase somatic awareness

EMBODIED NEW PRACTICES
Regular practices and actions aligned with commitments and new shape
Sustainability
Practicing well being

CURRENT SHAPE

NEW SHAPE

EMBODIMENT

generative somatics | Diagram designs: Querido Galdo, www.queridomundo.com

156

This model supports embodied transformation and healing from the impacts of trauma and oppression. We hold the definition of transformation as: you or we have transformed when our actions align with our values and vision, even under the same old pressures. The same old pressures are the social conditions and systems, difficult dynamics within our leadership, organizations, or relationships, and the ongoing changes of life.

New insight and understanding are important, and transformation is more than that.

Transformation is when we have new options and choices. We can make different moves and have different conversations that are aligned with our values, visions, and what we are committed to. We are connected to what we care about, and can think, relate, and act from there. Transformation gives us more choice and agency, while helping us to ask and answer the deep questions of creating meaning and navigating life. It allows us to develop more trust, coordination, and love. We can be with ourselves and others with more presence and attention. It helps us to build the skills that trauma and oppression did not teach us—and to use those skills toward equity, interdependence, and a radically different relationship to the planet. It is transformation that sustains over time. This is, in our lingo, the *"for the sake of what"* of this work.

Lastly, the social conditions that we are living and healing in change slowly. For most of us, the transformation that we seek—environmental justice, racial justice, economic justice, gender equity—is a lifelong commitment. Many of those conditions aren't likely to radically transform within our lifetimes. As healers, leaders, organizers, or movement builders, we have to be able to take transformative action and build transformative relationships within these pressures and these conditions.

Current Shape and New Shape

Let's revisit what we mean by shape. A shape is more than one's physical "body language," though it also encompasses that. Shape is the embodiment of our thinking and beliefs, how we connect and relate, the actions and nonactions that are accessible and habitual. It is also our emotions and emotional range along with our physiology and physical form. It is the embodied self within social conditions. These can be individual or collective shapes, such as family, community, groups, or organizations.

Our current shape is our current embodiment. It is our responses and reactions, embodied beliefs and ways of thinking, emotional range, ways of acting, and the action we don't know how to take. This is where we start from.

Our new shape is our embodiment when we have transformed through the various stages of the Arc and embody our commitments and cares—we can think, be, act, relate, and feel from them, even under pressure.

Circle One. Commitment, What Do You Care About, and Why the Body?

We begin with, "What do you care about? What do you want to heal and transform? What do you want to see in the world? What do you long for?" The body/soma is the ground of transformation. We change ourselves through the body—and the body will ask more from us than the mind will, in the transformative process. Somatic awareness, somatic opening, and somatic practices create sustainable change.

Circle Two. Regenerating Safety and Embodied Resilience.

In this circle, we explore and learn to cultivate our inherent resilience to serve healing, relationship, and collective action. We discover and work with conditioned tendencies and survival reactions that aren't working anymore. We build safety and boundaries from the inside out, while also dealing with the realities of material safety and social oppression. Through this more options for safety, belonging, and dignity are grown.

Circle Three. Somatic Opening.

We often need to deconstruct things to build anew. This is true in our somas as well. Our habits and survival strategies live in our tissues. Our automatic ways of reacting, relating, and thinking are driven from much deeper in our brains, hearts, and muscles than our ideas about them. These embodied strategies are also protective, and often taking care of previous hurts. Somatic opening allows what has been stored in the body to come forward and be felt. It allows what has been left incomplete, to complete, holistically. This aspect of transformation can feel disorganizing, unsettling, and often means we are touching our pain. Without it, however, we are placing new practices on top of old embodied strategies. Under enough pressure, the old strategies will win out. Thus, we need to allow the roots to come up and to give them their respects. On the positive side, this can feel like setting down weights that you have been carrying for years.

Circle Four. Healing Shame, Mutual Connection, and Conflict as Generative.

After somatic opening, we are ready to take on the big and important work of loving and being loved, dignifying and being dignified, in relationship, whether personal or in our work and movement spaces. Healing shame involves distinguishing somatically (not just mentally) what is and is not our fault, where we are over- or under-accountable, and how to forgive—especially ourselves. This makes more room for conflict to be generative, meaning we can build more trust and capacity through conflict, rather than splitting, appeasing, or being "right."

Circle Five. Embodying New Practices. Sustainability. Well-Being.

Throughout the change process we are taking on new somatic practices that serve each phase. Here, our embodied practices are aligned with our commitments and vision for the future. Embodied transformation and new practices mean our changes are sustainable. Well-being, happiness, grounded trust, and bold action become more familiar—even amidst the social conditions, and while working with others to create change and healing.

We keep changing. The arrow from new shape, back to current shape.

Once we have moved through the Arc, and new ways of being have become embodied, we get to keep growing. There may be a short or long phase of integrating the healing and changes, of noticing how you are living and relating differently. Then, we get to keep changing.

And finally, what does the embodiment mean in the center of the Arc? This refers to three things.

First: as we purposely engage in embodied change and healing processes, we become more embodied. That means we are more able to feel ourselves, our sensations and aliveness, our longings and commitments—and to organize our lives and relationships around them. We are able to feel and tolerate a wider range of sensations and emotions, allowing us to respond instead of react, to make choices rather than act in or act out. We also can feel others in a more present and grounded way. Whether we had been more numb to others or very sensitive to others, we can feel, distinguish, and not be taken over by the feelings.

Second: embodiment also means we get more and more connected to a built-in harmonizing force that is self-healing, self-generating, and invites learning and change. Embodiment encourages us to keep growing, to move toward more aliveness and possibility, to both soften and enliven. I tend to think of this pulse as a spiritual immune system. It asks us to keep healing, changing, and harmonizing. Through this, it helps us be more alive.

Third and finally: embodiment reconnects us to the vast history of life and the wisdom of three billion years of evolution. It brings us to the knowing of interdependence, even while our social conditions teach us individualism, how to "other," and build enemies. Embodiment rejoins us to being part of life on the planet and the deep resonance of living in relationship rather than dominion. There is intelligence in the felt sense. There is intelligence in the aliveness that moves in and through us. Embodiment allows us to access this and be reminded.

Each aspect of the Arc is detailed in the following chapters. Enjoy.

7

Arc Circle One— Vision and Longing

MISSING THE BOAT

It is not so much that the boat passed
and you failed to notice it.
It is more like the boat stopping
directly outside of your bedroom window,
the captain blowing the signal-horn,
band playing a rousing march.
The boat shouted, waving bright flags,
its silver hull blinding in the sunlight.

But you had this idea
you were going by train.
You kept checking the time-table,
digging for tracks.

And the boat got tired of you,
so tired it pulled up its anchor
and raised the ramp.

The boat bobbed into the distance,
shrinking like a toy—
at which point you probably realized
you had always loved the sea.

—NAOMI SHIHAB NYE

What do you want? What do you value? What do you long for? What is yearning to heal?

What do you want to be possible for your community or for the world? These are the questions we begin with, when looking to heal trauma or engage in personal or group transformation.

One of the things that captured me about somatics is that we begin with these questions of possibility. The body learns on "Yes." That means that we organize ourselves, our somas *toward* something. We think, act, and practice toward a possibility. It is harder to place our attention on stopping something without attending to what we are going to practice instead. It is much easier to fully engage a healing or change process, especially through the difficult times, when we have a vision big enough to compel us forward.

In the process of change, we will explore and understand the hurts and their impact, and assess if further support is needed. But, we do not start with asking what is wrong or look to diagnose the problem as the place to begin. We instead begin with exercising the muscle of imagination and possibility, toward what we want. We begin with what futures we desire, with what is drawing us.

Wanting and longing are somatic experiences. Where we find these desires are in the sensations, the body, and through the felt sense. "What do you want?" is not a theoretical question, or one solely to analyze. This is a question that gets answered through a felt, resonant experience. We will analyze and create strategies around getting there, assess where the desires emerge from, and more. And, we need to allow space for the questions of yearning and calling to be felt and answered from beneath the thinking mind.

There are multiple parts of our lives, and we hold multiple wants and commitments—for ourselves, our close relationships and families, for our work lives, our purpose and calling, for our communities and the broader social and economic conditions we live within, and for the natural world. We do not have to sacrifice one area for another. Rather we can grow our capacity to hold multiple dynamic cares and commitments.

In a politicized somatics we hold that through the change process (healing) we can learn to hold wider and wider circles of care. We can hold those for ourselves, others, and the future. We call this—I, You, and We. This means we can care for and take action for ourselves, for others, and for other communities and the environment. In doing so, we can learn to hold more complexity, without losing ourselves. We can learn to hold the cares and concerns of others, even if we are not familiar with their experiences or don't "relate" to them.

Declarations and Commitments

We begin with the questions of possibility and longings to get a deeper sense of what future we are changing toward. These questions are not always easy to answer, and often become the first part of the change process. More on that soon.

Let me first define what we mean by declarations and commitments. Declarations are a "speech act," as distinguished by Fernando Flores, PhD, a linguist and philosopher, and former Chilean finance minister and political prisoner. This means an aspect of language that holds action and coordination with others inherent to it. When we declare, we are intending and calling forth a future. We are mobilizing ourselves, and often others, into action to build it.

In somatics we understand declarations as an embodied competency. We develop the ability and skill to declare. This is to imagine possible futures, speak them aloud to others, and mobilize yourself and others toward them. This is a powerful skill for healing, for leadership, and for social change.

Imagination and yearning are somatic experiences that need to be practiced, and muscles that need to be built if they haven't been used often. Sometimes our imaginations have been discouraged, our yearnings denied and dismissed. Because of inequitable social conditions, particular peoples have been encouraged to imagine, to want, and to declare futures. Others have been systematically discouraged from doing this. Often those people with the most social privilege based on class, race, gender, and nationality are the best at declaring. And, are often declaring for themselves and others, without deeply considering others' experiences and desires. Those with the least systemic privilege often need to be reminded, encouraged, and empowered, through healing and political education, to declare and declare boldly.

We begin by exploring what and whom you care about, what you want and long for. And then, we'll craft this into a declaration—an imagined future that is compelling to you. This declaration becomes an internalized rudder and sense of direction. It becomes a commitment. Our declarations guide our healing, conversations, and actions toward what we care about.

Here are some examples of declarations, from people whose stories are included in this book:

I am a commitment to being a powerful leader, even in the face of people who do not acknowledge my leadership. (Spenta Kandawalla)

I am a commitment to healing my life into current time. (Nathan Shara)

I am a commitment to be in my skin without apology. (Lisa Thomas-Adeyemo)

I am a commitment to the transformative power of somatics serving social and environmental justice and collective liberation. (me)

I am a commitment to the harvest and feast. (Alta Starr)

I have had the opportunity to be with these folks, and they with me, in healing and living into these declarations. I am moved and inspired.

Most of our declarations ask us to change and heal. When we long for something we don't already have, or don't already embody, it asks us to grow and to become someone who does and can embody that yearning. I sometimes think of this as a spiritual trick, but in a good way. To have us long for what is beyond us, so that we keep growing and changing. Becoming.

Declarations are dynamic and organic. We may have one now, and work for the next years to embody it, heal into it, and bring it about. Once we have grown into it, the next declarations may emerge, the next horizon. To me, this is good news. Learning, growing, making a bigger difference, being more than we thought we could be, learning to be satisfied and appreciative without sacrificing our values, and more. We will craft declarations over our lifetimes.

Lastly, some declarations span beyond our lifetimes. We can care about something that will take longer than our lifetime to achieve. This is true of many things we long for in social justice movements: ending poverty, an equitable and environmentally sustainable economy, transformative justice instead of prisons, etc. These long-term declarations can still guide our lives and actions, and can live beside declarations that are focused on our more immediate lives.

Discovering What You Are Committed To: Types of Declarations

INHERITED DECLARATIONS

We live in families, communities, and social contexts that tell us consistently what we want or should want, and what we care about or should care about. We inherit declarations. We have them handed to us over and over again, as if they were the only things we should want. These can range from prioritizing money, cars, shoes, wealth, and more stuff, to an individualized "happily ever after" of monogamous heterosexual marriage, having kids, or finding a soulmate. Religious beliefs and norms also tell us what to long for and what not to want, who is righteous and who is a sinner. Culture also comes with values, meaning, and priorities. Some of these inheritances are powerful, meaningful, and align with who we want to be, and others do not.

We first want to get to know what we have inherited. What are the declarations that were given to us? To discover your inherited commitments, you can explore the following:

1. Look at the ads, images, and definitions of success, safety, desirability, and being powerful that surround us. What do you see? What does this tell you to want and care about? Who does it ask you to be? Even if we are reacting against this—"I won't be that!"—we may not yet be self-defining our commitments and longings.

2. If you had "turned out" to be just the person, and to have just the life, that your family or community wanted you to be, who would you be? What would you be doing? What would you care about? What role would you be playing?

3. If you had "turned out" to be just the person, and to have just the life, that society wanted you to be, who would you be? What would you be doing? What would matter to you? What would you be fighting for? Whom would you be against?

4. What did you learn to care about because of the dynamics in your family, or those that raised you? Because of your family's circumstances? Was there room to also find yourself, even if you had different cares, desires, and concerns than those that parented you?

It is useful to get to know the inherited declarations and how they are operating in us. This can help us see which of them we want to keep, and which are not relevant to what we care about. Some of these inherited declarations may actually be in the way of what we care about.

Our perception of and our actual possibilities are influenced by our social and economic conditions and our location in these. Those who are more oppressed can internalize this oppression, not feeling that they are allowed to imagine and imagine big. Those with more social privilege may follow the social norms of "success" not because it's what they long for, but because of the financial rewards and social privileges it grants them. Our lived material conditions (job, income, health care, access to schooling) affect what we can imagine and how we can pursue our declarations. It is much easier for some people to access learning, alternative health care, education, healing, and innovative or alternative spaces, than others. Even if some of these spaces consciously make themselves financially accessible to poor or working class people or people of color, many workshops, practitioners, and the like do not create environments that reflect oppressed people's experiences and needs.

Stepping away from inherited commitments can be scary. It may threaten something about your safety, belonging, or dignity. It may threaten your place within your family or community. Many, many queer and transgender people have had to face this in their families and closest relationships, in order to be themselves. If your longing does not have much room in the social norm, it can also be dangerous. As we learn what we long for, what we are committed to, we also need to assess what support we need and how we may need to take care of our safety.

Again, we are always living within social and economic conditions. These are shaping what we see as possible and affecting our imagination and choices. The more socially conscious we become, the more we can uproot these hindrances to our imaginations. We are always navigating our social conditions, yet often have choices well beyond what we have been told and taught.

SELF-DEFINED DECLARATIONS

As we begin to explore what we long for, want, and what our larger callings are, we learn to imagine beyond what we have inherited. We begin to find a deeper permission to discover, listen to, and then follow self-defined declarations.

A self-defined declaration is one we discover, cull from our life experiences, or maybe have always "known" but turned away from for various reasons. It is a declaration that invites us to become more of ourselves, bring our essential gifts, and risk loss and being predefined. Very often I see that self-defined declarations ask us to risk who we "should" be and discover and claim more of ourselves. In this, we tend to contribute more to others, build more connected and authentic relationships, take bolder risks, and allow more creativity. Self-defined declarations ask us to become someone beyond who we are now.

> That is how I learned that if I didn't define myself for myself, I would
> be crunched into other people's fantasies for me and eaten alive.
>
> (AUDRE LORDE, "Learning from the 60s")

We can begin to use the "muscle of imagination," by asking ourselves questions. By exploring, feeling, and listening for your answers. Some questions you can ask yourself are:

- What do you want?
- What do you long for?
- If you had permission or encouragement to long, want, desire … what would you want?
- Imagine you had the life that deeply aligned with your longings. What would that life be like?
- What difference do you want to make for others or for the environment?
- What feels like authentic expression for you?
- Who and what do you want to impact?
- How do you want to love, and be loved?
- What have you always known about yourself?
- What are you made for?
- What's calling you now?

Remember, there are many different domains of life. You can ask yourself these questions in any one of them. Some of the domains are—your love and intimacy, parenting, your community, your friends and family, your work, resources, leadership, your organizing, how you are involved in social change, your spiritual path, and more.

Know you will keep changing and evolving. Your declaration a decade from now will likely be different than the one you craft now. (Except for those declarations that stretch beyond your lifetime—those often remain the same.)

HEALING DECLARATIONS

There are times in our healing processes when it is vital to craft healing declarations. Sometimes we need to prioritize our healing, garner our courage to face what's painful, and to transform. A healing declaration speaks specifically to what you want to heal, and/or the outcome or vision of what's possible through that healing.

Some questions to ask:

- What wants to heal?
- What is possible in my life (love, leadership, etc.) if I heal?
- What wants to be more whole? What does more wholeness bring to my life?
- What is possible if I face what I need to face to heal?
- What do I want to leverage my courage for?
- What do I want that is requiring me to heal?
- What am I repeatedly struggling with that is asking me to heal?
- Why heal? Why feel?

Often, we are moved to heal because we are suffering. The pain has gotten to be too much, or the breakdowns in our lives are too hard, too problematic. Maybe people around us are encouraging us to heal, to deal. Creating a healing declaration can help define where you are going and what makes healing and feeling worth it. While healing does help us get away from pain—this is not enough of a declaration to sustain us through the process. Again, the body learns on "Yes." What do you want to heal toward?

Some healing declarations could be:

I am a commitment to knowing how to trust and being trustworthy.

I am a commitment to mutuality—both giving and receiving with dignity and generosity.

I am a commitment to being a dignified and flexible leader—through facing and mending my experiences of sexual violence.

I am a commitment to having my creativity and love be the center of my life—and healing the shame that runs me.

I am a commitment to centered accountability, mutual connection, and ease.

I am a commitment to being satisfiable.

I am a commitment to showing and sharing myself, and authentic relationships.

The phrasing of declarations is odd: *I am* a commitment to. We use this so that when we speak this to ourselves, we are identifying with it. We are becoming it and embodying it. Our declarations, our commitments are who we become.

A declaration may ask you to change particular relationships to be more authentic, to change your work or how you spend your time and days, or even to change how you parent. These disruptions may not be easy on you or some of the people in your life. We want to go about these changes as skillfully as we can. And, some people may be more invested in you playing a role they are familiar with, than they are invested in your declarations. Change is a disruption. This disruption is designed to bring more safety, belonging, and dignity, more contribution and purpose, more equity. However, disruption is disruption, and shifting a homeostasis is not always easy or welcomed by all in the short term. As we change, we want to respect and care for our children and those in our lives, while we also allow for the change that is being called for.

CO-CREATED DECLARATIONS

We are often creating declarations with others. This happens in our friendships and our partnerships, our families and our communities. Those who work for social equity are co-creating declarations through community organizing and by developing missions, visions, and strategies collectively.

Co-created declarations tend to take a bit more time and process to land. There are more people involved, taking care of bigger issues, be they family, organizational culture, community practice, or social and environmental justice. The joint declaration, like our individual declarations, becomes the guiding vision or the North Star for the group. We can collectively stay true to that declaration in the relationships we build, our practices, and our actions. We can assess—who do we need to be collectively, to embody our declaration? If it is an organization, we can assess—do our organizational systems and decision-making processes support our declaration? Do some get in the way of our declaration?

Questions groups can reflect on together:

- What do we care about?

- What do we want to create together? With what quality(ies) do we want to do that?

- What do we want to change or develop in our family? What qualities do we want to embody? Is there healing needed?

- What do we want to see in our community and in our region/country/world?

- What difference and change do we want to make?

- What do we want to change or end? What do we want to see instead?

173

- If we were successful, what would we have made possible? What would we have accomplished?

- How do we want to be as a group, and what growth does that require?

- Who do we need to be, how do we need to engage, to align with our values and vision?

- How do we want to work with conflict and our differences?

It is often easier to see and say what is wrong, than imagine what we want. It is important to analyze a situation and problem. In fact it is essential to see dynamics, and assess causes and root causes personally, organizationally, and socially. It is also vital to find and set a declaration. This can be so much harder for many reasons. We usually have not had as much practice at imagining what we want, as we have had practice in feeling and struggling with what's wrong. We may not be in a situation, family, or community where what we want is seen or supported as possible. What we want, we may have never seen, and thus we have to work hard to imagine it in a grounded way.

Here are some examples of co-created and collective declarations:

We are a commitment to deep partnership and growing our family, with both children and community.

We are a commitment to healing in our extended family through facing our history, and telling the truths that weren't told.

We are a commitment to be mobilized, aware, and accountable white folks, organizing for racial justice.

We are a commitment to reimagining and building the next iteration of a powerful, coordinated Black Left that centers and leads radical systemic change in the U.S., anchored in a global analysis and in relationship to global and national movements. (Black Organizing for Leadership and Dignity)

People are aware that they cannot continue in the same old way but are immobilized because they cannot imagine an alternative. We need a vision that recognizes that we are at one of the great turning points in human history when the survival of our planet and the restoration of our humanity require a great sea change in our ecological, economic, political, and spiritual values.

(GRACE LEE BOGGS)

PROCESS DECLARATIONS AND OUTCOME-BASED DECLARATIONS

People tend to first develop process declarations. These are declarations that focus on a process rather than an outcome. An example is: I am a commitment to healing my shame and internalized oppression. Or, I am a commitment to helping others heal their shame and internalized oppression. This is a powerful intention, and it leaves us to fill in what the intended outcome will be.

With a process declaration, we want to ask: If you were successful at that, what would be possible? Again, as an example, "If you healed your shame and internalized oppression, what would be possible?" Then, we begin to imagine the outcomes and possible futures. What would be possible could be a number of different things—loving and authentic relationships or bold and visionary leadership. It could be loving and clear parenting or taking up space in my life and the world. Get the idea? Imagining the possible future is essential for crafting declarations and learning to embody them.

Another example of a process commitment is: I am a commitment to being peaceful. This is a state of being. As you have probably experienced, humans have lots of states of being. Can we practice toward being more peaceful, more of the time? For sure. And, choosing an unchanging "state of being" as our declaration is a bit of a setup. Again, with this type of process commitment we can ask, "If you were peaceful, what would that give you? What would your life be like that is different than your life now?" As you can see, the answers to this question could be varied. We want to dig into the particulars of the desired future, and base our declarations on that.

Often a process declaration is a good instinct. It can point to what we want, or what we think the process is to get there. And sometimes the process we come up with is only part of what gets us there, but misses key elements of change. Sometimes our process declarations don't get us to where we want to be at all.

Here are questions to run your declaration through to help it be more grounded and outcome-based, and be more of a desired future to heal and grow toward:

- Imagine you already had that (the declaration/desire); how would your life, loves, leadership, family, etc. be different than they are now? Be as specific as you can.

- Pretend you already had that; what would it give you? How would you be changed?

- Imagine your process declaration was successful; what would it make possible for you?

- What would you have that you don't have now?

Then we want to craft a declaration that orients toward the outcome or desired future that was revealed through these questions.

If you have a process declaration and it feels highly motivating for you, good, keep it. Just also know the answers to the above questions so that you can notice and assess how you are doing, where your practices are and are not aligned, and when you get there.

Below are examples of outcome declarations. These are all real declarations that people crafted and worked with over months or years:

I am a commitment to have two children by the end of the year. (This happened!)

I am a commitment to radically prioritizing my health and well-being for the next twelve months to serve my vitality and purpose.

I am a commitment to having twice as much joy and creativity in my life (through healing my shame).

I am a commitment to publishing six pieces to forward environmental justice.

I am a commitment to ending the sexual abuse of children within five generations (2000–2125).

Our declarations organize us. They bring our attention to what we care about, and help us recommit our time, energy, conversations, and actions.

What if I Just Don't Know?

What if we don't know? What if this very question as to what we care about causes anxiety and uncertainty? What if the answer is a list of who we "should be" or what's wrong with us? What if we are just blank, and have no idea?

Sadly, if you have experienced trauma or oppression, this is often the case.

Unfortunately, trauma and oppression often leave us disconnected from our longings, desires, and commitments. In fact, traumatic experiences convey to our soma that what we want for ourselves and what we most deeply care about don't matter. Violation, neglect, community violence, and experiences of oppression tell us somatically that our being and our wholeness don't or shouldn't matter.

To protect ourselves from further experiences of trauma and oppression, we tend to hide away what we deeply care about. Shutting down and turning away from our longings can be good self-protection. It can keep what is most essential to us away from danger. Our survival reactions can tell us that all people are dangerous, and that if we show what we care about it will be used against us. Tragically, this does happen. Not with all people, but it does. I've worked with many survivors of torture or intimate violence who were clear that "There is no way I'm ever telling people what I want because they will use it to hurt me."

If this is your experience, there is healing to do to find and reveal what you authentically care about. It is all good—this is a fine place to start.

Many of us were never asked the questions: "What do you want?" "What's important to you?" "Who would you be if you were more yourself?" "What difference do you want to make?" Many of us were never offered a model of what it means to want something meaningful, pursue it, and achieve it. Many of us never had this reflected in mainstream media and the social narratives about our people, gender, or class. Many of us had the opposite shown—that we, or our people, could not achieve what we wanted, did not have human longings for love and safety, or were not powerful.

All of this then gets in the way of knowing what we want, need, and desire. Often discovering what we care about, what we want to leverage our courage and love for, requires its own process of change and healing.

Where Do Our Longings Come From?

This is a big question. Lots of people have different answers to this. Are our longings spiritual? Are they connected to our time, place, and conditions? Are they intergenerational? Can they be described by neuroscience and physics? We could say yes to all of these.

Through a somatics lens, here is what I have come to see.

We find our longings deep within our somas. Or, I could say, they come through our somas. When we discover what deeply matters to us there is a resonance, a pull, and usually some fear. Longing and commitment are compelling. Drawing us. We may not know how to get there, but the draw is there. I see the fear that is often attached to our longings as an intuition of the changes this declaration will require of us.

I also see that there is a preexisting capacity (spiritual or evolutionary pull) in our somas that orients toward more harmony, wisdom, and evolution. I don't mean harmony like everything is calm. Rather

I mean dynamic, interdependent harmony and growth, like nature—wind, water, air, grasses, soil, in a broader, dynamic system. This pre-existing somatic impulse asks us to grow, expand, and evolve toward more complexity and more simplicity. We can also override and ignore this, and it will have consequences. I have seen thousands of people connect to this inherent urge to grow, this pull, as they connect more somatically to the aliveness in themselves. It seems longings speak to us through the felt senses.

There is also an inherent pulse in us that moves toward healing. At times I saw this as a spiritual immune system, spurring us toward more wholeness. At other times I have seen the soma as a channel or riverbank for a more vast energy or aliveness. The more we transform, clear, and open those channels, the more information, harmony, and longing come to us. This embodied healing comes with wisdom and an impulse toward more life.

I see over and over again, that when we leverage our courage to sense, feel, and follow the deeper callings in ourselves, we are changed. We become more free. Healing—and healing from trauma—is difficult and painful. It is also liberating. It helps us become more whole, power-ful, and creative people, family and community members, and leaders for change.

Feeling and Complexity

I personally have a strong spirituality, not, however, a strong sense of reli-gion or monotheism. My spirituality is very connected to the land and mountains I grew up in, the sweet waters of the creeks, the silver spruce, and the billions of stars I lay beneath. While I have this, I also feel it is essential to ground and question my own spiritual interpretations. Just because we think something, does not make it true or useful. Just because we feel something, it is also not inherently true. Yet, much truth does come through feelings. As do habits, survival strategies, and reactions.

It is complex to talk about feelings. Our Western social con-text demeans feeling as hysterical, "female," and irrational. The individualism of our culture says feelings are singular, mine, and unique. Capitalism often manipulates our feelings and more unconscious needs into consumption.

We are not deeply developed in understanding the wide variety of experiences and information that come through feeling and sensing. To me, somatic healing and transformation are part of what can grow this very needed human skill in us. We want to be able to distinguish between the many felt experiences (feelings) including:

- Inspiration and guidance

- Creativity

- Habit

- Reaction

- Survival strategies

- Wounds (emotional, psychological, physical, and spiritual)

- Resilience

- Spiritual bypass

- What are our own, and what are others', feelings

Sometimes more than one of these is happening simultaneously, and we need to be able to distinguish between them.

Our social, cultural, and economic conditions leave us with deeply embodied beliefs. We are shaped based on our experiences and environments. Once embodied, this shaping, these adaptations and beliefs, can "feel" like the truth. We can also default to holding spiritual experiences as beyond the reach of the world or thinking mind. Spirit, God, or the Mystery also gets interpreted through social norms and economic conditions. This can lead us toward a spiritual bypass that is not useful.

Thus, whatever our longings, we also need to assess and analyze them in a broader context. We need to learn both to trust ourselves and callings deeply, and to educate ourselves to see the social conditioning that may be built into our desires and wants. Whom and what do our longings serve? Whom might they be impacting in a negative way? We want to engage all of our intelligences in discovering and crafting our declarations. It requires us to increase our internalized permission and self-trust, while also assessing and grounding our longings.

Finding Our Longings, Declarations, and Callings

First and foremost, we can find them through becoming more embodied in our somas. Being able to engage with and listen to the aliveness in you, your impulses, and what compels you brings a lot of information about what you care about.

Finding our longings and crafting declarations are an active practice. It doesn't just happen to us—rather, we are asked to apply ourselves. We risk, explore, act, and dig in to find what most matters to us, and how to align our lives with that. Even people who are well established in meaningful lives have had many instances of not knowing, many days of uncertainty, as they found their way. Discovering our commitments requires listening, looking, asking and being willing to hear, and risking.

These processes can help us to discover and deepen our declarations.

ASSESS AND LOOK UNDERNEATH

- Scrub out the inherited. Assess what you have inherited as commitments, and which of these still serve you and your life at the current time.

- Assess how your cares and concerns have been shaped by social conditions. Do you really want that? Or is that a way of understanding safety, dignity, or belonging that is more defined for you by broader conditions?

- What of the values, ways of being, and seeing the world do you want to preserve from your family and community? Which do you want to change?

FEEL AND HEAL

- Feel more—sensations and emotions. Allow more aliveness in and through you. Notice what makes you more alive. Notice what's calling you that you may be turning away from or that scares you.

- Being able to feel more of yourself often requires a purposeful path of healing, support, and what somatics calls de-armoring. De-armoring is a process of somatic opening, and shedding embodied patterns of numbing and protection. There is much more on this in chapter 10, on Somatic Opening.

- Heal the impacts of trauma and internalized oppression. These squeeze and limit your capacity to imagine, feel yourself, and have an internal sense of permission and possibility. There is more on this process in chapter 11, on Healing Shame.

LEARN AND STUDY

- Learn who else has done what you are called to. Who else has been down this path? What compels you about them? What would you want to do differently from them?

- Deepen your social analysis. Often as we learn more about history, social norms, and our context, we become clearer about what has shaped us, and who we want to be. Also, what we want to participate in, and what changes we want to help create.

PURPOSEFUL PRACTICE

- Make finding and crafting your declaration(s) a purposeful practice.

- Listen. Reflect. Engage actively in these.

- Make a daily practice of asking yourself the questions in this chapter. Write or draw about them. Do it for thirty days and see what you discover.

- Learn, inquire, discover in areas you are drawn to.

- Purposefully talk with others about your questions and what you care about.

SUPPORT

- Find at least two supportive people you can talk with regularly. People who are interested in you finding what you care about, and in your healing. Let them know the questions you have. Let them know the practices you are doing.

As we craft commitments, we want to dig in and start imagining. We want to engage our feeling and thinking. Again, we want to get into the details of the vision and future we are called toward.

Making Transformation Pragmatic

Somatics is about embodied change. Embodied healing. Transformation has happened when the change shows in our lives, in our relationships, and in our actions. We look to make our declarations actionable. Not overriding deep emotional processes, but rather interdependent with them. Once we have created a declaration, we want to ground it. Here are ways we can do that: *Conditions of Satisfaction, Actions, Somatic Practices, and a Support and Accountability Partner.*

Conditions of Satisfaction: How Will You Know When You Get There?

Conditions of Satisfaction (COS) are experiences and measures that let us know we are changing. They let us know that we are arriving at our declaration. They also act as markers along the path toward where we want to go. The funny thing about embodied transformation is that as we change, these changes become the new "normal." With this we sometimes don't notice our changes. Conditions of Satisfaction also help us to note where we have come.

COS are specific, as measurable as we can make them, and have a timeline. Here are questions you can ask to develop COS.

When you have embodied your declaration ...

- What actions will you regularly be able to take that you don't take now?

- What conversations will you be able to have that you don't have now?

- How will you feel about yourself, or your life, that is different from how you feel now?

- What is different about you?

- What is possible that was not before?

- What have you accomplished?

- What quality of relationships will you be in? How is that different from what you have now?

- How will people's assessments of you change? What do they say / think now?

We are looking for concrete action and outcomes from these questions, that we can notice, touch, and see. We may be looking for a shift in qualities as well, and can make those measurable by percentages or a scale. Each of these COS will be connected to a timeline. We ask, "by when ..." will you do, be, have this? This starts to put the changes on the ground and into action.

Here are some examples from the healing declarations earlier in the chapter, with the "by when" added:

I AM A COMMITMENT TO BEING SATISFIABLE

COS:

❏ I will notice what is working 60% of the time, before I notice what is wrong. (within six months)

❏ I will easily acknowledge others, appreciating what they give and bring, even when they, too, are complicated people. (within one year)

❏ I will notice and let myself feel sensations and emotions of happiness, contentedness, love, and ease—without going into denial about our world. I will increase my capacity to do this by 50%. (within six months)

❏ I will become a resource for those I care about, for hope as well as critique. They will let me know that. (within one year)

I AM A COMMITMENT TO KNOWING HOW TO TRUST AND BEING TRUSTWORTHY

COS:

❏ I will develop my skills in aligning my intention, my reliability, and my competency, in order to be trustworthy. I will have increased these skills by 50%. (within six months)

❏ At least four people I care about will say (without me asking) that I am more trustworthy, or that they can count on me. (within six months)

❏ I will look at others' intentions, reliability, and competency, to see if they are trustworthy. Do their actions, intentions, and words match up? I'll increase my ability to do this by 75%. (within nine months)

❏ I will purposefully extend my trust to people that match the criteria above. I will increase my ability to do this by 75%. (within one year)

❏ My automatic reactions of distrust will decrease by 50%, through my healing. (within one year)

I AM A COMMITMENT TO BEING A DIGNIFIED AND FLEXIBLE LEADER— THROUGH FACING AND MENDING MY EXPERIENCES OF SEXUAL VIOLENCE

COS:

❏ I will start seeing a skilled somatic practitioner who is knowledgeable about healing sexual trauma, and go at least three times per month. (within two months)

❑ I will feel and process my rage, and learn to have and integrate my anger. (within eighteen months)

❑ I will learn and practice new ways of setting boundaries and protecting my dignity—so that I can have boundaries and stay connected. (start now, and be good at it within one year)

❑ I will allow myself to feel and communicate the more vulnerable emotions and sensations underneath my anger or shutdown. (within nine months)

❑ The changes in my leadership will be felt and acknowledged by others. (within one year)

If your declaration has a very long time horizon, or is beyond your lifetime, please break down the COS into one-to-two-year segments.

Actions

Make an action plan. Usually there are actions our declarations require. Perhaps it is a conversation that is needed to move your declaration ahead. Maybe it is signing up for a class, school, or a community group. Maybe it is joining a social justice organization. Maybe it is getting support from a coach, mentor, or therapist. Actions are the things you need to do to move toward your declarations that have a start and finish date or are a one-time thing.

Somatic Practices

Somatic practices are daily and weekly practices that help support the embodied changes you are working on. Practices are just one aspect of embodied transformation, and an important one. Each practice should have a clear purpose or intention, be an embodied practice, and be repeated daily or weekly. Remember, somatic practices are about transforming ourselves—it is not about "managing" ourselves or looking/doing it right.

Daily practices could be:

- Center yourself five times per day, speaking your declaration to yourself.

- A meditation practice that has a clear intention toward your declaration.

- Daily walking or movement, feeling yourself and having it serve your declaration.

If you have been trained in somatic practices, there are many more to choose from: centered requests, offers and "no's," consent, extension, and more. Or you can add an intention to an embodied practice like exercise, dance, listening to music, martial arts, or cleaning your house. Just remember, somatic practices include a clear intention that serves your declaration, feeling yourself and practicing being embodied, and repetition.

New practices aren't inherently comfortable, but without practice they won't ever be comfortable. Let yourself feel the discomfort and practice anyway, toward what matters to you.

Support and Accountability Partner

We change in community. We change with support from and accountability to others. A support and accountability partner is someone you ask to formally be a support and ally to you, as you change. They may agree to two months, six months, or a year in this role. During this time, talk regularly (weekly, or every other week) and focus on your declaration, your COS, and practices. They can help support your changes and support you to be accountable to your declarations.

Also, ask others that are supportive of your declarations to give you their feedback. How are you doing? What changes do they see?

To Close

Begin with what you want. Even if what you start with is that you want to be out of so much pain. Or, you want to not feel powerless. Or you want connections that feel real. These experiences let us know we want something else and can start us on the path to healing and working toward what we do want.

Some of us may start very personally and some with the bigger picture of what we want for our communities or the world. Either is fine. And, we want to attend to both. Sometimes people who are more focused on their internal lives will stay internal and not attend to their lives in the world. Sometimes those very focused on social equity or their work will focus exclusively there, not attending to and including themselves personally. We have capacity and need for all of these. We are individuals with particular paths. And, we are people in families, communities, and part of the broader social and economic landscape. A full human life crosses all of these. Healing trauma crosses all of these, too.

PRENTIS HEMPHILL, somatic therapist and practitioner, teacher for generative somatics (GS) and Black Organizing for Leadership and Dignity (BOLD), and writer.

My first year learning somatics I resisted developing a commitment. I had three commitment sheets with half-written sentences, unprocessed longings, and questions.

Making a commitment is no small thing. It is, for me, a spiritual practice of projecting a longing forward, beyond the confines of my body. It's an insistence on something I haven't seen. It's fundamentally a promise to the work and risks it takes to manifest that future. It can be a scary thing.

For a long time the way I related to my future, and *the future,* was as the place where things were yet to happen, and where I responded accordingly. It was not a place where I could shape events for myself and others. It was definitely not a place informed by my vulnerabilities or my longings. I was aware that other people got to have commitments, they got to declare. And sometimes people made declarations that implicated my body, declarations that defined who I was or should be, and what our world would be like. While I was growing up, people around me had commitments around enforcing binaries and dichotomies. There were commitments to uphold white supremacy, commitments to conveying inherent superiority of all kinds. For the survival of my being, my body and self shaped into resistance, into a hypervigilance that scanned for safety and protected against these kinds of spiritual, emotional, and physical attacks. What we know of survival is that it keeps what most matters close, hidden, and protected in our depths. In that context longing became, at best, private. It became hard to tolerate until my own desires and longing, my own visions for the world, became hidden even to me.

So years later, sitting in my first Somatics room, being faced with the task of not only admitting my longing, but creating from it a guiding, salient statement, and believing, insisting on its fulfillment, I was overwhelmed.

The first commitment I committed to, that I allowed myself to really look squarely in the face, was: I am a commitment to giving and receiving love. Simple on the surface. Underneath it lay my fear of rejection, fear of intimacy, issues with self-acceptance, and struggles in my relationship at the time. To say the commitment out loud meant feeling the rush of all of these struggles, and ultimately the desire to know love in a way I could only sense, but had no memory for.

That commitment alone reshaped my life. In my journey toward embodying it, it had me assess my relationships, clarified my love concepts—for myself and others, and asked me to show up for the places in my life where love and care were really present, moving away from my hiding habits and tendency toward dissatisfaction, but into fulfillment, pleasure, and vulnerability. I found love, with me, and laid the foundation for relationships that have been more fulfilling.

It took a year of working my love commitment before something started to reveal itself as a social movement commitment. It took, I think, the work of deeply accepting myself, finding safety in my body and with others, before I felt safe enough to assert a vision for the world outside. What came was a commitment to building Black movement that held trauma healing at the very core. At first I was afraid to say it; who was I to make this declaration. It was certainly not something I could do alone and I wasn't sure I was the most qualified to lead here, but I was committed.

The thing about commitments is that once you say them, a path unfolds. The commitment coincided with my going back to school to become a psychotherapist. At the time I couldn't quite see how to explicitly bridge my political and organizing work with my therapeutic path. It had mostly been a plan to open a private practice, but one where Black and Brown, queer and trans clients could feel themselves whole and not inherently lacking, could look at me across from them and imagine that they could be understood, and a place where we could really talk about the way systems of oppression took root in our psyches and bodies. I believe we need these kinds of liberatory spaces for individual healing. Yet, the commitment I was articulating was pushing me to claim broader and bolder futures for my organizing and healing work.

This was 2012. By the next year, everything was shifting. Black organizing was experiencing a surge in energy, led by uprisings across the country and the world. Conversations around healing justice, resilience-based and cultural organizing were re-emerging and finding relevance in how organizers went about the work of liberation. Guided by my commitment I found myself in the middle of these conversations and efforts, learning and experimenting with how to infuse an analysis of trauma deeply in movement. My commitment brought me to Black Organizing for Leadership and Dignity, to National Queer and Trans Therapists of Color Network, brought me to my role as Healing Justice Director of Black Lives Matter. Each step finding my kin with similar commitments to learn and practice together. Each step helping me to clarify the role of trauma in our relationships, in how we organize, and even in how we dare to declare.

In the journey toward embodying this commitment there have been moments of significant fear, doubt, overwhelm, and external resistance. The map I'd created on my commitment sheet had me identify and develop mentorship relationships, intentionally connect and collaborate with peers, and bring my heart and care forward in conversations about trauma and Black movement. I didn't realize until I found myself in the middle of an ocean of fear that these steps were smaller, meaningful risks that made my commitment possible. My commitment itself was the lighthouse on the shore that called me forward into action and navigated me through my doubt.

Years into working commitments I wonder at times if our commitments are not only about what we want to see in the world, but if they are uncovering what's already there, just under the surface.

8

Arc Circle Two— Embodied Resilience

Just like moons and like suns,
With the certainty of tides,
Just like hopes springing high,
Still I'll rise.

—MAYA ANGELOU, from the poem "Still I Rise"

I finished this book in the heart of the Rocky Mountains, for me a deep source of resilience. It wasn't planned that way; I was running late on my deadline. Lucky for me. I got to sit at my writing table and stare out at the freshwater creek, smell the sweet and pungent spruce, and watch the ravens hopping around. In the morning I found moose scat, and on a dawn walk, the moose! I was quieted by the silence of the falling snow.

For me, being in wilderness connects me to resilience—I feel a greater harmony there, which then re-harmonizes me. I practice consciously letting go to the mountains, to those ancient stones, to the vast communities of trees. I respect them and listen to them. This returns me to a deeper center, to creativity, and a wide perspective. I feel right-sized in their massiveness.

As we delve into Circle Two of the Arc of Transformation, we are going to start with resilience. We'll explore our inherent resiliency—what brings us more alive, what alters our somas toward coherence and ease, what reminds us of the vastness of being alive. We will begin to recognize resilience in ourselves and others, and learn to practice it on purpose. Resilience deeply serves the healing processes of regenerating safety and somatic opening. It also serves living.

We Are Inherently Resilient

Somatics understands us as inherently resilient. Just as we are born with the inherent survival strategies of fight, flight, freeze, appease, and dissociate under threat, we are also born with inherent capacities for resilience. These include an impulse toward connection and touch; being moved by nature, animals, and stars; our inclination to dance, sing, and create; and our urge to play. If we think of children in supportive environments, these are all things they do.

We are born with an impulse toward contact and connection. Newborn babies, if placed after birth on their mothers' bellies, will move themselves to the breast to nurse. This is long before they can crawl. Babies search for faces and eyes. Staring into babies' eyes helps create what's called secure attachment—babies knowing they belong and are connected.

We are born with an internal capacity to grow and evolve. While learning and growth can be scary at times, we thrive with it. Brain development can happen throughout our lifetimes, and a key thing that builds new neuronal pathways, that grows our brain, is learning. Some of the things that build us the fastest are: learning a new language, learning to play a new instrument, or learning a new body-based art, like dance. Interestingly, music and dance are also practices that can evoke and help cultivate our overall resilience.

We are resilient and creative people. Our communities are resilient and creative. There are practices that can help us build resilience for ourselves, those we love, our organizations, and our communities. We can cultivate resilience.

> We have to laugh. Because laughter, we already know, is the first evidence of freedom.

(ROSARIO CASTELLANOS)

What Is Resilience?

Let's explore resilience in the context of trauma and healing. Resilience is the ability to somatically, holistically renew ourselves during and after oppressive, threatening, or traumatic experiences. We are able to shift ourselves, physiologically and psychologically, from traumatic hyperalert states to calmed, cohesive states. It is the ability to regain a sense of hope and imagine a positive future. Resilience allows for safety, belonging, and dignity to be reestablished.

What does all of that mean? Let's unpack it.

Resilience is our ability to bounce back—like moss after we've stepped on it, or to find our intactness again. It is our ability to "come back" to ourselves, to connectedness, and to positive vision, even when the experiences and conditions are difficult. It is our ability to stay connected to hope and goodness, and relate this to how we choose, act, and decide. Our resilience is part of how we live through very hard moments or times, and is what can support happiness, connection, and well-being.

Let's dig into the somatics of resilience. Resilience is a somatic experience. This means that we can discover, attend to, and practice resilience through the soma. States and experiences of resilience have us feel more of ourselves and more connected to ourselves ... like we can more easily rest inside of our own skins. It allows for more, rather than less, sensation, emotion, and aliveness, but it is not overwhelming. Resilience tends to be both calming and invigorating at the same time. It usually connects us more to others, to our environment, and to land or spirit.

If we were to notice the sensations of resilience, we might feel a sense of warmth and gentle movement, more ease or relaxation throughout the body, and of being bigger, wider, and deeper. There may be more aliveness and sensation in the chest and belly when we are resilient, and a stronger sense of being settled in the hips and lower body. We may feel more open and permeable, while still able to access our boundaries.

If we were to notice resilience emotionally, we'd likely notice a sense of enlivened calmness, curiosity, and connection. Many people say they feel hopeful, or open-hearted in a grounded and pragmatic way.

If we were to look relationally, resilience often shows up as feeling connected, wanting to give and receive, to be more patient and compassionate. Resilience can feel like an open, loving acceptance. Resilience can feel also like commitment and passion ... with spaciousness.

To contrast, in triggered or hurt states we tend to be somatically organized to be hyperalert, distrustful, and tracking others and the environment, or to be mobilized into fight, flight, freeze, appease, or dissociate. Any of these more triggered states tends to make us feel ourselves less deeply, and begin to numb and contract. We'll often separate from others, need to control others, or appease others. Spiritual bypass may sound like resilience, yet tends to make us numb and feel less of ourselves. It often is not grounded in actions that take care of ourselves and others. Spiritual bypass can show up as consistently avoiding boundaries or conflict, even when they are needed for healing or justice.

Many of the current resilience tools speak to the state of the brain and the areas of the brain that are most active in either a triggered or resilient state. This is useful and can help us not personalize the symptoms and states of trauma so much. But it can also fall into the camp of objectifying the body and brain, and separating out the self. The brain is an organ in the body, part of the central nervous system, and interdependent with the rest of the functioning of the body/self. When we are discovering our resilience and then cultivating it, we want to do this with all of ourselves—thinking, emotions, sensations, actions, and how we relate.

As we understand through somatics, being triggered or being resilient is more than just a temporary state. These experiences become what shape us and what we come to embody. Both safety and survival reactions, and resilience inform our overall shape. In many ways, the more we purposefully heal, the more we work with our safety shaping, and the more we cultivate resilience, the more whole and resourced we become.

What Is It Not?

Resilience is *NEVER* a reason or excuse to permit harm or oppression, or to ignore the harm and oppression many communities, children and youth, and poor and working class people face—as in, "they are so resilient." This is sadly thrown around too often by people who have systemic privilege. I think people can use resilience in this way to minimize or rationalize their own privilege, manage their helplessness, or excuse their own inaction.

Yes, people and communities are unbelievably resilient. And, trauma and oppression, inequity, and violence are devastating. Resilience is a tool for healing and creating just, loving, and sustainable conditions, not one to rationalize violence and oppression.

> There are those of us who recoil from the word resilience. It can be a sensitive subject, both painful and polarizing. Many see resilience as a possible antidote to the avalanche of adversity in the world. However, many trauma survivors, with experiences that are often minimized, marginalized or medicalized, are often frustrated by what seems like excessive funding for or fascination with resilience.
>
> (CHRISTINE CISSY WHITE, "Putting Resilience and Resilience Surveys under the Microscope")

Some of the ways resilience is being tested, researched, and used make traumatizing and unjust situations and conditions more tolerable or acceptable. There are resilience trainings for police officers that do not question systemic police violence against Black communities, poor communities, and other communities of color; or the militarization of the police. What if we instead funded increased community capacity for transformative justice and practicing collective resilience? There are many resilience and mindfulness trainings for military personnel that are aimed at keeping soldiers in combat for longer periods of time. These trainings do not question war, who benefits from war, or the thousands of people killed on the other side of the US military. I appreciate that these programs may serve individuals. Yet, in not questioning the broader purpose of the institutions, we are perpetuating violence and oppression. That is not resilience building.

Here is a broader call to understanding and researching resilience:

> RYSE Center in Richmond, CA, was born out of young people of color (YPOC) organizing to shift the conditions of violence, distress, and dehumanization in which they suffer, survive, succeed, dream, and die.... Every day, YPOC struggle, succeed, and exceed metrics of compliance. However, their compliance does not guarantee their safety, security, or humanity. Oscar Grant, Tamir Rice, Jordan Edwards, Michael Brown, Rekia Boyd, Alex Nieto, and too, too many others were all compliant. Yet we lost them to state violence. Individual behaviors, adherence, and achievements alone cannot bring healing or transformation from injustices long experienced and navigated daily by YPOC.
>
> RYSE is working to reimagine, uplift, and uphold metrics of liberation—where resilience is the baseline, not the benchmark. Where solidarity and resistance replace or enhance self-efficacy and civic engagement. Where systems are held accountable to their allocation and delivery of love, belonging, reparations—liberation.
>
> (KANWARPAL DHALIWAL, ACEs 2018 Conference and Pediatrics Symposium: Action to Access)

Again, resilience is an understanding and practice for healing and creating just, loving, and sustainable conditions, not one to rationalize violence and oppression.

Finding Resilience, Practicing Resilience

Let's find what brings us resilience and how we can practice it on purpose. First, let's do some somatic storytelling. When is a time, either recently or in the past, when you felt enlivened, peaceful, whole, hopeful, wise, or connected with everything—your version of resilience? This does not need to be connected to an experience of hurt or trauma; in fact it is better if it is not. We are looking for an experience in which you, your soma, felt many of the things we discussed earlier in the chapter—sensing and feeling more of yourself, enlivened and calm, connected or curious, or aligned with yourself and life.

When you find that experience, let's pay attention to the details of it, as if you were there again. What did you see, smell, and feel? Where were you? What moved you? What did you feel in your sensations, in your emotions? Tell, or imagine you were telling someone, the story of this experience.

Here is an example from Raquel Laviña, whose story is included in the final chapter.

One of my first, most visceral activist memories happened in the 1990s during the first Gulf War. I remember thousands and thousands of people in the streets and a megaphone being shoved in my hand for my first public speech. That moment calling for unity, not just a unity for peace but one born of stopping the war abroad and at home, made my blood and heart run in a way that connected to everyone else.

We can explore what inherently provokes or supports resilience in us. Here are some of the key things that research has shown bring us resilience. Which of these do you relate to? What would you add?

- Connection to nature, animals, and land

- A deep sense of spirituality that is experienced directly (not necessarily religion)
- Art, music, creativity, dance
- Helping and making a difference for others
- Experiences of loving and being loved
- Collectively: making music together, moving together, sharing purpose and practice
- Learning something that brings you joy or full engagement
- Imagining positive futures
- Play

As you review this list, what other experiences of your resilience come to mind? Elicit at least two more, and remember them in detail. Place yourself back in the experiences. Feel what resilience is fed and evoked for you. Feel how that lives in your soma. Finding these experiences we already have helps us get to know what brings us resilience, and what it feels like inside of us.

A last thing we can explore with resilience is "turning it up" and "turning it down." Settle yourself into one of your resilient experiences—feel it somatically. Notice your sensations, emotions, and thoughts. When you are inside of the experience, try turning it up. This means take the somatic volume knob and increase the intensity of the resilience. What is that like for you? What do you feel in your body?

Then bring it back to "neutral." Then try turning the somatic volume knob down. Decrease the intensity of the resilience and sensations. What is this like for you? What do you feel in your body?

More is not always better. What we are exploring here is what feels most resilient and enlivening *for you*. For those of us whose survival strategies might take us toward intensity, it may be that turning down the somatic volume is much more resilience giving. For those of us who may be over-contained, or wanting to decrease stimulation, turning up the somatic volume may be most resilient. Getting to know what works best for your soma, at this time, is what we are most interested in. As our somas and embodiment change, so often do our resilience and the "volume" that works for us. We want to practice in the zone that feels most nourishing.

As we get more familiar with the resilient experiences and resilient states, we can begin to practice them on purpose. We can begin to invite others into noticing and practicing as well.

Practicing on Purpose

Fear is a five-lane highway in the brain, while resilience a foot path through the woods. We can make that dirt path wider by walking it, over and over again.

> (ANDREW HUBERMAN, neuroscientist and tenured professor in the Department of Neurobiology at Stanford University School of Medicine, personal interview with the author)

There are three key ways to cultivate resilience. One is to purposefully find and do the activities that bring you resilience—daily, weekly, and monthly, while you notice your sensations and soma. The second is to notice moments and experiences of resilience and consciously feel, linger in, and somatically experience them. The third is to practice collective resilience with others. We can do this with our families, our communities, and our organizations.

Practice One. Let's say it is music, either making music or listening, that brings you resilience. Now we want to explore how often you can purposefully do this. Can you play or listen daily? Weekly? Can you find live music regularly? As best as you can, plan to purposefully engage in it, to do this practice, at least weekly.

When you are there, get present in yourself—feel your breath and sensations. Set your intention to allow and practice resilience. Then enjoy your practice. Periodically, pause and feel yourself. Allow the resilience to deepen in your nervous system, to get more familiar in your muscles and mood.

If you cannot access your place or practice of resilience weekly, do it as often as you can. You can also sit quietly with yourself weekly and elicit a time in the past in which you were playing music, for example. Take your time; get inside of the memory. Again, get present in yourself—feel your breath and sensations. Set your intention to practice resilience. Then enjoy your practice, remembering the experience in detail. Let this permeate your soma.

Practice Two. As you are living your life, notice the moments that become resilience-giving to you. Maybe it is the sound of a friend's laughter, or the sun shining through the clouds in a particular way. Maybe it is appreciation given or received, or a new urban mural on a nearby building. Let yourself notice the experience, and linger. Feel yourself, your breath, your back, the quality of emotion. Register the resilience in yourself. Practice noticing resilient experiences at least once a week.

Practice Three: collective resilience practices. When we think about collective practices that promote community resilience, we want to look at things that are already present within community. It may be long-standing cultural practices or rituals; it may be shared music, dance or movement, or another form of creativity. It may be shared connection to land and nature. It may be collective purpose and action. This is the first place to look, rather than bringing in something new off the bat.

In collective resilience practice, we want to name and set intention as to what we are practicing and why. How does this practice nourish our collective resilience, community, or alliance? Why are we doing it? When you are doing the collective practice, at some point, remind the collective to feel themselves, to feel all of us together and the collective aliveness. Let the resilience into the collective soma on purpose.

Two years ago I was at a memorial service for a Black, butch community member who passed unexpectedly, chef Yulanda Hendrix. The shock, and how beloved she was to community, mobilized many people into holding her family, the collective grief, and the many, many logistics of this loss. The memorial and celebration were beautiful and so congruent with who she was and how she lived. Near the end of the night, the crowd was clearing, and someone called a line dance in her honor. The music was blaring; we all moved together; it was joyful, alive, poignant, and beautiful. At some point someone called out, "Feel it!" There was our collective moment of sensing ourselves, the group, and the collective resilience we were sharing.

(This is included with permission from
Yulanda's partner, Lisa Thomas-Adeyemo.)

To develop collective resilience practice, we can explore:

- What resilience already exists in this group?
- What purposeful practice can we do together to cultivate this resilience? Examples are: singing, dancing, meditation, art, ritual, connection with nature, and gardening.
- What will more collective resilience serve? Examples are: our connectivity, our collective purpose, our alignment and action, healing, trust-building, well-being.
- When can we do this regularly? Daily, weekly, monthly? Plan for it. Depending on what the activity is, it may take ten minutes or an hour.
- I suggest that the resilience practice happen at least twice per month, even if the group is not together. The group can agree to a practice and time, and can all do it from their respective locations.

During the collective practice—invite everyone to be present and remind the group why we are doing the practice. Then do the practice.

Feel your sensations and feel for each other—let the practice deepen your collective resilience in a felt way.

When we're exploring collective resilience in communities that benefit from systemic privilege, it is important to engage resilience practices that also support the deepening of empathy, interdependence, and collective accountability for justice. How can practicing collective resilience support our collective courage?

Resilience and Social Justice Organizing

When we are organizing for social and environmental justice we can engage this question of resilience. What resilience is already present within a community, group, or organization? Are there other resilience factors we can introduce that help to make the group more hopeful, connected, and powerful? How can building resilience be a purposeful aspect of our strategy or campaign?

Integrating resilience into our healing work and our organizing for social justice helps to build courage and connection. It can help us both heal and be more able to deal with ongoing conditions of oppression. Practicing individual and collective resilience can help to uplift us and sustain together to create structural change.

We can keep asking:

- How would our communities, organizations, and work be different if we oriented to cultivate resilience? Our own, and that of other people and communities?

- How can we purposefully support each other's resilience and practice collectively?

- In times of increased stress, how can we both let ourselves feel the impact of it, and also return to practices of resilience?

The following is an excerpt from *Love with Power: Practicing Transformation for Social Justice* (2016). In this publication, the Movement Strategy Center highlighted a number of movement organizations integrating transformation into their internal and external work. The partnership with the National Domestic Workers Alliance (NDWA) and generative somatics was one of those.

> If you want to do work that is focused and with a big vision you need to work on yourself and your own limitations. I now feel a sense of liberation, more complete and energetic in my job as an organizer. I believe more in allies, collaboration, and community. My vision and my energy are open.
>
> (ARACELI HERNANDEZ, Day Worker Center director, Casa Latina)

Research on Resilience

There is lots of interesting and useful research on resilience. Many psychologists, neuroscientists, and trauma specialists are actively studying resilience in the face of trauma. I have included a few examples below. While these examples are more dated, I have included them because of their range, and because they consider resilience from different locations. They also consider diverse communities and contexts, not solely assessing resilience in white middle and upper middle class communities. If you would like to read more about trauma and resilience, a good place to start is the ACEs Too High website at acestoohigh.com (ACEs is Adverse Childhood Experiences).

Early Witnessing of Violence

Alicia Lieberman, PhD, is the director of the Child Trauma Research Program at University of California San Francisco (UCSF), and the director of the Early Trauma Treatment Network. This is a collaborative of four university sites that also includes the Boston Medical Center, Louisiana State University Medical Center, and Tulane University. This program is also part of the National Child Traumatic Stress Network, a forty-site national initiative committed to increasing the access to and quality of services for children exposed to trauma. Dr. Lieberman focuses her work on behalf of children and families from diverse ethnic and cultural origins, with primary emphasis on the experiences of Latinos in the United States.

Lieberman explored the brain development of children under the age of six who witnessed or were exposed to violence. She discovered some of the young people were able to "work around" those places in their developing brains that were most impacted by the trauma. The resilience factors for these children were a strong connection to one or more of the following: spirituality, animals, nature, or creativity.

- Spirituality—Not a religious practice or doctrine; rather feeling connected to something vast, that they could join and communicate with.

- Animals—Animals were a resourcing place to connect and give and receive care and contact.

- Nature—Trees, the sky, the ocean, being outside.

- Creativity—Drawing, dancing, making music, and singing.

These are very intuitive findings, when we look to people's lived experience.

Survivors of Violence

Judith Lewis Herman, PhD, is a psychiatrist, researcher, and professor at Harvard University Medical School. She is the director of training at the Victims of Violence Program at Cambridge Health Alliance, and a founding member of the Women's Mental Health Collective. She has studied trauma and resilience in many people and places, including child sexual abuse, domestic violence, and combat and political torture survivors. She was one of the first trauma researchers to affirm that the trauma of intimate violence is equally as valid and destructive as the trauma of torture or war. She brings a feminist analysis to her work. Herman is well known for her book *Trauma and Recovery* (1992), and for distinguishing single incident traumas and complex repeated traumas.

She found that the following psychosocial factors led to having a more connected and contributive life post-trauma:

- Help—the ability to help another during the trauma, or after traumatic experiences.

- Greater Meaning—the ability to make greater meaning and purpose of the traumatic experiences.

- Relationship—the experience of staying positively connected to at least one other person.

These may feel familiar or resonant.

I want to make a note about *making greater meaning from traumatic experiences.* This means the ability to find broader purpose through our experiences, or the ability to gain depth or wisdom from them. In turn, this can inform our life or work in healing, organizing, or helping others. Making greater meaning is not that violence or trauma was a "God-given" experience. Some religious traditions and new age spiritual narratives will collapse our capacity to grow and give back, with the idea that this "was meant to happen." Trauma and oppression are not spiritually destined. This is a vital distinction.

Imagining Positive Futures

Bessel van der Kolk, MD, a Dutch psychiatrist, has played an important role in broadening the definitions and treatments of PTSD (post-traumatic stress disorder). In 1984 he set up one of the first clinical research centers in the States dedicated to the study and treatment of traumatic stress in civilian populations. He holds child trauma as the largest public health crisis in the country. Van der Kolk is professor of Psychiatry at Boston University School of Medicine and president of the Trauma Research Foundation. He is one of the leading researchers validating body-based treatments for healing trauma.

I did a training with him a number of years ago in which he shared a very moving story and set of images. You can now find this story in his book *The Body Keeps the Score.* He was visiting a friend whose children were in elementary school across from the World Trade Center towers as they were hit on 9/11. Through the window of the classroom, the five-year-old saw the first plane hit, and the ensuing chaos. He reunited with his father and brother and they escaped through the fire and smoke. The next day he drew a picture, which he later described to van der Kolk.

The drawing had the Twin Towers with fire and smoke coming out of them, planes crashing into them, and people jumping out of the buildings. At the bottom of the towers he had also drawn black circles. Van der Kolk inquired as to what those were. The boy responded that they were trampolines for people to land on. "I was stunned," writes van der Kolk. "This five-year-old boy, witness to unspeakable mayhem and disaster ... has used his imagination to process what he had seen...."

This little boy had resolved what he was seeing through his imagination. He created a positive future for those people and for himself. That is incredibly resilient.

- Imagination—the ability to imagine positive and sustaining futures.

Many people use imagining different worlds as a resilience strategy. I think about science fiction writers who envision positive futures in their writing, and then share that with the rest of us. Artists also do the same. Imagining positive futures is vital for navigating violence, oppression, and systemic trauma. It is vital to lead us toward love, social justice, and a sustained planet.

We also need to ensure that imagination is used as a practice of resilience rather than a practice of denial. When it shifts over to denial of conditions or avoidance of healing, then imagination is more like dissociation and is being used as a survival strategy.

Collective Resilience

Pumla Gobodo-Madikizela is the research chair in Studies in Historical Trauma and Transformation at Stellenbosch University in South

Africa. She served on the Truth and Reconciliation Commission (TRC), a court-like restorative justice body assembled in South Africa after the end of apartheid.

Her work focuses on two paths of research, exploring how the dehumanizing experiences of oppression and violence play out in the next generation in the aftermath of collective historical trauma; and the study of empathy and what being moved to offer forgiveness entails. She wrote the book *A Human Being Died That Night: A South African Story of Forgiveness.* In her work and speaking she explores the process of forgiving in the aftermath of historical trauma, and the potential for dialogue, remorse, and forgiveness to break intergenerational cycles of violence.

There is little research about collective resilience. Gobodo-Madikizela has highlighted this in some of her work, however. She looked to Black South African townships after political assassinations and state violence during the South African apartheid regime. In these townships, activists and social movement leaders were targeted and often tortured and murdered.

She saw that communities that gathered with each other after the state violence, and engaged in ritual—such as song, drumming, and dance—showed a decrease in intra-community violence. Sadly, in communities that did not gather, or in which people were isolated, an increase in intra-community violence was shown.

- Collective movement, drumming, and song increased collective resilience and decreased intra-community violence after state violence.

From a somatics understanding of trauma this makes a lot of sense. The profound break of safety and connection, and the mobilization of survival reactions (fight, flight, freeze, appease, and dissociate) need to be addressed, or they take over. It can be understood that through collective practices that are body-based and resilience building, the survival mobilization and break of connection can be processed and reset, thus moving the collective from a hyperalert state to a more calm and re-cohered state in the brain, body, and relations.

These are important and particular examples of research regarding resilience. Fundamentally, we want to stay curious and discerning about resilience. We want to be able to practice it purposefully, in calmer as well as more stressful times, and have it serve both healing and structural change. Decreasing trauma, violence, and oppression is very resilience giving.

Resilience and Survival Strategies

Resilience and strategies to survive threat are both inherent in us. Sometimes there is a fine line between resilience strategies and our safety / survival shaping. Is a spiritual experience helping us heal or helping us dissociate? Are we helping others in order to connect and uplift, or to avoid feeling or including ourselves? Are we taking time alone to renew or are we isolating? The boundaries between resilience and safety shaping can be nuanced when trauma is involved, and important to pay attention to.

To understand and feel the difference between resilience and survival strategies we can look to our sensations, emotions, and our ability to act from a range of choices.

Resilience leaves us feeling more connected, more open, and with a greater sense of safety. Resilience practices leave us ready to take action toward a better future for ourselves and others. We will have a wider range of sensations and emotions with resilience, and believe it is okay to feel more and be more alive, rather than numb. Practicing resilience will help us respond rather than react, and leave us with more options.

Survival strategies, on the other hand, tend to leave us more numb, tight, or contracted, with less feeling. While these strategies have been smart and thus might feel "safe" or familiar, this way of surviving tends to disconnect us, leave us more alone or isolated, and feeling less whole. This shaping will move toward reaction, instead of response, and in the midst of this we often forget what we care about. This leaves us with fewer options, moving more from habit than choice.

We will focus in the next chapter on how to work with and transform our safety / survival shaping.

This distinction is true in our individual lives, and in our communities and movements. We have collective resilience and we have collective ways to survive. In one way or another, they all have taken care of us, but our collective resilience moves us toward hope, interdependence, and a vision for the future we want. Resilience, and practicing it, leaves us more creative and responsive.

ALTA STARR, writer, somatic practitioner, lead teacher for generative somatics, associate program director and teacher for Black Organizing for Leadership and Dignity (BOLD), and movement elder.

Look Back and Wonder.

Very little in my earliest years set me up for a satisfying, successful, or even moderately fulfilled life. My infancy and early childhood were marked with physical abuse bordering on torture that included forced feeding and elimination, as well as sexual abuse. I had few experiences in those years to establish any sense of wholeness, agency, or possibility. Like those Audre Lorde speaks of in her poem "A Litany for Survival," I was "never meant to survive."

Yet here I am, alive, and more, satisfied and joyful, competent, loving and loved. Yes, of course those early violations left behind obstacles in my path, and in my adolescence and young adulthood in particular, I experienced a lot of emotional pain. The impact of trauma from my childhood played out in my work life and relationships. School, work, and partnerships both professional and romantic were often, as one therapist commented, "Like trying to run a marathon with an invisible

250-pound weight on your back." Yet even during the hardest periods, I gravitated toward joy, beauty, and wholeness.

I was born in 1951, the same year that gospel diva Clara Ward wrote "How I Got Over," in celebration of her escape unharmed, along with her mother and sister and members of their group, the Ward Singers, from a group of white men that attacked them outside Atlanta as they traveled through the segregated South. It's a raucous, joyful, shouting song, structured around the chorus, "you know my soul look back and wonder how I got over." I know that wonder intimately, and that state of celebration. While my years of studying and teaching somatics have reduced much of the mystery, my sense of awe has only deepened.

Life compelled me toward life, and the more deeply I explore somatics, the more I see the transformative power of life itself. The more consciously we inhabit our bodies and surrender to the flow of life in us, the more it moves us toward wholeness, connection, and fulfillment. This core aliveness precedes and is independent of any trauma or wounding, and while many experiences can interrupt or distort our connection to it, this life force is always there, and we can intentionally strengthen our ability to access it.

Life itself drew me to cherish the beauty of pale sky and sunlight winking through a tangle of oak leaves, and the twinkling silver undersides of beech leaves reflecting summer sun. It drew me to music, and the sturdy steady rhythms of waves slapping against the shore. Life calls me to play, to speak made-up languages with my partner, take long quiet walks with old friends, and to wrestle with my dog. The more I answer life's call, the louder it sounds and the more avenues to it I discover.

Currently, through teaching somatics and embodied leadership and working as a somatics practitioner, I support others in accessing and cultivating this life force both as individuals, and in the collective tasks of building power for justice and liberation. One of the places I get to pursue that work is with BOLD (Black Organizing for Leadership and Dignity), a generative somatics partner. BOLD brings the embodied leadership methodology to Black movement leaders from organizing groups around the country. In BOLD, as a result of history and social context, even though our participants come from across the African Diaspora, have widely differing approaches to radical change, and are of different ages, classes, sexual orientations, and genders, we are able over the course of each year's training to build alignment around decolonizing our bodies as indispensable to achieving the radical social changes we want.

We got breathtaking evidence of how important embodiment is to liberation at our very first BOLD training in January 2012, at the historic Penn Center on St. Helena Island, South Carolina, one of the first schools for formerly enslaved African-Americans. We were teaching centering, a foundational practice, in which we bring our awareness into the present and come home to our bodies, relaxing our natural length, width, and depth. Centering is a powerful way to organize ourselves to act in alignment with our deepest values or purpose, rather than reactively.

So in the training I said, as we always do, "Notice the sensations in your body; drop your breath into your belly. Now center in your length, your full natural length, letting the top and bottom halves of your body connect and balance. Let your weight drop into gravity, while you let more breath and space into your spine ..." and BOOM, one of the participants, a tall large man, passed out!

He was okay, and sat up after a minute, then reported that he didn't know what had happened, only that as he was letting himself fill out in length, or trying to, he got woozy and light-headed, his mouth got dry, and he collapsed. What he figured out later, after talking with his mother that evening and journaling about the experience, was that

213

by the time he was thirteen, he was already over six feet tall. What he'd learned growing up in Birmingham, Alabama, in his muscles and tissues and bones, was that he needed to fold in on himself and make himself appear smaller.

Can you imagine how much contraction and tension he'd held in those back muscles just to make sure nobody, especially anyone white or in a cop uniform, ever noticed him and decided he was threatening? Such a simple and profound moment of insight, precipitated by inviting his body to relax into its natural length! Yet, the most profound work for any of us comes after such moments of opening, as we strengthen our awareness of how life is moving (or not) in our bodies and build new ways of being that allow us to live in service to our deepest concerns and commitments.

Social context, political realities, and history live in our tissues. Whatever our social location, our bodies are testaments to the dynamics of our world as well as our individual lives. Life adapts brilliantly so that we can survive, and those adaptations, however limiting (such as contracting the powerful long muscles of your back and legs in order to appear nonthreatening), are themselves dramatic demonstrations of life's wisdom. But the process of embodied transformation helps us connect to an even deeper wisdom. Dropping into and surrendering to our own life force allows us, for example, to be with contradictions—of which both life and social justice work offer us way too many—without going numb. Our own aliveness allows us to honor and stay cognizant of others' dignity. We can see, "Oh, that person's bullshit that so irritates me, that's just part of how that particular life is trying to survive. I don't have to be okay with it, but I also don't have to be in reaction to it. I can make choices and find ways of dealing with it that don't diminish either me or them." This competency is critical in movement work, where so often the pressures and pace drive us to treat each other as disposable at best and demonic at worst.

In a recent generative somatics embodied leadership training, we had a participant, a Black woman, who had developed a hard exterior to survive years on the street and in prison. As she started to thaw and to feel, years of grief began to pour out in tears and shaking, and she was frightened. She wanted to complete the course, but wasn't certain she would be able to stay as these emotions were so unfamiliar and disturbing to her. She spent a lot of the session on the edges of the group, quiet and only talking privately with the teachers. But by the last day, she spoke to the whole group, saying that while she didn't like "this feeling shit. Inside, I'm good, my spirit is good, and all this," waving her hand to indicate her tear-covered face and quivering hands and legs, "this is just the walls crumbling."

Coming back into our bodies isn't easy and takes courage, but aliveness itself is our strongest ally in the process, and the best news of all is that we can deliberately strengthen our ability to connect to it. It's just a matter of practice. We can practice by making time to do things that enliven and delight us, that spark our capacity to feel, that create greater openness in our bodies and emotions, and that connect us with others rather than leaving us isolated. By making time for life, we come more to life; by making time to experience awe, joy, beauty, and love.

Frederick Douglass knew how to do this, and his example is inspiring. We quote his speeches but ignore, if we've ever even known, that Douglass was a self-taught violinist. Think about the time it must have taken him to learn! He wasn't traveling around the country giving speeches against slavery in those hours. He wasn't writing for the *North Star* or debating strategy and tactics with his abolitionist comrades. He'd play spirituals, folk songs, and classical music for his family, out of love and for their delight. Surrounded by music, his son also learned to play and his grandson, Joseph Douglass, became a successful concert violinist, touring the country and the world for three decades, and becoming the first violinist of any race to record.

But I want to focus on the grandfather, and one anecdote from his travels in the British Isles between 1845 and 1847. Douglass spent almost two years there giving speeches, raising funds for the abolition movement (and to buy his freedom), and connecting with anti-slavery activists as well as those fighting their own battles for independence and justice. At one point, in Scotland, the travel and controversies got to him, and perhaps too, I like to imagine, a bit of homesickness. He bought a violin and locked himself away to play for three days, until, as one biographer puts it, "he was in tune himself and went out into the world—a cheerful man."

This might be one of the most important lessons we can take from this freedom fighter: a reminder that we too, in these troubling times, can nourish our connection to our aliveness, and *that it's our responsibility to do so.* I'd say, in fact, that building that connection, especially in community and our movement organizations, is as important as all the other things on our task lists for the revolution.

9

Arc Circle Two— Regenerating Safety

All aspects of embodied transformation are vital. Regenerating safety, in many ways, becomes a foundation for the rest. Regenerating safety helps us build the capacity to generate a sense of safety from the inside out, the ability to shift from hypervigilance to responsiveness, the ability to have boundaries and to make requests, to ally with others and let them ally with us.

Somatically, regenerating safety lets us both honor and transform survival strategies that exist at deeply embodied levels. When safety strategies have been practiced for years, they become mostly unconscious to us. The pain and betrayal of trauma and oppression alter our sense and reality of safety. Our strategies to navigate these experiences and conditions leave us in states of hyper-tracking or numbing, automatic distrust or over-trusting without grounding, of being "awake" to danger irrespective of the people or environment that surrounds us, ready to defend, avoid, or attack. Often these embodied survival strategies become part of our identities—"this is just how I am," or become most obvious in the repeated struggles we have with those close to us.

In this chapter, we want to move from reaction to response based on current-day context and content—recognizing the power, choices, and resources, as well as the internal resources and resilience we have in the present. Our aim in regenerating safety is to rebuild an internal sense of safety, boundaries, and consent. It is to develop our ability to feel the differences between our survival reactions and our capacity today. Then, to choose and act from our capacity today. Regenerating safety allows us to process the historical reactions still operating in our nervous systems, tissues, and selves; while also experiencing and integrating new, current experiences that leave us feeling more empowered. In this phase of change we also focus on building more skills in places we may not have developed them.

In the prior chapters we have explored the impact of trauma and oppression somatically. We have also dug into a different understanding of safety through the intersection of material safety, an emotional sense of safety, and increasing choices and our ability to make grounded assessments. All of this plays as a ground or backdrop to the healing we are exploring in regenerating safety.

I use the terms safety shaping and survival shaping interchangeably. By safety shaping and survival shaping, I mean any of the ways we have organized to protect and try to ensure our safety, belonging, and dignity. These are embodied, generalized, automatic, and understandable, and may or may not take care of what you care about now. Though we are focusing in this chapter on regenerating safety, safety is never truly separate from belonging and dignity. They are interdependent inside of us. Each of us will have our own balance of how these are experienced and how these were traumatically impacted or betrayed. For some of us, our safety strategies are organized to try to ensure physical experiences of safety—not being hit again, sexually assaulted again, having enough food or housing, etc. For others, the safety shaping is organized around preventing being left or isolated. Still, for others, these survival strategies can be primarily organized around not being shamed.

There are three aspects of regenerating safety: embodied practices, blending with the safety shaping, and allying. All of these are somatic processes in which we are transforming the survival reactions and strategies that have been embodied and generalized, and introduce new choices, practices, and an ability to assess from a present, empowered place.

We are rebuilding visceral and embodied experiences of safety and trust—of ourselves and of others.

I will discuss the principles of each aspect of regenerating safety here. I do not include all of the practices and processes. These are best learned and embodied through training, practice, and apprenticeship, and with feedback from a person competent in the work. It is not possible to learn embodiment through a book. We can explore the theories and processes, but to practice and embody them, we need to "go live."

Embodied Practices: Boundaries, Consent, and New Choices

We already have ways to protect ourselves, to have boundaries and communicate "no," to make requests, and to navigate our days. Some of these were learned as survival strategies to trauma and oppression. Some were taught to us by power-over social norms. Some were learned through good modeling. Others are developed through healing or political development or activism that was empowering.

Often what we are struggling with in healing and change are those survival reactions that we learned through hurt, and with which we are still trying to protect ourselves. These survival strategies may look like an automatic, fairly consistent "no," even to people and situations we want to connect with. Some might look like appeasing, getting along, automatically excluding our own wants and needs. Others may look like self-reliance, and the overwork that can come with this. Still others may look like numbing or not caring. Lastly, survival strategies can also show up as distancing, making space, and getting away from the storm.

Trauma and oppression have a profound impact on our experience of safety and our ability to generate safety. Most often we need to relearn and rebuild a lived sense of safety and the skills that support this, as well as taking care of material safety.

Embodied skills that often need to be relearned include:

- The ability to consent based on what is important to us.

- Boundaries that take care of ourselves, what matters to us, and take care with others.

- The ability to protect and defend ourselves through words and actions.

- The ability to notice what we want and proactively make requests, offers, and build toward these.

- The ability to hear and receive others' consent.

- The ability to be trustworthy and assess trustworthiness in others.

Each of these skills is an aspect of safety and navigating safety within our networks of relationships and social conditions. We want to rebuild these from the inside out, giving ourselves and our somas new choices, more flexible and responsive options for boundaries, requests while being responsive to ourselves and others.

The most important things we want to pay attention to in beginning to regenerate safety are:

- Do your current ways of establishing boundaries, consent, and self-protection move you toward more of the life, leadership, and loving you are committed to?

- While our embodied safety strategies are very convincing—they can feel "right," like the only move, and justified—are they responses or reactions? Do you have other choices? Other ways to respond?

- Can you have different boundaries in different contexts based on what you want and what you are committed to? Based on the group's aims?

- Do your boundaries include yourself and others?

The first thing we want to do in regenerating safety is build new embodied skills. Why this first? Our bodies and our somas will not let go of well-worn strategies for safety unless there is something that works to replace them. We can promise ourselves that the next time "that situation" happens, we'll say no, or have a clear boundary. Yet, if our historical adaptation to safety is to appease, we'll find ourselves in that situation again, saying yes, or being agreeable. Or, if our adaptation to safety is an automatic no, we may say that we'll relax and connect the next time, yet find ourselves fighting or saying no with conviction, and disconnecting instead.

The body won't let go of current embodied safety strategies—unless there is a better way to protect and have boundaries that serve safety, belonging, and dignity.

The body is wise. And it is habitual. The soma both wants to and knows how to heal. And, the deeply shaped strategies for safety, belonging, and dignity resist change because of the needs, sheer vulnerabilities, and hurts they are taking care of and protecting.

Safety strategies generalize in our psychobiology. Firing off when we do not inherently need them. No bad. This is how our embodied adaptations work. It is also why we need to transform them through the soma.

Developing new embodied skills requires purposeful practice. A new practice requires these five things.

- **Purpose.** For the sake of what do we want to learn a centered boundary? To consent in present time? Why shift that automatic yes or no or numbing to something that is more present and responsive? At the center of practice is a purpose.

- **Practice that is felt and embodied.** The practice is not a new idea or something to ponder, although that's good too. The practice needs to be a body-based practice connected to the above purpose. We are practicing being in our felt senses, listening, and feeling. We can practice it without a narrative at first, and then add a narrative that helps us practice for live situations.

- **Repetition.** We change through embodying new practices over time. Think not five times, but 300 times. While there is important and contradictory research about how many repetitions we must do to create muscle memory (300), to create embodiment (3,000), or to create mastery (10,000), we know it is about repetition—embodied and felt within a broader purpose.

- **New actions and results.** The new practices will show in your life, in how you live, act, choose, and relate. They will show up as an ability to have different conversations, to bring needs, ideas, and boundaries in ways that include you and are responsive to others' concerns. If these shifts are not showing up in new ways of acting and being, check what's missing about the other four components of a new practice.

- **External support and feedback.** It is hard to see our own embodiment. Once something is embodied in us, it becomes harder to perceive about ourselves. It is so integrated, it feels like who we are. Usually, if we ask the people we spend time with, they'll have a good sense of our automatic reactions and safety strategies, because they experience them. Thus, it is important to have trusted feedback from others who are committed to your transformation. How are you doing? Are your changes showing up in your life? Are you in the right practices given your healing or transformation?

Feedback, from a somatic vantage point, also involves noticing how your embodiment is changing, where these deeper safety strategies are located in your body, and practices to shift that. This type of seeing is cultivated through both somatic training and the development of a social analysis, so that the shaping of social conditions can also be perceived. It is helpful to have a trained partner in this process, whether a politicized somatic coach, somatic therapist, or somatic teacher.

Somatic practices to regenerate safety and rebuild a more internal locus of safety are varied. Here are a few that are beneficial for most of us to learn and embody through somatic practices.

Center. The practice of being present, open, connected, and anchored in your declaration. This practice is a baseline within our work. It is the somatic practice of being present and filled into yourself while staying connected to others at the same time. Centering is a way to purposefully organize ourselves in sensation and align with our physical structure—relaxed and balanced in length, width, and depth. Centering allows us to feel more aliveness, not to "calm down," numb or bypass our sensations or emotions; rather we practice being able to be present with all of it. Centering helps us to organize ourselves around our declarations and to make choices based on what we care about. It is a pragmatic and embodied place to return after being triggered or reactive. We dove into declarations in chapter 7.

Consent. Consent is about both giving and receiving permission. Consent means developing a present and centered yes, no, and maybe. All of these are valid. Consent is not a permanent answer. We can change our decision and pivot between yes, no, and maybe as needed. We also need to be able to receive and be responsive to yes, no, and maybe from others. This practice and embodied skill is vital for healing, leadership, and social justice work, given that the pressures of our conditions do not train us in consent.

Declines. There are many types of "no," depending on the relationship, the context, and the broader purpose of the boundary. We need a range. We can learn a connected, more intimate no; a boundary that redirects the person, conversation, or situation; a more powerful and nonnegotiable no. When we are saying no, we are saying yes to something more important to us. In your practice, also know what you are saying yes to.

A note: our bodies will hold our "no's" as contractions, numbing, disappearing, and more, until we develop a more proactive and embodied no that can be communicated to others. The body can tell the difference between the "good idea" of a no, and the embodied ability to have boundaries or decline.

Boundaries. There are many different kinds of boundaries, or ways to find and navigate space, safety, and relationship with others. Sometimes we can organize our boundaries in very spacious and open ways. For me, this happens when I am in the mountains or mostly surrounded by aspen and pine trees. The need to differentiate from the world is less for me there. These open, more permeable boundaries can be invited with people we love, have trust with, or are relaxed around. We also need to know how to organize ourselves to have more firm boundaries. In this we can show a firmer edge, have less permeability, and less welcoming of a closer contact. We want to have a range of ways to organize ourselves, our attention, and our field, or energetic space, as well as our bodies.

It is also important that our boundaries, whether more spacious or more firm, are organized in both our bodies and our fields. I know this may sound strange, yet we are reading each other's fields all the time. We can get offended when others do not pay attention to our field or override it. This energetic field that we live in is measurable through science and is perceptible by others. This field and what feels comfortable to us are shaped by time, culture, and context.

I see with many people and communities that have experienced trauma and/or oppression that boundaries can be held close to the skin. Almost as if they are not supposed to take up space and impact or influence others. We can understand why the experiences and messaging of trauma and oppression could shape us this way. This organization of boundaries, however, does not give one much room to live and move. Often to have a firmer boundary, a person will pull their boundaries in even further, which gives them even less space to maneuver and feel.

Imagine and feel that your boundaries are extended two to three feet outside of your body, beyond your skin. In this space you can have room to feel yourself, to notice and assess others, and to choose a more permeable or firm way to organize yourself.

Boundaries aren't an idea, they are a somatic reality. How we organize ourselves, our contactability or differentiation, is read and felt by others. We can organize ourselves for more and less contact. Here too we want to build choice, rather than having only one option, for many needs and contexts.

Requests. A request is a way to ask for what we need, want, and desire. It is a way to invite and engage others into what we are committed to and care about. It is a way to navigate conflict by revealing what it is we want or need. Requests start with "Will you?" "Would you?" "Are you open to?" and are followed by a specific request. Someone may say yes, no, or maybe in response. They may make you another offer instead.

Requests can be anything from "Will you hold me?" to "Will you take the lead on this project?" to "Will you work with me to align our values and how we are parenting?" Even "Are you open to being a support in my healing process?" A request allows us to begin to coordinate and then take action together. If we get a "no" to our request, we can reorganize ourselves and decide whom else to ask, or what our next choice might be.

It is useful to practice our requests before taking them live. Often our own discomfort and other safety strategies get in the way of making more centered requests, especially when they really matter to us. Once we have practiced, we can assess when the environment and timing are decent to make the request. Then we can ask: "I have a request. Are you open to hearing it?"

Offers. Offers are bringing ideas, support, or suggestions in the form of an action. What offers can you make that would forward your own healing or declaration? What offer can you make to another, that can serve theirs? To a community or organization? Offers help us bring what we care about to others, to build relationship, and to make things happen with others. Examples of an offer are: "I'd like to support you in your healing process. Would it be helpful to talk once a week about how it's going?" "I can give four hours per week on that project, and I'd like to offer to partner with you on it. Are you interested?" "I am happy to hold you. Would you like that?"

Again, it is good to somatically practice offers to help our somas learn, centering what it is to reveal ourselves, and to bring what we care about. We also practice to hear others' responses.

Let me give you two examples of using new practices within regenerating safety. Trauma, particularly intimate traumas like partner violence, child abuse, child sexual abuse, rape, and sexual assault, override a deep "NO!" in the survivor, whether or not it is ever articulated verbally. It breaks an integrity and boundary in the person. Somatically, the survivor will usually hold this "No" in their somas deep in the body. It may be in the pelvis, behind the heart close to the spine, up and down the anterior of the spine, or even deep in the intestines and abdominal tissues.

There is a "no" or decline practice we use in generative somatics called the "push-away." This is a way to practice a clear, powerful, and, if needed, forceful "NO!" for self-protection. All practices are done in a way that takes care of all people involved. Particularly when strength or force wants to be expressed in a practice, we want to assure that we address the physical needs of the people practicing. We then structure it so that it is aligned for them, and can be done from a present and physically centered place.

Because "no" was overridden and overpowered, we may have learned to no longer even try that kind of boundary. The soma, including the tissues, muscles, and neural pathways, may need to be reintroduced to the possibility of this kind of no. The push-away is a physical practice of just that—literally pushing away from center, with the arms, using your lower body strength as well, while feeling the impact of your push as the practitioner/practice partner is moved away. The legs and arms are some of our first protectors—we hold someone away, push, kick, hit, grab, and more, to self-protect. When we are hurt and threatened, there is a large amount of energy mobilized for this action in the soma. When it is prevented and overpowered, that energy and mobilization can collapse in on itself, or be held in the tissues as contraction or numbing. We usually do this practice standing, but it can also be done lying down from the massage table during somatic body-work with the legs, or energetically, if the impact of the movement does not work for someone's body.

I was working with a survivor of child sexual abuse and community violence, who also lives in the ongoing experiences of sexism and patri-archy. She is a cisgendered woman, European immigrant (white in US context), and working class.

As we prepared for the push-away, the somatic process already began. We were standing and preparing for a test practice, 1 was just getting the structure, and she began to sweat and to cry. "This is not possible. This will just make it worse." What had been learned deeply in her soma was just that: to assert, to fight back, to have boundar-ies, would increase violence toward her and others she loved. This is a profound internal dilemma too many survivors of violence find them-selves in. This embodied belief (which was true historically) was creat-ing havoc in her current life.

We went very slowly. Staying with the sensations, making space for the emotions, and getting into practice. Her survival strategies viewed this practice as a terrible idea. She chose to explore it and see. The first few rounds were bringing new information into her nervous system. She pushed away, it worked, I was moved back, the violence did not increase. In fact, no violence happened. She was still crying and sweat-ing and we could both see the curiosity emerging in her soma, as if there might be another experience or option available besides the sur-vival response.

We have to understand that in these moments in the healing pro-cess, many aspects of the past are happening simultaneously, alongside the present as well as a projected future. We make space for all of it. This is the lived experience.

We shifted into adding more strength to her push-away, engag-ing her lower body and center, feeling her sensations as we practiced. Eventually we added her voice, at first a "no" with no eye contact. She stumbled over it. Soon we added a clear and congruent "Get away from me!" We worked with this practice over a number of sessions, coming back to it on and off for six months.

For her, this practice brought new options into her nervous system that were just not possible without doing this level of healing. The soma wouldn't allow these actions until the stored hurt was addressed. Multiple experiences of sexual violence that she had had to navigate and survive within her family and extended community re-emerged through this process to be attended to. The impact and terror of these also need to be processed through the soma. We will discuss these processes more through somatic opening. Somatic awareness, practices, and opening are interconnected processes that we navigate through the transformation process.

The second example is about a group and consent. This took place in a social movement network that holds consent, agency, and respect as core to their values and political practice. The group was multiracial, multiclass, and multigendered in its makeup. For understandable reasons, the idea of consent was present, though the group's embodied skills to practice consent were not well developed. They were struggling to navigate relationships, power, boundaries, and difficult and dynamic political conversations—while practicing consent. Many of the breakdowns that ensued were solely interpreted as political differences, and splitting was imminent. Certain people were allowed to have boundaries and others not. You get the idea. Many of us have likely been in this dynamic in some organization or group.

We began by experimenting with some practices, with the larger purpose of the group guiding the direction of the work. Folks wanted to be more aligned with their values and analysis, and to learn together rather than split. Many conversations and other practices were relevant for this group. I am pulling out the consent practice because of how it worked for them. In varying configurations of pairs, groups of three and six, we practiced consent—a centered yes, no, and maybe, as a response to a request or proposal. Certain themes emerged through the practice. The majority of the cis-women and transgender people in the group had a much harder time holding a clear no. A large part of the group was very somatically reactive hearing no. Because of this combination, which is understandable given social conditions, the group was struggling. We dug into practice in pairs to get the options of a more viable yes, no, and maybe into each person's practice. Then we moved back to groups. Those who were having the hardest time hearing no got to practice hearing no from groups of three, feeling their reaction, and recentering. Those who struggled in saying no got to practice saying no to groups of four and five. We continued practicing centered maybe and yes as well, to feel the difference between an automatic yes and one based in assessment and choice.

The discussions that emerged were also key. Instead of making each other bad, we got to explore the reactions to no: what were these reactions trying to take care of? How else could that concern be addressed? What reactions had nothing to do with the purpose of the group? What was the cost of automatic reactions to the group's ability to connect, coordinate, and move toward its aims? Many people saw that their automatic reactions actually got in the way of their broader values and purpose. They also explored the palpable difference between a centered and grounded yes, and a yes that is avoiding a no.

This shared practice, and what it revealed to the group, allowed for different conversations, joint accountability to new practices, and coming back to curiosity and trust instead of blame-splitting. The challenges of doing principled organizing for social justice are many. The external conditions are overwhelming and dynamic. The ways we can sustain through these pressures, how we can assess, strategize, and work for change together, require skills not often handed to us.

To Recap

We develop new embodied practices first, so that as the soma opens through blending and allying, there are other ways available to navigate our days and choices. If the safety shaping has been taking care of boundaries by keeping others away, as that begins to process and let go, we still need ways to have boundaries. We put these new practices in place first so they are available and ready. New practices and options also support the soma in allowing the older strategies to let go.

Lastly, there are an I, you, and we to all of these practices. It is not an individualized learning of boundaries or requests that gets to be used free-form just for our own concerns. I have heard too many people come out of traditional therapy with an avid commitment to their own individualized boundaries, with no consideration for the family systems they are a part of, or the social conditions they may be perpetuating. The more privilege one has, the more likely it is for people to use new practices to perpetuate that privilege. Thus, we need to keep intersecting healing and transformation with social consciousness and participating in social justice.

The social norms and rules of the economy shape our capacities to consent, have boundaries, and decline. These conditions say much about who gets to request and offer, and who is meant to fulfill these for others. Because we have all been shaped by these conditions, we all can learn from and deepen these practices to serve interdependence, equity, and collective action.

Blending with and Appreciating the Safety Shaping

With new embodied skills for generating safety in practice, we'll go deeper. We want to attend to the older and more deeply held safety strategies that have been with many of us for decades. We want to get to know them, how they work somatically, and what they have been taking care of, as well as how they have been costing us.

Our safety shaping, at its core, has a protective intent, even when we may struggle with the symptoms and impact of the strategy. We can approach this shaping with respect, and be curious about how we organized to survive. How does this live in the muscles and connective tissues? What beliefs are embodied in these safety shapes?

What is the impulse in the shape—does it want to move, protect, run, speak, yell?

Through a somatic understanding of the soma, beliefs and contractions are interdependent. Emotional range—the ability to allow and express emotions, not repress or exaggerate them—and physical shaping are interdependent. I want to keep deobjectifying the body in how we understand the self and the process of healing, development, and change. Beliefs, emotions, our historical experiences, and worldviews all live deeply at the level of the physical body as well. We want to get very curious here. Through the body is the most direct way to contact the safety strategy at its root.

First let's explore these strategies. We form these safety strategies out of an adaptation to threat. That may be, or have been, a threat to our safety—physical, mental, emotional, and/or spiritual; to our belonging; and/or to our dignity and deep sense of worth. When these core needs are threatened and harmed, we will adapt and then generalize the adaptations. These adaptations show up in the soma as beliefs and self-concepts, as styles of relating, as habitual actions and nonactions, as contractions and numbness, and more.

These adaptations can look like:

- Contractions in the fascia, muscles, skin, organs, eyes, breathing patterns. This may be felt as tightness, slackness, or numbness. Sometimes parts of the body may feel blank or void.

- A constriction of the flow of energy, aliveness, emotion, and the impulse to move or express. This is held back through contractions in the tissues.

- A pushing-out or constant cycling of emotions or excitation. It can be like the soma does not know how to settle.

- A habit toward one of the following ways of dealing with aliveness, excitation, or emotion, with little tolerance of the others:

    ▸ awakening (seeking excitation, liking to start new things, feeling "safer" with lots moving);

> ► increasing (building energy, stirring up feeling, looking for the next possibility);

> ► over-containing (shutting down energy or aliveness, over-containing it before it grows, wanting excitation settled, grounded, organized); or

> ► completing (stopping or discharging the excitation quickly, getting it handled, managed, and done).

All of these will be connected to beliefs about these survival strategies as well. For over-containing, the belief might be that it is not safe to feel or "get out of hand." "What's the big deal anyway?" For automatic completion, it could be something like, it's bad to linger or feel too much, better to get it over with. For automatic increasing, the belief can be that the only way to be safe and seen is to show feelings and experiences a lot … you get the idea.

These safety strategies become fixed in the soma, not allowing other possibilities. They can feel that "it's just who I am," because we feel so little choice around them. Over time these strategies can cause other types of distress, such as not being able to connect in the ways we want to, not being able to build trust, not ever feeling safe, constant watching and tracking, and not being able to act in ways that are aligned with what we most care about.

Let's get curious about where these survival strategies and patterns live in the soma and body.

- When you feel protective, where do you feel that in your body? What shape, contraction, numbness, or slackness do you feel? What happens in your chest, eyes, pelvis, lower body, and connection to the ground? What happens in your back?

- When you feel threatened, what picks up in you? What hides itself away? What goes blank? Where is that in your body? How do you do that?

- When you dissociate or check out, how do you do that? From where do you leave? Out your shoulder or the back? Out of your head? Or do you tuck yourself down inside into your belly or pelvis?

- What parts of your body do you not feel present in? By contrast, being present would mean you can relax into, allow, and feel the aliveness in that part of your body. You can identify with it—"these are my hips, my ribs, this is my aliveness." Where do you feel present in yourself and where do you feel separate from or dis-identified with yourself and your body?

We also want to pay attention to our emotional range and where our emotions are more fixed.

- Can you feel anger? Do you feel this most of the time? Do you rarely feel it?

- How do you feel fear? Is it present in a low-lying way most of the time? Do you not really feel fear?

- Can you feel slight sadness as well as deep grief?

- Are happiness and joy accessible to you? Are you suspicious or critical of these emotions? Do you need to seem happy most of the time?

- Other emotions to ask these same questions about are guilt, shame, longing, satisfaction, ease, awe, and worry.

We want to build our somatic awareness and attention to be able to feel, notice, and live inside of ourselves. This allows us to connect with, work with, and transform the deeply held strategies for survival.

Blending

Blending is a core principle within a politicized somatics. It has a particular orientation within this approach and lineage. Here it is deeply informed by aikido, a noncombative Japanese martial art. Blending is so central because it works. The soma responds to it, consistently. Blending carries a philosophical underpinning as well.

What is blending? Blending is being very curious about what is. Then it is supporting what is, or moving with it, in the direction it is going.

Blending is not necessarily agreeing. It is not saying that whatever you are blending with is true. Rather, it is a way to be with a contraction, an emotion, a belief, a conversation, and even an action, that looks for what is at the center of it, where it's going, and what it is trying to take care of. We blend to get to know the core impulse inside of something, and to work with it effectively. We blend to help release the contractions in the tissues that hold so much unprocessed history. Blending deeply supports transformation.

Fighting against a survival strategy, or against the way the soma has organized to protect, does not work. It puts us at odds with ourselves and with others. We can stay in this struggle for a very long time, preventing healing, connection, learning, and the regeneration of safety and change.

Let me give an example. This particular person has a history of sexual trauma, and experiences the ongoing impacts from white supremacy and migration. He has a survival strategy of shutting down, not feeling, and positioning against people and situations. He wants to heal and to be more connected in meaningful ways with his community and family. He wants to have ways of feeling safe that don't involve them fighting so much. One of his embodied safety shapes is hardening his stomach and chest. He talks about this as keeping people away from him, and keeping danger at bay. He can remain on the inside and others are kept out. We want to blend with this hardening.

We don't want to just understand where it comes from or why it's there. This can bring insight but it won't change the safety shaping or give them new options. We don't want to tell the person to be more open. The safety shaping will read that as dangerous or even life-threatening.

Instead, we want to connect with the shaping on its own terms. We want to get to know it, without the agenda of getting rid of it. Where is it in the body? How does it harden? Is it hard like metal or wood? How dense is it? How much space does it take up? How much space do you have when it has hardened?

Then, we can explore. What is it taking care of? How long has it been doing that? If it had an impulse to act, what is the action? To hit, to run, to disappear?

We want to hold our attention with this spaciously, with curiosity. We then want to support this shaping somatically and emotionally in exactly the direction it's going. We want to verbally and physically affirm what it is doing and how it is doing it. We want to acknowledge how long it has been taking care of what it's taking care of.

Here's a different example. This person was neglected as a child, and asked to take care of others in ways that were way beyond their capacity. They were acknowledged for supporting others, yet acknowledged inconsistently. They are also impacted by sexism and gender norms and are working class. Some of their safety shape includes attending to others at the exclusion of themselves—putting their attention out on others and adjusting their needs and desires to fit what others need. One of the places this lives somatically is a leaning forward, their attention outward and in front of themselves. They have little sensation in their back, legs, or pelvis. Their eyes are somewhat fixed on the surface of the eyeball, looking outward. They come across as warm, attending to others, and quick to support.

Again, we can unpack and understand this shaping, and understanding alone will not change much. We can encourage them to include themselves, to have more boundaries, and that alone will not make much of a difference for them. Instead, it could have them feel like they are failing at change because they literally cannot do it. The safety shaping will not allow it until it has been addressed.

When we look at blending with this person, the first place we might focus is in the overall leaning and reaching forward. We want to be curious about how they do that in their body, emotions, and self. How are they more in front of themselves and not in their back? How far in front of themselves are they? How far forward do they want to be? What are they leaning out toward? Are they reaching? Toward whom or what? What works about being out of their backs and lower body?

What does this shaping take care of now? In the past? What's the impulse? To reach, to connect, to make contact?

Again we want to verbally and physically affirm what this shaping is doing and how it is doing it. We want to acknowledge how long it has been taking care of what it's taking care of. More on this process below, but first, a bit more on blending.

The Fist

This is a brief demonstration on blending. Take your hand and make a fist. Make it tight like it is taking care of or protecting something important to you. Then take your other hand and try to pry your fist open, as if you're trying to get it to change or act differently. What happens? What do you feel in your fist, and the rest of you? What's the quality of relationship with your other hand? Many people report that their fist gets tighter and resists the opening, that they hold their breath, that there's animosity between the hands. Now, you can let that go.

Next, make a fist again, the same way. Then with the other hand, bring a sense of listening and curiosity, no agenda for it to change. Wrap your other hand around the fist like you are present with it, and gently supporting it in the direction it's going. The fist may want more soft or more firm support. Do whatever feels best to the fist. What happens? What do you feel in your fist, the relationship with your other hand, and the rest of you? Many people report that their fist relaxes more, that their breath deepens, and that there is a good feeling between the hands. This may be a little weird, but it helps us feel what quality blending can bring in the soma.

When the soma is blended with, it will begin to change. When we are curious about what the contraction (numbness, overactivity) has been taking care of, when we support the contraction in the direction it is going, the soma will change.

When we have been struggling with the extra consequences of our safety shaping, it can seem odd to blend with them instead. This may seem like a wacky idea. Why support dissociation into more dissociation? Why support more tightness with tightness? Yet, it is what works. Over and over again. The pressures, experiences, history, emotions, and energy inside of this shaping get to be felt, processed, and eventually completed when we blend with the safety shaping.

BLENDING PROCESS

Client and Practitioner. In the following process I'll use the language of client and practitioner. I've never been comfortable with this language. My discomfort comes from the Western medical model's implication of the practitioner being the expert and "knowing." In this model, the client is perceived as either being passive or having something wrong with them. It is the embedded power dynamic and attached assumptions that are problematic. However, I am unsure what other words to use.

This is not a peer relationship. There are important differences in the roles, in power, and in accountabilities. I hold it this way: the practitioner does have power in this arrangement, and accountability to serve and help the client transform. The practitioner also needs to be accountable to the outcomes of change agreed to, and assure they have the right competencies for this. This role holds and guides a container for embodied healing. If they see they do not have the skills, they should refer to another practitioner that can meet the client's needs and goals. The client, the person coming for healing and transformation, is also active and accountable. The client should consider what they want, what outcomes and changes are important to them. The client should proactively bring intention and topics to the sessions. The client is both opening and risking, and in active intention in the process.

There should be transparency and alignment on goals and outcomes for the practitioner and client. It is important to check in on these at least quarterly. Both roles should both hold intent and accountability to these aims.

On to the blending process:

- A client can be sitting, standing, or lying down. Bring their attention to their sensations. Continue to ground this process in sensations, not just images or ideas.

- Explore with the client: How does your body/soma want to organize itself to feel safe or protected? Can you show this, slightly? Where do you want to contract or go slack, to numb or check out? Let your body do that, just 15–20%, while you feel yourself and sensations. Keep noticing how you do this.

- As a practitioner, slightly match the contraction (like supporting the fist), and support it in your intention, soma, and words in the direction it is going.

- Explore with the client: This shaping/contraction has taken care of many things for you. What has it taken care of? How has it been a part of your survival? How long have you been doing this? Encourage the client to stay 15–20% organized into the safety shaping.

- This is the aspect of blending that is curious. The aim is to get to know this shaping on its own terms.

- Next, explore what has this safety shape cost them? What are you wanting that this is in the way of?

- Then explore what acknowledgment or support this safety shaping needs. "If I was going to acknowledge all it has taken care of for you, what would I say? Maybe, good job, thank you for protecting me…?" Get specific words or phrases from them.

- As the client remains 15–20% in that safety shaping, feeling it at the sensation level, the practitioner can begin to affirm the contraction. Use the language they have given you. Pay attention somatically to what happens.

- Both practitioner and client notice what is happening in sensation, emotions, and internal process. Go slowly. The soma is what we are blending with. You as a practitioner should also be in your feeling self.

- Explore. "Does your body want to do that even more?" "Are there different words you want me to use, or do those work?" Affirm the safety shaping again.

- Keep feeling sensations, and allow emotions. Heating up, trembling, sweating, crying are all normal experiences as safety shaping begins to process. Notice any of these, and encourage your client to allow them, feel them.

- Continue blending with the safety shaping and affirming what it took care of while the soma releases.

- This process may be twenty to thirty minutes in length or more.

The aim of the blending with the safety shaping process is the same as that of supporting the fist. Allowing long-held safety strategies to be supported in what they have been doing, for oftentimes years. The experiences held within these contractions will often surface with this support. When they do, we continue blending and supporting, allowing these to process emotionally and through the tissues.

Include a physical blending as well. Informed touch is a powerful part of somatic work.

- Just as with the fist, we want to physically support the safety shaping as well, when relevant. Get consent to allow for touch.

- Assure that there is feeling and presence in your hands as a practitioner. Place them in ways that support the safety shaping in the direction it is going. For example, if the shaping is hardening through the chest, we could place one hand along the sternum and upper chest and another on the back behind the heart, adding a pressure that matches what the contraction needs. What we are doing here is taking on the role of the contraction for the tissues. This allows the tissues to soften, open, and allow more aliveness while the person is still protected.

- Blend the contraction with other support. Ask the person, "How else can we support this safety shaping?" You can use blankets (the weight or hiding can be helpful), pillows to cover areas of the body, sandbags for pressure, etc. Any of these can help support the contraction in the direction it is already going.

- Lastly, explore the impulse toward some action within the shaping. Is the impulse to flee, to fight, to dissociate? We can engage the felt imagination here if this impulse is not possible in the space. The client can imagine running while feeling their sensations, or imagine pushing someone away while feeling their sensations.

How you organize yourself as a practitioner matters. As practitioners, we don't want to merge or fall into the blend. We need to have a clear center in ourselves to ground in and return to. Having our attention fall into the client does not allow for a blend. Merging does not leave any space for blending. For those practitioners who keep more distance, it's important to remember that the client's soma can feel ours. We need to make contact in the blend, to feel them. We can slightly take on their shape (2–3%), match breathing for a time, listen to, and feel them. We want to communicate with our soma that we are supporting this safety shaping. Somas read for congruence.

While images and words (descriptors) are relevant to this process, most important are the sensations and shaping in the tissues. We want to bring the attention, both ours and theirs, to the sensations as the foundation of blending. Words are a useful connection point, but words are not where the change is happening. Understanding and reframing are not where the change is made. This can be hard to get when we have been trained so deeply in the verbal aspect of ourselves and transformative work.

That said, using the client's descriptors and words is also an aspect of blending. The word *lost* or *protected* means something different to each of us. It relates to different sensations, images, and associations in each of us. When blending, we want to use the language of whom we are working with, reflecting them rather than our own interpretations.

In this process, we are supporting the somatic releasing of the held energy, impulses, emotions, actions, and history that the safety shaping has been storing and navigating. Through this process we are blending with the contraction so as to allow the soma to soften and enliven. The protective reactions begin to move and resolve. As stories and experiences emerge, the practitioner can listen and affirm, while reminding the client to stay connected to sensation. As contractions let go and process, support the client in allowing this. Return to the blend, feel sensation, and acknowledge the safety shape. If emotions such as grief, anger, or fear come in the process, the practitioner can do the same thing—acknowledge the emotions, the depth of feeling, and help the client allow them, connecting to sensation. The emotion and somatic release will have their own arc of expression and then most often come to a natural end. Because the deeper safety shaping has often been with us for decades, and acted as a core part of our survival, we'll usually return to blend with it a number of times in the healing process.

By staying focused on the soma and the sensations as well as the emotions and content, we can support the change of shaping at its root. One of the things I deeply appreciate about somatics is this ground. Mostly, we just need to not get in the way of it, or get too overcomplicated, as we are blending.

There are many processes we can use to blend with and support the survival shaping. We'll talk about more in the next chapter on somatic opening. The principle of blending is key for healing trauma and the impacts of oppression. Blending orients toward curiosity of what is even when we may be struggling with the consequences of this survival shaping. It assists us in hanging in there long enough to get to know this shaping somatically, and how it lives in the tissues. Then physically, verbally, and in how we relate, we can blend with the shaping in what it is taking care of and in its unique organization.

As a final note for practitioners … if you choose to use this blending process with people you work with, please first practice it yourself at least five times, focused on your own safety shaping. Whether this is with a colleague or supervisor, practice will teach you many nuances of the process. I also hold it as part of our accountability as practitioners to know processes through our own experiences of them.

Allying and Being Allied With

The third component of regenerating safety is allying and being allied with. What do we mean by this? From a somatic understanding, we are social animals. We move in packs and herds like other social animals. We form community and connections, or try to. Isolation as it is used in prisons, torture, and intimate violence is deeply traumatizing for us because we are built as collective creatures. Alienation and exile, whether from a homeland or family, can leave a deep wound. The staunch individualism of US social conditions, as well as people being told to avoid, hide, and silence their experiences of violence, also have deeply negative consequences on us as people. Many of us are trained toward self-reliance instead of interdependence, isolating ourselves from help, connection, and growth. This aspect of the healing process helps us to re-weave this interdependence, somatically.

Through these years of work, I have come to see that there is a deep biological expectation within us, as social animals, to be protected or defended by others. We need to have people with us, for someone to have our backs, for others to help protect us. We don't want to be left alone, isolated, or left to harm. We need allies, partners, people we can count on. Most of us can also feel the other side of this—the want and impulse to protect those we love and identify with. Social animals move together for safety.

We are often left unprotected by the people around us, or those in our wider community, when we are traumatized. This adds another level of betrayal to the wounding. Whether this is neighbors not showing up when domestic violence is obviously heard, an unprotective parent in the face of abuse by another parent, or white people not taking action to end racism and the systems of white supremacy—when others do not step up to protect us it is deeply impactful. Trauma, as well as this non-responsiveness by others, often leaves us with a feeling of being alone, not cared for, or abandoned. Often we will develop strategies of self-reliance and/or a deep sense of distrust of people. This puts us in an essential discord with ourselves—we need people (belonging), or we want to stay away from them (safety). Then we are stressed at some level no matter which way we turn.

The mending and reconnecting of safety, belonging, and dignity are core to the healing and transformative process. Allying, in the context of somatics and healing, acknowledges this human need for safety and belonging combined, the need for being allied with, and works with the soma to address it. Again, there are a number of practices and somatic processes to do this.

In a somatic process of allying, the main orientation is to ally with the person based on what their soma needs to feel that others are with them. The body, not the thinking, will answer this question best. This is another form of blending. Let me give an example.

In a yearlong training, a cisgendered man in the program volunteered to do the ally demonstration. He had lived on the streets, homeless, for many years as a youth and had survived much violence, as well as been violent with others. He had been both poor and working class and is a man of color/Latino, US-born. He had been working hard in his own healing and worked with other men to end male violence.

Listening to his sensations and his body, I asked him how I could position myself with him, so that he felt, at a somatic level, allied with or protected. We began this process by trying out various positions. First, standing at his side—communicating "we are together in this; if they come for you, they come for both of us." Then we tried the other side. People's experiences on either side are often very different. We then tried me standing in front of him—"they have to get through me to get to you." Finally, at his back—"I have your back; I'll keep watch in this direction." During these various positions he was attending to the intelligence of the body. He was feeling what his body resonated with and what his body said no to. What felt like allying to him?

As the practitioner, we are looking for what works for the client's soma. Not our idea of what could or should work. While we are present and flexible, we are also staying connected to ourselves. Being present and congruent as a practitioner is felt by another's soma. Our incongruence will be felt too.

He told me that he didn't feel like I could protect him because the folks he faced on the street could kick my ass. Made sense to me. I am not a trained fighter. We just kept following what would work for him. He created an amazing setup. He asked me to stand and keep watch, while he lay down, so that he could rest. "You watch and let me know if anyone is coming," he said. "I can never rest, and I just want to rest." It was very clear to him where he needed me to stand. Lying down, he had his back to me and mine to him. We continued to follow his sensations and felt senses. He literally moved me inches to the left, until he found the place for me to stand that felt resonant. He took a deep breath and sighed audibly.

I also asked if there was anything he wanted me to say from my role. Often, there is. He asked me to periodically let him know that there was no one coming, or if there was, to tell him. I agreed.

My role was to keep watch and let him know if any danger was coming. I watched, I scanned, I took my role very seriously. I knew his soma could feel mine and was tracking mine. I wanted to ally in the way that worked for him. I watched more, I scanned more, looking about the room and out to the imagined horizon. I periodically told him that no one was coming. There was a potent silence most of the time.

What is vital is what happened in his soma. He sighed, breathed more deeply, sighed again. I asked him to just keep feeling himself and then also feel and notice that I was there. More breathing. Then he began to tremble. This is the soma processing stress, history, stored fight/flight chemicals, and more. The trembling was subtle and then grew. Then tears came. I just kept doing my part, and periodically checking in with him. Can he feel himself? Can he feel me? Keep feeling sensations and allow the emotions, as much as possible.

At this point it is all about supporting the soma as it processes and allows this release and reorganization to happen. He was having the opportunity to "rest," with another keeping watch. This allowed for the release of traumatic experiences through the soma, while a new experience of allyship was registering in his being, tissues, experience, and self-identity. This cannot happen through conversation alone.

This process continued for some time, with him feeling himself and feeling I was there with him, willing to support him on his terms. Because we were in a cohort of folks studying the work, their attention mattered too. The room was focused and still.

After about twenty minutes, the cycle of release came to a natural close, like the deep breath and calm at the end of a needed cry. He was ready to get up and we debriefed as a group. Some of the things he reported that most stayed with me were along the lines of: "I never feel like I can rest. I rested. I could let go and could feel you watching for me. I could feel others in the room watching for me. I have been alone, really, for so long, I didn't know this was possible."

Just so you know, all of this was as much of a surprise to him as it was to any of us. He didn't know that he needed to rest and be watched out for. His idea of what allying was for him was very different than what ended up happening. It was through the exploration of the process and the following of his soma that we discovered what worked for him, what he needed.

Ally processes for others can look very different. I have seen some processes where the person wants to hide behind the ally, others who want to disappear and have their ally say, "Nope, I haven't seen them," and still others who want allies at their sides, to be in it together. It is a unique process for each person depending on one's experiences of trauma and oppression as well as on their shaping. This process can be done multiple times, not just once, until the soma begins to know and even expect allyship again.

Lastly, as the practitioner or partner in the allying process, you need to be present and congruent. If there is an ally setup that you cannot do or don't want to do, you should let your partner/client know, and step out. The body tracks for congruence and presence. We can tell when someone is not present or not able to be present in the ways needed. If you cannot be present and with yourself and them at the same time, this can do more harm than help, when the aim is allyship. We need to know ourselves and limits well as practitioners, and be willing to be honest, not just helpful.

The ability to heal and process trauma preexists within us. The ability to be allied with, and to ally, is also deeply known to us. I think what we are doing is learning how to set the right containers, processes, and context for this to happen somatically.

A Note on Emotions

Emotions are very compelling to us as humans. When emotions are present, we are drawn to or sometimes repelled by them, depending on our shaping and the occurring emotion. When someone is authentically crying, it pulls our attention. When someone is fake crying, we can tell. Either way, emotions are a compelling aspect of being human. Somatically, emotions are a natural part of the release and reorganization process. They are not, however, the main measure of change or healing. The soma is. Emotions are often present as the soma releases and reorganizes.

Trying to stir up emotional release, or looking to emotions as the primary measure of change, is not helpful. As the soma processes old safety strategies, emotions and allowing a broader range of emotions will emerge. We can support and affirm these processes, while not making emotional discharge the goal. On the other hand, repressing emotions is also not helpful. Repressing or trying to move past emotions quickly requires somatic contraction or numbing. Healing is a process of learning to feel and allow more sensation and aliveness, and working with it skillfully. Lastly, many practitioners are deeply empathetic. This is a strength most of the time. What is not useful is attempting to soothe someone's emotions and pain, so that they don't have to feel it.

As stronger emotions begin to surface in the healing process, our focus is on feeling sensation and aliveness, while supporting whatever emotions are there. Emotions also move in and through the body. As practitioners we want to keep this link conscious for ourselves and the client. "Where do you feel that grief in your body? ... Just keep letting that grief move through your chest." We'll talk about this more in the next chapter, on somatic opening.

COLLECTIVE ALLYING AND SOCIAL CONTEXT

As with all aspects of healing and transformative work, social conditions are present in the room with us and between us. This means that the solution or need is not always the same in each context. It may be that the person being allied with needs or wants someone closer to their social location and experience of race, class, immigration, gender, disability, etc. Sometimes this similarity can help the soma feel known and understood, or have the sense of there being less labor required to translate experience. Sometimes a difference in social location is wanted and this is what creates a deeper sense of safety. At other times, the relationship of trust and competence is what's most important. Either way the dynamics of social location, power, and shaping by conditions are present. As practitioners we want to overtly acknowledge this and talk about the client's needs and requests.

Groups of people can also use an allying process based in the soma. In social movement contexts, this process can be useful for groups looking to ally with each other for a broader vision and social change agenda. Here is an example. During a transformative justice training hosted by generationFIVE, about forty-five people experimented with an allying process to help build deeper trust in the group. In preparing for more public actions, they also wanted to prepare for the differences in being public as adult survivors of child sexual abuse, and those who are allies and do not have this experience of trauma. Because child sexual abuse is so hidden and denied, being public about it can be very stirring for survivors, and needs preparation and support.

In the allying process, the survivors gathered and discussed where they thought they'd like the allies to be located in relation to them. Naturally there were differences amidst the survivors' needs and they looked to address these too. We used the same structure to experiment with: first, allies on the sides, then in front, then behind, etc. Everyone was tracking off of their own somas as well as attending to the collective. The survivors would report back what felt aligned and resonant for public actions. The structure they ended up with was a V, open across the front and thinner at the back. On the outside of the V were the allies, on the right and left sides, and two deep in the back. Those survivors whose somas relaxed with more "people padding" were closer to the middle, and those who felt alliance with more space were at the front. People moved around and adjusted themselves accordingly. Then we just let this soak in. Did anyone need to shift positions to feel more allied with, in their somas? Could the allies be present and congruent where they were? When the group was settled, we let the feelings sink in, and got to know this somatic sense of allyship.

The learnings were manifold. Many of the survivors commented on how surprising it was for them to feel the support of nonsurvivors, and to have the somatic experience of not having to do this alone. Many commented on how powerful they felt together, and that it gave them more courage. People felt this at a somatic level as an option, not just as a good political idea. The allies commented on how good it was to hear the range in what various survivors needed and to know what would work. Their intention to ally was there and now that could turn into an orientation and practice. Both groups commented on how much this could prevent misunderstandings and conflict. Having the felt experience of allying, and how we got there, gave everyone a pragmatic way to practice with each other. Everyone said they felt more prepared for public actions together. Naturally, with changing contexts and pressures, the way to ally could also change. Yet now there was a way to have that conversation and translate it through the soma, into actions and ways to be with each other that the group did not have before.

Often we'll get caught in progressive left political conversations about allying and getting it "right," as if there is one right way. There is not one right way. Blame does not help allying. Righteousness does not either. Pretending we are "all good" is also of no help. Often these are protective responses to unattended hurt and pain. Or they can be reactions of privilege that have not yet been unlearned and accounted for. These reactions or approaches to allying result in everyone becoming more tense and contracted, trying to "behave" or unskillfully expressing their pain. While these reactions are understandable given trauma and oppressive conditions, they don't help to build trust and capacity to coordinate together. Instead, it is useful to help the soma and collective have experiences of allying, build a range of options and flexibility, and through practice, assure that allyship is actionable and dependable.

Principles to follow in groups looking to ally together include: aligning on the bigger purpose of allying; centering those most impacted in this context; holding the complexity of people's intersectional locations; and blending with those being allied with. In this orientation to allying we are both being responsive to those that are most impacted in this context, and given our goals, inviting allies into practice in which they are present and congruent. The other principle is to base the practice in the soma, not solely in ideas and language. Allying can be learned and experimented with together, through the soma, to bring increased choice, healing, and more effective action together.

I am using the term ally in a particular and somatic way in this section on regenerating safety. Allyship, in general, is a joining or bonding together for a bigger purpose. This can happen between people, families, communities, organizations, political parties, and more.

In the context of movements for social equity and environmental justice, allyship is used to mean a few things. One is allyship interpersonally and in leadership. Here we can think of allying as an ongoing process. Here is a definition from the Anti-Oppression Network (www .theantioppressionnetwork.com): "Allyship is an active, consistent, and arduous practice of unlearning and re-evaluating, in which a person in a position of privilege and power seeks to operate in solidarity with a marginalized group."

Allyship is also required and used in building power for structural change. This can be organizations and alliances bringing their resources and membership bases together for a campaign. They can also be larger international strategies that bring movements and parties—even governments—together to effect broad economic, environmental, and policy change.

Trust

I want to end this chapter talking about trust. Trust is profoundly important in our lives, families, communities, and organizations. Trust allows us to take risks together, to grow together, to know and be known, and to create big visions. Trust can be built, broken, rebuilt, extended, and taken away. It is a dynamic process. And, for most of us, trust is confusing and imperfect. In the process of regenerating safety, in all aspects of healing really, we're expanding our ability to grant trust and be trustworthy.

As we have seen, trauma and oppression harm us in the realms of safety, belonging, and dignity, impacting our ability to trust. Trust is manipulated through our power-over social and economic conditions. Situations and narratives are twisted so that those in power are considered trustworthy, and those without power considered untrustworthy. Although it is those in power who are doing the most harm, economically, environmentally, and to people's lives. We can look at the US border and detention facilities as a current example.

Capitalism tries to sell us things to represent trust that have nothing to do with it ... alcohol, vacations, things to "make us" desirable or secure. We are pressured to trust the nation, the president, and the military. If you question the actions of the administration you can be viewed as unpatriotic and punished with arrests and detention. In this context our trust is impacted, and we still need to trust others, and ourselves.

What is trust? How do we assess it? How do we develop it in ourselves and with others? We can look at trust as having three main components, each of which we can practice and assess in others. Trust is intention + competency + reliability, all held within an analysis of systemic power and conditions.

Intention. The first thing we want to assess and align is intention. What is your intention? Can you explore what another's intention is? What are they meaning, going for, intending? What are you meaning and going for? Is the intention good, for a larger purpose, considering you, considering others or the organization, or the community?

Competency. Competency is having the relevant skills to keep your promise. It is having the abilities to take the actions you say you will. Oftentimes, a gap between intention and competence is where breakdowns in trust can occur.

Reliability. This is when we are able to align intention and competence in a repeated way, over time. This is when people know they can count on us, because it has been shown over time. This is where we can assess others as well. Will they show up over time aligned with their intention and with the relevant competencies?

Power and trust. We need to acknowledge structural power within trust, as well as dynamics of power interpersonally. Is there a person in the dynamic who has more power to define and to decide? How are they acknowledging and working with that power? If there are structural power differences, can these be named and worked with proactively? In addressing power, there are still the other subsets of trust, intention, competence, and reliability, that need to be built.

Breakdowns in trust come when any of the four components of trust—intention, competence, reliability, or addressing power, are missing. Perhaps there is competence and skill, but not a clear or good intention. Perhaps there is intention and reliability but not the relevant competence. Perhaps there is intention and skill, but an inability to address power—we'd hold this as a lack in one of the other three as well. We can assess in ourselves and others which of these skills is present and which is missing. Each of these can be worked on and practiced to increase trust and trustworthiness.

One of the key aspects of rebuilding trust is showing new actions, aligned with shared intention, over time. Another aspect of rebuilding trust, and this may be the more difficult one, is choosing to extend trust again after a breakdown. Extending trust after a breakdown asks us to reassess—is there a good enough reason to do this? What will be gained in mending this trust? For many of us, present-day breakdowns in trust hit up against recent or historical ways we have been harmed or endangered. This cascade can feel like rebuilding trust or extending trust again is impossible or just a bad idea. Here we are asked to address and continue healing these previous harms, until we can assess what's in front of us based on the current situation.

Because many communities and peoples are under ongoing threat by state and economic powers, trust is very complex. This grounding of intention, competence, and reliability offers an ongoing way to assess for and make choices about extending and building trust.

If people close to us, with whom we want to build relationships, are missing some of these skills, this can become a place of development. This is true within our teams, organizations, and movements as well. We can assess for and offer intention, competence, and reliability; as well as invest in developing these, within and between us.

Trauma and the impact of oppression tend to have us take on certain safety strategies around trust. Usually they are some combination of extending trust to people and situations that have not shown they are trustworthy, being unwilling (or unable) to extend trust to almost anyone. The first is often built out of situations where a child is dependent upon untrustworthy people, and needs to extend trust to survive physically, psychologically, psychically, or all of the above. The second is often built when there is a close person the child can trust, and much of the rest of their environment is threatening or dangerous. Our experiences of social conditions also affect the combination of these survival strategies around trust. The more consistently targeted our people, class, or gender, the more either of these strategies needs to be employed.

Most of us need healing and development around trusting and being trustworthy. How could we not, given the conditions? I also think many of us long to trust fully, or to get to surrender with some-one that way. Trust, as adults, is a risk and also a need. It requires us to continue to develop skills, really all the skills in the chapter, and it asks us to heal. Making grounded assessments about our own and others' trustworthiness takes cleaning up and developing our ability to make those assessments, grounded in intention and behaviors over time, rather than from generalized survival strategies.

We can each practice good intention, developing the relevant competence, and demonstrating trustworthiness over time. We do this while moving toward equity by being awake to social conditions and power. We can learn to assess trustworthiness and what might be missing. We can learn to extend trust grounded in assessment, and in choice.

To Close

Regenerating safety is an essential aspect of healing and transforma-tion. Our aim is to rebuild an internal sense of safety, boundaries, and consent. We want to move from reaction to response based on current context and content—our current power, choices, and resources; our current internal resources and resilience.

New embodied practices relevant to consent, boundaries, and requests; blending with the safety shape; and allying are all compo-nents of this change process. These are somatic processes in which we are transforming the survival strategies that have been embodied and generalized; and introducing new choices, practices, and an ability to assess from a present and more empowered place.

We are rebuilding visceral and embodied experiences of safety and trust—of ourselves and of others.

10

Arc Circle Three— Somatic Opening and Disorganization

For the raindrop, joy is in entering the river—
Unbearable pain becomes its own cure.
Travel far enough into sorrow, tears turn into sighing; in this way we
*   learn how water can die into air.*
When, after heavy rain, the storm clouds disperse, is it not that they've
*   wept themselves clear to the end?*
If you want to know the miracle, how wind can polish a mirror,
Look: the shining glass grows green in spring.
It's the roses unfolding, Ghalib, that creates the desire to see—
In every color and circumstance,
May the eyes be open for what comes.

> —MIRZA GHALIB (1797–1869), translated by
> Jane Hirshfield

Changing

Somatic opening is the depth of embodied change. In this aspect of the transformative process, what has been developed to help us adapt and protect can be transformed and allowed to process and heal. The embodied strategies that have helped us to survive and navigate our lives, loves, work, and the world can be changed and evolved. We can update our somas, allowing what we no longer need to survive to transform; and new knowing, ways of being, relating, and behaving to emerge.

Somatic opening allows what has been stored in the body to come forward and be felt. It allows what has been left incomplete, to complete, holistically. Without somatic opening, we are placing new practices on top of old survival strategies. Under enough pressure, the older, more embodied strategies take over. This aspect of transformation can feel disorganizing, unsettling, and often means we are touching our pain. This aspect of healing can feel like you are taking yourself apart, and the person you have known yourself to be is changing.

There were times in the deepest parts of the opening process for myself, when I felt unearthed, undone, and could not find a familiar reference point of "me." What I had known as "the way I am" was changing deeply. This was very disorienting. To stay with the changes, and not get in my own way, I would find and focus on my sensations. I'd center, balancing in my dimensions of length, width, and depth. I could sometimes also center in my declaration. Many times though, I just landed myself in my sensations, and called that "good enough" for a "self" for today. It was useful. I struggled with myself less when I could let what was familiar change. I grew my tolerance for change. I grew my tolerance for the unknown and for trusting an organic yet intentional process. Large changes have happened many times since then, and I continue to come back to sensations as a ground and a place to be and rest in the turmoil or unknown.

While somatic opening can be disconcerting, our habits and survival strategies that no longer serve us live in our tissues. Because they were built out of harmful experiences, we need to address them, and then change them through the soma. Our automatic ways of reacting, relating, and thinking are driven from much deeper in our brains, hearts, and muscles than our ideas about them. These embodied patterns will persist (that's what they are built to do) until we take action to get support, heal them, and engage new practices.

We often need to take things apart as we simultaneously build anew. We know this in social justice work—be it local or corporate policies that do not support equity; oppressive social norms; or global economic systems that concentrate wealth in the few and poverty with the many. What is not working, what is doing harm, needs to be stopped, uprooted, and changed. Rather than reforms to a broken and racist mass incarceration system, or carbon trading that does not radically reduce our carbon use or invest in renewable energy, we need new systems.

This is true in our somas, too.

What Is Somatic Opening?

In short, somatic opening is a combination of relaxing (softening) and enlivening, of the soma. It is the process of stuck, held, numb, or dissociated aspects of the soma being worked with so that what is contracted opens, and what has been held at bay can emerge and move. I know this can sound weird if it is unfamiliar to you, but it is very effective.

This is happening through the soma—again, that means through the tissues, emotions, and self. This is not working on the body, an objectified "it" or solely getting the kinks out of the muscles and connective tissues. Rather, we read and assess where the embodied strategies are in the soma and then work together to process these through the body, emotions, thinking, and making meaning.

By relaxation, we do not mean slack or collapsed. We do not mean relaxed always feels emotionally calm, either. Relaxed means that the muscles or connective tissues are not held in an ongoing pattern of contraction, or of slackness (as in giving up). Relaxation allows for a wider range of sensations and emotions. It allows for more aliveness. By bringing more aliveness to the embodied survival strategies and the actual impact of the wounding, what was stuck or stymied can process and move through. This allows what was incomplete, compartmentalized, or withheld to become whole again. What was held back (let's say you could not run, hit, speak, or scream) or what was pushed forward but not integrated (easy to anger, easy to cry, overreaching for contact) can now process and come to a completion.

In this somatic opening, as tissues change, so do belief systems; as emotions get to be felt, more ease and emotional range appear and fear decreases. As the soma both relaxes and enlivens, a range of emotions often appears, particularly those we were unable to have or integrate. This may be sadness and grief, anger, fear, and/or happiness and satisfaction.

Lastly, through the somatic opening processes, history that has been stored in the tissues can surface. Many people I have worked with or trained have said something like, "I have not thought of that in ten, twenty, forty years," as the tissues change and adaptive patterns release. I have come to see the body as both a holder of unintegrated stories, and as a storyteller. Many times our minds have held a different belief or narrative than our bodies. The ones in the body most often tend to be closer to the truth of our lived experience.

Advances in neuroscience are helping us better understand how this works in our psychobiologies. The body holding the experiences of trauma, while the mind distances, is part of how we manage threatening stress. How distant the mind and body are can depend on many things. It may have to do with the age or stage of development of the person being harmed (children), their relationship to those doing the harm (the closer and more dependent, the more likely), and/or the extent and longevity of the harm. We explored this in chapter 4: The Impact of Trauma and Oppression.

In bottom-up approaches [to processing trauma], the body's sensation and movement are the entry points and changes in sensorimotor experience are used to support self-regulation, memory processing, and success in daily life. Meaning and understanding emerge from new experiences rather than the other way around. Through bottom-up interventions, a shift in the somatic sense of self in turn affects the linguistic sense of self.

(PAT OGDEN, *Trauma and the Body: A Sensorimotor Approach to Psychotherapy*)

These memories can return during the somatic opening phase as the tissues and body change and the holding in them releases. People can remember something they have "always had a feeling about," or something they do not consciously relate to. It may come in images (like pictures or a movie), or it may come in sensations that carry a knowing. The content may be unclear while the sensations and process are very clear. The good news is that in somatics, it does not really matter. The main process is to allow the embodied patterns to relax and enliven; to move the emotions and impulses that are caught there through the soma; and to process and integrate the experiences in the body, emotions, and sense of self.

There is a Latina woman I worked with—second-generation, heterosexual, and middle class. She came to work with boundaries, dynamics in her extended family, and exploring what she wanted in the next phase of her life.

We reintroduced her to feeling and sensation, and explored her declarations. What changes does she want to see? We delved into practices with resilience, boundaries, and regenerating safety that were relevant in many aspects of her life. Her soma began both to soften and feel more powerful.

As we deepened into somatic opening and somatic bodywork, things took a turn. An experience emerged of an earlier trauma in her life. In high school, her boyfriend raped her. She tried to tell her friends and they mostly dismissed it, saying that she was having sex with him anyway. The social norms of sexism, "boys will be boys" and "if you consent once, you consent always," were already ingrained into those young women and men. She broke up with him soon afterward, struggled on her own, and then "buried it." "I just moved past it," she said. She was now in her early forties.

She was taken aback, thinking that this was well in her past. It wasn't, however. She had developed many survival strategies to deal with it, yet the terror, the shame, the helplessness were right there in her tissues. She had a very difficult time softening her stomach and abdomen, and felt a disconnection from her pelvis. The way she had made it through the rape, and the deep impact of that trauma, emerged from her soma. The safety strategies she developed from this experience were also connected to her current struggles with boundaries, communicating to her family what she needed, and prioritizing herself amidst broader family dynamics.

This became the next piece of our healing work together. Through this process, she was able to face the impact of that experience and how it had cascaded into other parts of her life. The resilience and boundaries we had worked with began to root much deeper, and a more "filled out" sense of self emerged.

In somatic opening we shift from the embodied adaptive survival patterns running our behaviors; to our values, cares and commitments, and deep sense of knowing—our resilience and choices getting to lead. Through somatic opening we are disorganizing old embodied patterns, processing what these strategies have taken care of, and reforming into an embodiment with more choice, purpose, and connection.

Healing Interrupted

Let me start with a story. Some years ago I was driving down a busy street in San Francisco, four lanes all in one direction and timed lights. We came to a large intersection, crossing another four-lane street. The car in front of me ran that stoplight. A woman walking with a number of children had already started to cross the street. To avoid being hit by the car, people ran, and the kids scattered. The person who drove through the light kept going and disappeared over the next hill. I pulled over to see what was happening.

People were afraid and upset. One little boy, who looked about eight or nine years old, had thrown himself onto the pavement, in order to not get hit. The woman, who I guessed was his mom or caregiver, looked shocked, overwhelmed, and frightened. She was yelling at all of the kids to get onto the sidewalk. She tried to herd all the kids together. The little boy made it onto the sidewalk, and started crying while his body began to tremble. In her upset the woman grabbed his upper arms and shouted, "You're fine! You're okay! Quit crying. Stop crying!" I had compassion for her. It was easy to understand how afraid she must have been, and what it would have meant if any of the children had been hurt. It seemed she was trying to contain and control the situation, and likely her own fear as well.

And, that approach had a very particular impact on that boy's soma. She was demanding that that little boy stop what he was instinctively doing. When we understand trauma and mobilization through the soma, what he was doing was exactly natural and self-healing. His shaking, trembling, and sobbing were the brain/body processing all the cascade of chemicals and energy that were just mobilized to save him, that helped him dive out of the way of the car.

After a successful escape, this mobilization needs to be released through the body and emotions to return to a calm and cohesive state, and to be able to actually recognize that he was successful at protecting himself and is okay. This is its own process. The protective mobilization is one process—fight, flight, freeze, appease, and dissociate—taking some action. The coming down off it back to a coherent state and self is a whole other process. This tends to be where we run into trouble. As did the boy and the woman.

When the woman grabbed him and insisted he stop crying and shaking, he did what most kids would do. He tried to do what she said.

We will keep adapting and trying to behave for both safety and connection, even when it means we have to override a deeply inherent and healing process in ourselves.

To stop this natural process in his soma, he had to begin to contract and hold back all of that trembling and crying. He started to squeeze his jaw, tighten his eyes, and hold his arms down at his sides, pulling them into his body. He began to breathe shallowly. He tightened himself to try to stop all of the release. Remember what it's like to try to prevent yourself from crying? To try to stop crying once it starts? We do the same thing: hold our breath, squeeze our eyes and jaws, swallow, "push it back down."

Instead of coming down off of the protective mobilization through crying and shaking, he was forming contractions to hold it at bay. To stop it. This disallows the cycle to complete and instead stops it midstream. We then need the contractions and somatic patterns to hold it. This may burst out later as tears "for no good reason" or anger, or dreams, or it may stay held in the tissues and contractions, acting as a baseline patterning for the next charged experience.

In the best-case scenario, the boy could have sat or lain down on the sidewalk as an adult just sat next to him to ground him and encourage his natural process—"It's fine, just let all that come. All those tears are fine. Let all that trembling happen. That's good. Just feel yourself. I'm right here." He may have said how scary that was, asked if everyone else was okay ... whatever was there, we'd make room for allowing the soma to process. Then, it would end. It does not last forever. The emotions, chemicals, and energy move and then it's complete. Likely, he then would have taken a few deep breaths, like kids do after a big cry. And he would have been ready to move on. You may know this process from children in your life.

This process would have also allowed him to recognize that he "made it," he acted, and it was successful. This could have registered in the soma as being safe again, rather than the energy and state of protective arousal being what's held there (I am not safe ... I am activated).

That's what we're built to do. The soma knows how to move from a protective and mobilized state, to take action, and then to let this activation process through the body and emotions, returning to a present and coherent state. We know how to do this and it requires a supportive context. When that process is allowed and supported by the social and relational context, we are impressively good at processing through scary experiences and protective mobilization. Evolutionarily we have been doing this for thousands of years ... we were also prey to carnivorous animals. We needed to mobilize, act, and then return to a present and calm state.

Energy Flow

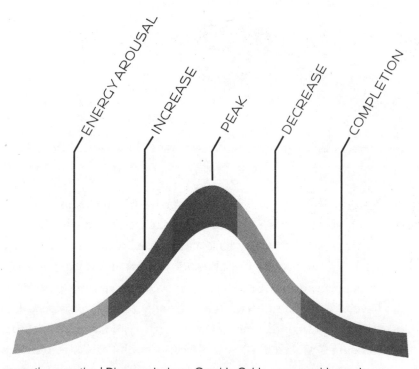

generative somatics | Diagram designs: Querido Galdo, www.queridomundo.com

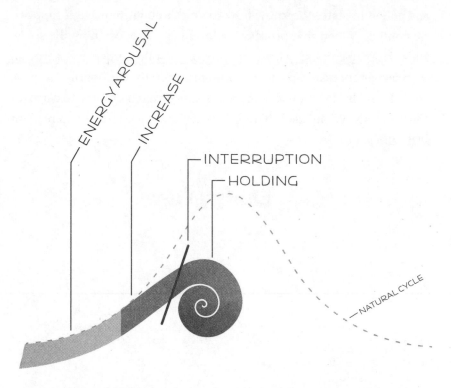

**Energy Flow
Interrupted**

generative somatics | Diagram designs: Querido Galdo, www.queridomundo.com

This process could have been supportive for the woman too. We could have also acted as a ground for her and explored what her soma needed for support. She may have also needed to shake and cry. That would have been a totally normal response to what just happened. This is what happens to any of us when we have a threatening experience.

I have thought about that moment many times, and wished I had had a skillful way to intervene. I offered support and help, and her focus was to contain it herself. I get it. It's very complicated. In our social norms, a stranger helping with parenting or caregiving is mostly con-sidered off-limits. I am white and she is a woman of color. Everything happened very quickly, and in the blur of the moment, I could not find a respectful, graceful way to engage her. I have replayed the scene in my imagination many times, wishing that I could have skillfully done so, to allow the natural self-healing to happen.

This story is one way to see how experiences get stored in our bodies and the inherent capacity to process through them gets stifled or stopped. This results in contractions, in numbness, in fear, and related beliefs being stored in our tissues. If we are in a context to allow the mobilization, the sensations and emotions to move all the way through us, they can process through to completion and integration. Other-wise they get stuck, the tissues contracted or numbed, and the process caught midstream.

How Do We Contract and Shape?
A Useful Model

Many somaticists have models of how the body holds, contracts, and numbs—from the fascia to the connective tissues, muscles, and organs. This then connects to our emotional range and sense of self, and to the self in relationship and in action. The following model of how we contract and compartmentalize was developed by Wilhelm Reich (Aus-trian, 1897–1957). He was a student of Elsa Gindler (German, 1885–1961). Many Western-based somatics traditions use this model. This model has been adapted, adjusted, and added to by many. He used the term *armoring bands* to describe the patterns that are typically devel-oped to manage arousal or aliveness that cannot be allowed. There is more information on Reich and Gindler and the lineage of this work on this book's website (www.thepoliticsoftrauma.com).

The usefulness of this model is that it helps us begin to perceive the patterns of constriction in the soma. You can notice these in yourself and in others. While these embodied patterns are built to serve our safety, belonging, and dignity, they also constrict and limit other sensations, emotions, and actions. A protected heart does not only feel less pain, it also feels less love.

The sensations and aliveness in our bodies move in multiple directions, up and down, side to side, and front and back. The next time you are excited (in a happy way), notice how your sensations and emotions move. Usually excitement is an all-over increased aliveness (vibration, quickening), with a concentration of feeling in the chest, and a movement upward. Or notice your sensations and aliveness when you feel lovingly connected. This often feels like a warming of the chest and stomach along with a settling or relaxing lower into the body at the hips and legs. Often there is an opening and softening of the chest, back, and heart, softening of the eyes, and the boundaries of your skin or edges becoming more permeable.

Armoring bands, or patterns of contraction, run horizontally in the body, helping to prevent or lessen sensation, emotion, aliveness, and movement. As a brief example, I met a woman at a workshop who ended up participating in a demonstration with me. I could see somatically that her arms were disconnected from her body at the shoulders (through somatic armoring, not literally). It was as if they moved separately. There was aliveness in her torso but not in her arms. I did not know what this was for her, or make up a story. I was just observant and curious.

In the somatic bodywork demo, I worked with her chest, shoulders, and arms. Through our conversation and the de-armoring in the session she revealed her trauma. She had been a concert pianist as a young adult, studying with master pianists and finding her way to a top international music school. She and one of her younger teachers fell in love. Because of the gender rules and taboos within her culture and religion, her parents took her out of school, and kept her locked in their house for the next year. In resistance, she quit playing piano, to her own great loss as well. All of this surfaced as we explored somatically reconnecting her arms and bringing life into them again. Our physical and psychological strategies are interdependent.

I feel very respectful of the soma and our shaping. I had no idea what was to emerge in that session. She shared that she was shocked and amazed about the disconnect of her arms. She of course knew the experiences, but did not know they lived like that in her body. As she worked somatically over time, the coherence of her torso and arms returned, and with that many forms of her creativity. She did not, as far as I know, return to piano.

I encourage you to explore the image below and feel it by trying it on yourself, and noticing the effect—physically, emotionally, psychologically, and relationally. What behaviors and actions might they allow for, or not allow for? You may recognize yourself and your own shaping as we go through this. Observe others too. What do you see in their shaping? Where and how do you see your own or others' adaptations in the body, rather than just getting an impression or metaphor?

I encourage us to practice seeing the shaping in the soma, and to make space between that perception and our automatic assessment of what it means. These assessments can be useful too, and they are influenced strongly by social conditions. We want to be able to perceive our own and others' somas, and then use that information in a way that serves growth, connection, and vision, not to deepen oppressive social norms and stereotypes. Our first move is curiosity: what do I perceive in the soma/body? What might this shape or armoring serve?

People have many different bodies. This image of armoring bands is shown on a body that has four limbs. All bodies, all people, no matter our ability, have shaping, aliveness, and constrictions or adaptive safety shaping. There are patterns in the human body as to how this constriction works, and each of our shapings will be unique. Each of these armoring bands runs around the entire body, not just across the front. At the end of the chapter I have detailed what some of the armoring along these bands can look and feel like, if you want to dig in further.

Armoring Bands

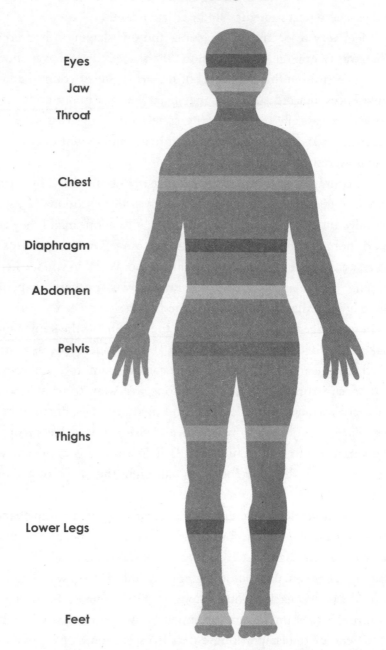

Eyes
Jaw
Throat

Chest

Diaphragm

Abdomen

Pelvis

Thighs

Lower Legs

Feet

generative somatics | Diagram designs: Querido Galdo, www.queridomundo.com

Supporting Somatic Opening

There are many processes to allow the soma to soften, enliven, and allow what is withheld or stuck to process. As we dive in here I want to set some reference points for how we know what somatic opening is and isn't.

The following are core markers of somatic opening:

- Felt senses. We will be able to feel this process in the body and through the felt senses, body, and emotions. Dissociation or unintegrated emotional catharsis is most often *disconnected* from the felt senses. We want to come back to sensation again and again, as a ground for the process.

- Resilience and declarations are at hand. In somatic opening, we keep resilience close by. This is not to contain or stop a somatic opening process, but rather to support it. By knowing what we (or a client) are committed to and what brings them resilience, we can connect with this as needed in somatic opening. When an aspect of the opening process becomes too intense, we can access resilience as a counterbalance. When we don't want to feel something, we can be reminded of what we most care about and why we are healing (declaration). Somatic opening is fundamentally making more lived room for resilience and what we most care about.

- The tissues will change. As we work with this aspect of healing, the holding, numbing, and pressing forward in the tissues will change. This means a shift from dense and unyielding to supple and receptive, or from slack and empty to pulsing and dynamic. Where reaching and longing may not have been possible, it becomes possible, not just because of an emotional and psychological change, but because the armoring in the tissues that learned to disallow longing, changes. The chest, eyes, and arms can long for, again. If boundaries were overridden, the tissue muscles and connective tissues that held back the making of boundaries as a safety strategy can change. This is part of what allows those actions and conversations to now be accessible.

- Aliveness is allowed through the person and body. By aliveness I mean sensations, emotions, somatic impulses, images, and thoughts. In somatic opening, through process and touch, we are inviting what is hardened to soften, what is numb to come back to life, what is withheld to surface, and what is pushed forward to relax back. In this, what these embodied strategies have been protecting, repressing, or serving can be revealed and worked with. Emotionally this may be the terror of being attacked, the isolation of intimate partner violence, the shame and rage of transphobia or racism, the grief of being disconnected from land. This can also be the impulses, whether expressed or withheld, to defend, yearn, run, fight, cower—each of these has a mobilization that is felt at the physical and emotional levels. This does not mean the full action needs to be taken. Rather, it means that the mobilization of that impulse can be supported to complete its arc in the soma. Safely, pushing away, hitting, kicking, and other ways to self-defend may be a part of this process. We are following the protective impulses in the soma. We can also use the felt imagination, imagination connected to the sensations, to follow the impulse—for instance, to run. In all of these processes we are taking care of the client and the practitioner. This is not disconnected catharsis, but rather an embodied allowing of the impulses that weren't allowed to happen.

- When withheld or compartmentalized experiences begin to process, there are predictable somatic experiences that happen. This may look like a subtle or more overt trembling, shaking, heating up and sweating, coughing, laughing, and crying. Often emotions are an integrated part of this experience in tears, anger, joy, relief, etc. The somatic release and processing are the core of somatic opening. Here the tissues, patterns, beliefs, and experiences withheld in the soma are restructuring.

- As we explored in the last chapter, emotions are a natural part of the release and reorganization process. They are a normal part of being human. Emotions are not, however, the main measure of healing. The soma is. Sometimes, in trauma healing, people can get focused on an emotional release that overrides or gets separated from the soma. This means they are expressing emotions but not connected to sensation and their bodies. I look at this as a disconnected catharsis. This, in and of itself, can be a safety strategy or conditioned tendency. Meaning that there is a pull for big emotional release (anger, sadness) so as to not feel what's happening in the soma. I have had to interrupt someone's crying to bring them back to their sensations and to themselves in sessions. This can seem odd, but an emotional override does not make for somatic opening. As practitioners, this is where we need to be well developed in both emotional and somatic processes. We can notice congruence—the tone of voice, the sensations and connection to the body, and the emotional expression are all connected and related. Or we can notice incongruence—the quality of voice, the emotional expression, and the sensations and body are disconnected. This could look like a tight chest and jaws, while the person reports they are feeling happy. This could be tears, while the soma looks unenlivened or dissociated.

- There are results that will show through the somatic opening process. We will be more able to live inside our own skin and in ourselves, that is, to be somatized. Our emotional range will increase and be integrated—we can allow and be with a wide range of emotions in ourselves and others. The same thing will happen with sensations and a wide range of aliveness. Differentiation happens, where we can tell the difference between the traumatic experiences and what is happening now. Between our skills, choices, and power then and now. Between what is happening in us or is happening in someone else. We are better able to work with current challenges and hurts.

Through somatic opening, I see that a deeper self-acceptance develops. This is not an override ("it's all okay"), or positive self-talk, or an under-accountability. Rather, it is an integration of experience, a decompartmentalizing, and a freeing-up of energy, that can be used to live well now, in a complex world. Overall, positive changes will show up in our daily lives, actions, and choices. Others will notice our changes.

> Sometimes a breakdown can be the beginning of a kind of breakthrough, a way of living in advance through a trauma that prepares you for a future of radical transformation.
>
> (CHERRIE MORAGA, *This Bridge Called My Back: Writings by Radical Women of Color*)

Somatic Opening Processes

In this methodology we use a number of processes to support somatic opening. These include somatic bodywork, blending processes (emotionally and physically), enlivening processes, and embodied storytelling. While I can speak to these in writing, they are not learned this way. So I'll point to them here, and have offered resources as to where to learn these practices in the Resources section on this book's website (www.thepoliticsoftrauma.com), if you are interested.

One of the most effective and efficient ways to support somatic opening and the connected processes is somatic bodywork. We hold this as an essential aspect of the methodology.

Somatic bodywork uses skilled touch, breath, conversation, imagination, gesture, voice, and emotional processes to support the shift from contraction and dissociation to openness and embodiment. Practically, this means processing the experiences stored in the psychobiology through the emotions and body. Massage can temporarily relax a muscle or contraction, but the shaping or armoring in the body will not shift unless the concern that contraction is taking care of (safety, love, protection, shame, terror, escape) is processed. From a neuroscience perspective, the body is the easiest doorway into working with those experiences, protective mobilization, emotions, and memories that are related to trauma. The body more quickly accesses the aspects of the brain (the amygdala, the limbic and stress centers) that are most involved in surviving traumatic experiences and "storing" them. The body is a much quicker doorway than language, because these necessarily quick reactions to traumatic experiences bypass the language centers in the brain.

Somatic bodywork uses informed and benevolent touch, connected to breath patterns and conversation. Somatic bodywork techniques support held patterns in the soma and tissues to either soften or enliven or both. Breath patterns oxygenate the body, helping the tissues to shift from the inside out. Increasing the oxygen in the body shifts the pH, which in turn increases the metabolism in the tissues and the oxygen uptake. For the nerds among us, you can look up the Bohr Effect.

While there is a particular lineage to the somatic bodywork in this methodology, humans have been touching each other to support healing for as long as we have existed. A trained, present touch and attention, an ability to see holding in the soma and help it to reawaken or let go, and a capacity to be with and help guide the related emotional and meaning making processes, are invaluable for healing.

We are in movement. From our cells to our blood and endocrine systems, to our thoughts, we are in motion. We are also spacious. While it is commonly believed that we are mostly water, really we are mostly made up of space. Somatic bodywork allows places that have been stuck, clogged, numbed, or contracted to begin to move internally again. It makes space again. When our system has not been used to this, sometimes we don't know how to let sensations, pressures, aliveness, and emotions happen and go through their natural arc. The natural arc of this aliveness, whether emotion or sensation, includes a beginning, then an increasing, which expands to fullness, and then releases to completion or expression.

Let me give you a brief example of somatic bodywork.

I had the opportunity to do somatic bodywork with a nine-year-old, who was going through a divorce in his family. He was also getting a lot of pressure and some shaming from his father to "perform" better at school and not be so fastidious. This child is fastidious in his nature. The culture and class of each parent's home, now that they were split, was very different, and he had to navigate this going back and forth. His adaptive shaping was beginning to show with his chest being pulled in and back and his shoulders collapsing. He is white, and his gender identity and sexual orientation are yet to be seen. It all seems very fluid now.

He lay down on the table. I told him that we would be talking, and paying attention to the feelings in him and the images, while I worked with him. We found a pressure that worked for him. We tried some easy breath patterns. What blew me away was how quickly he was able to feel his aliveness, and feel it changing, moving, and easing; and what this told him. Children have fewer years of armoring in them than we adults. At first, most of the aliveness was in his head, back, and belly. His chest showed less movement. We worked there with breath, touch and pressure points, conversation, and inviting more opening. He could easily bring his attention there, and went from unsure to easeful as his chest softened. "It's easier to breathe now ..." he said. "How is that for you?" I asked. "Good." He continued, "There's a blue ball in there ... well, it's a blue diamond planet, that's shining ..." he continued. I asked about the feeling inside of the blue diamond planet. He said, "Happy."

Most of the aliveness now was in his upper body down to his belly. I asked if he could let it run down his legs too, like he was one big piece. He said, "Hold on, lemme see." "Okay, there it is! I feel it all the way in my feet now!" He described the aliveness as buzzing, vibrations, and sometimes jumpy. I asked if he liked it. "Yes," he said, "it feels like me."

He dropped very deeply into himself as we worked. It was a quiet internal state, yet very much awake. In that state I asked him if I could remind him of something, and he gave me permission. "Sometimes we need to be reminded that we are okay, we are good.... Nothing is wrong with you." This is a big thing to say to anyone, and most of us have many defenses against letting that in. His body adjusted, his jaw pushed out, one fist clenched ... then he relaxed. I said it again, "Nothing is wrong with you. You're good, just as you." His arms jumped a bit, his shoulders rolled in, and then softened back. I said it a last time. I asked him how that felt in him, and what was happening in his body. He kept his eyes closed and said softly, "That's right. I forgot ... I almost forgot that nothing's wrong with me."

Then I asked who he knew, loved him. Out came a very long list of people including his cats. He was great. I wanted to cry with the poignancy of it, and the beauty of his capacity to de-armor and heal with just a little support.

Blending, as we used in regenerating safety, is the principle of supporting the contractions or embodied patterning in the direction it is going. It is assuming intelligence in the tissues and reactions. Through supporting the contraction we take on the holding for the soma/person, deeply validating these adaptive responses. This support, rather than trying to edit or change the shaping, sees it, hears it, and listens to it on its own terms. This has the effect of letting us discover what it's taking care of underneath the surface behavior or contraction. Blending supports the contractions in softening and enlivening.

We use blending processes verbally, emotionally, and physically in somatic opening. Physically this involves supporting and taking on the pressure of a contraction for the body, again, supporting it in the direction it's going, rather than trying to "open it up." We might support the curving in of the shoulders, the contraction of the thighs, the denseness in the chest, or the disappearing of the pelvis.

Emotionally, we linger with and make room for the emotions that are there, again not immediately moving to solve, understand, and even express them. We stay with the sensation of the emotion, its location in the body, and make space for its own shape and movement. Putting our attention on the sensations and emotions, we can attend to and allow what is there to be felt and known. Emotions have movement to them. Sadness may start as heaviness in the chest, or an aching heart. If we stay with it, it may then be pressure in the throat, and then come forward as tears or sobbing, and sound. This may be strange to break down, but most of us have gotten so good at over-containing, fixing, or even blurting out our emotions, that the somatic process can get overridden.

In conversation and listening, blending is being present with and affirming the embodied narrative. This does not inherently mean agreeing; rather the blending is against a backdrop of a larger change process—which a broader declaration is guiding. This can be matching the language another uses. If they use the word *broken* to describe how they feel and you reflect back "you feel damaged," this can have a very different resonance in their soma. They may feel missed, or like you don't get it. Just as happiness and joy can mean very different things to a person. When we are working with healing from trauma and oppression, we are in very sensitive and vulnerable terrain. Joining the person in their world linguistically, while not mimicking them, is an important part of blending somatically.

We blend with the soma through somatic bodywork, resilience practices, the processes of supporting the safety shaping, and the ally process.

Enlivening processes are those that invite and allow aliveness and energy to move through the soma. Many of us have over-contained the life and power in us for very understandable reasons. Enlivening processes allow an experience of having more energy and aliveness move through you, than is your norm, while also being connected with others. This is for the broader purpose of healing and transformation, or the person's declaration.

We do this through somatic bodywork, partner practices, and specific movement practices.

Lastly, somatic opening can be supported through embodied storytelling. This is an opportunity for us to purposefully tell specific aspects of our life experiences that have deeply shaped us. This is a more familiar practice in therapeutic processes. The somatic orientation within this process is particular. We explore what has shaped us, what has informed our conditioned tendencies, or survival strategies. What their benefit and cost have been in our lives. And, where they live in the soma. We can also use this to explore and get to know our resilience or our longings, and how these live in our somas. We can use embodied storytelling to explore how we make or stay away from connection, how we were shaped by our social location and social conditions, and more. This process is less about getting to know or tell the story, and more centered on how we have been shaped and how this lives in the soma. It is telling a story while we are in ourselves, our bodies and sensations, for the telling. Of course, being listened to by someone who can be present with all the aspects of our telling is the other half of storytelling.

The Cycle of Emotion

During this phase of healing, somatic opening, we will encounter deep emotions. This is an inherent part of touching where we are wounded and allowing it to heal. Emotions and emotional expression follow a predictable cycle. The cycle of emotions can be like an ocean wave building to fullness and crashing on the beach, then reintegrating into the ocean. The aspects below can give you a sense of how to be with emotions, and to allow the full process somatically. In healing from trauma and somatic opening it is helpful to have someone else with you. This allows you to feel more fully while they can hold the space or ground.

1. Sensations and emotions emerge. In the first stage of the cycle, emotion shows up as a sensation or a felt sense. The emotion may be a response to either a current or a past experience. Then you have a choice. You can turn away from the emotion or you

277

can open toward it. There are times when putting an emotion on hold is a good way of taking care of yourself. Holding emotions down doesn't work as a way of life, however. The longer you brace against emotions, particularly those wrought by trauma or oppression, the longer those emotions will run your life. Instead of turning away from the emotions, you can choose to welcome them. You can do this by bringing your attention to the emotion in your body and slightly softening.

2. As you attend to or turn toward the emotions, they intensify and increase. In stage two of the cycle, you turn your attention toward the emotion, feeling your way *into* the sensation. When you do this, the emotion tends to intensify and reveal itself. This stage can often be the scariest. Feeling your emotions means learning to tolerate these sensations in your body. When we feel our emotions, we want to also feel our bodies.

3. Emotions grow to a point of fullness, like water about to spill over the top of a bowl. Stage three brings the emotion to fullness. The emotion grows in its charge and sensation. You may feel like you are about to cry. Your chest may overflow with joy and pleasure. You may want to kick, push, or yell.

4. Emotions release and are expressed bodily. Stage four brings release. Depending on the emotion, you may experience this release gently or it may be very intense. You may sweat or blush, weep or sob, shake, kick, laugh, yell, or become overheated or very chilled. This expression is the release of the emotion. Surprisingly, the full expression of even the most intense and scary emotions usually lasts only twenty minutes at most. Again, we want to feel our bodies and emotions at the same time. This lets emotions move through us in an integrated way.

5. Intentionally complete the cycle, in stage five. Draw upon your resilience and commitments. After the expression of emotion, you may find relief, peace, renewed energy, and a sense of healing or

transformation. This is the completion of the cycle, or what some people call *integration.* Take time to be with yourself. Acknowledge that you are complete with this feeling.

As you face, feel, release, and complete emotions connected to trauma, you will begin to experience more choice and self-trust, and be more at ease with a wider range of emotions within yourself and with others.

On, with, and through the Body

In this methodology, we distinguish between working on the body, with the body, and through the body. On the body sees the body as an object or machine, and a series of interconnecting parts. By manipulating, fixing, or trading out these parts, we manage the machine. Many allopathic medical approaches work on the body this way. I am not dismissing this as it's sometimes useful and needed.

With the body holds the body as a partner or an important informant. Sensations, and their information within, matter. We are partnering with the body because it is useful, helps us to heal, calms us down, etc. In this orientation we still hold the "self" as different from the body. The body is relevant yet not fully deobjectified. Many forms of meditation in the West, and many body-based approaches, orient this way. While we are attending to the body in a more intimate way, we are not necessarily living inside of ourselves as a dynamic living organism. I think it is very hard for us who have been soaking in an objectifying view of the body, mind over matter, God separate from the flesh, intellect paramount over empathy, to fully deobjectify the body. It takes a committed process.

When we work through the body, we hold the self and the body as inseparable. As the self changes, the embodiment changes, and as the embodiment changes, the self changes. This orientation deobjectifies the body/self fully. We are living and dynamic organisms, interdependent with others, the dirt, the air, plants, stars, and the oceans. My experience is that this knowledge is most accessible and actionable through the body. We also know of our interdependence through science, and we can experience it in spiritual or transcendent moments. When we reassociate, come back into the livingness of the soma, this knowledge is inherent. Working through the body invites and allows a more holistic healing, and orientation to practice and growth.

When we make whole again the body and self, other questions arise, like what is the consciousness in us? Is there an animating force running in or through us? How do we understand spiritual experiences, and those that seem so far beyond or dissolving of the self? Is there a self/soul/spirit that continues after we die? I love these conversations and many peoples and traditions have many ways to answer them. I have my own experiences, answers, and ongoing questions. What I want to highlight is that these questions, and the transcendent experiences they point to, are embodied experiences. Even those that allow the self to dissolve are happening through our somas. I think the body has profound spiritual capacities. I have seen again and again that the more deeply we live in our somas, the more we access a knowing of interdependence and a seeming contradiction of being both matter and animating source. Yet this too is of one fabric. As we experience spiritual and nondual experiences, it is through the soma that we bring them into action in our lives and in the world.

Somatic Opening and Groups

Groups of people, teams, organizations, and alliances have collective conditioned tendencies (CTs) and safety shaping, and can experience somatic opening in a purposeful change process. The collective CTs or adaptations are shaped from the individual histories of the people involved, particularly those leading the group. They are shaped by the cultural shaping of the collective—is the group primarily Black, indigenous, Chinese, Korean, Arab, Central American, white? Is the group racially and culturally diverse? Is its majority people of color or white? Is the group primarily immigrants, undocumented? The gender and class mix; the purpose of the group; and the broader social norms and systems of white supremacy, capitalism, patriarchy, and others shape the group. Lastly, the CTs and safety shaping of the group are influenced by the current social and economic conditions they are facing or organizing to change.

As with individuals, there needs to be a larger purpose for the group to want to transform and move through somatic opening. Perhaps they will become more aligned and powerful as a group, and more connected and better able to work with the pressures of the conditions. Perhaps they will heal from wounds they share, or build resilience and better thrive. A group can use the somatic opening processes here to transform collectively. The attention is on both the individual and collective opening and requires many more facilitators of the process.

Generative somatics, the organization we do this work through, has a long-term partnership with the National Domestic Workers Alliance. They are one of the fastest-growing labor rights organizations in the United States. They are run by women of color with a majority women of color membership. I love and respect many things about NDWA, including their orientation to uplift some of the lowest paid, least benefited, and often trafficked workers—nannies, domestic workers, and home health care workers. They organize in ways that reflect the lived and real experiences and intersections within these workers' lives. They work across immigration rights, labor rights, ending state violence, and with a feminist and anti-racist orientation. They also center love and care work in how they organize for change. I could go on.

We codesigned a leadership development program called Strategy, Organizing and Leadership (SOL) with NDWA. This is a sixteen-day (four, four-day sessions over a year) program integrating embodied leadership, trauma healing and resilience building, organizing skills, and broader strategy. In the third session we focused on somatic opening through embodied storytelling and somatic bodywork. The broader commitment was to support and increase their leadership, connectivity as a group, and ability to be resilient and strategic amidst the pressures of organizing for dignity and workers' rights.

During this session there were about sixty domestic worker leaders, doing guided somatic bodywork on each other. We pulled the bedspread and pillows from all of our rooms to make spaces for everyone to lie down. The cavernous conference room was filled. The care and attention in the room were palpable. We guided the breath patterns, questions, and hands-on techniques in Spanish and in English. After this session many people said some version of, "I never get cared for that way, that was so good. I am always caring for others." Or, "I've never told anyone that before ... no one has ever asked." It was powerful, and revealed the dignified need these leaders have to be asked, listened to, and to have access to relevant healing spaces. These women (almost exclusively) have experiences of migration trauma, racism, sexual assault and intimate partner violence, separation from their own families, and poverty. The healing plus organizing are vital. To these leaders, the experiences of healing and being listened to deeply are easily translated to how they organize, their ability to connect with other members, and the bold risks they take in campaigning.

To Recap

Somatic opening is the core of embodied transformation. Without it we are placing new practices on top of old contractions, and under enough pressure (intimacy, children, leadership, conflict, movement successes, and challenges) these survival strategies will take over. Through somatic opening we are able to recognize, attend to, and process the impacts and wounds we built these safety strategies around. We are able to somatically unravel patterns that no longer serve our lives and visions, and make room for others that do. We are able to return to the dynamic aliveness of embodiment and live inside of our own skin, amidst others. We increase our ability to choose, rather than react, based on our intimate and for-the-world declarations.

Detail on Somatic Armoring and Shaping

Here is further detail to help us perceive and feel the armoring and shaping within the soma.

Ocular Band: This constriction or banding includes the eyes and the back of the head. It can show up like a squeezing and tightening around the eyes and forehead, and upper cheeks. The eyes can get fixed in many different patterns. We can harden the eyes, not letting others in or our internal world out. We can chronically squeeze the eyes, like we are suspicious or squinting. Other ocular armoring can look wide-eyed, like the eyes are caught in a state of shock. The ocular band can also communicate a fixed emotion, like sadness or anger or worry.

The optic nerve goes from the back of the eyeball directly into the brain. In this, the holding in the eyes affects the fascia throughout the body and the brain. More tension here communicates more tension to the brain and fascia, while more relaxation communicates just that.

Try on various occipital armoring. What happens in you? What's familiar? Who do you know whose eyes have hardened? How does this impact you? What shaped that in them?

Mandibular Band: This includes the jaw and cheeks, occipital ridge (the base of the skull), and face. Tightening the jaws chronically is a great way to hold things back and down … words, feelings, thoughts, perceptions. We can contain what comes up through the chest, belly, even the pelvis, by bearing down on the jaw. The mouth and jaw are our main editors—assessing what to let out and what to let in. What does a set jaw communicate?

The jaw is physically designed for the teeth to not touch and the tongue to relax while the lips are closed or slightly parted. I see very few jaws like this without some conscious somatic opening work. Many of us hold our teeth together and jaws tensed. Many people push their tongues into either the tops of their mouths (feel the jaws tighten) or the bottoms of their mouths.

Holding and tension at the occipital ridge, where the muscles attach to the skull, can have the effect of holding back, making it physically difficult to cry. It can seem like "holding your head above water," or a stiffness or "properness."

Each of us develops a "social" face. Our faces are very expressive, like our eyes. Yet, faces can also become hardened or fixed in an expression. Some of us have a more consistent look of worry, or sadness, or anger. Some of us have learned to not let how we are show through our faces, as a way to navigate our worlds. This social face can soften, again allowing more range of expression, emotion, and connection.

Try on various mandibular armoring. What happens in you? What's familiar? What do you see in others? What does a contracted jaw, lips, or cheeks keep in or out?

Thoracic Band: This is the constriction throughout the throat and neck. I sometimes think of the neck as the cork in the bottle. Through contraction in the throat and jaw most things can be held down. We still have some expressions in English that speak to this like, "swallowing it," whether words or emotions.

Emotions have movement and sound. Sadness can well in the chest and then come forward as tears and sighs or sobs. Anger can be felt in the lower body, arms, and legs, and also rise up and have voice. Happiness can be felt similarly. Impulses to protect ourselves also have movement and sound—whether it is verbalizing boundaries or needing to push someone off, this mobilizes our bodies toward action and sound.

Voice comes through the throat for many—through the hands for those who use sign language. We use the term "caught in my throat" for not being able to express an emotion or feeling. This is often literal. The contractions in the throat don't allow the expression of emotion or voice. In trauma and when we are very afraid, we often can't speak or vocalize, or were not allowed to.

Our jugular vein runs near the surface in our necks. Openness and surrender, in a trusting sense, relax and open the throat. In a loving and safe sigh, or an authentic big laugh, we move the head back, opening the neck and throat. We can associate the neck with trust and positive surrender, and with the opposite, of holding on, repressing, and protecting.

The back of the neck is the cervical vertebrae, below these the thoracic vertebrae. Any injury like whiplash, being choked, or sexually assaulted can impact the neck and spine, and we will brace to protect the physical body—as well as protecting our inner being.

Try on various ways to armor your throat and neck. What happens in you? What's familiar? What do you see in others? What sound, yearning, and aliveness are allowed out? What is allowed in?

Chest Band: This is where the big pumps of the heart and lungs live, wrapped by the ribs. The chest houses our heart (the organ) as well as our emotional heart. The chest houses our lungs and allows or constricts our breath.

We tend to experience this area as the center of many of our emotions. We'll often touch our chest in speaking about something that moves us, or being "heartbroken." Allowing ourselves to be "open-hearted" translates into softening and enlivening the chest, breath, shoulders, and back. We are more porous or permeable.

Contraction around the chest is typical and understandable, given experiences of trauma and the impact of oppression. When we are mobilized into protection or if we are shocked, our breath moves into the top third of the lungs, making oxygen more available to the large action muscles. Kept there, it produces anxiety. Breathing lower in the body, belly and chest breathing, relaxes the tissues and calms our emotional and physical state.

Armoring of the chest and back can show up many ways. We may feel a density in the chest, like it's a block. We may bear down or harden the chest to prevent feeling and impact. The ribs are actually designed to move and are flexible in a nonarmored state. Or the chest cavity may feel very thin and flat, clogged, empty, or hollow. The chest may be pushed forward, or collapsed inward, backing up the heart or protecting the breasts.

These styles of armoring can be instinctive, as well as socially reinforced, ways to manage safety, belonging, and dignity. Pulling our hearts back out of harm's way is a natural impulse, but there are also trends of "style" where media images of women's bodies have the chest collapsed inward as "beauty." Other eras show the breasts pressed forward as desirable. We live in a context of social and cultural fixation on women's and trans people's breasts. All people with breasts navigate this, and armoring or dissociating from the chest is one way to deal with the attention and public projections.

When we collapse our chests it makes it harder to breathe and to take up space. We often collapse our length as a result of pulling the chest back. This can be an attempt to make ourselves less noticeable, or indicate that we are not a threat or not sexually "provocative." This can dovetail deeply with female gender training, and race and class constructs around who is allowed to take up space. Many transgender people have to navigate their experience of having a chest and/or breasts, both in a deeply personal relationship to their own bodies, and within the profound social pressures of a binary gender system.

On the other hand, puffing the chest out is also deeply instinctual and socially reinforced. We see this move in other animals as well. Birds, chimpanzees, and gorillas will puff out their chests, just as other animals like bears will stand on their back legs to appear bigger. Appearing larger, they can seem more threatening, to discourage aggression from others. We also can puff out our chests, and held there, this can be a style of chest armoring. "Barrel-chested" is another way this type of armoring can look. Social images and male gender training include this puffed-up chest—being threatening before threatened. Again, race and class constructs also influence our strategies.

The chest and upper back are designed, in a relaxed state, to be flexible, allowing deep breaths in the belly and chest. The rib cage can expand front to back and side to side as we breathe. The shoulders are built to drop and relax on the skeleton, and not be held up with the musculature. The organs should also be able to relax, rather than be constricted by the holding around them.

What do you notice about your chest and upper back? Try on various ways to armor your chest band—collapsed in, pressed forward, hardened, empty. What's familiar? What do you see in others?

Arms and Hands: It's interesting to me that we call our arms limbs, like trees. Not all of us have arms and hands, and the impulses and functions listed here are part of us, whether we do or not. Arms and shoulders are structurally connected to the ribs and chest. Arms are and do many things—they gather things and people toward us, hug and hold, open and welcome another, reach toward, and express our longing and yearnings. Arms make boundaries, pushing away, holding at bay, hitting, pushing back. These can be used to build good relationships, or be protective, or aggressive. There are many forms of music we play with our arms and hands. The palms of our hands have one of the highest concentrations of nerve endings in the body, making our ability to feel and distinguish things tactilely quite sensitive.

So we look at armoring in the arms and hands—where has our capacity to reach and yearn, make boundaries or self-protect, been hindered? Where have these experiences and our adaptations to them remained in our tissues?

Diaphragm Band: The diaphragm, solar plexus, midback, stomach, kidneys, and more, are affected by this armoring band. A way to understand this banding is this: in order to sing, yell, scream, or gasp—any kind of powerful or fast breath—you have to engage your diaphragm. The expression "I got the wind knocked out of me" refers to this part of the body. Or the emotional expression of feeling "punched in the stomach" is pointing to this area.

Armoring in this area can feel like an ongoing tautness, a pushing outward, a feeling of being tucked in and under the ribs, even a holding on for stability. You might feel little space in this area, a density, or it may feel like a large cavern. I have heard people experience each of those. Contraction here can help to separate the areas below—the belly, pelvis, and lower body, from what is above—the heart, voice, and head. Contraction or numbing here can feel like the opposite of relaxation, ease, and space.

This is complicated by the fact that in the US media there seems to be a cultural obsession with taut core muscles, low body fat, and the fabled six-pack. Yes, strong core muscles are good for our overall health, and muscles should also be able to relax and soften. We, and muscles, are not built to be taut and "at the ready" at all times. Muscles have a contracted and relaxed range. An ongoing tension through to the solar plexus and abdominal region weakens the muscles, and pressures the internal organs. All of this pressure can also put us into complex relationship with our own bodies and result in us wanting to distance from our own stomach and abdomen.

A chronic state of contraction or slackness also affects the vertebrae—this region includes the thoracic vertebrae dropping into the lumbar spine. Armoring here can be experienced as a pushing forward, like you are trying to get away from something, or a pulling back, shortening the front of the body.

What do you notice about your diaphragm, stomach, and midback? What qualities do you feel there, both on the surface and internally? Is there a lot or a little sensation and aliveness here for you? What's familiar? What do you see in others?

Abdominal Band: Moving down the body, the abdominal band comes next, including the lower belly and small of the back. Within this area are small and large intestines, bladder, and more. This is a dark, cavernous, mysterious part of the body. It's a good place to hide. What usually happens with the armoring band around this area is that we lose access to the lower part of our body, our pelvis, our genitals, our legs, and a deeper connection to the ground.

Armoring in this area can be tension or slackness, numbness, a sense of density, or an inability to feel or access this part of the soma.

Many people will talk about their form of dissociating or getting away, including tucking themselves deep inside. When asked where, invariably people will point to the lower intestines. People often experience this as the place they have "tucked things away." Many find that this is where difficult experiences they have not had the opportunity to integrate get "stored."

What do you notice about your abdomen and low back? What qualities do you feel there, both on the surface and internally? Is there aliveness and sensation here for you? Can you connect from your lower belly back to your pelvis and lower body? What's familiar? What do you see in others?

Pelvic Band: Next we have the pelvic band, which includes the many muscles and ligaments connecting our lower body and our torso, front and back. Our largest muscles are here, the gluteus maximus, as well as the genitals, anus, and perineum. The femoral arteries run through our hips.

Often the armoring in this area appears as a chronic contraction or a "leaving" this area of the body. Getting away from what is there, or from traumatic experiences, by moving up and out of the pelvis. If you are willing, try doing this and feel what you have to contract and abandon to get out of your pelvis. Sexual trauma can cause a whole range of armoring and compartmentalization in the pelvis and can deeply affect your experience of sexual pleasure, intimacy, and aliveness.

Pelvic armoring can also show up as the pelvis pushed forward or tilted back. Wearing high heels, a sexualizing cultural practice focused on women and trans women, moves the skeletal structure out of alignment, tipping the pelvis. Anytime we are habitually out of structural alignment, we are fighting gravity. The human body is designed to take the pressure of gravity primarily through the skeletal system, not the muscular system.

So many social and religious factors target our sexualities. Many are taught that human sexuality and pleasure are shameful, wrong, or bad. Queer people are targeted across religions and often portrayed as sinners or sexually perverted. And we live in the age of hookup apps, making many kinds of sex easily available. Lots of sex doesn't inherently mean that we are present and connected in our pelvises, or in our sexual expression. Research on the long-term impacts of child sexual abuse shows consistently higher rates of pelvic disease and struggles with fertility. From a somatic perspective, this makes a painful kind of sense, given that the body's resources get directed toward core survival functions during trauma—respiration, circulation, and survival strategies are prioritized over other vital functions like digestion and reproduction.

I think of the pelvis as the doorway between the upper and lower body. If this is blocked, it is difficult to be one whole piece or soma. Opening through the pelvis lets us rest our weight into gravity and the lower body, making it easier to find and feel the ground. It can allow us to align the pelvis, ribs, and head structurally, and to have a dropped and open attention. The lower belly and pelvis are the center of gravity in our bodies.

What do you notice in your pelvis? Where is there aliveness or where may you feel more numb or blocked? Is there an open doorway between your torso and your lower body? Do they feel connected or disconnected? Can you feel yourself as one piece from feet to head? Can you drop your attention to your belly and pelvis as the center of gravity?

The Lower Body: Legs and Feet: Let's move to the lower body. Not all people have lower limbs. The orientation of the lower body toward ground, expression, and an impulse toward certain types of protective mobilization are relevant whether we do or do not have them.

As adults we may not think of the legs and feet as expressive, yet in babies and young children we can see this. Babies tend to move and scissor their legs when they are hungry, when they are happy, and when they see someone they love. If you watch little kids getting frustrated or starting to fight, their legs are usually the first part of them to become active. They kick their legs in tantrums, and stomp, and wrestle with their legs.

The lower body offers us a lot when it comes to protective impulses and action. We use our legs and feet to run away and run toward, kick, push away, and more. A wide range of emotions gets expressed through the legs as well, including anger, fear, and even love.

When we are contracted through the lower body, the legs and/ or feet may feel leaden and heavy, missing, and blank, or like you are floating just above the ground rather than being settled onto the earth. The legs can hold a low-grade anxiety, revealed in tapping or shaking the foot regularly. Armoring can show up like a pulling in, or pulling the legs closed, with the inner thigh muscles (adductors). It may be that one uses their lower body for sports, dance, or exercise, that they are well coordinated, but that they are not in their legs.

Many of us spend many hours sitting. This also shapes and patterns our lower bodies, generally creating less access in ourselves.

We are electrical systems. Electrical systems need a ground. I'll often think of the pelvis and lower body this way, as our ground for aliveness and energy. The more we can live inside of the pelvis and lower body, the legs and feet, the more experiences, vision, and energy we can ground. When these lower parts of ourselves are accessible, we can drop our attention and energy down, in a very pragmatic way, into our bodies. This allows us to "ground" in a wide variety of situations and lets our thoughts, emotions, and aliveness literally have a place to also ground.

To Close

Every armoring band relates to the others. We are one integrated system that can also very skillfully compartmentalize. As one set of contractions starts to shift in a particular banding, the increased sensation or aliveness will affect others. Often in somatic bodywork, we will work with the contractions above and below the central contraction so that there is room for sensations and emotions to move, when the central contraction softens and enlivens.

I want to also ask that we do not overgeneralize symptoms and experiences based on this somatic understanding of the body/self. If you are struggling with something physically, please also check out your symptoms with a skilled medical provider, be it an acupuncturist, osteopath, allopathic doctor, or naturopath. We want to stay curious as to what brings us healing and well-being, and get the range of support needed.

NATHAN SHARA, trauma therapist, educator, and writer, and lead teacher and practitioner for generative somatics.

I've come to understand somatic opening not as a moment in time, but as a long, and at times painfully slow, thaw back toward wholeness.

As a kid, I would sit stock-still trying not to breathe whenever my father lost his temper. Curling my shoulders in around my chest, I tried to be so small and quiet that he wouldn't hit me—as though if I tucked in far enough, there wouldn't be anyone left to hurt. While he towered over me shouting, with just the slightest movement of my fingertip, I'd write all the things I was thinking but didn't dare to say against my thigh. "No." "You're wrong." And: "I will never be like you." In hindsight, the spark of resistance behind those words is what I've been following ever since then. It is what led me to committed engagement in liberatory struggle and to the communities I'm grateful to be part of now. But the stillness and the quiet have come with me too.

The only child of Indian immigrant parents, it's no coincidence that my childhood anger found its expression in written form. With heavy emphasis placed on family privacy and academic achievement as key strategies for survival, books had become both my resilience and my escape. The breadth of places and stories that I encountered through reading carved out a parallel universe of imagination and possibility inside me. Though my home life remained volatile, the richness of my internal life—shaped by writers such as Gloria Anzaldúa, Audre Lorde, and Paula Gunn Allen—carried me through till I left my parents' house to go to college.

By the time I came to generative somatics in my mid-twenties, my world had expanded considerably. I had come out, first as queer and soon after, as transgender. Volunteering at a domestic violence shelter had brought me deeper into feminist antiviolence movements, and my involvement in students of color campus organizing had politicized me further. Seeing how racism and homophobia impacted my friends' and my own sense of safety and well-being, I was pursuing a degree in social work. I wanted to support other queer people of color in healing, and was really hoping I'd figure out how to work through my own shame and anxieties in the process. While leading a support group for queer and trans people on body image, I was introduced to Staci Haines's work. With little understanding of what I was getting into, I applied to participate in the eighteen-day Somatics and Trauma course.

I think it's fair to say that somatics initially appealed to me intellectually. The concepts and principles offered an entirely different framework for understanding trauma and healing than anything I'd heard in social work school. However, many of the practices left me feeling like I was missing something. Others around me were having significant experiences, with tears and trauma stories pouring forth. That wasn't happening for me. I was often so caught up in wondering whether I was doing the practice right that I had little to report during the debrief afterward.

As time went on, I realized that this itself was part of my conditioned tendency. I'd become skilled at figuring out what was expected of me, and performing it. Most of my attention was usually spent scanning others, to figure out what that was. My own feelings and emotions weren't something I knew how to access while I was with other people.

The paradox was that, on the outside, my life was full of people. I had friendships, intimate relationships, and was involved in several political projects. However, while I often got excited about some new person I'd met or an organization I'd just learned about and threw myself into it completely, when disappointment, irritation, or conflict inevitably arose, I'd withdraw. While politically, I believed in generative conflict, I watched myself consistently play out patterns of avoidance and denial instead.

During those early days of somatic practice, as I learned to shift my attention to feeling and sensing rather than thinking, I kept getting an image of a cavern inside my chest. While most of the cavern was a vast and cool space beginning just behind my sternum, there was a small and glowing room at the very bottom, full of books, a big armchair, and a crackling wood fire. As we explored how our survival strategies had taken care of us, I started to identify the ways that tucking in when confronted with violence had allowed me to maintain a sort of intactness, deep underground, behind my heart. I knew who I was and so long as I kept that hidden, I was safe. I could be content and have my dignity in solitude. At the same time, I was lonely and longed for connection. I wanted to be seen and known and understood. Which required something that I had no idea how to do.

We often say that somatic opening is the part of the transformative process when we've started to let go of our deeply ingrained ways of being and surviving, but don't yet embody the skills to show up consistently in alignment with our commitments. It entails facing into parts of ourselves that we've avoided. And it requires that we feel the sensations and emotions that we learned to contract around, either because they were overwhelming to feel, or because they threatened our ability to stay safe, connected, and worthy.

In my case, I realized I had to confront the terror and shame that I felt about my own anger. I had seen how toxic and damaging expressions of anger could be, and I still held to that promise that I'd written against my thigh—that I would never behave that way. And yet, in that persistent way that trauma confuses the scale and stakes of things, even the slightest blip of irritation felt to me like I was becoming my father. In response, I had completely overdeveloped my brake system. I'd learned to stop my breath, contract my solar plexus, and still my face at the slightest hint of frustration, making sure that nothing harmful would make it from my insides out to the surface. As I received somatic bodywork more regularly, I slowly came to recognize that the impulse within all of that contraction was a loving one. Fundamentally, I didn't want to cause more harm. As I started to entertain the possibility that maybe I wasn't a terrible person who had tricked people into believing otherwise, it became more possible to contend with the human-sized liabilities of how I was navigating my relationships. While I had never been loud or physically aggressive, I was confronted with the ways that shutting down, withholding, and pulling away can hurt people too.

I developed a new commitment sheet, outlining practices and actions I could take to update my relationships into current time. One practice was that if I was upset, disappointed, or angry with anyone in my closest circles, I would address it directly within a week. I used somatic practices such as the jo kata, centered grab, and spirited commitment to dignity to build my capacity to stay aligned and on purpose in the face of my terror at making this type of impact. After seven months, I changed it to within seventy-two hours. It hasn't been without bumps, but over five years later, I am in deeper and far more trusting relationships with my friends, comrades, and colleagues as a result.

In the decade since I first came into this work, many things have changed and some have not. I still love to read. My voice still gets quieter during especially difficult conversations. But rather than living at the bottom of a cavern deep inside my chest, I now inhabit the whole of my body. I no longer expect love to come find me in the depths of where I'm hiding, or to take up residence within my internal world.

Instead, I am in a loving partnership, sharing a wide and vibrant life that includes many things that I never could have imagined.

In 2016, my partner and I traveled to India, where I was able to reconnect with much of my large and loving extended family, whom I hadn't seen since before I transitioned, fourteen years earlier. Since then, I've also become part of putting on a weeklong political action camp committed to supporting and mentoring the next generation of young South Asian organizers.

These days, I spend much of my time supporting individuals, groups, and political formations to engage conflict using transformative approaches to justice. My work with survivors of intimate violence, people who have caused harm, and the networks and communities around them is a place of ongoing practice, learning, and contribution that I know I could not offer without the healing work I've had the support to do. The compassion I've been able to find for my own survival strategies has allowed me to support many other folks who tend toward over-containment, minimization, and shutdown in the face of pressure.

While there are still plenty of times that I struggle, the richness and expanse of my current life hold far more than I came in with. I am part of a fierce, loving, and imperfect community, and more and more, when I feel scared, angry, or uncertain, I reach out to the relationships around me for support. I practice revealing the very parts that I least want to share, and when my friends express love and reassurance, I practice believing them. The quiet, stillness, and isolation of my earlier years have transformed into a life that also includes voice, action, and connection. I've come to understand somatic opening not as a moment in time, but as a long and at times painfully slow thaw back toward wholeness.

11

Arc Circle Four—
Healing Shame,
Interdependence, and
Generative Conflict

I can tell by the way the trees beat, after
so many dull days, on my worried windowpanes
that a storm is coming,
and I hear the far-off fields say things
I can't bear without a friend,
I can't love without a sister.

> —RAINER MARIA RILKE, from "The Man Watching,"
> translated by Robert Bly

Healing shame, deepening interdependence, and learning to work with conflict as something that can be generative are all essential in healing trauma. I'd say these are essential processes for leading a skillful life, though they are also not easy. Engaging in these processes requires deep encounters with painful aspects of healing, a true sorting of accountability and helplessness, and a truing of our longings for connection and justness.

When healing from trauma, we must also heal shame.

Given all of that, healing and taking action for justice take courage. Each of us has that courage. This does not mean we are not afraid; rather it means we build the road by taking it. We gain courage and confidence, skills, and freedom from shame by taking the risks required.

After somatic opening, we are ready to take on the big and important work of loving and being loved, of dignifying and being dignified in relationship—whether personal relationships or in our work and social movement spaces. Healing shame asks us to distinguish somatically (not just mentally) what is and is not our fault, where we are over- or under-accountable, and how to forgive—especially ourselves. This creates the space and skills to take bigger risks, to deepen relationships, and to be more accountable in a centered and clear way. This transformation makes room for conflict to be generative—meaning we can build more trust and capacity through conflict, rather than splitting, appeasing, isolating, or being rigidly "right."

These processes come at this place in the Arc of Transformation because we've now been able to clarify our declarations, cultivate resilience, and get to know and work with conditioned tendencies and survival strategies. We have been developing other skills and practices like embodied boundaries, requests, and recentering. We have also been blending and working with somatic opening to holistically process the traumas that impact our safety, belonging, and dignity.

I'm going to start with healing shame because it is so defining for so many of us. This is a multiphase process, which becomes a set of practices over time. Trauma, the shaping from oppression, privilege, and internalized oppression all leave us with shame. Later in the chapter we'll address mutual connection, conflict as generative, and being with contradictions.

What Is Shame?

First let's look at what the experience of shame feels like and then unpack how we see it somatically. Shame is the generalized sense that we are wrong, bad, tainted, stupid, that it is *all* our fault. It is a deep and often hidden feeling that something is very wrong with us. Shame is the pervasive sense that we *are* wrong, not that we *did* something wrong.

Shame is, sadly, a normal and predictable impact of trauma and oppression. Because something integrous has been torn, something that knows wholeness has been harmed and shattered, we are left with shame. This violation can be due to direct experiences of physical or sexual violence, verbal abuse, and neglect, or due to the more generalized, negative social messages of not belonging or worthlessness that target oppressed peoples. This violation can also come at the hands of historical traumas or state violence. Shame is present due to a break in our innate integrity and worth—from the very intimate to the systemic.

An image I use when trying to understand and work with shame is that of a pine tree. If there is an axe cut in a tree, sap will flow there. This both shows the place of the wound and seals that area of wounding. Shame works like this somatically.

The impulse inside shame is to hide, disconnect, and make sure no one finds out about who we "really" are. It can pull our attention to ourselves alone, worrying and judging, rather than being able to be truly present with others. It often feels like if shame is seen, all will be lost. If we are seen in what is so terrible about us, we fear we will be cast from belonging, or even the possibility of belonging, forever. This is a very difficult experience and set of emotions and contractions. Shame tends to drive many not-so-life-affirming behaviors when it goes unaddressed.

Often, we carry the shame of people who came before us, as well as people who have harmed us. We want to ask ourselves, "What of the shame I am carrying is mine, and what may belong to the people who harmed me or who benefits from this oppression?" If we assume a level of interdependence among us all, we likely carry a mix of our own shame as well as that of others.

Many of us have taken actions that we need to be accountable for or that we regret. There are times in our own lives, and with the people with whom we live and work, when we have done harm. We can feel guilty or ashamed about our actions or way of being. In this case, it is important that we allow our guilt or shame to lead toward centered accountability and mending with others, while honoring dignity and humanity. It is not always right to jump to "It's not your fault" in every situation of shame. Instead, we can look to mend these harms through connection, conversations, and new actions.

We live amidst social norms and systems that tell us lies to concentrate wealth and power in the few, while shifting harm and blame to those most exploited. This makes addressing shame even more complex. Shame is confusing because it generalizes, like our other survival strategies. We become confused about who's done the harming and who has been harmed. We often feel deeply ashamed about experiences where we have actually been hurt, and confused or defensive about ways we participate in harm.

People who repeatedly do harm, whether intimate, community, or state violence, have to deeply bury, compartmentalize, and create defensive or self-righteous narratives or spin to manage their shame. With that denial, so goes their empathy.

Healing shame allows us to imagine a positive future for ourselves and others, to reconnect authentically, and to take action toward what we care about. It encourages centered accountability, rather than being under- or over-accountable. It lets us explore forgiveness, without it being an "override," avoiding collective accountability and change. Many people talk about the deep relief of not being so driven by shame, and the freedom they feel in its place.

What is the difference between guilt and shame? Guilt can lead toward new action and mending. Shame often leads us to try to hide it, to isolate, or to defend. Thus, shame requires healing.

The Somatic Role of Shame

As with other impacts of trauma and survival shaping, we understand shame as an embodied experience. If we could have talked or thought our way out of shame, we would have already.

Like other survival shaping, shame has a protective role—it is taking care of us by hiding what is too overwhelming to face, and by giving us a sense of agency in a context where agency may have been taken away from us. Shame takes care of helplessness. How do we understand this somatically?

There is another metaphor we use called the shame trampoline. Imagine bouncing on top of the trampoline are all the beliefs, internal narratives, negative stereotypes we have internalized, and other shame-based feelings. What would yours include? What's bad about you, or wrong with you? It may be things like: I am bad, tainted, ugly, too much, too little, stupid, too smart, perverted, unworthy, a burden, disgusting, never meant to be, etc. Or things like: it is all my fault, if I could have …, if I were just more …, if I were just less …, and on and on. These are painful to name. Many times this deeply internalized sense of shame is raced, gendered, classed, about ability, and more. Shame can feel anything from terrible to debilitating.

By bouncing on top of the trampoline, shame cycles round and round, spurning other survival strategies, like "try harder," "I don't care anyway," and more. Shame is very distracting—it holds our attention and tends to make our lives smaller. It also never lets us see, feel, and grapple with what's "under the trampoline." This is where shame becomes protective, even though it causes suffering. Underneath the "trampoline," or shame-based contractions, are the deeper wounds of trauma. These are the experiences of helplessness, terror, deep grief, agony, abandonment, and rage. These are very difficult experiences and emotions to face and to feel. Shame becomes a distraction to these, keeping our attention on what's wrong with us instead. Shame, in this protective way, also allows us some agency. Some sense of still having power by it being "our fault." Helplessness, abandonment, and even rage can be overwhelmingly vulnerable.

It is important to understand this somatic role of shame, however, because it informs how we then work with it to transform. As with many things in somatics, to transform it, we must get closer to it.

Healing Shame

Given the depth of shame, the process of healing it takes place in phases and over time. It needs to be in connection with at least one other person, because of shame's impulse to hide. The aspects of healing shame include: education and social context, blending with shame (opening), "spirited commitment to dignity," centered accountability, and cultivating forgiveness (including self-forgiveness). Some of these later phases will become practices that we can continue throughout our lifetime.

It is also our accountability to assess with our clients or practice partners that one is sufficiently in the embodied healing process (Circle Four on the Arc of Transformation) to enter these waters. Healing shame comes later in the Arc because it requires the ground of a strong declaration, access to resilience, the new skills that regenerating safety can bring, and experiences of somatic opening. We begin this aspect of healing by knowing: What wants to heal now? What do we want to get from healing shame? How is that connected to what's most important to us?

Education and Social Context

First we must explore and talk about what shame is and its protective role somatically. Then we need to dig into social conditions, oppression, and privilege. So many people are blamed in the social narrative and policies for things that have nothing to do with them. The profound criminalization of Black people is one example. This is projected and enacted daily onto Black communities, and affects folks deeply. Another example is the negative stereotypes and the local and state policies behind them that are stacked against transgender people. Another is the ongoing invisibilizing and blaming of Native peoples while continuing to take their lands and resources. All of this projects and perpetuates blame and shame, but in the wrong direction.

When someone is healing shame, we need to have enough conversation, offer enough political education, so the person has grounding to know what is their responsibility (their actions) and what is not (their survival, community and social conditions, limited options, etc.).

Let me give an example. There is a Filipina woman who immigrated to the United States to try to help lift her family out of poverty. She has worked as a domestic worker for years, sending the majority of her earnings back home. She left when her youngest child was eleven years old, and that child now has children of her own. She has not met her grandchildren in person. She has not seen her own children for over twenty-five years. She is seventy-six and still working. She feels ashamed that she is not there for her children and grandchildren. She feels ashamed that some of her employers withheld her pay when they realized she was undocumented. She feels ashamed that she was sexually assaulted when she was a child.

What of this shame is hers? This does not mean she does not feel the emotions of shame, but the loss of access to her family, the economic conditions that left her with few options to support them, being sexually abused, and targeted as an undocumented immigrant are not her fault.

The Philippines has been economically dominated and influenced by the United States for decades. The United States has either installed or supported political leaders that have partnered in exploiting rather than uplifting their people. Economic migration is often one of the few choices left for many people to feed their families. The dynamics of who gets access to documentation in the United States is very classist and racist, even though the economy depends on immigrant labor. Once undocumented, one's vulnerability to being used or exploited increases, and there is often no place to turn.

This dynamic of misplaced blame is also present in intimate partner violence and child abuse. The personal abuse is often righteous and blaming, while the people attacked feel bad and ashamed. Too often the person being violent is believed and protected over those who are harmed. We can see this in innumerable examples of children being labeled as bad or "inviting" of abuse, adolescents being trafficked or pimped and being criminally charged, and "non-protective" mothers losing parenting rights to the abusive parent.

Hopefully these examples help us see why it is vital that we ground ourselves in deep understanding of power-over political and economic systems and social norms, as well as how power-over plays out interpersonally, most often backed by these broader systems. We need to understand this broader misuse of power as we unpack and heal shame.

In holding this as a joint understanding, we can begin to at least mentally understand the differences between what is our "fault" and accountability and what is not. This does not heal the shame, but gives us a grounding to come back to as we move through the broader shame-healing process. As we engage in the process of healing shame, we both can share a foundation and analysis of what is and is not our accountability. This does not take away from emotions or the impacts of violence and oppression, but lets us place accountability where it belongs throughout the process.

There can also be complex and contradictory dynamics involved in shame. We want to be able to hold all aspects of these dynamics, intersecting healing and accountability. It isn't useful in healing to try to explain away why someone caused harm, if they did. Even when there is a larger set of conditions, if we hurt someone, we want to acknowledge that too. I have worked with many people who were sexually abused as children who then, as young people, sexually abused another child. We need to hold each aspect of this. We need to hold that they were hurt and abused, which in turn set them up to hurt another. And to hold that they hurt another. Grounding ourselves in a transformative justice orientation, we can have a broader understanding of personal and social forces, heal the complexity of shame, and support centered accountability at the same time.

Lastly, because healing shame is a very deep process and one that is affected by conditions, it is also important that power differences, and differences in social location, between the practitioner and client or between the practice partners are named, acknowledged, and any needs or requests addressed.

Blending with Shame (Opening)

We have worked with the principle and practice of blending in both regenerating safety and somatic opening. It is again useful in transforming shame. Here its use is probably the most counterintuitive for people. I have seen through many years of training, that this moment of naming and blending with shame can seem like exactly the wrong thing to do. Yet it works. It frees up the shame and lets us enter into the terrain and essential healing that has been avoided or protected by shame. It lets us somatically get "under the trampoline."

What does this mean? Because shame wants to not be seen, wants to stay hidden to prevent the assumed consequences, people are mostly alone in their shame. When people share content of shame, how badly they feel about themselves and what they deeply believe is wrong with them, mostly we try to talk them out of it. We try to comfort them by saying, "That's not true, don't you see...." Or, we tell them all the good things about themselves. However well-meaning this is, it leaves people again alone with their shame and, perhaps, feeling even worse about how they feel about themselves.

Instead what we want to do at this phase of the healing process is blend with their shame. We are not "agreeing" with them, but rather affirming and actively being with these deep and embodied experiences of shame. What does that look like somatically? Given that shame wants to be hidden away, we usually sit next to a client/practice partner, looking in the same direction, feeling them and connected in with them. As the practitioner, this is a very important time to be centered, soft, and hold a steady and accepting ground. As with all somatic processes, we track this process through the soma, attending to sensations, somatic release, emotions, and the psychological processes involved.

As we are with a client/practice partner, we ask, what is shameful about you? What is bad or wrong about you? This is a very direct question and inherently welcoming of their shame. When they answer, we acknowledge what is. The person healing might say, "I wasn't smart enough to figure out how to make it stop." We can then reply, "You weren't smart enough to figure out how to make it stop." We are just being with their shame as is—not trying to talk them out of it or get away from it. They might say, "I am disgusting." And, the practitioner again is present and reflective of this, saying, "So, you are disgusting." Each of these may get repeated many times, as the person feels themselves and the contractions begin to melt.

After three or four reflections of their shame, we check in. How are you? What are you noticing in your soma? Sensations? Emotions? How are *you?* Often they'll be heating up, trembling may begin, or tears may come. Often people have either never said these things aloud, or no one has been able to stay with them while they have. Then we continue asking again, what is shameful, bad about you? What else? For some, it is one theme that runs deep. For others, it is a network of shame that has many pieces. Whatever it is, we are present, reflect, ask, and stay with them. Often the experiences that drove the shame into them, surface. We encourage these as embodied and felt stories, letting them surface, acknowledging and reflecting them, and helping the person stay very connected to their felt senses.

This process is about breaking a deep isolation of shame. It is about letting the soma de-armor and allowing those deeper experiences of trauma to process. There can be a point when the emotions and experiences of the trauma become the focus of the process. All good. The main aim, as in somatic opening, is to allow what has been compartmentalized, stored, and contracted to be felt, move, reach the surface, and process. This may be terror and trembling and crying. This may be grieving, with sweating and sobbing. This may be a nuanced letting down internally, the organs relaxing some, or the hips feeling the ground while the person becomes quiet, yet alive. We stay with them, blending, and being a ground for the deeper work.

In this process, there will be a natural arc to the opening: an entering into the terrain, an increasing of intensity, an opening and somatic release, and then a completion of that phase and some space. This process is not about getting rid of all the shame; rather in skillfully navigating this arc somatically. Given the role shame plays, how deep it is, and the ongoing pressure of conditions, this process can be done as many times as is useful for the person healing. If you are a practitioner, it is also important for your own ongoing transformation as well.

Helplessness is one of the most difficult and traumatizing experiences. Whether we were helpless to protect ourselves, or helpless to save or protect another, it can be devastating. At some point in the process of healing shame, our helplessness is met. We take on so many strategies and contractions to avoid helplessness. Meeting it, being able to be with it, with the support of another, is freeing. Eventually we can move from feeling like we won't survive feeling our helplessness, to its being processed and integrated. Once the charge and contractions have moved from the soma, we can arrive into a clearer state of acceptance: "I was helpless. I had very few choices given the context ... I could not make more of a difference then." From our current state of resourcefulness, resilience, and development, we can be with helplessness of the past. We can also develop the ability to hold the contradiction that now we have power, choice, and volition, while helplessness is also part of our real experience.

Language is very important in blending with shame. It is important to use the same language that the client uses when reflecting back their experience to them. If they say disgusting, use disgusting. If they say horrible person, or selfish, or stupid, use that. This tends to be the hardest part for practitioners in learning this process as the statements are not "true," nor would we want to hurt someone. The process is nuanced and subtle. It is about meeting a person where they have been isolated, and allowing the soma to shift. The soma responds to blending, again and again. It is part of how we work and it needs to be done skillfully. I suggest learning and practicing this process first with support and supervision from someone who is skilled in it.

Spirited Commitment to Dignity

After the vulnerable work of blending with shame, we move toward getting a new experience into the soma. Spirited commitment to dignity is a process with others that realigns us with dignity, power, and connection. It assists in the processing of shame through the soma and is a felt reminder of our inherent worth and interdependence. This is a partner practice, and can be done with a practitioner or in a group.

As the soma processes such vulnerable experiences, as we reveal both shame and what's underneath it, it is important to bring resource, connection, and aliveness into that opened space. This helps to reorganize us in connection and dignity.

This is a hard practice to describe ... think expressing full power and vitality. Think connection and people fighting FOR you. Think fighting FOR what you most care about.

There are various ways to do this process. We tend to use Thai pads, a plastic bat, and a couch, or large pads and a staff (or *jo*). This process can also be done with no impact, what we call an "energetic" version. These practices come from martial arts traditions, but that is not how we use them here. The core principles of this phase of healing shame are connecting aliveness through the body (power), with connection with others (the opposite of isolation), and with dignity. This is so important to do with others because we are seen and supported, dignified by others, and centering our declaration. It interrupts the isolation and over-containment of shame, while nourishing us.

In one of the personal stories at the end of this chapter, you'll hear more about this practice.

Centered Accountability

When we have been navigating a deep sense of shame and trauma, often we have not learned or practiced centered accountability. There is often little in our family, community, or social contexts that models this for us. Our social norms tend toward polarization, blame, or litigation, rather than a nuanced ability to hold complexity and encourage accountability, mending, and justice.

Centered accountability can hold complexity—both be accountable and know what is *not* our responsibility, while staying connected and in relationship.

Often we will lean toward being under- and over-accountable, as a reaction to a much deeper sense of shame and worthlessness. When we feel a deep sense of being "bad" or ashamed, we can be over-accountable for things that have nothing to do with our actions, and simultaneously be under-accountable for things that are in our purview. Both over- and under-accountability tend to happen quickly and automatically, just like a conditioned tendency or safety shaping. These reactions help us to get away from the triggered sense of being bad, caught, blamed, or our shame revealed.

In this phase of the healing shame process, we want to explore, through conversation and practice, under-, over-, and centered accountability.

What is over-accountability? Over-accountability is taking on blame, responsibility, and fault automatically. It is taking this on for people and situations that we may have wanted to be able to affect (or want to now), yet did not or do not have the power to do so. An example of this is a young child trying to stop domestic violence in their own household, or a child wanting to protect their siblings from physical or sexual abuse, while being a child themselves. This sense of over-accountability and helplessness can last for many years and inform many survival strategies. These impossible situations and the helplessness that they experience are often what we are working with through the process of healing shame.

Other examples of over-accountability are internalizing the narratives of oppression and blame perpetuated by power-over conditions. These can show up as: not being the "right" kind of immigrant, not "making it" financially when you have worked hard for the American Dream, being too Black, being not Black enough, wishing "your people" would "act right," not being the "right" gender, needing to be "more" able-bodied, and more. This oppression gets internalized and felt as shame.

Over-accountability as a reaction can also show up as a generalized shame for positions of systemic privilege. This shame does not mobilize connection and action; rather it moves toward polarization, proving, blaming, defending, or an immobilizing guilt. This type of over-accountability can show up as being ashamed of and embarrassed about your entire class (wealthy, US, or other First World nation), or race (white), or gender (cis-male), etc. It is essential that those of us with systemic privilege are engaged in changing ourselves, our people, and in social justice. This is much more effective from a centered accountability than from an automatic over- or under-accountability. These automatic reactions ask us to work with our own healing, so that we can engage centered accountability in our work for justice and liberation.

What is under-accountability? Under-accountability is avoidance of, dodging, deflecting, and/or denying of accountability. This too is an automatic reaction when driven from shame, often happening more quickly than we are aware of in the moment. Later we may feel ashamed, guilty, or see our part, yet not take action to be accountable. Instead, we may again hide our sense of shame and "move on." We are under-accountable when we avoid affecting things within our spheres of influence, or don't face mistakes and impacts we have had with good intent and responsibility.

Under-accountability can show up for the same reasons we react with over-accountability. It may also be intensified if the traumas included overt blaming and shaming, being degraded or humiliated. Power-over conditions can focus these kinds of blame on groups of people. These same systems can train more privileged groups into under-accountability and being unaware of their roles in harm and oppression, or seeking comfort from that information, rather than engaging it for change.

Let me say a few things about codependency, since it is a word that gets thrown around a lot in our daily speak. Codependence can be both over- and under-accountable. Taking responsibility for circumstances or an addiction that is not our own can be reactive over-accountability. Not having boundaries, or doing self-healing work, or facing one's own fears and trauma can be the under-accountability of codependence. I find that the mainstream solutions to codependence are often overly individualistic, and can exclude our interdependence. This does not mean we should self-sacrifice (over-accountability), but it also does not mean individualism and only taking care of "our side of the street" are the solution (under-accountability). Centered accountability can make grounded assessments of people and situations, know ourselves, and look to how we can affect—or not—for the better.

Let's explore how over- and under-accountability live in the soma. Let's do this somatically. When was a recent time you reacted from either under- or over-accountability? Place yourself back there. What was happening in your muscles? Your breath? Were you leaning forward or back? What was happening emotionally? How were you or weren't you connected with yourself? With another? We want to get to know this state or this shape. When we react from over- or under-accountability, we are in a pressured or stressed state. We are often in our conditioned tendencies or even safety shaping. We want to get to know how we do that, and how that shapes us.

A somatic practice you can use is something we call "walk in/walk out." This is a simple practice of causing pressure. With a partner, face each other with five to six feet between you. One partner stays in place and the other moves toward them. Come slightly closer than is comfortable to the person who is in place. Hang out there for the count of fifteen. You do not necessarily have to look at each other the whole time. Mostly, notice what happens somatically, and how you organize yourself under pressure. Notice what happens when they then back up. Do this three times, noticing how you organize under pressure. Then, you can add content related to the situation in which you were over- or under-accountable. Before the partner approaches, give them a line to say aloud. It could be as simple as saying your name, or "I need to talk to you," or "That didn't work." Whatever is relevant to your situation. Again, learn what happens in you under this particular kind of pressure.

As we do with conditioned tendencies and safety shaping, we first get to know the shape/state and *how* we do that somatically. Then we want to explore what the automatic reaction may be trying to take care of. What is it trying to either protect or keep us from feeling or knowing? What is it costing us? We can look to the processes in regenerating safety to further address what is needed here.

Centered accountability is what we want to develop through the healing shame process, and continue to deepen and practice throughout our lives. Centered accountability can hold complexity, both be accountable and know what is *not* our responsibility, and stay connected and in relationship. No small thing. These embodied skills can make a decisive difference in intimate, community, and organizational relationships and dynamics.

How do we practice centered accountability? First, we prepare ourselves for it by addressing the other aspects of the healing shame process, particularly blending. The other components of healing through the Arc are relevant here too: having strong declarations, resilience and regenerating safety, and somatic opening. We can then use somatic practices to learn centered accountability, and evolve this as a choice, even under pressure. As an example, let's take the walk in/walk out practice again. In the first round you got to know your automatic reaction under pressure. This is the baseline so that you can notice when you may be tweaked or what we call "grabbed." This time, center yourself (see practice in chapter 7), speak your declaration to yourself, then have your partner move toward you. Instead of just staying in place, step toward your partner. Do this in a centered way, as if to engage the conversation out of your declaration, connected to yourself and to them. We call this entering. Repeat. When you are ready, have your partner add content. This type of holistic practice helps our nervous systems, muscles, and emotions learn new moves.

Our assessments and our listening to and engagement with others are very different from a centered state. I think getting good at centered accountability is a lifelong practice.

Perhaps the most complex question in the section is—what is within our scope of accountability? In some ways, knowing the truth of interdependence, we could say that as adults, everything is within our scope of accountability. We are accountable for the health of the living systems on the planet, each other, and all life. This orientation can throw many of us into a reaction of over- or under-accountability, from the sheer size of it.

If we can orient to this concept from a place of centered account-ability, we can hang in with the complexity. We can find our particular role that helps to serve the whole. We can help build collective power toward sustainability and justice. We can deepen our centered account-ability through getting feedback and growing our social and political consciousness. We can be a part of a local or national social or environ-mental justice organization and join collective action.

One of the things we can do as an ongoing practice of centered accountability is welcome questions and discomfort. This is the kind of discomfort that allows us to learn, to not know, to risk, and to change. Being able to be with discomfort, to have space within ourselves for sensations and aliveness that are somewhat disrupting while also stay-ing connected to ourselves, allows us to be in centered accountability.

A genuine apology focuses on the feelings of the other rather than on how the one who is apologizing is going to benefit in the end. It seeks to acknowledge full responsibility for an act, and does not use self-serving language to justify the behavior of the person asking for-giveness. A sincere apology does not seek to erase what was done. No amount of words can undo past wrongs. Nothing can ever reverse injustices committed against others. But an apology pronounced in the context of horrible acts has the potential for transformation. It clears or "settles" the air in order to begin reconstructing the broken connections between two human beings.

(PUMLA GOBODO-MADIKIZELA, *A Human Being Died That Night: A South African Story of Forgiveness*)

Cultivating Self-Forgiveness and Forgiveness

Are we forgivable? That's a big question. Are you forgivable? Are others?

Many of us have been shaped by institutionalized religious interpretations of forgiveness. Many of these interpretations ask victims to forgive those who have offended, with little or no accountability or reparations from them for the harm caused. "Forgive and forget" may have the intention of easing a victim's pain, but it is often used to allow people, leaders, or the state doing harm to continue unchallenged. This makes forgiveness complicated to unpack and use for healing, transformation, and justice.

Another way to understand forgiveness is as an offering—the opportunity to be in right relationship again. It is an opening to transform relationship, rather than harboring hate, vengeance, or resentment over time. Harboring these, while understandable, becomes their own set of contractions or wounds to sustain. The kind of forgiveness that is an opportunity to be in right relationship again can be cultivated toward ourselves and others. An opportunity to come into right relationship means there is change and action toward accountability on the part of the person, people, or state systems that have done harm. It opens the possibility of a new relationship and of mutual dignity that is nourished. Forgiveness should feel both freeing and empowering. In this way, forgiveness is not used to deny, but to open and transform.

Let's start with self-forgiveness. I often find this more difficult for people than forgiving others. Our shame, trauma, internalized oppression, and mistakes conspire to create much more self-loathing than self-acceptance. Self-forgiveness is an act and a practice. This practice helps us soften with ourselves, heal what is under the "trampoline," and get out of automatic reaction. Cultivating self-forgiveness helps us to cultivate centered accountability and self-acceptance, too.

> If you haven't forgiven yourself something, how can you forgive others?
>
> (DOLORES HUERTA)

A practice we can use is the "Even If" practice. This can be done with a practitioner or practice partner, or with yourself and a piece of paper. Let's start with the paper. Here write, one line at a time, the things you somatically believe are your fault (usually these are the things we continually feel shame about). Remember, much of what we are ashamed of is not actually our "fault." Yet, the beliefs run deep and need to be tended to. This is not easy, yet in this way we can directly cultivate self-forgiveness connected to what we are ashamed about.

Then, with your practitioner or practice partner, go line by line: "Even if ... (fill in with content from your sheet), I am forgivable." Your practitioner or practice partner can then say it as well: "Even if ... (use the content just shared), you are forgivable." This is again a practice we somatically track in ourselves or with clients. We want to attend to the reactions and responses in the soma, and follow them in the process. Some people have a reaction of disbelief the first few rounds, with a piece of content. Then it might move to sadness or anger. We want to work with this until the self-forgiveness feels somatically viable.

Here are a few actual examples from people I have worked with over time:

- Even if ... I lied, I am forgivable.
- Even if ... I betrayed my (friend/partner/family), I am forgivable.
- Even if ... I didn't fight back, I am forgivable.
- Even if ... I tried to be loved by them, I am forgivable.
- Even if ... I could not save my sister, I am forgivable.
- Even if ... I denied who I am, I am forgivable.

- Even if … I didn't tell anyone, I am forgivable.
- Even if … I turned away from my community, I am forgivable.

If you want to ritualize this and practice on your own, you can create a space where you attend to this daily. Choose a container or bowl and a special space. Again, write one aspect of shame on a piece of paper, fold it, and place it in the bowl. Keep going until your list is complete. Then, daily, center yourself, pull your one slip of paper, and practice "Even if …, I am forgivable" with whatever is on that paper. Do this for ninety days, every day choosing a piece of paper. If you feel complete with one of them, you can place it open, under the bowl. I think you'll be amazed with how much shifts and opens when we purposefully cultivate self-forgiveness as a focused practice.

Self-forgiveness opens more room for right action. When we are less burdened by shame, we can see situations more clearly, make assessments based on what we and others care about, consider the conditions we are in, and take right action. When something we are ashamed about was our responsibility, we can look to the best ways to mend the harm, and practice centered accountability.

Let's now explore forgiving others. Forgiving others—intimates, family, community, the horrors of history, etc.—is a complex conversation. How do we support transformation, forgiveness, and accountability? In which situations? When does this give us more personal and collective peace or empower us? When does this bring healing and more choices? When does it move toward denial or justification? These are vital pieces to consider as we contemplate forgiving.

I hold forgiveness as a very personal choice, and one to explore throughout one's healing process. An automatic or instantaneous forgiving early in healing is usually a glossing-over of the impact of the trauma or pain. Holding resentment or a desire for revenge over time also has a cost to us, however. That too lives in our somas. I see that we can heal deep wounds, open ourselves to love, life, and commitment without forgiving the harmful actions, violence, and oppressive forces. It is a question of how we hold them internally and with others.

*At one point in my own healing process, I was grappling with my father's com-
mitted denial of and unwillingness to face his sexual abuse of me and other
girls. I saw that if I closed my heart off to him, I was closing my heart off to
others as well. I could not close off a special compartment just for him, although
that would have been helpful. Rather, I decided an open heart was better than a
closed one, for my life. That required feeling a bunch of hurt, grief, and rage as
I sorted through how to work with my hurt and his ongoing unaccountability.
While I extended my hand to righting our relationship many times, he never
took it. This was mine to then heal, too. There is a long story between then
and now, including transformative justice attempts and a focus on both healing
and accountability. What was vital to me, alongside my own mending, was to
assure he not hurt anyone else. I would not say that I have forgiven him, because
in me this lines up too closely with denial. Rather, I would say my heart is clear
about him, I can hold what was beautiful and terrible about him, and I wish
him no harm. If he were ever to approach me with accountability, I would be
open to that conversation. To me, this leaves me freer.*

I am committed to a transformative justice approach to accountability and healing. I see that most people who do harm, also have the
capacity for transformation in the right context. That context is particular. I speak to this more in the final chapter, on the connections
between personal and systemic transformation.

I hold the practice of forgiveness of self and others, and centered
accountability as lifelong practices. I see they cultivate compassion,
dignity, and courage. These seem relevant and necessary in our world.

Skills of Interdependence

Experiences of trauma and oppression break apart safety, connection,
and dignity, leaving these needs at odds with one another, leaving us
more compartmentalized and separate from each other. The healing
work of regenerating safety, cultivating resilience, somatic opening,

and healing shame allows for these core needs to reconnect and begin to operate in support of one another. This gives us the ground for mutual connection, more capacity to navigate contradictions, and the ability to work with conflict as generative. To me, these are the embodied skills that let us build close and trusting relationships, grow intimacy, and coordinate skillfully with each other toward larger visions for change and justice.

These capacities also allow us to continue navigating social and economic conditions that separate us, privileging some over others and harming some more than others. Because of these conditions and our commitment to change them, I think we need these skills even more.

Mutual Connection

Mutual connection allows us to hold the cares, concerns, and needs of others, as well as our own. It is an embodied capacity to widen our circle of care, without disappearing ourselves. We can deepen our practice of empathy and interdependence while being self-responsive. Mutual connection allows us to hold complexity without going into reaction, and needing to make another bad or ourselves bad. This means holding our own complexity as well as that of others. This embodied ability is something most of us need either to learn or more deeply cultivate.

One way that many of us default in connection is by popping out of ourselves and leaving our own boundaries, commitments, and needs behind, so as to negotiate relationship with others. Both experiences of trauma and oppression can train us into this. This was a strategy that at some point took care of, or even now takes care of, safety, belonging, or dignity. But once this strategy becomes embodied and generalized, it leaves us few options for mutual connection because we are not fully included.

Experiences that can have us develop this as an adaptive strategy are: needing to track one's environment for ongoing danger; needing to track a particular person and their emotional state; intimate violence or child abuse where connection had some chance of decreasing violence; situations of ongoing sexism, racism, and homophobia; state violence or surveillance; and more.

Somatically, this safety shaping can look like a leaning forward, attending to, and in ways merging with others while not being able to feel ourselves deeply. Often this means being very sensitive to others, but not responsive to oneself. It can also look like shrinking ourselves somatically, pulling in and not taking up space. This means keeping our boundaries inside of our own skin, rather than extended outside of ourselves, making some space to move and choose in. This safety shaping allows others to define the dynamic and environment, rather than doing that mutually.

Another embodied pattern for connection is the opposite—not being able to really feel and authenticate others. This can also come from fear and hurt, and can be shaped by privilege. Sometimes blocking others out, hardening ourselves, and not feeling others was the best strategy. This too can be safety shaping that gets embodied and generalized—meaning we can't not do it. Experiences that can create this shaping are parenting or schooling that is degrading, invasive, or isolating, social training (class, gender, race, nationality) that overindividualizes, makes one "better," or gives pressure to "know," be "right," or be the decider. Trauma or social norms that shame one's sensitivity, or degrade their ability to feel others, can also have us shut down that capacity.

Mutual connection in its simplest (this does not mean easy) form is being able to feel ourselves (our sensations, boundaries, emotions, commitments) while feeling and being curious about another's experience at the same time. Can you feel your own back while you are interacting with others? Can you feel your center and know what you care about, while being curious about and sensing another? Can you consent—say yes, no, or maybe based on your own needs, commitment, and boundaries—while dignifying the other person's needs, commitment, and boundaries as well? Can you hear and respond to yes, no, and maybe, act accordingly, and stay with yourself? These practices, grounded in our own sensations and sensing others', are the somatic capacity of mutual connection.

Lastly, vulnerability and authenticity go a long way toward building mutual connection. Again, this does not inherently mean agreeing; rather it means including and being with. In a practice we do, we ask questions like: "What do you care about?" "Who matters to you?" "What are you made for?" while doing two things. One, we practice staying connected to ourselves (sensations) and sensing the other. Two is that we let the "body" answer the question, rather than the thinking, which tends to be more authentic. Our thinking tends toward more automatic answers, or what we think we "should" answer.

Here are some things we can practice for mutual connection:

- Feel your own back while talking with others.

- Move your attention back and forth between your own cares, concerns, needs, and boundaries, and another's. Include both of you, even if it's complex.

- Increase your ability to feel your own aliveness and sensation, even when it's more than you are used to.

- Increase your curiosity by placing your attention on others, asking more questions, and authentically wondering about another. Feel yourself as you do this.

- Feel your own sensations while touching others. When touching hands or hugging—feel for them, their temperatures, textures, and pressures, and feel you—be in your own center or back. And, notice yourself being touched.

- Make centered requests, offers, and boundaries, while also feeling and attending to others having them too. This does not mean it all works out all of the time, but it does mean we are attending.

- Practice overtly consenting, and ask others for their consent. This can be across a number of situations, not just sexual intimacy.

- Expand your tolerance of complexity—not just as an idea, but that you can be present with more complexity and keep connected to yourself somatically. We can increase our ability to feel and be with our discomfort, and a wider range of emotions.

- Practice being self-responsive. We need to be inside our own skin and to feel, to be self-responsive. Examples include: go to the bathroom when you need to, rather than waiting. Notice when you are hungry or not, and respond. Notice when you have a request or boundary, and practice making it.

- Grant yourself and others permission to take up space, if they do not usually. This is a practice of expanding, likely being uncomfortable, yet expanding somatically.

In groups, practicing mutual connection is more complex because there are just more people. There are more needs, boundaries, cares, and concerns to attend to while also including ourselves. Groups need similar embodied skills and practices to thrive. Groups can practice and get good at mutual connection, making requests and offers, and having boundaries that take care of the individual, the group, and the broader purpose. A team or group can also practice being present with each other, bring their cares and concerns, and be curious about others'. It is easy for people in groups to either dismiss their own needs for the organization's or group's, or to default to forgetting the group's purpose to focus on their own needs alone. Neither of these is sustainable or ends up being successful long-term. Mutual connection allows us to widen our circle of connection.

Contradictions

We live amidst many contradictions. We internally have many contradictions. Because contradictions are inherently complex, we often need to grow our capacity to recognize them and navigate them skillfully, instead of from reaction, to make choices.

In doing systems change work, organizers and strategists look to the inherent contradictions in economic and social conditions as key places of change. These contradictions—like increasing poverty and a shrinking middle class while the elite are getting wealthier—are places where these systems can be consciously pressured to change and new systems forwarded.

In healing work, relationships, and group dynamics, we also address contradictions, but in a different way. Here, contradictions are the pressures where more than one contradictory thing is true or felt. These pressures often produce an impulse to polarize, position, and separate. Most of the time, this is not useful within meaningful relationships, in trauma healing, or a group that is trying to accomplish something purposeful together. Instead, we can leverage contradictions for transformation and growth.

Here are some examples of contradictions:

Many of us also love some of the people who hurt us. This can be true in family violence, intimate violence, and community violence. The contradiction can be that we are enraged at, or even hate, someone and love them at the same time. In a close relationship where there has also been harm or betrayal, this is normal. Love, hate, wanting to get away and stay close, can all happen at the same time.

Under the pressure of these kinds of contradictions, we can try to choose one or the other—to shut down our love of them or to deny our hurt and anger, to leave and block them out, or to stay and let harm go unaddressed or be minimized. Polarizing, positioning, or choosing *one or the other* tends to not work. It does not address the whole of what we are experiencing, the complexity of dynamics, and leaves us with fewer choices.

There are also pressures and conflict in groups when working for change. Someone within the group may harm another or act in ways that are not aligned with the group's values, and also be a contributing member to the group. They have done harm and benefited the group. How do we deal with this skillfully in a way that can advance transformation?

A group was working toward transformative justice around community violence within a working class community. The community was organizing to forward alternatives to the police and the ongoing incarceration of their community. A robbery with physical violence occurred and the community began to split about calling the police. In this polarization, the nuanced assessment of safety, accountability, and organizing for alternatives began to get lost amidst people's hurt and fear.

Contradictions of these sorts ask us to hold more complexity without polarizing, get wider instead of positioning, while also keeping boundaries, openness to change, and compassion intact. How do we do this? This takes somatic capacity and the ability to navigate contradictions.

In working with contradictions somatically, we are learning to make space for all the aspects of the contradiction, rather than polarizing. This allows us to make more grounded assessments of a situation and conditions, align with our vision and values as much as possible, and make strategic choices—all while keeping sight of relationship and not throwing each other, or ourselves, away.

One practice we can use involves naming the contradiction and assigning each "side." The people representing one side are given the themes, words, and mood of that part of the contradiction. The other side is given themes, words, and mood that correspond to the other aspects of the contradiction. Those dealing with the contradiction stand in the middle. Both sides start talking from their position at the same time, just like a contradiction. Neither side of a contradiction, whether inside of us or external, tends to wait its turn.

In this practice those grappling with the contradiction first let themselves be impacted by it, and feel their own reaction or protective response. Maybe they shrink inside of all that pressure and what seems unsolvable. Maybe they have the impulse to choose a side in reaction. The goal of this first round is to let ourselves get to know our reactions to the contradiction.

Next, we center ourselves somatically, and connect to our broader purpose and commitments. This could be your individual commitment to healing or leadership, or a group's broader social change commitment. This time, when the sides start in their positions, those in the center both let themselves be touched by it (we are not trying to become unaffected) and recenter somatically. They practice internally, somatically, getting wider and expanding to be able to hold both sides of the contradiction. As the contradiction goes on, the practice is to center, connect to the broader purpose, and get wide enough to be "bigger than" the contradiction and either/or.

Through this practice we learn both our reactions to the pressures of contradictions and what is possible when we expand and include, while being connected to ourselves and our purpose somatically. Over and over again, I have seen people find new interpretations and choices, heal where it did not seem possible, and, in some cases, resolve the contradiction. Somatically, it is possible to find a third way.

A client was working to heal from intimate partner violence, but he still needed to interact with his ex because of sharing children. Through working somatically, he could hold the harm, violation, and hurt his ex-partner had caused, while also acknowledging that his ex was a contribution to the kids' lives. The children's safety and well-being were naturally central in this process. His ex-partner had been very accountable about the well-being of the children, yet was only now beginning to be responsible for his violations to my client. Through working with contradictions, this client was able to hold the pain and the love, and assess the changes in his ex-partner based in current time. This helped him make more grounded choices about himself and the children, and their time with their other dad.

Conflict as Generative

What is generative conflict? Conflict is inevitable. If we are taking risks, loving deeply, and working for change, we need to plan on conflict. What we do with it makes all the difference. Generative conflict is conflict that leaves us more connected, learning, and positively changed on the other side. It is conflict that can deepen trust rather than rupture relationship.

As a reminder, we talk about trust as intention + competency + reliability. Often in conflict, one of these is missing or ruptured in some way. The impacts of trauma often have us feel more protective or brittle in conflict, roll over inside of it, or try to avoid it altogether. None of these lets us engage conflict as generative. We need to do our own healing, our own change work, to be able to show up for a different kind of conflict.

The benefits of knowing how to do this, and how to practice it, are innumerable. I think of the many relationship rifts that can be prevented and the many movement splits and polarizations that can be shifted to more connection and more collective power. There is a great amount of learning we can garner. It looks worth it to me to get good at generative conflict.

There is not a step-by-step how-to, but there are embodied skills we can develop that help us grow this capacity. Many of them have been explored in this chapter and this book. Here are some highlights.

To practice conflict as generative:

- Have a declaration that is bigger than the conflict. This can include a value for having conflict be generative, or the vision of an organization, or for social justice. You can define yours. Keep it close and keep recentering on it.

- Have an awareness and analysis of systemic power and its relevance in the conflict. Our social conditions are always with us.

- Know your trauma reactions and survival shaping—these will likely get elicited in conflict that matters. Your healing and development work with these will decrease your reactivity in conflict.

- Notice that others will likely be captured by their safety strategies too. Look for the concern behind the reaction. It is trying to take care of something.

- Be emotionally and politically accountable, not rigid. This means use all of your emotional and relational skills, even if someone else isn't using theirs. Keep your political analysis close by, stay connected to your values, and don't get rigid in a position. Don't make the other "wrong." It is nearly always more nuanced.

- The more you have worked with healing shame, centered accountability, and self-forgiveness, the easier generative conflict gets.

- Practice curiosity and listening for what is behind the behavior or the position someone has taken. Listen behind your own as well. Share this as much as you can: "What I am trying to take care of is...." Or, "I am afraid of...."

- Make assessments based on actions and context. If someone's words and actions don't line up, note their actions over time. This tells us what's embodied and what we can likely count on.

- Embodied skills like requests and offers, boundaries, blending, knowing how to recenter when you get triggered, making and receiving assessments, mutual connection—these are all important to use during conflict.

- The ability to tolerate the sensations and feelings of complexity, in yourself and others, is key. We can keep growing into this through practice.

- Pay attention to the collective soma during the conflict ... what's too much, what's too little? What underlying concern is not being spoken or is being fought for but not acknowledged? Conflict will have tension—and we want to watch for too much, and too little, for the group's soma. We want to stay with dynamic tension that can lead toward growth, learning, and change. Different groups have different capacities for tension. Different people have different capacities for tension. Attune toward not too much and not too little for the collective soma.

Generative conflict does not mean it will always work out. It does not mean we won't have any more conflict. We may choose to change a relationship, or ask someone to leave a group or organization, even when conflict has been generative.

It does mean that *how* we do conflict creates more possibility, and does not create more damage. Generative conflict tends to leave relationships with respect, albeit differences, rather than people feeling trashed, shamed, or discarded. Conflict as generative can radically deepen a group's commitment and clarity. It can strengthen the bond and longevity of a partnership or friendship. It can help us all practice more centered accountability. It can cultivate more wisdom. Generative conflict leaves us in better shape and more trusting for the next conflict.

RJ MACCANI, parent, lead teacher for generative somatics, staff at Common Justice, co-founder of the Challenging Male Supremacy Project, and leadership team for generationFIVE.

I find it nearly impossible to imagine what sex would mean to me had the abuse not happened. I was six when a much older boy at my babysitter's house, one of her son's friends, first pulled me behind the couch and rubbed himself against me—arousing himself and causing me to be aroused. It felt like he kept me back there forever, hidden from the other kids busy watching TV or wrestling on the nicotine-stained carpet. It was the first, and by far the mildest, of the many times he found a way to get me alone and sexually abuse me. I didn't have language then to understand what was happening. He told me to keep it a secret. He told me that if anyone found out, they would think we were gay—I knew that was supposed to be bad. One time his friend, the babysitter's son, found him on top of me. He made fun of us, and nothing else happened. I don't think he told his mother and, either way, no one came to make it stop. The abuse continued until I found the words to tell him to stop, and was able to avoid his advances. My babysitter died soon after, and I never went back to that house.

After that I became interested in sex and masturbation in a way that seemed well ahead of most other kids my age. Something like innocence was still present in me, but amidst the sweetness and excitement of kissing games, note-passing, and puppy love crushes I felt a gnawing sense of something being off, that something was wrong with me. I went to a new school in seventh grade and remember meeting a girl in homeroom who seemed as fast as me. She was flirting, and I was freaked out. Maybe she had been abused like me, I thought. And if she was then she could probably see in me what I thought I saw in her—what I didn't want anyone else at school to see. I figured we were probably both messed up, and so I made sure to keep my distance.

As I became more sexually active in my late teens and early twenties, I became promiscuous to a fault. I hooked up with almost anyone that wanted to, regardless of whether she was a near stranger, a good friend, my good friend's ex, or my supervisor. I damaged or completely lost friendships and ruined important working relationships. There were times I was pushy, cajoling a friend or girlfriend into having sex when I should have gone slower or stopped altogether. I was causing harm.

Though I was navigating an inner sense of turmoil, and increasingly distraught over lost relationships and the harm I was causing, there was little in mainstream American society that suggested to me as a young white man that I should stop acting this way. But it was also during this period that I became politically active. Involvement in my high school's gay-straight alliance, solidarity actions with the Afrikan Student Union and striking sanitation workers on my university's campus, the global justice movement, and struggles against police violence in my hometown all connected me to other ways of seeing the world and social relations. I began to engage and identify with feminist and womanist critiques of patriarchy and white supremacy. While this was clarifying in many ways, I began to feel a sort of triple shame: the abuse I've experienced makes me dirty, I am bad because I've done abusive things, I am wrong because I reproduce systems of oppression. I numbed myself with wine and weed. I began to relate to my own sexuality more critically but still felt haunted by the sense that I wasn't completely in control. I didn't know how to transform the underlying dynamics that might continue to wreak havoc in my own and others' (personal and political) lives.

My healing began when the work I was doing with prison abolitionists and women of color feminists led me to generationFIVE, an organization seeking to address child sexual abuse from a transformative justice perspective that was leveraging somatics to support this mission. Until then I had not made the link between my political commitments and my own life experiences of abuse. I began sharing with family and friends that I had been sexually abused as a child. I felt relief and anger in connecting with other survivors. I wasn't so dirty and different ... but why the fuck were there so many of us? Breaking our isolation together, we used digital stories and theater to engage wider publics in our conversations. In smaller circles I also began discussing ways my own behavior had been harmful or abusive. This felt even more difficult than coming out as a survivor.

Generative somatics courses facilitated deeper healing and transformation. Through practices such as bodywork, blending with shame, and emotional/political autobiography, I experienced the release of long-held contractions in my system that were locking me into patterns of thought and action that were incongruent with my chosen values. I began to touch into and feel the emotions my shame was protecting me from—helplessness and rage about the abuse I'd experienced, deep grief about the harm I had caused. I was able to let these emotions be expressed, and to reveal and experience these parts of myself in connection with other people. In the early years, I would often still get drunk or high in the evenings during the courses. Over time, though, I no longer needed or wanted to do so. I felt safer in my own skin, more comfortable with a wide range of emotions, and confident that I could keep good boundaries with those around me.

And I don't feel shame anymore about the ways I was abused. I do still feel guilt and some shame for the harm I have caused, though I don't feel trapped by these feelings. If anything, they provide a felt ground that informs my own sense of right and wrong. There were many factors—first experiencing sex as a power relation, learning white male entitlement, or being reactive in my own shame—any one of which alone may have been enough to lead me to engage in messy, unprincipled, and sometimes abusive sexual behavior, and yet none of them are excuses. I can come to understand these root causes, even find a way to forgive myself for falling prey to them, and still follow through on a transformation process that means I never again take such harmful actions and that I attempt to make things as right as possible.

Rather than hide from my own past, or from others who are hurting or have hurt like me, I found myself continuing to move toward greater integration and connection. In 2008, I began to proactively support women in my social networks who were challenging the sexual assault they'd experienced. Later that year I joined with a couple other men to form the Challenging Male Supremacy Project, a volunteer collective collaborating with feminist, queer, and trans justice groups working to end gender-based violence, build transformative justice, and contribute to broader social movements. A large part of our work involved engaging other men in individual and group processes of accountability and transformation. I draw so much resilience from working with others to foster healing and disrupt patterns of violence.

In 2014, on my thirty-fifth birthday, I participated in the closing day of the School of Embodied Leadership. I declared myself a commitment to family and transformative justice. I finally felt brave enough to dedicate myself to a positive future, and to braiding together two challenging and lifelong paths. I practiced fighting for this commitment in our closing *randori* practice, in which a dozen of my comrades held striking pads and cheered while I elbowed, kicked, and screamed for what I most deeply long for and care about. And then I held pads and cheered for each of them. I've rarely felt more alive, connected, and clear than in that circle. That feeling moves within me to this day, alongside everything else.

XOCHITL BERVERA, queer Latina organizer, lawyer, movement builder, and teacher/trainer, founder, and director of the Racial Justice Action Center, and teacher for generative somatics.

At the Racial Justice Action Center, we have two grassroots organizing projects. Women on the Rise centers formerly incarcerated women, while Solutions Not Punishment is a Black trans–led collaborative. Both are focused on ending criminalization, divesting from our criminal legal system, and building power in marginalized communities. In every meeting, there is always a lot of experience with arrest and incarceration in the room, as well as experiences of having been cast out of families, jobs, homes, and communities.

Shame is a powerful, shaping force in the work we do. Part of the "work" of our current criminal legal system is to systematically and persistently shame the people who have been caught up in that system. This systematic strategy of shaming people is part of what we are fighting against. Standing up to shame and fear is a critical part of our organizing.

When I was a young organizer in New Orleans, I experienced the smallest taste of how that system can create shame inside of us. I was arrested and spent just one night in the Orleans Parish Prison. Some friends and I had been leaving a bar when we saw the police beating a man. They had him down on the ground and were kicking him. An officer pulled out a Taser and Tased him repeatedly. I had recently graduated from law school and was young and full of naïve beliefs about my "right" to observe. Before I could say anything, the cops grabbed me, spun me around, handcuffed me, and threw me into the back of the patrol car. They said a lot of things, but what I remember most was how they were laughing at me.

Inside the jail, I remember two specific moments. The first was right after I was fingerprinted. They sent over the one LatinX deputy, who implied he was an immigration official. He lowered his voice, spoke to me in Spanish, and tried to convince me that I should just "tell the truth" and admit that my license and documents were fake. As an organizer, a politicized Latina who clearly knows there is nothing wrong with my being an immigrant of whatever status, I was amazed at how ashamed this made me feel. I was being accused of being something he clearly thought was shameful—and accused of being a liar and a fraud on top of that.

The second moment I remember was during the discharge process. The woman at the discharge station lay down a piece of paper for me to sign, after which I would be let go. But I, again, being young and an organizer, wanted to read the piece of paper. When she tried to hurry me, I said, "Hang on, I have a right to read what I'm signing." The woman slammed her hand down on the paper, pulled it away, and said to the deputies, "Take her back." It was another six hours before I was called back to her again, at which time I, of course, signed the paper with no questions or comments, eyes lowered, having "learned my lesson."

I spent the next two days in bed. What I remember most was not feeling righteous anger at the system, or indignant, scared, or sad. All of those feelings would have made sense. But instead what I felt was a deep disgust, a self-loathing, a blaming of myself for what I perceived as being naïve, stupid, and weak. I blamed myself for getting into that situation, blamed myself for how much such a "small incident" impacted me.

When I finally made it back into my office, my coworkers applauded. They were proud that I'd stood up to the cops, tried to stop a man from being beat. They wanted to hear about it, called me "brave." I was shocked. My shame was so deep that being celebrated was the last thing I imagined—or could tolerate.

Shame, I realize now, was a reaction to being in a place where it was undeniable that I had very little power—and people had tremendous power over me. Instead of letting myself feel the depth of that powerlessness, I responded as if the demeaning treatment was an accurate reflection of who I was, that I deserved it—I must have done something to make someone treat me like that. At that moment, some part of my psyche preferred to blame myself because at least then I kept a sense of agency, a sense of power. That felt better than to acknowledge just how totally powerless and scared I was inside that jail. That insight came years later through somatics—that one of the functions shame often serves is to keep you from the more overwhelming feelings of terror and powerlessness.

Many of our members and leaders at Women on the Rise and Solutions Not Punishment have had way more experience in the dehumanizing spaces of prisons and jails. They've served ten, fifteen, twenty years. One of our new organizers, who was inside for ten years, said at our last meeting, "When I first got out I thought, oh I'm just not going to tell anybody [that I was incarcerated]. I'll explain the gap in my resume and I'm going to start over. But then I found Women on the Rise, and I realized I can tell my whole story—and that has freed me." This is how organizing works. In her words, "If I can tell my story without shame, then hopefully I open the door for other people who think that they have to hide. We have this incredible strength from incarceration. We've overcome a great deal to be here. How do we move forward based on that idea of ourselves?"

It's part of the American cult of individualism to think that we can heal ourselves, that we can figure it out ourselves. What I see over and over again is that it is the sharing—the practice of interdependence and connection—that can break open the very protected isolation of shame.

That's why it's so important to have storytelling in our organizing, so there are times and places of possibility to move out of shame. It won't happen every time. We all have rote stories. We often use stories to hide. But to do storytelling in a different way opens up the possibility. Sometimes somebody opens up and shares something vulnerable and it invites the rest of the group to do so. Shame puts layers over itself so that it won't be seen. Once it's out there and seen and responded to, its power is greatly diminished. Healing becomes possible.

Then we have power together as a group.

One example of this was when one of our Solutions Not Punishment organizers, Juan, was pulled over by the police and his gender marker didn't match what he was perceived as by the cops. We got the tapes afterwards so we could hear what they called him. They called him "a thing," and joked around with each other, "What are we going to do with it?" They threatened him with a genital search and finally arrested him.

After we got him released, he wanted to organize around what had happened. He shared that he'd been arrested so many times before, spent time in jail, and never felt like he could stand up and fight back. But with the larger community that we had built, he felt he could make some different moves. He made these powerful videos where he called on all of our allies and friends and said, "Come." He said, "I am not a thing or an it. I am trans. I am proud. I won't let them take my dignity. I and my people and community deserve better."

We organized a march to the police station to demand an apology and policy changes from the police department. When we were setting up the action, we had him, as the primary organizer, practice where he wanted to stand, who he wanted on either side of him, who he wanted behind him, and if he wanted anyone in front of him when we went into the police department. We went to the station in an eight-person configuration. Outside, other people held the banner and chanted for two hours while we negotiated. It was an ally practice in action and it was beautiful. By the end of the day, the mayor and the police chief had both issued a formal and public apology and pledged to make changes. Then they went on to adopt the strongest standard operating procedures in the country for interactions with trans and gender-nonconforming people.

That was standing up to shame. That was organizing at its best.

12

Arc Circle Five—
Embodying Change

*Embodying a new shape requires us to come to
terms with the understanding that the practices
that got us here may not be the ones that will take
us forward. It requires us to consider ... what are
the practices that will not only allow us to celebrate
this new shape, but to embody it?*

—RICHARD STROZZI-HECKLER,
personal interview with the author

Embodying New Practices and Sustainability

Throughout the embodied transformation process we are taking on
new somatic practices that serve each phase. We begin to get more
present and connected to sensations, emotions, and the aliveness in
our somas in Circle One, while we explore what we care about and
long for. Here, we make declarations. In Circle Two, we get to know
our embodied conditioned tendencies and safety shaping, as well as
new practices around resilience, centered boundaries, and requests. In
Circle Three, somatic opening, we purposefully deconstruct what no

longer works, allow deeper healing, and expand our capacity to feel a wider range of sensations and emotions. New practices can root deeply when we do somatic opening work and then attend to healing shame, centered accountability, and cultivating forgiveness in Circle Four. This also lets us deepen mutual connection, be more resourced in working with contradictions, and practice generative conflict. Each phase engages somatic practices to help us heal, transform, and be able to take new actions, have new conversations, and build trust.

Somatic awareness, somatic opening, and somatic practices, held within broader conditions, are relevant to each phase of the Arc of

Somatic Transformation

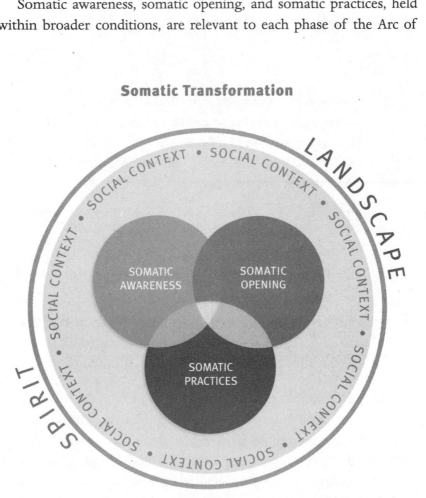

generative somatics | Diagram designs: Querido Galdo, www.queridomundo.com

Transformation. Each phase asks us to develop our sensing, to shift somatically through opening, and to engage in practice to build relevant skills.

We've arrived at Circle Five on the Arc of Transformation, embodying new practices and sustainability. Here, our embodied practices begin to be more and more aligned with our declarations and vision for the future. Here, the healing and changes we have worked hard for, we have risked for, and we have been willing to feel deeply for, become sustainable. We say we have transformed when our new practices align with our declarations and desired changes, even under the same old pressures. I like to say they are aligned at least 85% of the time, because living and our social conditions are complex. We make mistakes, we are taking new risks, and we have bigger visions—we need some learning room. In this circle, well-being, happiness, grounded trust, and bold action become more familiar, even within the current social and economic conditions, and even as we are taking collective action for social change. We become more whole as people. We are becoming this "new shape."

What Embodied Competencies
Serve Our Transformation?

Throughout the change process, and again in this phase, we ask this question: what embodied competencies serve our declarations and our transformation? What ways of being, what ways of relating, and what actions serve our life and our work? Here is the place to focus on deepening those embodied practices and helping our somas generalize them. In this phase, we can consciously deepen these practices and attend any further somatic opening that this requires of us. I think of this as the time to practice a range of options, so we are not stuck with one type of boundary, one way to connect, or one response under pressure. We develop a range of actions, choices, and ways of being so we can respond rather than react. We can keep our declarations and values close, and forward these. We can contribute powerfully to the groups we are a part of.

First, we return to purposeful practice. To review, the five parts of a somatic practice are below. You can also review the more thorough version in chapter 9, on Regenerating Safety.

- **Purpose.** For the sake of what do we want to learn a new embodied skill? What serves our declarations ... a centered boundary or consent based in present time?

- **Practice that is felt and embodied.** The practice is not solely a new idea or something to ponder. The practice needs to be body-based, include the sensations and emotions, and be connected to the above purpose.

- **Repetition.** We change through embodying new practices over time. Think not five repetitions, but 300 and 3,000 times. Practice is about repetition over time, embodied and felt within a broader purpose. Plan on practicing daily.

- **New actions and results.** The new practices will show in your life, in how you live, act, choose, and relate.

- **External support and feedback.** It is hard to see our own embodiment. It is important to have trusted feedback from others who are committed to your transformation.

From a somatic understanding, we are always practicing something. It is either a default practice or one we have chosen to forward our transformation and well-being. Is what you're practicing aligned with what you are committed to? With your values and visions?

New skills are developed somatically so that they become more than good ideas—they become natural actions and habits. We want to not only know about boundaries, but be able to take the action of having boundaries in the course of our days, relationships, healing, and social justice work. We don't want to leave centered accountability as a good theory, but rather embody it and be able to act from this place under pressure.

We can now explore which practices we want to deepen. Given many of our community and family experiences, and because of oppressive conditions, there are fundamental skills that many of us don't learn to embody, such as: having boundaries that take care of ourselves and others, mutual connection and intimacy, moving toward what is important to us, and building trust amidst conflict, among others. Other survival skills become embodied, like hypervigilance and distrust, appeasing, and aggression. Many of these will have loosened and changed by this phase. Now we want to deepen the new practices.

Some of the embodied skills that many of us need to learn or relearn are below. What do you want to embody more thoroughly?

Presence and Embodiment: *Being able to feel and engage with a wide range of sensations and emotions.*

- Ask: Why feel? How can it benefit me and others if I were more present? What is possible if I allow more feeling? Why is it worth facing what stirs me or makes me feel uncomfortable?

- Center in length, width, and depth, and in what is meaningful to you. Length: dignity for you and others. Width: connection and belonging (I, you, we). Depth: history and ancestors, deep longing, meaning, and calling. Center in your declaration and what most matters to you.

- Embodied meditation practice.

- Bring your attention to your sensations as a regular practice. Learn from the information they bring.

- Widen your capacity for emotions, from awe and happiness to anger, sadness, and fear. Practice being with your own emotions and those of others.

- The more we can be with our sensations, the more we can be with our emotions without fixating on the stories and experiences that go with them.

- Somatic bodywork.

- Other practices for those who have trained in the work: center in action, centered transition (two-step).

Generativity: *Taking action and risk, creating, and envisioning possibility based on chosen values.*

- Ask: What do I care about, want, long for? What do we care about and long for? If I/we were to set a direction toward a vision, what would it be? This can be personal, interpersonal, or social.
- Ask for and give positive assessments and feedback.
- Commitment practice: tell other people what is important to you, your vision, and longing. Ask what they care about.
- Resilience practices.
- Make centered requests and offers toward your declaration and others' declarations.
- Other practices for those who have trained in the work: blend and lead, extension, collective extension, centered grab, somatic request, and offer practices, jo "take the center line" and overhead strike/extension.

Setting Limits: *Embodied boundaries with others and self, including "no," insisting, and discipline.*

- Ask: Where do I need to say no? What/whom do I need to say no to, in order to be able to say yes to something more important? Can I be with someone saying no to me? Can I negotiate? Is there anyplace I need to insist or quit? Is there a place I want/need to be disciplined?
- Centered "no" practices.
- Ask for and give useful negative assessments and feedback based on your declaration or another's declaration.
- Other practices for those who have trained in the work: intimate declines, push-away practice, insist and quit, grab-center-face, jo insist and decline.

Mutual Connection: *Presence with self and others simultaneously, felt sense of belonging, intimacy, community. Consent—yes, no, and maybe.*

- Ask: Can I feel my own and another's needs/desires/wants and not disappear or invalidate either one of us? Where do I want to feel more intimate and connected? Do I want to build a deeper sense of belonging or support others in doing so?

- Practice mutual connection. Feel yourself and sensations while also feeling and noticing others.

- Stand next to one or more people and widen your feeling sense to include them. Stay connected to yourself as well.

- Blending practice.

- Consent practice.

- Other practices for those who have trained in the work: coordination (partner two-step), hand on heart/chest, blend, embodied consent—yes/no/maybe practice, rowing, partner jo kata, the five notes in the chord of CFEEB—center, face, extend, enter, blend.

Impacting and Leading: *Influencing, choosing, intending, and taking action based on chosen values.*

- Ask: Given what I care about or am committed to in my life or community, where do I need to know how to influence change? Where would I like more choice and/or to be a part of direction setting? Where do I need to take action toward my vision?

- Make requests; offer vision or proposals.

- Offer feedback to move forward your vision and those of others.

- Engage your declarations and conditions of satisfaction. Take action toward them.

- Ally practice.

- Other practices for those who have trained in the work: extension and partner extension practices, blend and lead, pads, requests, offers, hand on heart/chest, extension rowing, offer somatic assessments, 31 jo kata.

Centered Surrender: *Trust of self, other, land, and Spirit. Being influenced from center. Letting go while keeping your center.*

- Ask: Where might it be potent for me to let go? What difference would it make if I could viscerally trust more? What/whom would I trust to surrender into? What might that give me that I don't have now?
- Practice being trustworthy: intention + competency + reliability.
- Practice extending trust to others.
- Open palms: Center and open palms (thumbs out) to your sides so that the chest opens. Breathe and feel.
- With whomever you hug or hold, let yourself be hugged or held (receive somatically).
- Resilience practices.
- Somatic bodywork.
- Other practices for those who have trained in the work: blend and be led, jo surrender practice, somatic bodywork with disorganizing pattern.

Compassion and Love: *Giving and receiving; permeability; appreciation, with self, others, and the world. Pleasure.*

- Ask: Why is it worth loving open-heartedly, when pain will at some point be a part of it? Why is it worth letting others' love in? Why is it worth letting others feel my love? How do love and compassion make a difference in my life and others' lives? My community?
- Offer your authentic and grounded appreciations to others.
- Invite and take in real and grounded appreciations from others.
- Somatic bodywork.
- Resilience practices.

- Notice daily what is beautiful to you in your world. Feel the sensations of that.

- Notice and look for pleasure. When you are feeling pleasure, let yourself linger with it, and feel it 5% more.

- Other practices for those who have trained in the work: permeability; somatic bodywork on chest, upper back, and legs with "Ahh" breath pattern; blend and welcoming; blend with jo; giving and receiving love practice.

Unknown and Contradiction: *Being with death, change, contradictions, and unanswered questions.*

- Ask: Where are the contradictions in my life and community? How can it benefit me and others to welcome and be with them rather than denying them or rushing to solve them? Which of these contradictions are resolvable and which may not be? What are the unanswered questions for me? What might I gain by leaving them unanswered for now?

- Contradiction practice.

- Embodied meditation practice. Allow yourself to feel "contradictory" sensations, or make space for unanswered questions.

- Practice being with your own and others' more intense emotions instead of trying to change, contain, or fix them. Feel your own sensations as you do this.

- Other practices for those who have trained in the work: collective contradiction practice, ally practice, collective 1–31 jo kata, somatic bodywork belly and pelvis.

Centered Accountability: *Being responsive to self, others, and wider community. Able to differentiate intention from impact. Apologize, repair, and forgive.*

- Ask: Where do I need to be accountable? Where might I be over- or under-accountable out of trauma, oppression, or privilege?

Are there people and situations in which I need to apologize and repair? Ask for an apology? Can I forgive when it is appropriate?

- Ask for and give assessments such as: How am I doing? Is there any way I am acting that I need feedback on, or gets in the way of my declarations or our relationship?

- Learn. Do ongoing education and politicization about collective and systemic forces.

- Join. Join an organization that is taking collective action for social and/or environmental justice.

- Shame healing blend practice.

- Self-forgiveness practice.

- Practice apologizing from center (not shame or blame).

- Allow others' apologies in from center.

- Other practices for those who have trained in the work: grab and grab-center-face with over-accountability, under-accountability, and centered accountability. Shame healing blend.

Well-Being and the Other Shoe

I have noticed with most people, at this phase of healing, that there is a need to practice and become familiar with well-being or happiness, of being touched by the world but not taken over by it. Does this make sense? Often at this phase people say things like, "I am not used to being happy. When is the other shoe going to drop?" Or, "I am doing well … I mean shit is happening, but I am good. Is this okay?" Or, "I feel more powerful, happy, and on it, but also calm. That's weird."

There are many ways to describe what is happening here. One way to understand this is that your healing is outweighing your wounding. Or that your inherent resilience and dignity are getting reconnected with safety and belonging. It can be understood that your survival shaping has shifted and your present-day, more resourced self is more embodied. When our embodiment changes, so do our identity and how we know ourselves.

Mostly this oddness is upon you because you have been diligent in your healing, committed to your transformation, and connected with others in the process. You have changed. You have grown. You have more embodied capacity to generate safety, belonging, and dignity, and make those aspects work together.

In this transition it can feel strange to not be hyperalert most of the time. It can "not seem like you" to extend trust or let go of something easily. You may have newfound curiosities that you find draw your passion, and you are wondering about yourself. This is all good. If well-being is unfamiliar, let it be unfamiliar and keep getting used to it. If trusting feels strange, same thing—keep exploring it and let yourself get to know it. If mutual connection, or giving and receiving love is happening, and you feel unsettled, let it teach you. If you find yourself having centered boundaries, and then feel guilty automatically, let yourself have centered boundaries and practice appreciating that you know how to do that now.

There is not another shoe that's about to drop. And, there are many metaphoric shoes dropping in our world every day. But the feeling of staying alert because it might be coming is what's changing. You can let it change. We are more aware and skillful when we are relaxed and present. We are more powerful and connected when we have many options for responding.

Knowing Our Conditioned Tendencies

This phase of embodied transformation is also a place to cultivate some acceptance for our conditioned tendencies. Our conditioned tendencies and safety shaping have gotten a lot of attention through regenerating safety, somatic opening, and healing shame. Much will have changed. We can continue to get to know our CTs and shaping, especially those that get stirred up under pressure. In knowing them and how they operate in our sensations as tension or numbness, as our automatic moods and interpretations, we can be more at choice and less reactive out of historical shaping.

In getting to know this shaping at a new level, we can more deeply appreciate what it was trying to take care of and how many years we practiced it. As we have new moves and practices, we can find more compassion for the ways we needed to survive or navigate. Because there is less charge, hurt, and history held in the soma at this phase of healing, we can work with the **habit** of the conditioned tendencies. Not all of our conditioned tendencies go away; some of them do, and some of them become part of our ongoing growth and path. We want to be aware of, responsive to, and accountable for them.

Ongoing and Dynamic

On the Arc of Transformation you'll also see that from new shape there's an arrow back to current shape. Once we have embodied change, it then becomes our current shape. The good news is that we can continue to grow, evolve, and change throughout our lifetimes. What is happening in our lives and the context of our lives also change. The conditions in which we are living also change and are dynamic. As we grow, as we have new commitments and new phases of life, new things are called for from us. We can continue to move through the Arc intentionally.

Change is ongoing and dynamic in our organizations and movements as well. Even very successful organizations or alliances have phases organizationally. Different phases call for different types of leadership, systems, and engagement. In our broader visions for equity and sustainability we need different types of practices and organization for dismantling exploitative systems, for building scalable alternatives, and for governing through deep democracy.

We can hold this continuous change as good news, and have the practices and embodied processes to engage the change.

Somatics and Trauma Healing
Process in Review

Healing is powerful, difficult, and liberating. We avoid pain for a reason. We avoid trauma because it's devastating. We are drawn toward our agency and being more whole, because it is deeply known in us. I think our somas want healing and yearn for interdependence. We transform to have more access to our lives, to our love, to our power.

Here is a review of the healing process through the Arc of Transformation.

- **Choose and commit to heal and transform.** This is a time to explore what we want to heal and what it is going to take. How do we want to feel more whole, more alive, more agency? While it takes commitment and courage, we can bring our whole self— our emotions, sensations, mind and body, our relationships—into the healing. This is a good moment to find support, allies in your healing, and engage with others.

- **Find your soma, discover your declarations.** We start with beginning to identify with our somas again, to live into ourselves again. This means beginning to welcome sensations, emotions, aliveness, and practice. We discover our declarations. What is important; what do you/we long for? We learn to declare and to ground it in what becomes both felt and tangible. We begin to practice.

- **Resilience and regenerating safety.** We rebuild an internal ability to generate safety, boundaries, and consent, and begin to feel the difference between this and survival reactions. We take on practices, blend with the safety shaping, and learn allying. Purposefully bringing in resilience as something that is inherent in us nourishes our healing, and helps us be more resourced in our lives and conditions.

- **Opening—completing the trauma through the body.** Trauma and our survival shaping get stored in us. It is like there are stories in our muscles and numbness holding our histories of hurt. During somatic opening we feel our wounding, our painful emotions, and let them move through us to help heal. We let the reaction we could not have, be had, so as to mend. We may feel deep grief and then relief, anger and then more power, ashamed and then self-compassion and forgiveness. During opening, we decompartmentalize, becoming more whole.

- **Healing shame, mutual connection, and conflict as generative.** "You didn't get hurt alone; you can't heal alone." We need community, support, and connection to help us heal. We learn to let people and love in, that there is nothing wrong with us. We learn deeply that oppression and being hurt are not our fault. We also learn to practice centered accountability, self-forgiveness, and generative conflict. We get better at loving and being loved. We get better at working with contradictions.

- **New embodied skills, practicing wellness, taking collective action for change.** Trauma and oppression leave us knowing how to do some things and not others. Maybe we know how to take care of others and not ourselves; maybe we know how to only feel anger and not our sadness or self-compassion. Now we can learn and embody the skills we need to live, love, and lead well. We can join or continue to join others in transforming the social and economic conditions that harm; and build those that support equity, cooperation, sustainability, and the sacredness of all life.

Healing is for ourselves and for others. Sometimes we start healing through collective action. Sometimes healing leads us to collective action. This interdependence of healing and social action, of loving internally and externally, is affirming of life. Yours and ours.

Part 4

Healing and Social Change:
We Are in It Together

13

Personal and Systemic Transformation

The kind of change we are after is cellular as well as institutional, is personal and intimate, is collective as well as cultural. We are making love synonymous with justice.

—PRENTIS HEMPHILL

Healing trauma, making ourselves more whole again, and changing society and the economy are distinct yet interdependent processes. They can work powerfully for and toward each other, or they can be at odds.

I think many of us in this generation of social justice and healing are asking the question of how personal and systemic transformation can powerfully serve one another. How can we best reveal the need for each, in coordination with the other, toward the world we desire? This is not a new inquiry, or even a new integration; it's just new for our moment and context. I think many of us are exploring and experimenting with how personal and systemic transformation can become not only integrated and co-serving, but inseparable. How both can be fully engaged, each energizing the other, each making the other more effective.

I believe we need to engage both personal and systemic transformation, for the liberatory future we imagine and need.

Let's look at the processes of systemic change first.

Social Change Takes Structural Change

Social change is not just a change of many individual attitudes. In some ways, that may be the easiest part of social change. Many people's attitudes about racism or climate change have shifted, even in the last decade, but the systems driving white supremacy and climate destruction have not. In fact, they have intensified within the United States under the current administration.

Social change means transforming the economic and governing structures we live and operate within. It means transforming from a power-over worldview, to a power-with paradigm—one that assumes interdependence and equity with all life. It means that economy shifts radically from exploiting the earth's biosphere and the majority of people, to one based in equity and a renewable and interdependent relationship with the living systems that allow for life—ours included. At this point, if we don't, we are facing dire consequences within the next 75–150 years.

> Just Transition is a framework for a fair shift to an economy that is ecologically sustainable, equitable and just for all its members. After centuries of global plunder, the profit-driven, growth-dependent, industrial economy is severely undermining the life support systems of the planet. An economy based on extracting from a finite system faster than the capacity of the system to regenerate will eventually come to an end—either through collapse or through our intentional re-organization. Transition is inevitable. Justice is not.
>
> (MOVEMENT GENERATION, *From Banks and Tanks to Cooperation and Caring: A Strategic Framework for a Just Transition*)

Systemic change focuses on shifting power—the ability to define and decide on reality and resources—from being concentrated with the few most privileged, to those most affected by the power-over system and to the collective. Systemic change works to radically change the economics of global capital—where it comes from and whom it goes to. Systemic change transforms the systems that promote an amassing economy and power-over conditions like mass incarceration and for-profit prisons, food systems based on monocropping and chemicals, into a just and restorative economic system. This is no small task. But, it's necessary for life on the planet to continue and thrive.

The means to change systems are varied and unique. History shows that it takes community-based organizing and mass movements to create systemic change. In mass movements, millions of people are engaged in changing the worldview, the governing structures, and the economy. It takes campaigns to change policy and governing structures. It takes all of these to change who governs and how we govern. Systems change requires disrupting the status quo and building alternatives.

Those who have been doing this work for decades are our best guides. People have devoted their lives to becoming excellent organizers, community leaders, political educators, and social change strategists. They are thinking locally, nationally, and internationally. For those of us who have not spent the majority of our time doing this, or built our competence, we can join and support those who have.

Some of the things organizers are focused on doing are:

- Mobilizing and organizing people in their communities or workplaces

- Developing and implementing local and national strategy

- Building and running campaigns to change policy, resources, and practice

- Affecting electoral politics—running candidates, influencing who governs

- Policy change, and implementation and enforcement

- Building alternatives: food, transportation, local economies, restorative and transformative justice

- Political education

- New worldviews and communications, changing hearts and minds

- Preparing communities and leaders to govern

- Organizing dissent and resistance to oppressive policies, violence, and conditions

Our current social and economic conditions shape millions of people into the power-over worldview, practices, and embodied survival strategies. Even if many, many individuals grow and change, that does not directly translate into a change in the economy or governing structures or the military. Nor does it translate into a radical mainstream shift of worldview from individualism, amassing wealth, disconnection from the planet, or supremacy. Malls are being built, forests cut down, and success is being defined by capital, even as mindfulness spreads in the West.

Structural change alters the systems in which we live so that millions of people can be shaped by equity, interdependence with the biosphere, and cooperation. Humans have a wide range of potential—from incredibly empathetic, cooperative, and creative to demeaning, awful, and violent. What gets cultivated in us has a lot to do with the social and economic conditions we reside within. To me it's more social than personal.

What are we moving and organizing toward? Many brilliant people are exploring this question and working on both disrupting the status quo and building the new.

- From global capitalism based on concentrating wealth and exploiting resources and people, to local and sustainable economies and fair labor.

- Collective ownership of the commons: water, air, lands, etc.

- Changing the cultural narrative and paradigm from power-over to power-with, including the safety, belonging, and dignity of all peoples. The narrative shifts from accumulation and exploitation, to sustaining and interdependence, and from suffering as virtuous to happiness as virtuous.

- Collective practices aligned with cooperation, democratic processes.

- Generative conflict, empathy, wisdom, and collective well-being.

- Right-sizing humans in relationship to the earth's regenerative natural systems.

- Self-governance.

- Healing and addressing historical traumas, reparations.

- Transforming ourselves from the impact and embodiment of power-over conditions, violence, intimate violence, and other harms.

- Using restorative and transformative justice to address harm, safety, and accountability.

- And more....

Again, Movement Generation has done a beautiful job at articulating a shift in conditions; they call it a change from an Extractive Economy to a Regenerative Economy. You can find their framework at https://movementgeneration.org/justtransition.

It's Possible

Systems change can be confusing for many, and overwhelming for most. I think the ahistorical and individualistic nature of US culture is part of this confusion. We are generally taught to be forward-looking, and not to pay attention to the broad patterns of history—even as we are deeply affected by these patterns. These patterns tell us about small groups of people concentrating power and wealth, of how enemies are built and wars justified, and how patriotism is redefined depending on the power elite of the decade. History, if we look, also tells us about why white supremacy is such a powerful ongoing struggle in this country, why patriarchy is still the norm, and why we think ownership of the commons—land, air, and water, is even possible. History helps us understand our moment, and see a different future.

Individualism, in connection with this, tends to keep our attention on our own—either that I'm taking care of my own and the "other" is not my responsibility, or I made it (or didn't) because of my own singular efforts and others should do the same. This keeps our attention on our own lives and maybe those near to us by family or community or region. This is the ungrounded myth of "pulling ourselves up by our bootstraps" with hard work alone.

Capitalism, tied to individualism and a lack of history, also makes systems change confusing. Buy it, own it, and accumulate become the signs of success, and even the offered markers of safety, belonging, and dignity. Of course, accumulation has little to do with any of these. Having access to good housing, healthy food, health care, education, meaningful work, and community has lots to do with them, however, as do equity and clean water. Capitalism has us put our attention and time into accumulating, being successful, and "safe" in those terms, and meanwhile undermining our real security—the health of the planet, meaningful community, and knowing how to have generative conflict and interdependence with each other and the rest of life.

Finally, when I talk with people who generally have shared values, care about others and the planet, systems change can still seem overwhelming and feel so big. I get it. It is. I hear many people say something like "I care, I vote, I try to buy (organic, local, fair trade, etc.), I recycle … I don't know what else to do." We can think of voting every two or four years as being our only way to affect policy, governing, or the economy. Or we can assume that changing our own individual attitudes is what we can do. These are both important, but not enough to change systems. I hear others say, "Why get involved at all? It doesn't make a difference." This too is understandable, especially if one's experience shows them that. However, people organizing in their communities, regions, states, and countries has such a long proven history of success in creating change.

I think mostly we have not been taught what to do to be a part of systemic change. Finding the road there is not always easy, but it's possible. Here are some ways:

- Join organizations and alliances that are focused on equity, changing the economy, and environmental justice. Most of these organizations use organizing and base building as a main means toward equity and sustainability. "Join" means go to meetings, volunteer your time, bring your resources, money, and otherwise, to serve the purpose of the organization, and more.

- Continue to educate yourself about our conditions and how we are and can change them toward equity and sustainability. You can do this through self-study, political education, and joining groups doing the same. You can learn, deepen understanding of your own social location, and how you show up well and most powerfully for change.

- How deeply can you get your life, money, resources, and time aligned with the values of equity and environmental justice? If you have more than you need, ask yourself the question, how much do you really need? What do others need? What does the future need? Have this conversation with someone who does social change work. And, act accordingly.

- In the places where you live and work, join others to shift and equalize power: who decides and who has and controls resources? How can your organization serve equity and environmental justice? You can organize with others to change policy and practice. Assess, is your organization working toward something else, instead? If so, what does it consider success? Who benefits and who pays?

- Support and help build alternatives. This can be alternative local food systems, this can be restorative and transformative justice, this can be renewable energy and non–fossil fuel–based transportation, etc.

- Lastly, you can participate in dissent. This can be online, in the streets, in your neighborhood, and more. Let yourself be counted based on what you value, based on the community and world that works for the whole, not the few.

None of this is that easy or comfortable, because of the conditions we live in. This can feel like swimming upstream and in some ways, it is, when we are changing systems. Yet, our actions, where we place our love, time, and resources, are what we help build. For ourselves, for others, and for the future. What do you want to help build?

Sites of Shaping/Sites of Change: Transformation. In chapter 2, and throughout the book, we have explored how we are shaped at each and every Site—from the personal to the institutional and historical. We are shaped by, hurt and/or privileged by, and somatically adapt to power-over social conditions through the Sites. This is embodied in us even when we don't agree with the values or structures of these systems.

The great news is that we can also shape and affect these Sites toward what's more life-affirming, toward change. Below are examples of ways we can work to transform at various Sites. As we discussed, the larger the Site, the more people it impacts and the more people it takes to change the systems and norms of that Site. The change is then sustained by new systems, by a shift in worldview, and by new collective practices.

Each Site requires a different means to change. One means of change cannot be easily imported to another. I have heard therapists say, "If everyone just did their healing work, the world would be different." But this doesn't map over like that. The systems operating at the scale of global economy or a two-party democracy don't change just by individuals changing. I have also heard social change organizers dismiss healing as "soft skills" and unnecessary, saying if we can just change oppressive policies and/or shift who's in power, people's lives will change. While I appreciate this view, I also think it is not a one-to-one match. Trauma, sexual assault, and the impact of intergenerational oppression need particular attention and healing.

The means of change, as well as the skills and experiences needed to create change, at each Site are different. The scale of operation at each Site is different. Creating purposeful change at the various Sites can, however, complement one another, if done within a broader vision and purpose for the change, and with a shared understanding of power. Transformation and trauma healing for individuals and families can support and serve institutional change and vice versa. They can make each other stronger, and more lasting.

Individual: We can heal traumas, we can become more powerful and loving, we can choose more than we react, with purposeful, intentional healing and practice. How do we change and grow as people? Biologists, acupuncturists, psychologists, and medicine people would all have different answers to this. Somatics sees that we, as people, can change through intentional transformative work and embodied practice, over time. Most often, this is guided and supported by someone with more experience and competency in the areas we are committed to transforming or healing.

Family and Intimate Networks: As we discussed in chapter 2, to change family culture and practice, to change intergenerational family trauma, we can engage family systems therapy, ceremony, new facilitated conversations and/or new collective somatic practices. Bringing more information and resources into the family system is usually a part of these processes. Healing intergenerational wounds; finding new ways of addressing conflict, accountability, apologies, and amends can have a huge impact on an intimate network and family system, culture, and practices.

Community: Community usually changes purposefully through community organizing. The aims of the organizing are defined by the community, and those people (and lands) most impacted by power-over systems. This is important because the perspective and experiences from this position are unique, and usually bring with them a broader view. Community organizing might shift local policies and practices, may increase resources and access to good food, education, art, and outdoor space. It may organize and educate a community toward equity and environmental sustainability. Communities can also practice alternative local economic alternatives and transformative justice. Bringing more information and resources into the community is usually a part of these processes.

Institutions: We change institutions purposefully through organizing, campaigns, movement building, communications (changing hearts and minds), building alternatives to scale, dissent, and more. These then affect electoral politics, governing and financial institutions, and academia (what gets held as history, reality, researched, and studied). The fundamental economic, governing, energy, and business systems need to be shifted to equity and environmental sustainability to create power-with conditions.

Social Norms and Historical Forces: Social norms are shifted as institutions are. Historical forces are ours to learn from and then address their collective shaping. Specific processes like reparations can address historical traumas and current systems of oppression.

Landscape and Spirit: Again, in this model, we hold that landscape and Spirit mostly shape us. Of course, we impact land and other elements deeply. The changes at the other Sites help us shift how we are treating and relating to land, water, air, forests, and more. We can restore land, water, and air by massive cleanup and restoration efforts, and by drastically shifting our use of fossil fuels, toxins, and extraction of minerals, etc.

We want to know the differences in how people, communities, and systems are changed, so that we can work with each effectively. This also helps us to better integrate personal, community, and systemic transformation—and again have these processes serve each other.

Healing trauma, making ourselves more whole, and changing society and the economy are most effective, most transformative, when done interdependently. We need to engage both personal and systemic transformation for the liberatory future we imagine and need.

Healing Can Serve Social Change

As we see, social and economic change takes people, leaders, organizers, cultural workers, strategists, and ... more people. It takes people who are able to coordinate with each other, take courageous action together, and build toward an interdependent vision and purpose. It means we need to be able to invite and tolerate change based in liberatory and life-affirming values. Even when it gets hard. How do we be these people? How can healing serve all of this?

We are shaped by life, by our experiences, both positive and traumatic. Because of our safety strategies and power-over conditions most of us need to heal and transform to be able to live our values. We can heal and transform to be more whole, to hurt less and love more, to gain courage, and to have our values and actions become more and more aligned.

There are many, many things that trauma healing and embodied transformation can bring to our lives and communities, and to serve social and environmental justice.

- Embodied healing helps us become clearer in how we are seeing and assessing ourselves, others, and the situation at hand. It can also help us become clearer at assessing opportunities and challenges within social justice work.

- Healing widens our range of skills, from having clear yet dignifying boundaries, to being able to connect and hold our own and others' needs. These skills serve our relationships and build trust.

- Trauma healing allows us to develop presence, and the ability to be present with a wide range of people, emotions, and situations. We become less reactive, more responsive, and more connected to what we care about. Each of these capacities serves our lives, leadership, and our organizing for systemic change.

- Embodied practice helps us learn to hold and be creative with the inevitable contradictions we face. Contradictions are present in our social justice organizations, in healing and trauma work, within alternative models like transformative justice, and even within our experiments to combine healing and movement building. We need to be able to work with them well, and create possibilities rather than more breakdowns.

- Trauma healing and embodied practice let us engage in generative conflict. This can prevent splitting and group reactivity, and lead instead to more trust, holding more complexity, and leading more effectively together. Through healing we don't throw each other or others away so quickly. Instead, we learn to build each other up.

- Embodied healing can help us learn to be powerful and relevant allies. We can engage the deeper work of unpacking privilege and changing our reactions. We can also learn to "let in" allyship, extending trust instead of skepticism.

- Lastly, trauma healing supports us in being able to love and be loved better. We can mend and be happier, while we are navigating a complex world in which we choose to live and act from our values.

How We Change

Somatics is fascinated with the *HOW*, more than why. *How* are we shaped, how do we cultivate resilience, how do we practice, how do we transform? This makes somatics both pragmatic and deep. Somatics gives us a practical and applicable understanding of *how* we embody what we do, and how we can change.

A politicized somatics invites us to ask different questions: How can we build resilience into our campaigns? How has this community been traumatized, and how has that shaped them? How can our organizing approach be particular to this shaping and support healing? What do we want to practice together to build more connection and coherence? What embodied skills do we need to have our actions better aligned with our stated mission? How can we do conflict well? A deeper understanding of how people heal and transform helps us know how to more effectively engage people in change.

In understanding more about how we are shaped, how we survive, and how we heal, we can more powerfully connect with people. We can become more whole and engaged people and help others do the same. We can engage change that responds to safety, belonging, and dignity, personally and in service of an equitable and ecologically sustainable future for all life.

Challenging and Setting Direction

There are a number of things we need to challenge and change as we look to more deeply connect politicized healing and social change. I want to flag these here. What we do and how we practice over these next years will be defining. Because these fields are not fully institutionalized in the United States, we can have a powerful influence in how embodied healing, somatics, meditation, mindfulness, and other transformative practices can serve systemic change. Will our growing understanding of embodied practice, trauma healing, and neuroplasticity be used to serve equity and sustainability, or be left to individualism, a "mindful" military, and moneymaking? It is up to us and how we organize to shape these fields.

Individualism is a strong pressure within trauma healing, psychotherapy, and other one-on-one healing traditions. Healing, boundaries, self-care, and our measures of transformation can be held for the individual alone. Are you feeling better? Are you in the relationships you want? What matters to you? What boundary do you need to have? These are all important guiding questions, but if we stop there, we are likely to repeat or reinforce power-over conditions and an individualism that does not ultimately serve healing or equity. We can use trauma healing to support individuals while we also acknowledge the conditions in which we are shaped and are healing. We can use healing to support people to be more engaged and active in changing these conditions. This, in turn, can also support their healing.

Most formal training as therapists and healers is depoliticized. Political education, addressing the traumatic impact of oppression and privilege—and its integration into healing, most often has to be sought outside of formal training. This is true for most formal somatic training as well. The vast majority of the research in neuroscience addressing trauma, mindfulness, and resilience is the same, depoliticized and focused primarily on the individual, outside of addressing social conditions. We can actively challenge these spaces to integrate not only a social analysis but also the practice of participating in social change.

We also need to question many self-care approaches that lead us to individualism, classism, and external soothing. Is being self-responsive and caring deeply for ourselves important? Yes, absolutely. Yet, we need to question how self-care gets constructed and for whom, and what we think "self-care" will bring us. Self-care is being commoditized: what can we buy—from candles, to stones, to spa treatments—to soothe ourselves? These things are being used to comfort ourselves from stress, overworking, from hurt and confusion—from the pressures of capitalism and power-over conditions. Middle class to owning class white people are primarily the "target market" for most of these products. The goal of self-care can be represented as an ongoing, unchanging state of calm and "well-being." I don't see that as self-care, or even as possible.

Instead, I see that we are dynamic, that change is constant, and that we can grow to be more alive, more connected, and more present. In healing trauma we can access more steadiness, increased calm, less anxiety, and more peace. Self-care can become a practice of sustainability, healing, and generosity. It can be reflected in our daily practices and practices within our organizations. This is deep internal and collective healing work.

Concepts like transformation, mindfulness, and "embodied" are gaining popularity in the mainstream. Transformative practices are being shaped by capitalism, individualism, racism, and sexism, and, in turn, perpetuating those systems. Without an understanding and integration of social conditions, these practices are mimicking and forwarding power-over systems and worldviews ... even if that's not the intent.

Mindfulness, meditation, and yoga practices in the United States are a good example of many well-meaning people, with authentic desires, who are also shaped by capitalism, white supremacy, and patriarchy. Many of these same people are (inadvertently) perpetuating power-over systems and frameworks through these practices and their organizations. Mindfulness has an app—actually many—as does yoga. The app in and of itself is not the problem; rather the capitalizing—taking the practice out of its path, not sourcing where it comes from, shifting the aim to moneymaking—is the problem.

It is rare to hear a yoga or meditation teacher, teacher training program, or researcher discuss the cultural appropriation within the meditation, mindfulness, and yoga "movements" in the States. These practices have been brought from deeply collective cultures into an individualistic cultural frame. Many things get lost in that translation. Who claims, owns, leads, and makes money off of these is part of the appropriation. These practices are originally part of larger coherent paths of community and spiritual development. This too is often missing from the teaching. Most of the nationally known leaders in mindfulness, meditation, and yoga and the research of these practices are white, male (yoga has more women), straight, and many wealthy. These locations of privilege shape who and what are perceived and who and what go unseen, who defines and who benefits.

It is also uncommon to hear teachers, teacher training programs, or researchers connect meditation, mindfulness, yoga, or embodied practice to ending white supremacy and racism, heterosexism, and transphobia; or to taking action to address social inequities or environmental justice. This seems a natural fit, given the values embedded in most of these practices. As disheartening, most meditation, "transformation," and yoga institutions are not working to address and promote equity within their own organizations. The aim is not solely to "diversify" these organizations and teacher training programs; rather it is to integrate a deep understanding of power-over conditions, and to have transformative path and practice serve to transform these. Many practitioners of color, working class, and queer practitioners have been diligently asking these institutions to widen their understanding and analysis over the last twenty years, but it has been slow going. Thanks to all of you who have been doing, and continue to do, this organizing work.

Lastly, mindfulness, resilience, meditation, and embodiment practices are being used and researched to help ease the stresses of capitalism and the traumas of war. This use of transformative practice is unethical to me, when it is not connected to changing the root cause of the harm. I, of course, want people to suffer less and to access healing. I do not want people to struggle with PTSD; rather I am committed to their transformation. But promoting resilience and meditation while continuing to elevate war and violence, and support the concentration of wealth with a few, is counterproductive and harmful.

I recently attended one of these types of conferences. The yearning I saw in people for practice and meaning was real. But the container for it did not address systemic questions. Capitalism and individual success were the driving force, and those who presented were often the embodiment of that. As an example, Google attended the conference and had a special meeting room. They requested private, Google-only sessions with various national teachers. Those invited gained more status in the overall conference space. The questions for Google were about mindfulness in the very intense tech world, practices for people to be less stressed, etc. Google was not asking about how transformative practice could help change their terrible record on equity, racism, and sexism within their company. The Google sessions were not questioning the concentration of wealth in the tech world, next to the toxins, environmental waste, and unequitable labor practices that help to build that wealth. Nor was the profound gentrifying effect of Google and other large tech companies acknowledged or taken on as a part of transformation.

I want to appreciate and affirm the longing for practice, for depth, and for meaning. And, it cannot be truly had without challenging how these approaches play a part in the continuation of suffering, however well-meaning, and the very separation of personal and systemic transformation. With the increased popularity of transformation and embodiment, it is essential that we as healers, and people who care about change, integrate a social analysis and social action into transformative work. Meditation, mindfulness, yoga, and somatics can serve to powerfully transform us, engage our communities of practice in social change, and be a force for equity and ecological sustainability.

Quality of Practice

Like organizing and movement building, healing and deep personal and interpersonal transformation require their own set of skills. They require mentoring, learning, and practice to do well—to be able to help people make real and sustainable changes in themselves, their lives, and their leadership. Given how important healing trauma and its connection to systems change are, we want to take care of the quality and integrity within this work.

Healing and transformative work asks us to become emotionally competent and hone a sensitivity to what is happening on the surface, as well as deep below the surface within people. It asks us to learn to perceive dynamics in people, teams, families, and group relational systems.

Trauma healing requires that we become deeply familiar with and skilled in the range of emotions and embodied states that are predictable in both survival and healing—from rage and grief to delight and happiness. Safety strategies that come from fight/flight/freeze need to be understood, while new practices like resilience and grounded trust need to be familiar and transferable. Trauma healing and transformational work also asks that we understand and can facilitate a change process that includes the past, the current time, and invests in a different future. Because healing and embodied transformation asks people to be so vulnerable, healers need to have a high standard of skill and accountability. I think we should assure that the risks people take to heal become part of depthful and pragmatic change. This requires us to be rigorous in our work and in our own ongoing practices and learning.

Wherever we train and develop our transformative skills, we can explore the lineage and account for the aspects of appropriation. The living lineage and accountability of this somatic methodology are on the website for this book at www.thepoliticsoftrauma.com. Because of the length of this book and the lineage, we decided that online was a better location. Please check it out. In our places of learning healing and transformation, we can also assure they are holding and integrating an analysis of power-over conditions and social action. We can ask that the teachers and organizations connect social transformation to personal healing. If this is not possible, know that you will need to supplement your training with other organizations providing political education and an organizing framework. And lastly, we can look for learning environments where we can deepen, practice, and get feedback to become skillful and accountable as practitioners.

To Close

I am excited about the many innovations and experiments people are forwarding to interconnect personal, community, and systemic transformation—this being just one. What are the embodied ways of being, leadership, and relating that can best serve equity and sustainability? How can trauma healing and embodied practices help to make our organizing, organizations, and work for systemic change more powerful, more compelling, more connected? How can healing help us transform the impacts of oppression and get to be more whole people and leaders? How can it help us be more accountable for our privilege and show up skillfully for change?

These questions continue to guide me in this work. What questions are guiding you and yours?

I see that when both personal and systemic transformation can be fully engaged, each energizing the other, each can make the other more effective toward the liberatory future we need.

DENISE PERRY, co-founder and director of Black Organizing for Leadership and Dignity (BOLD), longtime organizer and movement elder, and teacher for generative somatics.

I started organizing more than thirty years ago where I learned the craft on the streets of many southern towns guided by mentors who saw something in my determination. The craft of organizing has always been associated with leadership. I would never define myself as a leader but I have grown to understand the correlation of the two. There were many twists and turns to my role as a union organizer and, after ten years, it landed me in South Florida. Shortly after arriving I had agreed to co-found an organization in the historical Black neighborhood of Miami with a former coworker and friend. After eleven years as director, I decided it was time to leave the organization so that it could grow in new directions. While on sabbatical I met a colleague who had been doing somatics and incorporating the work into a few organizations in a way that was intriguing to me. We soon partnered to create BOLD, Black Organizing for Leadership and Dignity. BOLD is a project that was a vision started about nine years ago by two Black directors whose organizations had been doing leadership development work. The discussion that started BOLD was a question about what is the infrastructure needed for Black organizing to thrive in a way that is needed in this moment.

The work of Black organizing is so fundamental to societal change, and in many ways there hasn't been the kind of infrastructure to allow the work to really grow to its greatest potential, since the periods of the Civil Rights Movement or Black Power Movements. We've seen resources decreased not just financially but holistically. By holistic, I mean the ability for us to do this work in the full essence of who we are, the full essence of Black life. Being rooted in such a politicized, capitalist country, oftentimes it's difficult for us to separate what really gives joy or what's really important because we can find ourselves settling for a source of soothing that is outside of ourselves that fills a void.

Then there was and is the State's attack on Black people for speaking out against and critiquing the system and its impact of oppression on Black people. This put a lot of people in fear about doing the work that builds power and facilitates liberation. BOLD's vision is to create the infrastructure for transformative Black organizing, and recenter the requirement to liberate Black people. The liberation of Black people will liberate all oppressed peoples. This is not done by Black people alone but it is done by the leadership of Black people. BOLD is building the leadership of Black organizers.

The current organizing conditions have created silos, competition, tokenism, and transactional functions. BOLD's work is to challenge all of these limiting conditions by creating curriculum, conditions, and experiences that give participants the opportunity to live and practice into new ways of being.

We have created Maroon space. This is a profound political act when you look at the history of Maroonage around the world. BOLD Maroon space affords participants to be who they are, to be in community as their full selves, to learn and teach one another, to try new concepts, to study, to be held well.

Our trainings are taught through three domains: Transformative Organizing, Embodied Leadership, and Political Education. These are fundamental to all organizing and organization building. They sit on a foundation of somatics as a methodology, which allows us to do this work beyond simply thinking. I continue to witness how people are impacted by it. Witnessing the most authentic responses to see others and be seen.

Black community lives so much of our lives in what W.E.B. Du Bois coined as double consciousness. This dual life facilitates insecurity, fears of being too much or not enough, and an overall weariness. The movement is not free from anti-Blackness, which is what we are navigating through double consciousness. What is at stake is our mental and emotional health, the ability to resource our organizations, and State repression.

There are so many beautiful stories of BOLDers' experiences. One participant literally came in with the fatigue of an elderly man. During the course of the sixteen days of training, he shared his life stories that were felt by all of us. His aliveness grew each session and at the end of the program, the old man became a vibrant, joyful person. His opportunity to be seen, for people to listen to his story, for him to be able to shed tears in front of his comrades, to be challenged politically, to see his work from a new paradigm, was enriching to all of us. What he now brings into his work and organization is a new sense of possibility and aliveness that is compelling.

I think what has opened folks' empathy, vulnerability, and curiosity is a process that affords people the opportunity to reveal how we have been shaped to be who we currently are as individuals. This is a model that we have borrowed from generative somatics. The tool is made of concentric circles also known as Sites of Shaping/Sites of Change. The tool helps us step away from assumptions and open a perspective that begins to say, "Oh. This is Miss Mary. She is more than this one moment." Miss Mary now can be understood as shaped by her intimate family, community, society, and we can increase our curiosity about how this shaping impacts how she shows up, what her view of the world is, and how we can connect with her. Once you begin to understand this and do it for yourself, you can't look at another human being and just be like, "Oh, we disagree, so I don't like you." Instead, it increases both curiosity and empathy for your actions or inactions. It allows us to be able to see ourselves more clearly and to accept and appreciate who we are, why we do the things we do. This must be a felt understanding before we can discuss and begin any transformation.

One of my favorite BOLD courses is our Praxis. This is where we take all of the theory and put it into action. We get on a campaign and practice within the high stakes of making a difference. This process increases the pressure; we are no longer talking amongst ourselves about what we think will happen when we employ new organizing skills. We bring ourselves face-to-face with people on the streets, in their homes. At this point the organizing and somatic lessons blend in real time. The further they get into the element of the practice, the better the outcome of their work is. What may first have been a feeling of "I'm just here to deliver something" might get 30% of the people to engage. But when they say, "Oh, I actually need to listen here. I actually am curious about them," they increase engagement to 50%. When they bring their self-awareness into the conversation and increase their physical and emotional connection, that connection moves them to 80% engagement! This now creates an environment of relationship building, where the organizing really begins. We see this in the results of the work over a week's time. The participants' number of contacts increases, the number of folks making commitments increases, and there is an ease and excitement for the work over time. This is not an easy process. The participants work hard, many hours each day, to build this muscle, to do this organizing work they feel called to do.

The BOLD team is committed to the success of each participant; therefore, we practice giving and receiving assessments. Assessments are rooted in supporting people to achieve their commitments and visions. We observe all participants in a variety of situations and provide assessments in service to their transformation. It is not always easy to help folks see themselves.

BOLD's commitment to Black organizing demands that we build conditions that afford folks the opportunity to experience the power of breaking isolation, to be with others who share experiences, fears, hopes, or visions, and connect with vulnerability and empathy. We live in a society that has created conditions that "others" our community. Our commitment to Black organizing demands that we teach the political tools and practices of Transformative Organizing for Black liberation as the antidote to our current conditions.

RAQUEL LAVIÑA, deputy director of National Domestic Workers Alliance (NDWA), longtime organizer, and teacher for generative somatics.

One of my first, most visceral activist memories happened in the 1990s during the first Gulf War. I remember thousands and thousands of people in the streets and a megaphone being shoved in my hand for my first public speech. That moment calling for unity, not just a unity for peace but one borne of stopping the war abroad and at home, made my blood and heart run in a way that connected to everyone else. As powerful as we were, showing up night after night, it didn't stop the war. My takeaway was that you can mobilize a lot of people but if there's not a systematic way for people to build power beyond protest, you can't change systemic issues and form a new vision.

I got into organizing because it brings people together over a long period of time, develops their leadership, and wages campaigns for change. At the same time, I was working at a domestic violence shelter, supporting families in immediate crisis and in a lot of trauma, and they were taking incredible risks to change their lives. I found, as a person who was both an organizer and a service provider, that healing and activism were treated separately from each other. But the separation didn't make sense; people often brought their trauma to activist spaces, and individuals leaving the movement to heal didn't make our organizations stronger, or make our organizing a source of healing. My question became how do you build a movement that can engage hundreds of thousands over a long period of time, that can build power to win systemic changes and transform the people who are making and benefiting from the changes?

That's what led me to seek healing methods connected to social change, and eventually somatics. In 2008, generative somatics, which believed in the enduring tie between social and individual transformation; and Social Justice Leadership, where I worked, which worked with grassroots organizations to advance the analysis, organizing strategy, and personal transformation; began a leadership development program with the National Domestic Workers Alliance (NDWA), where I now work.

NDWA aims to be a home for domestic workers. The history of domestic work as an industry is connected to the history of this country in that domestic work—which is mostly done by women, Black women, women of color, and immigrants—is among the lowest paid work. Domestic work lies at the intersection between patriarchy, capitalist economy, and racism, which creates an industry where the lowest paid workers contribute to the functioning of this country without the proper respect and dignity paid to the workers or the value of their work. With a country whose eldest and youngest make up the majority of the population, those who take care of our homes and families are needed more than ever, making the care industry one of the fastest growing in the entire economy. Domestic workers care for families and homes no matter the working conditions. We say "Domestic Work Makes All Other Work Possible," meaning that workers who are caring for the homes and families enable employers to pursue their careers and jobs.

NDWA imagines an economy that centers care, where all families and homes are well taken care of—both those of the employers and the workers who care for them. NDWA took on the challenge of building power so that the women, women of color, and immigrants who are taking care of homes, and whose work is undervalued, have the ability to shape their own working conditions, either with their employer directly or across the industry; where families are supported to receive care; and where domestic workers can help to shape the broader economy and democracy.

The collaboration between NDWA, generative somatics, and SJL led to a lot of experimentation inspired by the possibility of embodied leadership and working class women really living in a whole, full, felt sense of their own power. And if that was possible, how would that accelerate the kind of power that we want to build as a movement and the vision of a more just future for all people?

The SOL program (Strategy, Organizing and Leadership) had a focus on analysis and organizing strategy—bringing in somatics built upon the tremendous amount of care and resilience that members already had. We really saw change from the first day of our first retreat to the last day of our fourth retreat—the amount of sun that came from the middle of everybody's core was unbelievable. They were taller, like literally physically taller, from the first day to the last day. Their dignity was so much more intact and their access to their brains and their hearts and their bodies was so much higher, you could see it; it showed up in them physically. They would walk into leading our national assembly. They would walk into the senators' offices to advocate for a Bill of Rights. They walked to negotiate with their employers for better wages. They brought that full sun, and it just made a huge difference. You could see it happening live, within one year, for eighty workers at a time.

There's a fact: when you are really practiced in your centering, then your presence can grow and people can feel that, and it inspires the center in them as well, whether or not they're actively doing it. That was happening in the Alliance. You could see that it changed how much access people had to their own dignity simply by being around people who were actively feeling their dignity.

When we're organizing, we want higher wages and access to benefits, the dignity of the worker to be seen, and for the employers and their families to truly be cared for—that kind of organizing unlocks something different than just a reform. It enables us to see whole people, both workers and employers, and make transformative change for a more just economy and democracy. Transformative organizing demands that we think bigger. Sure, everyone wants better employment standards, but we also need dignified workplaces free of the need to deal with sexual harassment. We all need women of color, Black women, immigrant women in office making laws, and taking back the democracy. It's more complicated than other kinds of organizing, but the wholeness makes it worthwhile.

Our training structure usually incorporates four retreats. By the time we get to the third one, there's a lot of storytelling and we work our way up to doing bodywork. Every single time it is one of the most profound moments. This is day sixteen with each other by this time with the same group of women. We pair them up, and they learn how to just be there for each other, through breathing patterns, through talk, through a little bit of touch. We're usually in a big room, and it's like thirty-five pairs of women all in the same room. They're just holding space for each other. You get to see people for the first time getting to say something, let something out, whatever it is. Whether it's a lot of laughter or puking or body shakes, and there's just a welcome for that to happen and no judgment about it. And they just don't get that, ever in their lives, because they're like, "I have to take care of my family. I have to take care of this family I work for. There's so many other things. I'm the rock, so I can't ever truly relax and let go, and just be seen for exactly who I am." They get that in the bodywork session.

Here's a striking example—one of our affiliates in Chicago runs a worker center that's for both day laborers and domestic workers to gather, find fair work, and take collective action. They noticed that the men would do most of the talking and women would be on the sidelines taking care of details, and making sure the center was clean—which felt the total opposite of the value and dignity everyone was committed to. The power they were feeling by being part of a movement and the leadership development they were doing, including the SOL program, sparked their willingness to challenge deeply held gender norms. They started talking about rules for the space where everyone shared in leading and caring for the center. The women stayed centered and united when opening up huge conversations about gender and patriarchy that happened over and over and over again until the men began to train each other in the new norms instead of making the women shoulder that burden. That process of standing in their dignity and being willing to interact—not shunning the men, not walking away, not taking it on and martyring themselves—but saying, "We're going to keep talking with you about if we're building a workers' movement, we have to be equal, we have to fight for each other's dignity, and that starts in our own center."

One of the things that's really important in thinking about building transformative leadership within domestic workers, that translates out to all leadership, is that domestic workers get to see all kinds of life. Especially those in the cities, going from the neighborhoods that are the most poor, traveling into the neighborhoods that are the most rich, 'cause that's where they're working. Every day of life the range of humanity is seen. And then the work that you're doing—no matter how bad your employer is, the act of cleaning their bodies or cleaning their home is super intimate, and so you have to see somebody's humanity no matter what. Even if they're treating you like you're not a human, you have to reserve a part of you that is just like, "I see the dignity of this person, even if they don't see mine."

We think of how the practice of doing that, and then adding this fullness of themselves, means something for the kind of leadership that we want to have in a broader movement. They're not denying the bad treatment that they might get. They're not ignoring the exploitation. They're very able to be clear about the exploitation, and very able to be clear about how everyone deserves humanity. There's something in that that I think is very useful for how we think about how leadership can be transformative leadership.

From that place, the kinds of strategy we can make opens up, the kind of demands we can create opens up, the kind of ways we deal with each other opens up, and how we are as we show up as leaders opens up.

Critical Context

Power-Over:
An Intersectional Analysis

Indians think it is important to remember, while Americans believe it is important to forget. America has amnesia.... Certainly, there is a passion for memory loss in American thought.... Americans may be the world champion forgetters.

—PAULA GUNN ALLEN, "Who Is Your Mother?
The Red Roots of White Feminism"

Americans believe in the reality of "race" as a defined, indubitable feature of the natural world. Racism—the need to ascribe bone-deep features to people and then humiliate, reduce, and destroy them—inevitably follows from this inalterable condition. In this way, racism is rendered as the innocent daughter of Mother Nature, and one is left to deplore the Middle Passage or Trail of Tears the way one deplores an earthquake, a tornado, or any other phenomenon that can be cast as beyond the handiwork of men.

But race is the child of racism, not the father.

—TA-NEHISI COATES, *Between the World and Me*

A s we explored throughout the book, we are deeply shaped by the social and economic conditions in which we are living—they are active shaping forces in our lives, loves, struggles, relationships, aspirations, identities, and choices. They are more than ideas or perspectives; rather, our social conditions inform our conscious and unconscious ways of relating, our practices, and our actions. Conditions shape our neurobiology; they live in our tissues. There is nothing wrong with this. This is how we work. The tricky thing is, however, that even when we do not agree with the norms, they get in anyway.

Take a moment and let yourself notice your automatic and embodied associations with the following words. Feel and perceive the embodied images, senses, and meaning these words evoke automatically in your soma. If you want to, take a piece of paper and write these embodied associations down.

Leader. Maid. Immigrant. Terrorist. Freedom fighter.

Survivor.

Poor. Rich.

Transgender. Woman. Man. Intersex.

Race. Racism.

God. Nature. Earth.

Marriage. Polyamorous. Single.

Colonization. Genocide. Discovery of America. Indigenous peoples.

Lesbian. Gay. Bisexual. Queer.

What value, intention, race, gender, and class did you associate with each of these?

I would guess that most of our automatic and embodied associations with these words are strongly defined by our conditions, and who we are in those conditions. Most of these words have no qualities associated with them—no good or bad, worthy or unworthy. Many have no gender, time, nation, or intent connected to them. Yet, my guess is, we fill these in. We fill these in with the inheritance and training we get from the larger social norms in which we live. We may or may not agree with our own embodied associations. And yet, we may think, react, and relate from them.

Social conditions have everything to do with defining what's real, what's possible, what's seen and felt, and even what's imaginable. They describe to us who and what are valued and cared for as well as who is easy to disappear and demonize. Social conditions are deeply relevant to identifying the root causes of trauma, and thus, to healing from trauma.

This section is an introduction to some of the history and conditions in which we are looking to heal from trauma, and prevent it. This is a high-level look at an intersectional analysis, a starter. Each of the sections below have volumes of research written on them, and are worth digging into much more deeply. There are many books, movies, organizations, and theorists who can deepen our knowledge and help move us into action. The section has definitions and examples of these systems at play. Again, the Resources section on the website www.thepoliticsoftrauma.com will have more on where to continue to learn and get involved.

Let's explore the power-over conditions we are living inside of and an intersectional analysis of these conditions.

Power-Over: The "Land of the Free ..."

We can talk about social and economic conditions in all human societies. For now, I am going to focus on, and give examples primarily from, the United States. It is the context in which I am writing and working, and is a major global player in power-over. This is inseparable from an international context, however. The economy is international, and land and peoples are harmed and exploited internationally to concentrate wealth and decision-making power.

Conditions in the United States are based on a politics and economy of domination, or power-over. The United States is founded on colonization—the forced removal and killing of hundreds of thousands of people and societies who were living in this land for

15,000–50,000 years or more. The core of the US economy and wealth was built on chattel slavery—the forced removal of peoples from their homelands in Africa, Europeans profiting from their sale, and decades of unpaid labor in conditions of poverty and violence. The cotton industry was key to creating US wealth. Lastly, the US economy and society are built on unpaid reproductive labor—the unpaid labor, primarily of women and children, to birth, feed, raise, and sustain other humans and the community. This is also racialized and class dependent.

All of this was done inside of a broad narrative of manifest destiny and dominion over the earth.

Until my sophomore year in high school, I thought that Columbus discovered America. Because I am from Colorado and there are strong indigenous communities there, I also knew that there were peoples here before European settlers. But I did not know how to place all of this together, alongside Thanksgiving. Thankfully, my history teacher had us read Bury My Heart at Wounded Knee *(Brown 1970). I got, for the first time, a clear view of the colonization of the United States and the devastation, as well as the resistance and agency, of the indigenous peoples of this land. I was also devastated. I cried, I asked questions, and it restructured my worldview. On some level, I realized that if this myth of Columbus, the creation myth of the United States, was so partial and skewed, what else that was fundamental was not aligned with life, dignity, truth, or justness? I saw that I had been handed a worldview that may not be grounded or anywhere near true.*

Here is a map of the United States and the many peoples who lived here for thousands of years before colonization, and continue to today. This is from a project led by Aaron Carapella in Broken Arrow, Oklahoma. After years of looking for authentic maps of the Americas he decided, "It's time to make a REAL map of Native America, as WE see it."

The Indian wars have never ended in the Americas.

(LESLIE MARMON SILKO, *Almanac of the Dead*)

In the 19th century, manifest destiny was a widely held belief in the United States that its settlers were destined to expand across North America. There are three basic themes to manifest destiny:

The special virtues of the American (European immigrants) people and their institutions

The mission of the United States to redeem and remake the west in the image of agrarian America

An irresistible destiny to accomplish this essential duty.

> (ROBERT J. MILLER, *Native America, Discovered and Conquered: Thomas Jefferson, Lewis & Clark, and Manifest Destiny*)

John Louis O'Sullivan was an American columnist and editor who used the term "manifest destiny" in 1845 to promote the annexation of Texas and the Oregon Country to the United States. O'Sullivan was an influential political writer and advocate for the Democratic Party at that time. While manifest destiny never had a coherent and articulated philosophy or set of strategies and policies, it was upheld, touted, and then widely felt as a conviction in the morality and value of expansionism and American exceptionalism. Andrew Jackson, the US president from 1829–37, advocated "extending the area of freedom."

We can still hear this as a central narrative in US imperialism today. There is a strong ongoing dissonance between the national narrative of freedom and democracy, and the ongoing institutions of war, oppression, and corporatization.

> Investors, monarchies, and parliamentarians devised methods to control the processes of wealth accumulation and the power that came with it, but the ideology behind gold fever mobilized settlers to cross the Atlantic to an unknown fate. Subjugating entire societies and civilizations, enslaving whole countries, and slaughtering people village by village did not seem too high a price to pay, nor did it appear

inhumane. The systems of colonization were modern and rational, but its ideological basis was madness.

(ROXANNE DUNBAR-ORTIZ, *An Indigenous Peoples' History of the United States*)

Dominion over the earth is a Christian concept from Genesis 1 that has had a huge influence within the building of US culture since settler colonialism. It states: "Let us make humankind ... and let them have dominion.... Be fruitful and multiply, and fill the earth and subdue it; and have dominion over the fish of the sea and over the birds of the air and over every living thing that moves upon the earth" (Genesis 1:26–28). This adopted cultural narrative gives rise to institutions and norms that destroy biodiversity, lack environmental sustainability, and prevent an understanding of humans and nature as profoundly interdependent. Humans are nature.

To infuse this concept of dominion over the earth into mainstream culture, the Catholic Church and the colonization of the Americas worked hand in hand. The Catholic Church fueled the perception of peoples in these lands as "savage" and in need of "saving," underscoring the rights of the colonizers to take, rape, and kill. The majority of "Indian schools" were run by Catholic and Christian organizations. These were used as tools of colonization, destroying indigenous language, culture, and social and family ties. These schools are known to have been places where violence and child sexual abuse were rampant, a large part of that destruction.

Private ownership of land and nature also came with colonization and the Church. The Catholic Church is one of the top three largest landowners in the world, and the only one that is not a nation. Can you begin to see and feel the interdependence of social conditions and trauma? How we need to understand one to heal or change the other?

In the United States and many Western cultures, individualism is held as paramount while interdependence is underrated. The "I" as a singular person is of utmost importance, holding more weight than the "you," the "we," or the "all." When we think of success, mainstream culture trains us to think of *my* success, what do *I* want, what are *my* dreams, what am *I* achieving? Or, what do I want for *my* children, *my* family, or those *I* most identify with? We usually do not ask ourselves, what does my success cost others or the environment? Or, how can my success nourish others and the environment? What do we most need? Or, how can we take care of the commons?

I am not saying that all aspects of individualizing are negative. Some are beneficial as well. An individual breaking away from family and community can interrupt dynamics of violence, creating more focus and personal freedom. Individualism as a core organizing principle, however, is limited and has consequences for the "we." Individualism trains us to leave others and the planet behind quickly, can breed a type of competitiveness, and a blame of those not succeeding. Individualism can also leave us lonely.

Most everything we do and have has actually come from interdependence with others and the planet. This includes what we each ate today, our clothing, this book, and the computer I wrote it on. Humans are fundamentally social animals. We organize ourselves collectively in groups, communities, towns, and cities. Individualism is at odds with this evolutionary biological reality.

We live in an increasingly commodified capitalist system. This means people, seeds, soil, water, and more are productized for sale and profit. People are not seen primarily as community or citizens, but rather as consumers. In modern capitalism, profit is the fundamental measure of success—not happiness, not collective well-being, not the sustainability of life.

As we are taught to be consumers before community, our culture says that objects bring meaning, money brings worthiness and belonging, and that those without it must not be as worthy. We are convinced that our collective energies should be used for increasing wealth and sequestering our own.

The more social and economic privilege one has—that is, access to resources, to education, to being reflected in the media and culture as having worth and dignity, and more decision-making power in one's life or the life of society—the more one tends to interpret their experiences as their own and as individually earned. On the other hand, the more our community, peoples, gender, sexual orientation, or class is impacted negatively by broader social conditions, the more we tend to see and understand that experiences are not so individual. They impact us as individuals, but are constructed and driven from something much larger, by an economy, social norms, and institutions with more power and ability to define reality. Or, those of us impacted negatively by conditions may also internalize them, assuming something is wrong with us, or our peoples, and strive to be or become the norm—even when this may be impossible to succeed at.

> When you are accustomed to privilege, equality feels like oppression.
>
> (UNKNOWN, in Frances Causey, *The Long Shadow*)

When our peoples have been systematically denied and harmed, we need to relearn our histories. We need to find the stories, the images, and knowing of other models; beyond colonization or slavery, examples of self-determined women and transgendered people, Maroon societies, practices deeply connected to the planet and stars, and more.

We also need to know of those who came before us in social movements—their visions, collective power, learnings, and shortcomings as well as the backlashes that too often undermined and were meant to destroy these liberation movements. This is a part of personal and community empowerment, as well as trauma healing.

Power-Over: An Intersectional Analysis

What is an intersectional analysis? It is an understanding of these systems, and how they are mutually reinforcing. It helps us understand *how* the concentration of wealth and decision making remains with the

few, and *why* the identity of those few is so predictable. Intersectionality also helps us understand solidarity, and how power-over systems
harm the majority while simultaneously working to position the rest
of us against each other.

My understanding of intersectionality is grounded in third-wave
feminism, and the teachers I had the great opportunity to learn from,
including Chandra Mohanty, bell hooks, Audre Lorde, Mary Beth
Krouse, Edith Swan, and others. In my years of social change work
this has been deepened by partnerships with Raquel Laviña (National
Domestic Workers Alliance), Spenta Kandawalla, Chris Lymbertos
(Arab Resource and Organizing Center), Denise Perry and Alta Starr
(Black Organizing for Leadership and Dignity), Sumitra Rajkumar,
Cindy Wiesner (Grassroots Global Justice), and many more. Political
education is lifelong. I want to appreciate Catalyst Project for supporting my ongoing development and all of the political education they do
with white people. While my social justice "homes" have been capacity
building organizations, not base building organizations, I have learned
so much through our partnerships with them. Thank you.

Below are primary systems that create intersectional power-over
social and economic conditions.

Capitalism/Economic Exploitation: This is the process of exploiting people for their labor and the earth for resources, in a destructive
and an unsustainable way, to concentrate wealth within an elite. This
includes concepts and social narratives, financial, corporate, government, and social institutions to both validate and perpetuate an exploitative economic system.

Capitalism is a bit of a sacred idea in the United States. When one
starts to question the processes and outcomes of modern capitalism,
outside of very specific academic and progressive left circles, it's amazing how quick the reaction can be, and how common. "This is the best
economic system there is!" "More people have money here than anywhere!" "Are you a communist?" "What do you mean, socialism instead

of capitalism? That didn't work; people are poor there" (often pointing to the prior USSR or Cuba). This reaction points to how merged the ideas of the United States, democracy, and capitalism have become. Democracy and capitalism are not the same thing—in fact we could say they are contradictory in principle.

Capitalism is an economic system based on wealth accumulation, through private ownership of the means of production, and running these to produce profit. It is based on wage labor, and paying those creating the products at a lesser rate than the sale of the products earns. It concentrates the accumulation of wealth and decision making with the owner, and inherently does not allow for the wealth of all people or workers—because this would limit profit.

Capitalism also relies on the use and exploitation of natural resources that do not account for the cost of the destruction of ecosystems or of their repair. Producing stuff, selling stuff for a profit, and throwing stuff away so that we buy more stuff at a profit are the cycle of capitalism simplified. It assumes ongoing growth, on a planet that does not operate that way. The earth's biosphere (a biosphere is the global sum of all ecosystems) is a closed system (besides solar and cosmic radiation) based *not* on unending growth and accumulation, but on ecosystem interdependence, renewal, and regeneration.

Neoliberalism is a philosophy about how societies in which capitalism prevails should be managed.

> Neoliberalism—the doctrine that market exchange is an ethic in itself, capable of acting as a guide for all human action—has become dominant in both thought and practice throughout much of the world since about 1970. Its spread has depended upon a reconstitution of state powers such that privatization, finance, and market processes are emphasized. State interventions in the economy are minimized, while the obligations of the state to provide for the welfare of its citizens are diminished.
>
> (DAVID HARVEY, *A Brief History of Neoliberalism*)

White Supremacy: The concept and related economic, corporate, government, and social institutions that perpetuate the idea of whiteness as dominant and defining. Also called racism.

The idea of whiteness was created in the 1800s in the burgeoning United States to quell alliances being built between European indentured servants, African enslaved peoples, and indigenous peoples to resist and stop colonization and slavery. To break the alliance, European servants were given a way out of indentured servitude, access to land ownership, and were offered a means to "upward mobility" to join the other European colonizers. They were identified as white, and "like the settler class," able to make their way in the new land. This did break many alliances, and further codified the racist economic policies and cultural narrative. Before this time European immigrants identified from whence they came, as German, English, Italian, Swedish, etc.; and as class-based.

White supremacy is perpetuated through economic and financial institutions, corporations, government and policies, the military, and the media. It is also perpetuated through individuals and groups.

Enslaving African peoples, and using their unpaid labor for wealth creation for European/white people, is a profound historical example of white supremacy, intertwined with colonialism and economic exploitation. Another is the exploitation of Chinese people for labor in building railways in the West, or the World War II internment of Japanese people in the United States and the confiscation of their homes and resources.

Current examples of white supremacy are many. Here are some examples below.

Mapping Police Violence is a research-based organization that shows the dynamics of police violence (www.mappingpoliceviolence .org). Here are some of their findings. As you read these numbers please remember that the numbers represent people with children, families, dreams, and lives.

- Police killed 1,147 people in 2017. Black people were 25% of those killed, despite making up less than 13% of the population.

- Black people are three times more likely to be killed by the police than white people.

- In 2015, in fourteen of sixty of the largest cities' police departments, 100% of those people killed were Black.

- Levels of crime in US cities do not make it any more or less likely for police to kill people.

- 99% of cases in 2015 have NOT resulted in any officer(s) being convicted of a crime.

The Dakota Access Pipeline is also based on white supremacy inseparable from colonization and genocide. This pipeline violates Article II of the Fort Laramie Treaty, which guarantees the "undisturbed use and occupation of" reservation lands surrounding the location of the pipeline. The pipeline was moved from its original site because of the risk to the drinking water of the North Dakotan capital, Bismarck, should there be a leak or spill. This is also true for the Standing Rock Sioux, a sovereign nation. Thousands of indigenous peoples and allies gathered in solidarity to protest the pipeline; and center indigenous rights, and the sacredness of water and the earth.

Patriarchy: The concept and related economic, corporate, government, and social institutions that perpetuate the idea of maleness as dominant and defining. Patriarchy also includes heteronormativity. This is the assumed "rightness" of heterosexuality as the defining way of sexual and intimate relationships while other expressions are perceived as aberrant or perverted. Patriarchy also assumes a binary of male and female as the only sexes with man and woman as the only genders. Patriarchy is also called male supremacy.

Patriarchy shows up in many ways. One is ongoing wage gaps based on gender. The following are current statistics on equal pay for equal work, based on gender as well as race and gender combined (US Department of Labor 2014). Women have a 21.4% wage gap in comparison to men *for the same work*. This means women make 78.6% of what men make.

If we add the lens of race, here is what we see. Compared to white men, women earn the following percentages, for the same work:

- Asian women—83.5%
- White women—75.4%
- Black women—60.5%
- Latina women—54.6%

Also, the higher the educational degree, the greater the wage gap.

Patriarchy also is expressed in how violence against women, children, and transgender communities is sanctioned, normalized, and perpetuated. Here are some of the statistics around violence against women and children. These are of course experienced as very personal and intimate traumas, and the rates make them a societal issue as well. It is vital to understand both.

- One in four girls and one in six boys will be sexually abused before they turn eighteen years old.
- 34% of people who sexually abuse a child are family members.
- 12.3% of women were age ten or younger at the time of their first rape/victimization, and 30% of women were between the ages of eleven and seventeen.
- 27.8% of men were age ten or younger at the time of their first rape/victimization.
- More than one-third of women who report being raped before age eighteen also experience rape as an adult.
- 96% of people who sexually abuse children are male, and 76.8% of people who sexually abuse children are adults.

- 325,000 children are at risk of becoming victims of commercial child sexual exploitation each year.

- The average age at which girls first become victims of prostitution is twelve to fourteen years old, and the average age for boys is eleven to thirteen years old.

  (NATIONAL SEXUAL VIOLENCE RESOURCE CENTER 2015)

Here are further statistics regarding transgender people.

A 2013 report from the National Coalition of Anti-Violence Programs (NCAVP) found the following about violence against transgender people, showing that trans women of color are most at risk:

- 72% of victims of anti-LGBT homicide were transgender women.

- 67% of anti-LGBT homicide victims were transgender women of color.

The NCAVP survey further shows that, "Transgender people of color were 6 times more likely to experience physical violence from the police compared to white cisgender survivors and victims." Transgender people overall were seven times as likely "to experience physical violence when interacting with the police" than cisgender victims and survivors.

Further research about income and income disparity shows transgender people are "four times as likely to have a household income under $10,000 and twice as likely to be unemployed," compared to the general US population (Sears and Badgett 2012).

During the writing of this book, I watched the hearings for the latest Supreme Court justice, Brett Kavanaugh. This was a spectacle of social norms and power-over systems. Here are some of the dynamics of patriarchy that were playing out:

- "Proof" from the current criminal legal system (evidentiary laws) does not reflect the realities and dynamics of sexual assault and rape, or the real psychobiological strategies engaged to survive trauma.

- There is incredible social pressure "not to tell," to self-blame, and to minimize the violation, and a simultaneous dismissal of survivors' voices when they do tell. These are all dynamics of male supremacy.

- "They both seem believable" was often quoted in the media. What does this even mean? If you are trained in trauma, or the context of patriarchy and sexual violence, you know that 99%-plus of people who sexually offend deny their actions, that the majority of people who know the offender defend him, and that 99%-plus of survivors of violence are telling the truth.

- Orrin Hatch was an embodied example of male supremacy. When he, his power, and his definition of reality were decentered or challenged, he did what a power-over system does ... he threatened, attacked, and discredited.

Christian Hegemony: The concept and related economic, corporate, government, and social institutions that perpetuate the idea of Christianity as dominant and defining.

> One of the longest-standing systems of institutionalized power in the United States is the dominant western form of Christianity that came to power when the Romans made Christianity the official religion of the Roman Empire in the fourth century. Christian Hegemony, the everyday, pervasive, deep-seated and institutionalized dominance of society by Christian institutions, Christian leaders, and Christians as a group, has deeply shaped our lives.
>
> (PAUL KIVEL, *Living in the Shadow of the Cross*)

While many have experienced and been inspired by the Christian faith for giving, humility, spiritual growth, and within social justice movements, it is a complex story. If we look at the institutions of the religion, many are used to perpetuate harm, environmental destruction, and the concentration of wealth.

> The US Constitution famously prohibits any religious test or requirement for public office. Still, almost all of the nation's presidents have been Christians and many have been Episcopalians or Presbyterians, with most of the rest belonging to other prominent Protestant denominations.
>
> (DAVID MASCI, PEW Research Center)

There has never been a Muslim, Buddhist, Jew, atheist, or person with another major religious affiliation serving as president of the United States. The anti-Muslim, Islamophobic, national narrative has been on loudspeaker since 9/11, and is used to target Muslims, Arabs, South Asians, and anyone perceived to be from these groups. The narrative combines anti-terrorism and anti-Muslim spin to fuel hundreds of policies including new immigration laws (the Muslim Ban), creating wars, and funneling billions of dollars on the military and surveillance.

Along with the Catholic Church, other Christian beliefs and organizations including Puritan, Presbyterian, and Episcopalian were also used to support slavery and colonization, the torturing and killing of people as witches, and more. As discussed above, Christianity and the mission systems were central to colonizing the Americas through conversion and forced schooling, often connected to getting access to needed resources like food and water. Christian missionaries are still very active today, also often tied to resource development projects. In 2010 an estimated 125,000 missionaries were sent from the United States —primarily to countries with less economic access (Johnson, n.d.).

Evangelical Christianity is one of the biggest supporters of Israel today, wanting to assure the success of the State for their own eventual return. Meetings between evangelical leader Billy Graham and Zionist leaders began in the late 1960s. This is another example of Christian support of ongoing settler colonization of Palestine. Ending anti-Semitism is not, however, a central tenet of evangelical Christianity.

In October of 2018 there was a mass shooting at the Tree of Life or L'Simcha Congregation synagogue in Philadelphia. Eleven people were killed and seven wounded. This was the deadliest attack on the Jewish community in the United States. The stated motivation was the synagogue's participation in the Hebrew Immigrant Aid Society (HIAS), a nonprofit that provides humanitarian aid and assistance to refugees. This is another example of intersectionality, combining anti-immigrant sentiment with deep-seated anti-Semitism.

Lastly, Christian beliefs are used to demean sexuality and the body as sins, and demean people who are not heterosexual or cisgendered. Christian beliefs and institutions are used to determine women's subservient roles, both within the church hierarchy and within private and spiritual life.

You can see how Christian Supremacy intersects with Economic Exploitation, White Supremacy, and Patriarchy.

Imperialism: To further understand the broader context of power-over conditions, we need to speak about imperialism as well. Imperialism is a nation or state's policy and practice of extending their dominion through taking land and territory, or gaining economic and political control over other areas and peoples. This always involves the use of power and force, either military or economic. Most imperialist nations, including the United States, deny their use of imperialism. They instead find or create an enemy and justify their tactics by saying it is in the name of freedom. Familiar?

> Every empire, however, tells itself and the world that it is unlike all other empires, that its mission is not to plunder and control but to educate and liberate.
>
> (EDWARD W. SAID, "Blind Imperial Arrogance")

Puerto Rico is a good example of US imperialism. In 1897, Spain granted Puerto Rico a *Carta de Autonomía* (Charter of Autonomy), which, after four hundred years, would give Puerto Rico its independence. General democratic elections were held in March 1898 and the first "autonomous" government of Puerto Rico began to function on July 17, 1898. Just eight days later, on July 25, Nelson A. Miles (the Commanding General of the US Army) invaded Puerto Rico as part of the Spanish-American War. When the United States won the Spanish-American War, it annexed the former Spanish colony of Puerto Rico, as part of the December 10, 1898 Treaty of Paris.

> The American who led the invasion, Gen. Nelson A. Miles, promised liberty to Puerto Ricans. He also promised prosperity and "the advantages and blessings of enlightened civilization."
>
> Puerto Rico was stripped of land and natural resources by US banking syndicates. By 1934, the theft was so extreme that Puerto Ricans organized an island-wide agricultural strike. In response to this strike the Yale-educated Chief of Police, whose father owned the Riggs National Bank, promised that "there will be war to the death against all Puerto Ricans."
>
> (NELSON DENIS, *War Against All Puerto Ricans*)

Puerto Rico continues to fight for its independence from the United States, as a commonwealth.

Many imperialist nations work together to maneuver for power and resources. A current example is the United States and the State of Israel, occupied Palestine. While there is much purposefully generated confusion in the States about Israel, Palestine, the United States, and Britain, the history is clear. The British created the settler colonialism of Palestine by way of Jewish Zionists. The United States and Britain continue to support the ongoing settler colonialism, displacement, and dispossession of the Palestinian people and the lands they tended to for centuries. Israel is necessary to the US and European powers to control the Middle East and its oil production.

> The standard Zionist position is that they showed up in Palestine in the late 19th century to reclaim their ancestral homeland. Jews bought land and started building up the Jewish community there. They were met with increasingly violent opposition from the Palestinian Arabs, presumably stemming from the Arabs' inherent anti-Semitism. The Zionists were then forced to defend themselves and, in one form or another, this same situation continues up to today.
>
> The problem with this explanation is that it is simply not true, as the documentary evidence shows. What really happened was that the Zionist movement, from the beginning, looked forward to a practically complete dispossession of the indigenous Arab population so that Israel could be a wholly Jewish state, or as much as was possible. Land bought by the Jewish National Fund was held in the name of the Jewish people and could never be sold or even leased back to Arabs (a situation which continues to the present). The vast majority of the population of Palestine, by the way, had been Arabic since the seventh century AD. The mythic "land without people for a people without land" was already home to 700,000 Palestinians in 1919. This is the root of the problem, as we shall see.
>
> (JEWS FOR JUSTICE IN THE MIDDLE EAST)

Starting in 2019, the United States will give Israel $38 billion over the next ten years—$3.8 billion per year, which is $10.41 million per day. This aid to Israel amounts to more than half of all direct military aid the United States provides worldwide. Simultaneously, in 2018–2019 the United States cut aid to Palestine, and as a consequence tens of thousands of Palestinians are no longer getting food or basic health services. Palestinians are refugees in their own lands, living in open air prisons, literal refugee camps, with limited access to hospitals, jobs, and other services.

Why in the United States is it considered anti-Semitic if we speak out against the apartheid State of Israel? We can be committed to the liberation of Palestine, and also for Jewish people's freedom and the end of anti-Semitism. These are not contradictory, but the national narrative is spun as if they were.

> Occupation, curfew, settlements, closed military zone, administrative detention, siege, preventive strike, terrorist infrastructure, transfer. Their WAR destroys language. Speaks genocide with the words of a quiet technician.
>
> Occupation means that you cannot trust the OPEN SKY, or any open street near to the gates of snipers tower. It means that you cannot trust the future or have faith that the past will always be there.
>
> And if you face all of this death and indifference and keep your humanity, and your love and your dignity and YOU refuse to surrender to their terror, then you know something of the courage that is Palestine.
>
> (SUHEIR HAMMAD)

Ableism: It is important in this intersectional analysis to also speak to ableism. Ableism is the making "real and whole" of able-bodied and -minded people, while making "unreal and un-whole" people with disabilities. This too is systemic, operating in the economy, government, media, health care, and more. Many of those working for the safety, belonging, and dignity of people with varying abilities use Disability Justice as a framework for organizing, education, and freedom.

> A Disability Justice framework understands that all bodies are unique and essential, that all bodies have strengths and needs that must be met. We know that we are powerful not despite the complexities of our bodies, but because of them. We understand that all bodies are caught in these bindings of ability, race, gender, sexuality, class, nation state and imperialism, and that we cannot separate them. These are the positions from where we struggle. We are in a global system that is incompatible with life.

There has always been resistance to all forms of oppression, as we know through our bones that there have simultaneously been disabled people visioning a world where we flourish, that values and celebrates us in all our myriad beauty.

(PATTY BERNE, Sins Invalid)

In closing, power-over depends upon violence, threats of violence, coercion, and a steady stream of misinformation to work. People(s) don't inherently want to give up their dignity, self-determination, or safety, or to be without resources. This must be taken through many forms of denigration and violence. Power-over is supported by vast cultural narratives, including media, religious beliefs, and government propaganda (e.g., the Patriot Act) that validate and uplift inequity, war, nationalism, patriotism, and the worthiness of these few, while suppressing and minimizing information that shows us otherwise.

These intersectional power-over systems operate in conjunction with each other. It isn't effective to understand one alone, because of how deeply they operate together.

What Does This All Mean?

In summary, if we look from a US frame, power-over social and economic systems, and accompanying social norms, go something like the following. This is not all-inclusive, and it can be painful—

- Some win, at others' expense. This is just how it works. They probably worked harder anyway, or deserved it more.

- Wealth and resources are concentrated in the few. And they deserve it. If others would just work hard enough, be smart enough, be innovative enough, etc., they'd have it too.

- Men rule. They are inherently stronger, more rational, more dependable, etc. The more you act like them, the more power you can accumulate.

- If you fall outside of the man/woman gender norm, or the heterosexual norm, you are aberrant.

- White is right. The most progress has been made by white people. They know, are in control, are inherently more worthy.

- Dominion over the earth. The earth is here for man's use. Man is the top of the evolutionary chain or created in God's image.

- The "able"-bodied and -minded are the true contributors. Others have little to give, or tax society.

- Christianity is the true faith. You can be saved if you convert. Christianity has supported the most progress.

- The smart, the privileged, the wealthy decide and define. They deserve to.

- Violence, including rape, is an acceptable means to gain domination and might. It is an acceptable way to spread freedom and democracy. It is acceptable, and even still legal, in many states to rape your wife.

- Boys will be boys ... including sexually assaulting, raping, and being physically violent.

- War is part of the economy. We are too much at risk if we don't have an offensive military. We are spreading freedom and democracy. We are protecting others. We are making money.

- The circle of care and empathy does not need to extend beyond myself, and those I identify with or strive to become. Get your own. Or, only give when you have extra, and are well credited for it.

- Manifest destiny. We deserved this land, this country, and we do not need to make amends or reparations to indigenous or African peoples. That's in the past. Why are they dwelling on it?

- There are no commons—the collective ownership and sustainable use of waters, forests, lands, air, oceans, etc. The most innovative and lucrative strategy should get the commons.

- The earth, land, and resources can be owned. Not owning and leveraging the ownership of land is primitive. Not developed. Not progress.

That is painful. Is it familiar? How does one heal from this and in this context? I believe there is so much we can further when we integrate an intersectional analysis, a grounded understanding of power-over conditions into our trauma healing models.

Lastly, I have included the questions from chapter 2, to help us continue to dig into and understand power, access, and conditions.

- Who is (systemically) offered safety, belonging, dignity, and resources? Whom is it taken from, to do this?

- Who is (systemically) denied safety, belonging, dignity, and resources? And then, blamed for it?

- Who benefits from this system/policy/norm/war? Which people, communities, and nations benefit?

- Who suffers from this system? Who pays—with their health, labor, and lives?

- Who decides? Who defines reality, the dominant narrative, history, possibility?

- Which peoples and what natural resources are exploited to concentrate wealth, power, and decision making in the few?

- Who is poor and who is wealthy? Which people, which countries? How is this perpetuated? Whom does this serve?

- How are the poor, the exploited, and the victimized described by or blamed in the dominant narrative?

For those of us working in trauma healing or social change, I invite us to also ask:

- What does it take to transform how power-over social conditions have been embodied in us, even when they are not what we believe in?

- Even when our thinking might have shifted, have our actions changed? Has how we spend our lives, time, and resources changed to align with these values?

- What does it take for us to work collectively, when there has been so much wounding between us and our peoples? When these power differences still operate? If, when under pressure, we tend to polarize and make each other wrong?

- If you are a healer, therapist, or practitioner, have you joined organizations and organizing for social justice? If not, why not?

- If you work in social movements, have you integrated an understanding of trauma and healing into your strategy and work? Have you accessed healing and transformation for yourself and your organization?

Who we are matters. How we understand our world matters.

AFTERWORD

As the field of Somatics/Embodiment in the West is growing out of its adolescence it's prudent for us to remember that it's been alive throughout the world since humans have inhabited the earth. While there've been extraordinary teachers who introduced somatics into the fields of emotional and physical health in the first half of the twentieth century, our hunter gatherer ancestors knew something about the power of feeling, sensing, and collective action thousands of years ago. To live an embodied life was critical for these first humans for the purposes of safety, surviving, healing, and a resilient community life. In other words, the fundamental tenets of somatics and an embodied life are our birthright; we might even say they are part of our DNA, part of our essential makeup. But they've been pruned out of us by our educational system's emphasis on cognitive memorization, rational thought, and placing concepts above wisdom—a system that puts us in our heads describing life, instead of living life. Somatics promises a life quite different in that it opens the possibility of human beings becoming self-healing, self-educating, and self-generating. This goes beyond just memorizing facts and figures, but organizing ourselves toward agency and fulfillment. There's nothing inherently wrong with rational thinking, we're rational beings, but by putting it above feeling, compassion, intuition, self-knowing, and wisdom we've sacrificed the heart of our humanity.

The success that the early Western somatic practitioners attained in curing themselves and others by turning the attention to the life of the body substantiated the idea that we could play a part in our own well-being. This focused the field of somatics toward a healing modality of physical and emotional health. This spawned countless forms of body-work, dance, movement therapies, biofeedback, and a body-oriented psychotherapy that reside under the broad heading of somatics. In addition, a growing number of universities now offer degrees in somatics in their psychology and philosophy departments. Strozzi Institute has set the standard for Somatic Coaching, and creating an Embodied Leadership culture in teams and organizations. It's good work, it's growing, and many are helped by it. May it continue. May it evolve.

We are now at the threshold of somatics' next contribution to not only our individual health, but to the health of the society and the planet. I submit that one of the reasons we can so easily pollute our water and poison our air is that we are out of touch with our bodies and our sensing; one of the reasons that most conflict quickly precipitates to violence is that we're out of touch with our bodies; and that one of the reasons there's a growing gap between those that have and those that don't have is we are out of touch with our bodies. When we don't reside in our bodies we are unable to feel. When I say feel I don't mean "have a feeling" or "have an emotion" although that may occur. I'm referring to feeling and listening to the core life energy, the animating principle that moves through us and is the repository of three billion years of intelligence. An intelligence that authors mutuality, interconnectedness, and interdependence. Our current educational paradigm teaches us that knowledge is the result of distancing ourselves from what we are to learn. We are instructed to look at our subject from afar, to intellectually dissect it, compartmentalize it, and then put it into manageable, logical order. Our capacity to sense and feel takes a back seat—and with it a direct relationship with life, with our soul's desire, with what truly matters to us. As William Blake said, "Man has no body distinct from his soul." The discipline of somatics is a powerful medicine in not only reclaiming our health, but healing our planet, and building a just, equitable society.

The Politics of Trauma: Somatics, Healing, and Social Justice, by Staci K. Haines, is a timely and sweeping perspective on how the art and science of somatics can contribute to righting the ills of the major issues of our times: social inequity, environmental injustice, trauma, and disenfranchisement. This is an ambitious, visionary book that proposes a radical new view of the intersectionality of individual healing, community restoration, social conditions, and trauma. This is a must read for therapists, coaches, and counselors, as well as those who are working in the social and environmental justice fields. It will inspire you, provoke you, and touch your heart. I can't recommend it enough.

Over the past fifty years I've had the privilege and honor of helping spread somatics and embodiment practices over five continents in such varied sectors as education, medicine, NGOs, psychology, government, nonprofits, military, technology, Fortune 500 companies, and Olympic and professional athletics. Being part of how somatics has evolved over a half century has been rewarding, and at times a heavy lift. I now feel deeply gratified to have *The Politics of Trauma: Somatics, Healing, and Social Justice* be a significant next step in understanding how our efforts at holistic healing cannot be separate from social conditions; and sustained social activism cannot be disconnected from healing trauma.

I attempted to introduce somatics into more diverse communities than the middle and upper class white demographic that typically came to the work. I introduced somatics to prisons and jails, HIV organizers, as well as the homeless. My intent and heart were committed to the democratization of somatics, but my social analysis lagged behind and I had no grounded strategy for how to bring it to more diverse communities. At this time my work was influenced by a meditation practice, aikido and other martial arts, and bringing bodywork and somatics to the helping and educational professions. Staci Haines has brought this vision to fruition.

Staci is a colleague of mine. She has been a teacher at Strozzi Institute and at one point ran the organization. I have taught in her organization, generative somatics. Through our collaboration in numerous projects I have increased my knowledge of how social context intimately and broadly shapes who we are; and if we don't include it in healing, leadership, and social equity what we do will be incomplete. I see that working for the justice of all living things—the water we drink, the air we breathe, the plants and animals that feed us, the majesty of the night sky, all of our brothers and sisters in the human family—is part of the spiritual path. Her work and research in the field of trauma are solid and effective. Time and again her work has shown that the shaping power of social conditions, integrated with trauma healing, allows people to be known and their actual lived experiences reflected and addressed. Oppression and inequity cause trauma. *The Politics of Trauma: Somatics, Healing, and Social Justice* clearly illustrates how the partnership of healing and social action, of personal and social change, creates the healing and transformation we seek for a life-affirming and equitable future for our planet and ourselves. Reading this book will prepare you to participate in a much needed future of love and rigor.

—RICHARD STROZZI-HECKLER,
Founder of the Strozzi Institute

GLOSSARY OF TERMS

The glossary of terms is to support you in digging into the book. Maybe a word or concept has been defined, yet as you come to it again in the book, you're like … "What was that again?" Turn to your handy glossary! These are divided into Political and Social Justice Terms, and Somatic Healing and Therapeutic Terms. Usually folks are more trained in one or the other. It takes time to deepen into a field and understand its distinctions. I hope this is a useful resource for you.

Somatic Healing and Therapeutic Terms

Allying/Allyship: In the context of somatics and healing, allying and allyship address the inherent need for safety and belonging by supporting the expressed needs of another's soma to feel supported and not alone. Somatically being allied with is a key component of regenerating safety.

Blending: A core principle in somatics of joining with. This is joining with a contraction or habituated shaping in the soma, rather than trying to break it up or unlock it. The assumption behind this blending is that there is intelligence in the protective patterning. Blending helps the soma to open.

Centered Accountability: A way of accepting and engaging with responsibility for harm, unintended or intended, that doesn't engage in under-accountability (avoidance or deflection) nor over-accountability (taking on fault or blame automatically). Centered accountability seeks to hold complexity, to both be accountable and know what is not our responsibility, and to stay connected and in relationship.

Declaration: A commitment to a desired future. A "speech act," an aspect of language that holds action and coordination with others inherent to it. When used in somatics, declarations guide our healing, practices, and embodiment, as a core longing or vision. A declaration involves developing the skill to imagine possible futures, speak them aloud to others, and mobilize oneself and others toward those futures.

DSM-V: DSM stands for *Diagnostic and Statistical Manual of Mental Disorders*. It is the manual published by the American Psychiatric Association that lists all classifications of mental disorders. It is currently in its 5th edition. Post-Traumatic Stress Disorder (see below) was first introduced in the DSM-III in 1980, and was controversial at the time. Its definition and understanding have evolved significantly with each edition.

Embodied Transformation: Sustainable healing and change, aligned with our vision and values. This change is holistic including behaviors, beliefs, and ways of relating. It is more than new insight; rather we can sustain the desired changes, even when under pressure (positive or negative pressure). Embodied transformation is possible when we work through the soma, and integrate somatic awareness, somatic opening, and somatic practices. These are held within embodied resilience and the broader social conditions.

Generative Conflict: Conflict that results in increased trust, deeper learning, and centered change. Numerous practices and change processes support the skill of generative conflict including: extending trust, being trustworthy (intent + competence + reliability), awareness of systemic power and social conditions, understanding of one's trauma reactions and survival shaping, embodied resilience, holding complexity, and the ability to recenter under pressure.

PTSD: Acronym for Post-Traumatic Stress Disorder, a diagnosis in the DSM. This is a compilation of symptoms that develop in some people who have experienced shocking, painful, violent, or threatening event(s) and/or oppressive social conditions.

Regenerating Safety: The somatic processes through which the location for generating safety returns to being internal, rather than being caught externally. This does not disappear the external challenges to safety, but rather reconnects the person or group to the current time resources, resilience, power, and influence they have to affect their safety. The somatic processes for regenerating safety include: somatic practices for boundaries and requests, blending with the safety shape, and the ally process.

Resilience: An inherent capacity to find wholeness, beauty, and hope. Resilience is inherent. Many experiences support our resilience. It is also our ability to somatically, holistically renew ourselves, during and after oppressive, threatening, or traumatic experiences.

Safety Shaping/Survival Shaping: Adaptive embodied strategies oriented toward retaining and maintaining a sense of safety, belonging, and dignity. Fight, flight, freeze, appeasement, and dissociation are automatic reactions to threat that can become generalized in our somas as safety/survival strategies. These adaptations become automatic somatic responses under any perceived or real threat to safety, belonging, and/or dignity, or just under the pressures of living. They leave us with fewer choices, and ways of relating actions.

Shaping: Embodied patterns. We are all shaped—we embody patterns and schemas through adaptations for safety, belonging, and dignity, through both traumatic and resilient experiences, as well as through the cultural and social conditions in which we were raised and/or live. These adaptations result in patterns of emotions, beliefs, behaviors, and physical patterns that become embodied habits.

Soma: The interconnected thinking, emotions, actions, relating, and worldview, embodied. We use soma as a way to show the interdependence of all of these aspects and the body.

Somatic Awareness: Conscious attention and the developed capacity to sense and feel physical sensation, emotions, and aliveness of the body/soma/self and the environment. Both internal and external information comes through the felt senses. Increased somatic awareness gives us access to this information. Dissociation and other adaptations can have us disconnected from this ground of being. We can learn to "live inside of our own skins" again.

Somatic Bodywork: A process for somatic opening that includes conversation, touch, breathing patterns, gesture, and emotional processing to work directly with the places in the soma that have held traumatic experiences or are hypervigilant or numb, to support the shift from contraction and dissociation to openness, aliveness, and embodiment.

Somatic Opening: A part of the process of deconstructing embodied shaping and habits in the soma. The intention is to transform learned reactions that no longer serve the person or group, allowing for sustained change and healing. Key principles in somatic opening are: supporting the contraction, or blending; connecting more resilient places in the soma with more stressed or numb places; allowing more aliveness to move through the soma connected to purpose; and opening the tissues to allow for more aliveness and sensation to flow.

Somatic Practices: Body-based practices that support the development of new skills and competencies aligned with a person or group's declarations and intentions. Somatic practices include: an intention/purpose, feeling, and sensing the body-based practice, repetition, and feedback from others. They result in actionable change, meaning you can do something you could not before even under pressure. Somatic practices can help us develop many embodied skills including: presence, generativity, setting limits, mutual connection, impacting and leading, centered surrender, compassion and love, working with the unknown and contradictions, and centered accountability.

Tracking: The process of observing posture, gaze, facial expression, muscle tension, breath, vitality, movement, and internal sensation. In somatics, both the practitioner and client engage in tracking the client's somatic experience during the healing process. Tracking can also be based out of trauma and has more of a sense of watching for danger or hypervigilance.

Trauma: Experiences, series of experiences, and/or impacts from social conditions, that break or betray our inherent need for safety, belonging, and dignity. It results in these inherent needs vying against one another instead of working together. Traumatic experiences cause a somatic contraction and "shaping" that becomes unresponsive to current time experience. This survival shaping does not take in new or current time information. Rather, the psychology, physiology, and relationality all remain organized around protecting from the same or a similar harm, without taking in new information.

Political and Social Justice Terms

Ableism: Negative stereotypes and systemic oppression targeting people with disabilities. This is systemic, operating in the economy, government, media, health care, and more. Ableism is the making "real and whole" of able-bodied and -minded people, while making "unreal and un-whole" people with disabilities. See the Disability Justice framework in chapter 1.

Activism: Efforts to promote social change through direct and distinct action (e.g., signing a petition, writing a blog, going to a rally, or organizing such activities). This is distinct from organizing.

Allyship: An active and consistent practice of unlearning and re-evaluating, in which a person holding systemic power seeks to end oppressions in solidarity with a group of people who are systemically disempowered. Allyship, in general, is a joining or bonding together for a bigger purpose. This can happen between people, families, communities, organizations, political parties, and more.

Christian Hegemony: The concept, and related economic, corporate, government, and social institutions that perpetuate the idea of Christianity as the dominant and defining religion.

Disability Justice: A liberatory framework that intersects equity, access, and freedom for all people with disabilities to social and economic justice for all people. This framework was created by Patty Berne and Sins Invalid, www.sinsinvalid.org.

Economic Exploitation: The process of exploiting people and the earth's resources, through the use of concepts and social narratives, financial, corporate, government, and social institutions, for their labor and resources, in a destructive and an unsustainable way, to concentrate wealth and power within an elite.

Environmental Justice: A movement and framework that understands the interdependence of the oppression and exploitation of poor people, communities, and countries with the exploitation, pollution, and unsustainable use of the resources of the earth. See Movement Generation (movementgeneration.org) and Asian Pacific Environmental Network—APEN (www.apen4ej.org) for more.

Equity: An evolving term in social justice. Equality that is systemic. Systems that are based in safety, belonging, and dignity, access to resources, for all people, fairly and equally distributed, in sustainable relationship with the earth.

Global Capitalism: A racialized economic system wherein economic distribution and production are owned by private entities in order to accumulate profit. Capitalism forwards private ownership as opposed to government ownership or a commons. A system where corporations are left to pursue profits with little intervention from governments, and often subsidized or bailed out by these same governments. Global capitalism transcends national borders, and seeks out cheap labor, natural resources, and fewer safety and environmental regulations to increase profit. This system concentrates wealth and power in an elite and 1%.

Global Climate Change/Climate Crisis: Global climate change is a long-term change in the earth's climate, an increase in the average atmospheric and ocean temperatures, caused by human activity since the mid-twentieth century. The adverse medium- to long-term effects of global climate change have been named the Climate Crisis, and pose a very real and ongoing threat, not only to our continued existence as a species, but also to the earth's ability to support life.

Healing Justice: A wide range of frameworks and practices that integrate a social analysis of power, oppression, and privilege with healing traditions and social action. It is specifically used to support resilience, healing, and transformative work for oppressed people's and social and environmental justice movements. The term is actively being defined within social movements and by politicized healers currently in different places and contexts.

Heteronormativity: The social norms, concepts, and related economic, corporate, government, and social institutions that perpetuate the idea of heterosexuality as being right, normal, God-given, and defining, and all others being aberrant.

Homophobia/Transphobia: Homophobia is the fear, hatred, discomfort with, or mistrust of people who are lesbian, gay, bisexual, or whose sexual orientation does not conform to heteronormative expression. Transphobia is the fear, hatred, discomfort with, or mistrust of people who are transgender, thought to be transgender, or whose gender expression doesn't conform to traditional gender roles. Homophobia and transphobia are systemically perpetuated.

Imperialism: Imperialism is a nation or state's policy and practice of extending their dominion through taking land and territory, or gaining economic and political control over other areas and peoples. This always involves the use of power and force, either military or economic.

Individualism: The idea that freedom of thought and action for each person is the most important quality of a society, rather than shared effort, equity, and/or responsibility. It is the idea and related systems that hold the interests of the individual as ethically paramount, promoting and valuing independence and self-reliance.

Organizing: Outreach and engagement with people who have shared interests and are often impacted, through privilege or oppression, by a specific set of conditions (e.g., a base of domestic workers are mostly working class women of color and poor white women who have a shared interest of fair labor conditions and who are impacted by racism, patriarchy, class exploitation, etc.). Through organizing, people mobilize to change hearts and minds, policy, economies, and governments.

Patriarchy: The concept and related economic, corporate, government, and social institutions that perpetuate the idea of maleness as dominant and defining. Patriarchy includes heteronormativity and is also called male supremacy.

Politicized Healers: Practitioners who may be trained in a variety of healing traditions and who incorporate an analysis of structural power and social change. Healing practitioners who bring an understanding of the impacts of trauma, oppression, and privilege; and the means to help transform these into more love, power, and collective action. Politicized healing interrupts the individualism of mainstream therapeutic approaches.

Power-Over: Cultural, economic, and social systems (and individual ways of relating) that utilize coercion, dominance, violence, repression, and/or exploitation to concentrate wealth, resources, and/or power in the few.

Power-With: Cultural, economic, and social systems (and individual ways of relating) that are organized to promote equity, interdependence, mutuality, and a sustainable relationship/practice with the earth and the earth's resources.

Social Analysis: The perception and assessment of power, resources, and decision making and their distribution within a society and economy. It understands the deep personal impacts of social inequities but does not overpersonalize systemic issues (e.g., if a person's racist attitudes change, racism ends). A social analysis allows us both to perceive and make assessments of the Sites of institutions, social norms, and historical forces, and integrate this meaning into our healing, transformational, and social justice work.

Social Change: A change in the structures and systems of an economy and society toward equity, justice, and sustainability with the earth and natural resources. This includes, and is not limited to, systems and institutions of: governing, finance, media, food, energy, transportation, education, health care, military, and laws/policies. Social change also helps to change hearts, minds, and actions. There are of course power-over strategies for social change that are also active.

Social Norms: The implicit and explicit rules of a society defining who gets access to resources, safety, belonging, and dignity and who does not. The defining of the "rules of engagement" socially, economically, and in relationship to the earth, land, and natural resources.

Structural Oppression: The systematic mistreatment and degradation of specific groups of people, based on race, gender, sexual orientation, ability, and class; supported and enforced by the society and its institutions. The majority.

Structural Privilege: The systematic prioritizing and uplifting of specific groups of people, based on race, gender, sexual orientation, ability, class, supported and enforced by the society and its institutions. Laws, rules, customs, and institutions support the rights, humanity, and privileges of some, while simultaneously denying these to others. The minority.

Transformative Justice: Transformative justice is a liberatory approach to violence and harm, which seeks safety and accountability without relying on alienation, punishment, or state or systemic violence, including incarceration or policing. It is an approach that seeks healing, justice, and accountability, while also organizing to transform the ongoing social conditions that allowed the abuse to occur. It is rooted in an understanding of trauma and resilience, as well as organizing and systemic change.

Westernized/Westernization: The process in which societies come under or adopt influences from Western (Eurocentric or the United States) culture in areas such as industry, politics, philosophy, values, diet, clothing, language, etc.

White Supremacy: The concept and related economic, corporate, government, and social institutions that perpetuate the idea of whiteness as dominant and defining. Also called racism.

RESOURCES AND
LINEAGES/ACCOUNTABILITY

Please find Resources for further learning and development related to *The Politics of Trauma*, as well as the Lineages and Accountability of this work, on the book's website at www.thepoliticsoftrauma.com.

REFERENCES

Chapter 1

Chomsky, Noam, and Edward S. Herman. 1988. *Manufacturing Consent: The Political Economy of the Mass Media.* New York: Random House.

Galeano, Eduardo, Mark Fried, and Jose Francisco Borges, trans. Mark Fried. 1997. "Window on the Body" from *Walking Words,* p. 9. Copyright © 1997 by W.W. Norton & Company. Reprinted with permission.

Huberman, Andrew. 2016. "Presence: Living and Working on Purpose. Session One: What we know and what we don't know about the soma (body/mind)." Webinar. https://strozziinstitute.com/program/for-coaches/webinar-on-demand-presence.

Sacks, Oliver. 1989. *Seeing Voices.* New York: Vintage Books.

Sins Invalid and Patty Berne. n.d. 10 Principles of Disability Justice. www.sinsinvalid.org.

Strozzi-Heckler, Richard. 2014. *The Art of Somatic Coaching: Embodying Skillful Action, Wisdom, and Compassion.* Berkeley: North Atlantic Books.

Chapter 2

Lorde, Audre. 1984. "The Master's Tools Will Never Dismantle the Master's House." In *Sister Outsider: Essays and Speeches.* Ed. Berkeley: Crossing Press. 110–114. 2007. https://collectiveliberation.org/wp-content/uploads/2013/01/Lorde_The_Masters_Tools.pdf.

Chapter 3

Angelou, Maya. 1993. "On the Pulse of Morning," in *On the Pulse of Morning*. New York: Random House.

Bier, David. 2018. "Trump Might Not Have Gotten His 'Muslim Ban.' But He Sure Got His 'Extreme Vetting.'" *Washington Post*. December 10, 2018.

Black Lives Matter. n.d. www.blacklivesmatter.com.

Coates, Ta-Nehisi. 2014. "The Case for Reparations." *The Atlantic*. June 2014.

DeGruy, Joy. 2005. *Post Traumatic Slave Syndrome: America's Legacy of Enduring Injury and Healing*. Milwaukie, OR: Uptone Press. www .joydegruy.com.

Duran, Eduardo. 2013. *Hozhonahaslíi: Stories of Healing the Soul Wound*. www.youtube.com/watch?v=WU_bJMplzGQ.

Herman, Judith Lewis. 1992. *Trauma and Recovery: The Aftermath of Violence—From Domestic Abuse to Political Terror*. New York: Basic Books.

Hosseini, Khaled. 2003. *The Kite Runner*. London: TKR Books.

National Sexual Violence Resource Center. 2015. www.nsvrc.org.

Sullivan, Shannon. 2015. *The Physiology of Sexist and Racist Oppression*. New York: Oxford University Press.

Chapter 4

Baldwin, James. 1971. "A Conversation between Nikki Giovanni and James Baldwin." *SOUL!* www.youtube.com/watch?v =eZmBy7C9gHQ.

Bass, Ellen, and Laura Davis. 1992. *The Courage to Heal: A Guide for Women Survivors of Child Sexual Abuse*. New York: Harper & Row.

Cambridge Learner's Dictionary. 2012. 4th edition. s.v. "flee." Cambridge, UK: Cambridge University Press.

Davis, Angela, and Kristin Henning. 2017. "How Policing Black Boys Leads to the Conditioning of Black Men." NPR. May 23, 2017. www

.npr.org/sections/codeswitch/2017/05/23/465997013/opinion -how-policing-black-boys-leads-to-the-conditioning-of-black-men.

Merriam-Webster Dictionary. 2016. s.v. "appease," "fight," "freeze." Martinsburg, WV: Merriam-Webster, Inc.

Ogden, Pat. 2006. *Trauma and the Body: A Sensorimotor Approach to Psychotherapy.* New York: W.W. Norton & Company.

Oxford Dictionary of English. 2001. s.v. "appease," "dissociate," "fight." New York: Oxford University Press.

Ridley, Matt. 2006. *Genome: The Autobiography of a Species in 23 Chapters.* New York: Harper Perennial.

Ridley, Matt. 2003. "The Genome Changes Everything." Edge Foundation, interview online. www.dnalc.org/view/15405-Chromosome -10-gene-which-creates-cortisol-Matt-Ridley.html.

Siegel, Dan. See a list of his many books in this book's Resources section at: www.thepoliticsoftrauma.com.

Van der Kolk, Bessel. 2015. *The Body Keeps the Score: Brain, Mind, and Body in the Healing of Trauma.* New York: Penguin Books.

Vocabulary.com. Accessed June 26, 2019. s.v. "fight." www.vocabulary .com/dictionary/fight.

Whittier, Nancy. 2011. *The Politics of Child Sexual Abuse: Emotion, Social Movements, and the State.* New York: Oxford University Press.

Chapter 5

Black Organizing for Leadership and Dignity (BOLD). n.d. https:// boldorganizing.org.

hooks, bell. 1994. *Outlaw Culture: Resisting Representations.* New York: Routledge.

Kahn-Cullors, Patrisse. 2018. *When They Call You a Terrorist: A Black Lives Matter Memoir.* New York: St. Martin's Press.

National Sexual Violence Resource Center. 2015. Centers for Disease Control study.

Roy, Arundhati. 1999. *The Cost of Living*. New York: Modern Library.

Chapter 7

Black Organizing for Leadership and Dignity (BOLD). n.d. https://boldorganizing.org.

Lorde, Audre. 1982. "Learning from the 60s." In *Sister Outsider: Essays and Speeches*. Ed. Berkeley: Crossing Press. 138. 2007.

Nye, Naomi Shihab. 1980. "Missing the Boat." Reprinted by permission of the poet from *Different Ways to Pray*. Portland, OR: Far Corner Books.

Chapter 8

ACEs Too High. n.d. acestoohigh.com.

Angelou, Maya. 1978. From the poem "Still I Rise." In *And Still I Rise: A Book of Poems*. Copyright © 1978 by Maya Angelou. Used by permission of Random House, an imprint and division of Penguin Random House LLC and Little, Brown Book Group. All rights reserved.

Castellanos, Rosario. 1988. *A Rosario Castellanos Reader*. Austin, TX: University of Texas Press.

Dhaliwal, Kanwarpal. 2018. ACEs 2018 Conference and Pediatrics Symposium: Action to Access. San Francisco, CA.

Gobodo-Madikizela, Pumla. 2003. *A Human Being Died That Night: A South African Story of Forgiveness*. New York: Houghton Mifflin.

Herman, *Trauma and Recovery*.

Huberman, Andrew. 2016. Personal interview with the author for the Strozzi Institute.

Van der Kolk, *The Body Keeps the Score*.

White, Christine Cissy. 2017. "Putting Resilience and Resilience Surveys under the Microscope." ACEs Study, Adverse Childhood Experiences, Resilience. February 5, 2017. https://acestoohigh.com /2017/02/05/trashed-4.

Zimmerman, Kristin, and Julie Quiroz. 2016. *Love with Power: Practicing Transformation for Social Justice.* Movement Strategy Center. https:// movementstrategy.org/b/wp-content/uploads/2016/07/MSC -Love_With_Power.pdf.

Chapter 9

Anti-Oppression Network. n.d. www.theantioppressionnetwork.com.

Chapter 10

Ghalib, Mirza, trans. Jane Hirshfield. "For the raindrop." Copyright © by Jane Hirshfield and used by permission.

Moraga, Cherrie, and Gloria Anzaldua, eds. 2015. *This Bridge Called My Back: Writings by Radical Women of Color.* 4th edition. Albany, NY: State University of New York Press.

Ogden, *Trauma and the Body.*

Chapter 11

Gobodo-Madikizela, *A Human Being Died That Night.*

Rilke, Rainer Maria, trans. Robert Bly. 1981. "The Man Watching" from *Selected Poems of Rainer Maria Rilke. A Translation from the German and Commentary* by Robert Bly. Copyright © 1981 by Robert Bly. Reprinted by permission of HarperCollins Publishers.

Chapter 12

Strozzi-Heckler, Richard. 2018. Personal interview with the author. June 2018.

Chapter 13

Hemphill, Prentis. Teacher for generative somatics (gs) and Black Organizing for Leadership and Dignity (BOLD). www.prentishemphill.com.

Movement Generation. n.d. *From Banks and Tanks to Cooperation and Caring: A Strategic Framework for a Just Transition*. https://movementgeneration.org/justtransition.

Critical Context

Allen, Paula Gunn. 1986. *Sacred Hoop: Recovering the Feminine in American Indian Traditions*. Boston: Beacon Press.

Allen, Paula Gunn. 1984. "Who Is Your Mother? The Red Roots of White Feminism." In *Sinister Wisdom* 25. Iowa City: Women's Press.

American Psychiatric Association. 2013. *Diagnostic and Statistical Manual of Mental Disorders*. 5th edition. Arlington, VA: American Psychiatric Publishing.

Asian Pacific Environmental Network (APEN). n.d. www.apen4ej.org.

Berne, Patty, and Sins Invalid. n.d. www.sinsinvalid.org.

Brown, Dee. 1970. *Bury My Heart at Wounded Knee*. New York: Henry Holt.

Causey, Frances. 2017. *The Long Shadow*. Passion River Studios. 2018. DVD, 74 min.

Coates, Ta-Nehisi. 2015. Excerpts from *Between the World and Me* by Ta-Nehisi Coates. Copyright © 2015 by Ta-Nehisi Coates. Used by permission of Spiegel & Grau, an imprint of Random House, a division of Penguin Random House LLC and The Text Publishing Company Pty. Ltd. All rights reserved.

Denis, Nelson. 2015. *War Against All Puerto Ricans*. New York: Nation Books.

Dunbar-Ortiz, Roxanne. 2014. *An Indigenous Peoples' History of the United States*. Boston: Beacon Press.

Genesis 1:26–28 (New Revised Standard Version).

Hammad, Suheir. Author of *Born Palestinian, Born Black: & The Gaza Suite,* 2010, Brooklyn: UpSet Press; and other books of poetry and political commentary.

Harvey, David. 2005. *A Brief History of Neoliberalism.* New York: Oxford University Press.

Jews for Justice in the Middle East. n.d. www.wrmea.org/jews-for-justice /the-origin-of-the-palestine-israel-conflict.html.

Johnson, Todd. n.d. Center for the Study of Global Christianity at Gordon-Conwell Theological Seminary in Massachusetts. https:// gordonconwell.edu/faculty/current.

Kivel, Paul. 2013. *Living in the Shadow of the Cross.* Gabriola Island, BC, Canada: New Society Publishers.

Mapping Police Violence. n.d. www.mappingpoliceviolence.org.

Masci, David. n.d. PEW Research Center. www.pewresearch.org/staff /david-masci.

Miller, Robert J. 2006. *Native America, Discovered and Conquered: Thomas Jefferson, Lewis & Clark, and Manifest Destiny,* 120. Westport, CT: Greenwood.

Movement Generation. n.d. movementgeneration.org.

National Sexual Violence Resource Center. 2015. www.nsvrc.org /sites/default/files/publications_nsvrc_factsheet_media-packet _statistics-about-sexual-violence_0.pdf.

Said, Edward W. 2003. "Blind Imperial Arrogance." *Los Angeles Times.* July 20, 2003. www.latimes.com/archives/la-xpm-2003-jul-20-oe -said20-story.html.

Sears, Brad, and Lee Badgett. 2012. "Beyond Stereotypes: Poverty in the LGBT Community." July 3, 2012. Williams Institute/TIDES.

Silko, Leslie Marmon. 1991. *Almanac of the Dead.* New York: Penguin Books.

Tribal Nations Maps. n.d. www.tribalnationsmaps.com.

US Department of Labor. 2014. www.dol.gov/wb/stats/earnings _2014.htm#Ratios.

INDEX

Christian Hegemony, 396–398
Church
    Christian Hegemony, 396–398
    colonization of the Americas, 387
    sin, 41, 398
    spiritual safety, 135–136
Circle One. See Arc Circle One (vision and
    longing)
Circle Two. See Arc Circle Two (embodied
    resilience); Arc Circle Two (regenerating
    safety)
Circle Three. See Arc Circle Three (somatic
    opening)
Circle Four. See Arc Circle Four (healing
    shame); Arc Circle Four (interdependence)
Circle Five. See Arc Circle Five (embodying
    change)
cisgendered women sexual abuse survivors, 54
climate change, 80. See also environmental
    justice
    structural change, 354–357
clinicians, relevance of somatic definition of
    trauma, 88
Coates, Ta-Nehisi, 84, 381
co-created declarations, 173–175
codependency, 311
collective allying and social context, 247–250
collective conditioned tendencies (CTs),
    280–281
collective resilience, 208–210
colonization
    multigenerational impact, 81–82
    Palestine, by Israeli State, 104–106, 397–401
    United States, 383–389
combining healing with organizing for social
    justice, 59
commitments, 165–167. See also declarations
    co-created declarations, 173–175
    Conditions of Satisfaction (COS), 183–186
    discovering what we care about, 177–178
    finding longings, declarations, and
        callings, 181–183
    healing declarations, 171–173
    inherited declarations, 167–169
    outcome-based declarations, 175–177
    Prentis Hemphill's story, 188–191
    process declarations, 175–177
    self-defined declarations, 169–171

communication
    consent practice, 228–229
    declines, 223
    offers, 225–226
    push-away practice, 226–228
    requests, 225
Community Site, 49–50, 361–362
compassion and love, 32, 344–345
competency, 251
conditioned tendencies (CTs)
    collective, 280–281
    knowing, 347–348
Conditions of Satisfaction (COS), 183–186
conflict as generative, 324–327
connection
    connecting individual trauma with
        systemic trauma, 84–87
    connecting resilient places or states, 28
    mutual connection, 31, 343
consent, 219–229
    group practice, 228–229
    mutual connection, 343
    somatic opening, 259–260
contraction, 75–76
    contract and shape model, 265–268
    diaphragm band, 288
contradictions, 321–324
    unknown and contradiction, 32, 345
COS (Conditions of Satisfaction),
    183–186
The Cost of Living (Roy), 133
The Courage to Heal (Bass and Davis), 120
creativity, resilience, 206
CSA. See child sexual abuse
CTs (conditioned tendencies)
    collective, 280–281
    knowing, 347–348
cultural appropriation of meditation, yoga,
    and mindfulness, 367–369
cycle of emotion, 277–279

D

daily practices, 187
Dakota Access Pipeline, 393
Davis, Angela, 115
deafness, 23
de-armoring, 182. See also somatic opening
    bodywork, 274–275

ABOUT THE AUTHOR

 STACI K. HAINES is the cofounder of generative somatics, a multiracial social justice organization bringing Somatics to social and environmental justice leaders, organizations, and alliances. Staci is a senior teacher in the field of Somatics; she designs and leads programs in Somatics and trauma, embodied leadership, and Somatics in organizations, as well as leading teacher training programs. She has a somatic coaching practice that serves social movement leaders and trauma and violence survivors and has been working and teaching in the field of Somatics since 1997.

Staci is also the founder of generationFIVE, a social justice organization whose mission is to end the sexual abuse of children within five generations through survivor leadership, community organizing, transformative justice approaches, and movement building. Additionally she is the author of *Healing Sex: A Mind Body Approach to Healing Sexual Trauma* (Cleis 1999, 2007), a how-to book offering a Somatic approach to recovery from sexual trauma and developing healthy sexual and intimate relationships. *Healing Sex* has been nationally recognized and translated into German, Japanese, and Spanish. A DVD of the same title was released in 2005 (SIR Productions, Spanish subtitles).

Lastly, Staci has presented at numerous institutions including Oberlin College, Smith College, UC Berkeley, and Stanford University, on issues such as Somatics and social justice, the interdependence of personal and social transformation, and the power of embodied practice, and has presented at national and international conferences.